C0-BXA-250

Medieval Lives c. 1000–1292

Medieval Lives c. 1000–1292: The World of the Beaugency Family is a gateway into Europe during the Central Middle Ages. Through charting the lives of the Beaugency family, this book delves into the history of Western Europe and explores the impact of the changes and events of the period on those who experienced them.

The Central Middle Ages were years of profound transformation, and through the two centuries in which they lived the Beaugency family experienced many of the key developments that have characterized the period, such as the launch of the crusades and the emergence of a commercial economy. By following the lives of the family, this book instills a deeper understanding of the significance that human experience has on our ability to truly comprehend the crucial historical events of the age. It personalizes the history of the Middle Ages and provides students with a unique insight into the culture of the period.

Containing maps, genealogical tables, over thirty images, a large collection of previously unpublished archival sources used throughout the book, and accompanied by a companion website with interactive features, *Medieval Lives c. 1000–1292: The World of the Beaugency Family* is a portal into the lives of the Beaugency family and an ideal introduction to the Central Middle Ages.

Amy Livingstone is the H.O. Hirt Professor of History at Wittenberg University (Springfield, Ohio). She is author of *Out of Love for My Kin: Aristocratic Family Life in the Lands of the Loire, 1000–1200*, and several articles on noblewomen and noble families. She is also co-editor of *Writing Medieval Women's Lives* and the journal *Medieval Prosopography*.

Medieval Lives c. 1000–1292

The World of the Beaugency Family

Amy Livingstone

LONDON AND NEW YORK

First published 2018
by Routledge
2 Park Square, Milton Park, Abingdon, Oxon OX14 4RN

and by Routledge
711 Third Avenue, New York, NY 10017

Routledge is an imprint of the Taylor & Francis Group, an informa business

© 2018 Amy Livingstone

The right of Amy Livingstone to be identified as author of this work has been asserted by her in accordance with sections 77 and 78 of the Copyright, Designs and Patents Act 1988.

All rights reserved. No part of this book may be reprinted or reproduced or utilised in any form or by any electronic, mechanical, or other means, now known or hereafter invented, including photocopying and recording, or in any information storage or retrieval system, without permission in writing from the publishers.

Trademark notice: Product or corporate names may be trademarks or registered trademarks, and are used only for identification and explanation without intent to infringe.

British Library Cataloguing-in-Publication Data
A catalogue record for this book is available from the British Library

Library of Congress Cataloging-in-Publication Data
Names: Livingstone, Amy, 1961– author.
Title: Medieval lives c.1000–1292 : the world of the Beaugency family / Amy Livingstone.
Description: First edition. | Milton Park, Abingdon, Oxon ; New York, NY : Routledge, 2018 | Includes bibliographical references and index.
Identifiers: LCCN 2017056515| ISBN 9781138677081 (hardback : alk. paper) | ISBN 9781138677098 (pbk. : alk. paper) | ISBN 9781351041980 (ebook)
Subjects: LCSH: France—Social life and customs—To 1328. | Families—France--Beaugency—History—To 1500. | Beaugency (France)—History.
Classification: LCC DC33.2 .L585 2018 | DDC 944/.52—dc23
LC record available at https://lccn.loc.gov/2017056515

ISBN: 978-1-138-67708-1 (hbk)
ISBN: 978-1-138-67709-8 (pbk)
ISBN: 978-1-351-04198-0 (ebk)

Typeset in Garamond
by Florence Production Ltd, Stoodleigh, Devon, UK

Visit the companion website: www.routledge.com/cw/livingstone

For the Thompson Lads: Gordie, Sam and Will
The Lights of My Life

Contents

Abbreviations

AD	*Archives départementales*
ChV	*Chartes vendômoises*
CMPD	*Cartulaire de Marmoutier pour le Dunois*
CMV	*Cartulaire de Marmoutier pour le Vendômois*
GV	Geoffrey of Vendôme, Letters
LDSM	*Le Livre des serfs de Marmoutier*
NDB	*Cartulaire de Notre-Dame de Beaugency*
OV	Orderic Vitalis, *The Ecclesiastical History*
Père	*Cartulaire de Saint-Père de Chartres*
RHF	*Recueil des historiens des Gaules et de la France*
SA	Charles Cuissard, "Sommaire des chartes de l'abbaye de Saint-Avit"
SCO	*Cartulaire de Sainte-Croix d'Orléans*
STV	*Cartulaire de l'abbaye cardinale de la Trinité de Vendôme*
Tiron	*Cartulaire de l'abbaye de la Sainte-Trinité de Tiron*

Illustrations

Documents

Maps

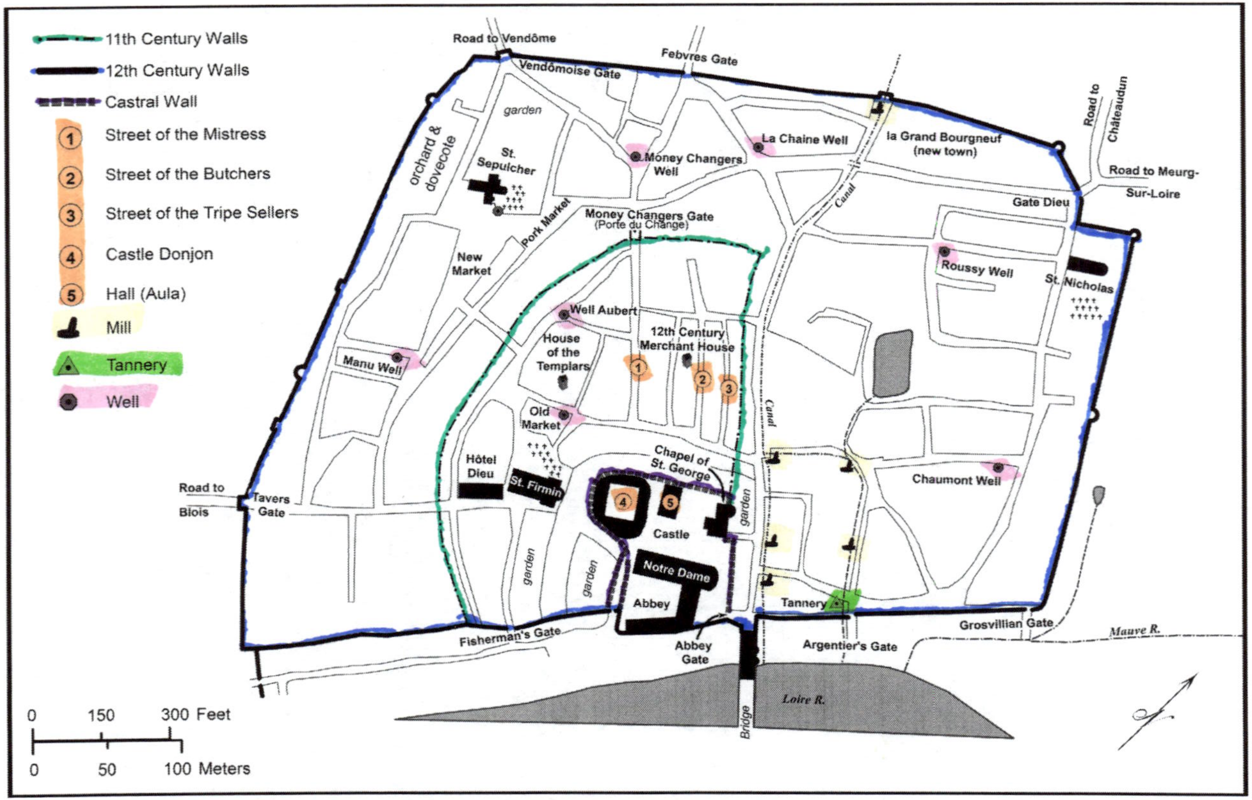

Map 1 Beaugency in the Middle Ages

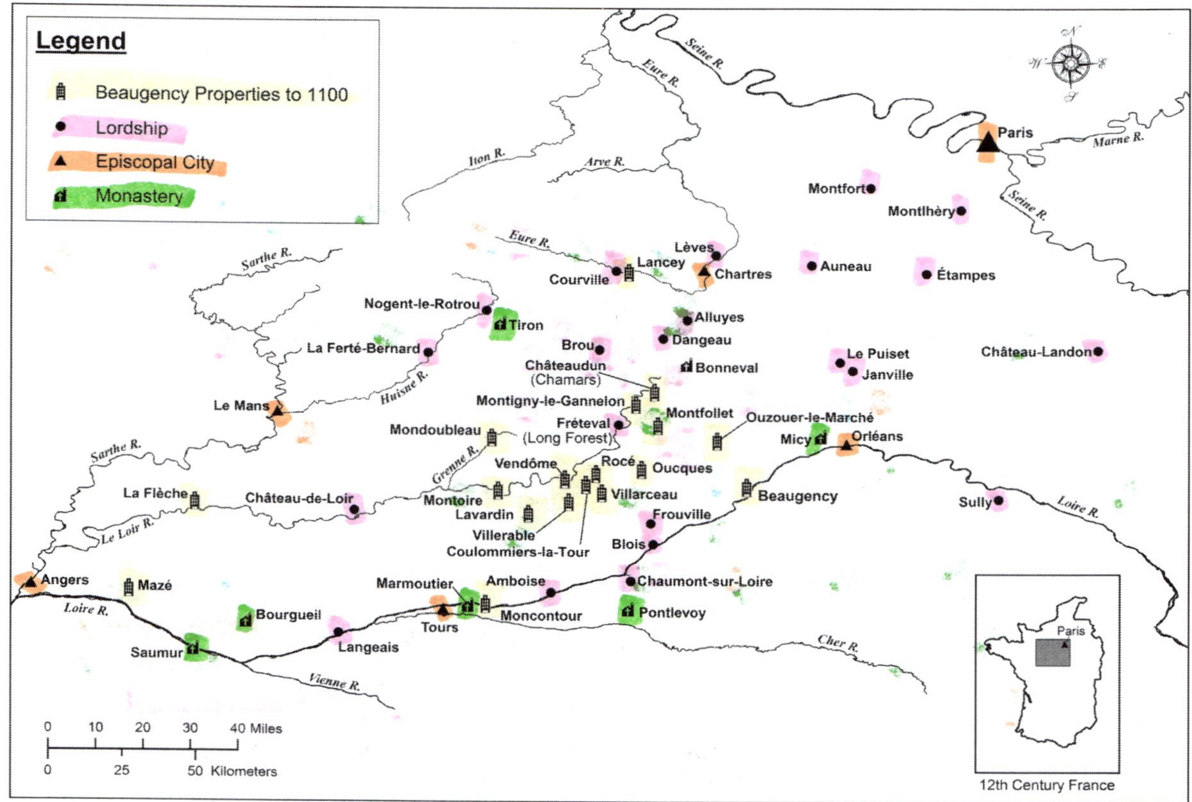

Map 2 Beaugency properties to 1100

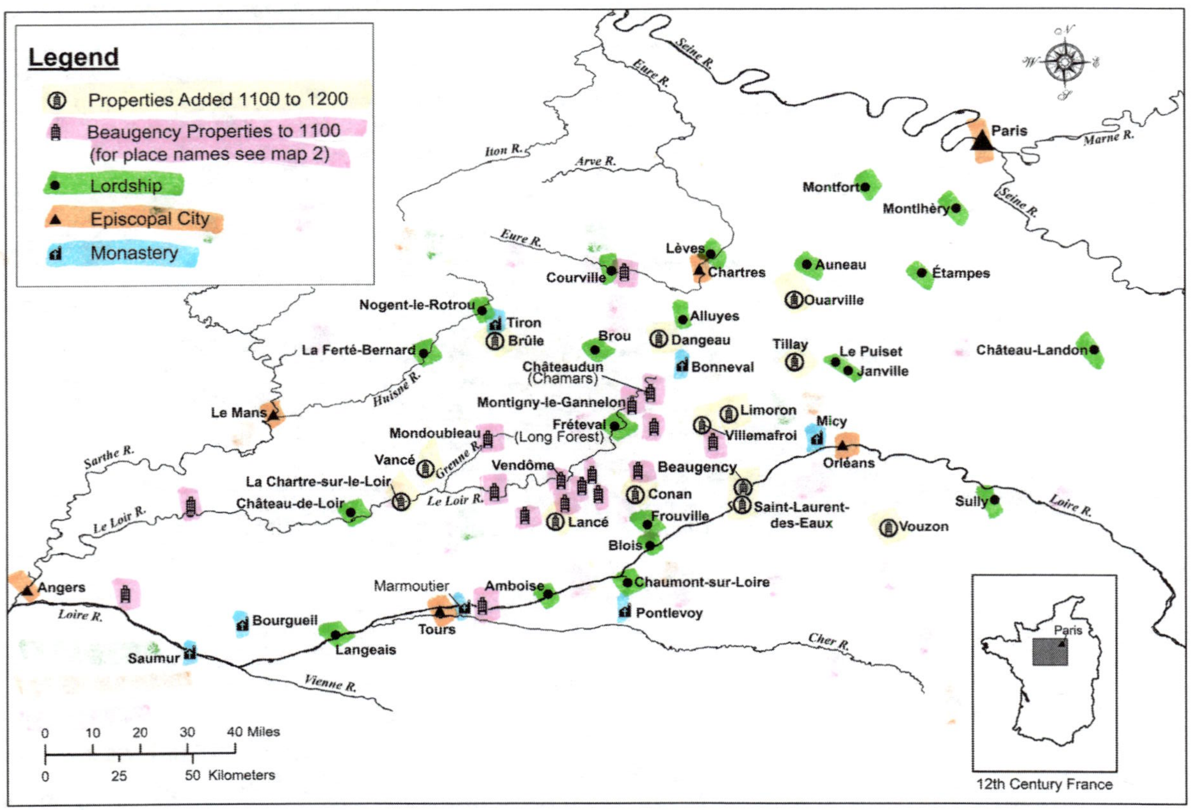

Map 3 Beaugency properties added from 1100 to 1200

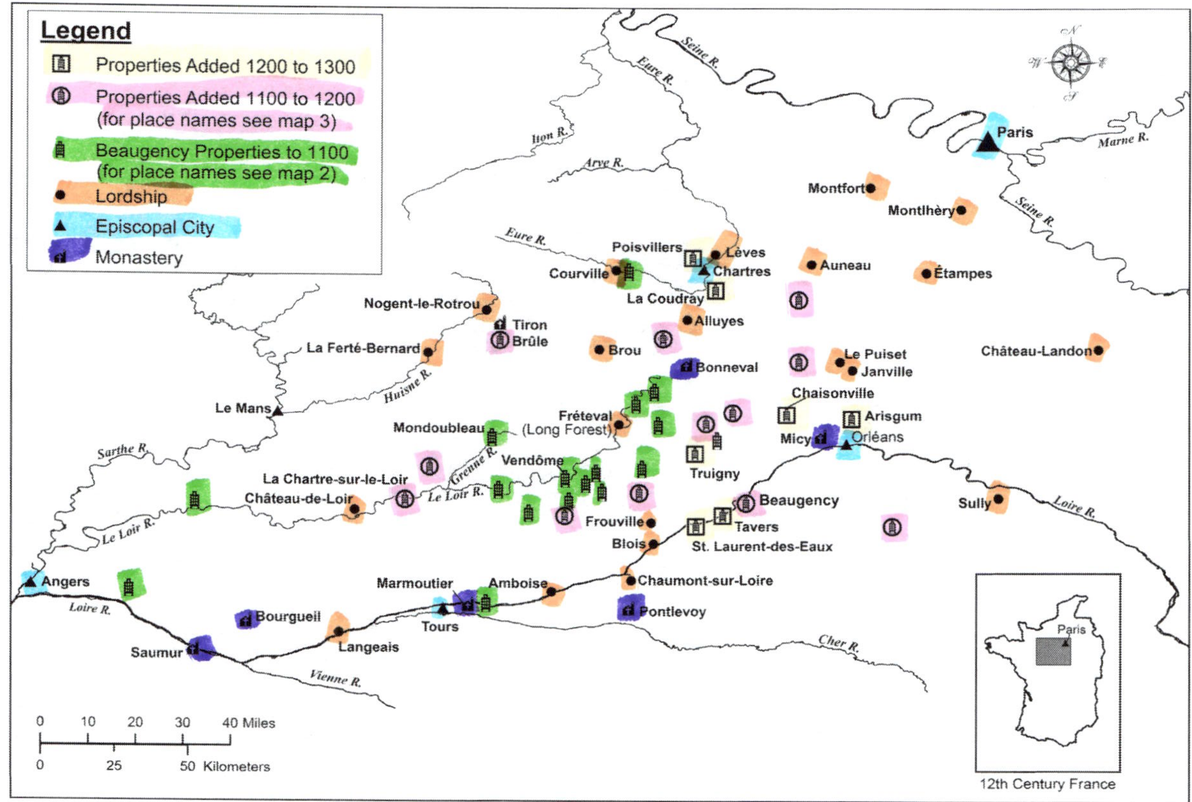

Map 4 Beaugency properties added from 1200–1300 and the Totality of Beaugency Patrimony c. 1050–1300

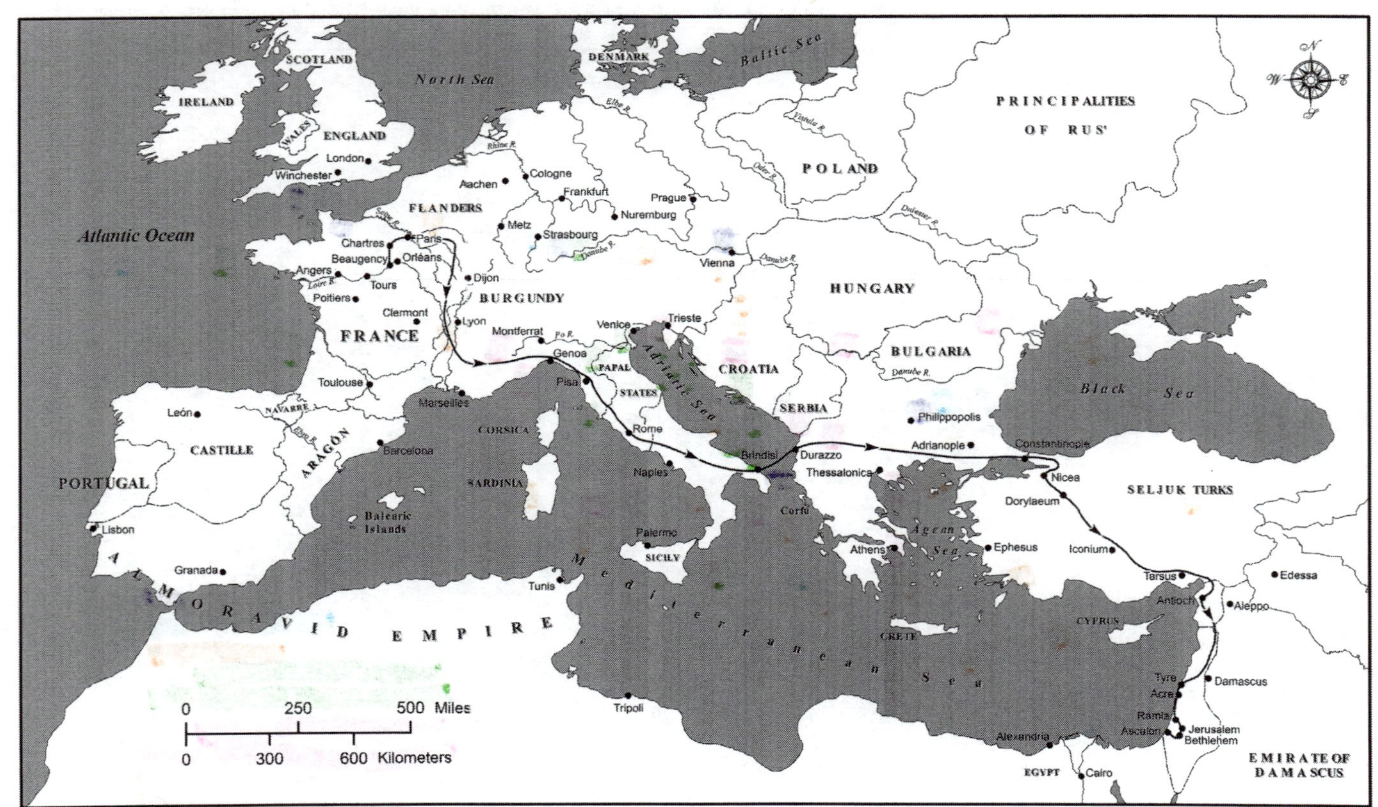

Map 5 Lord Ralph I on crusade

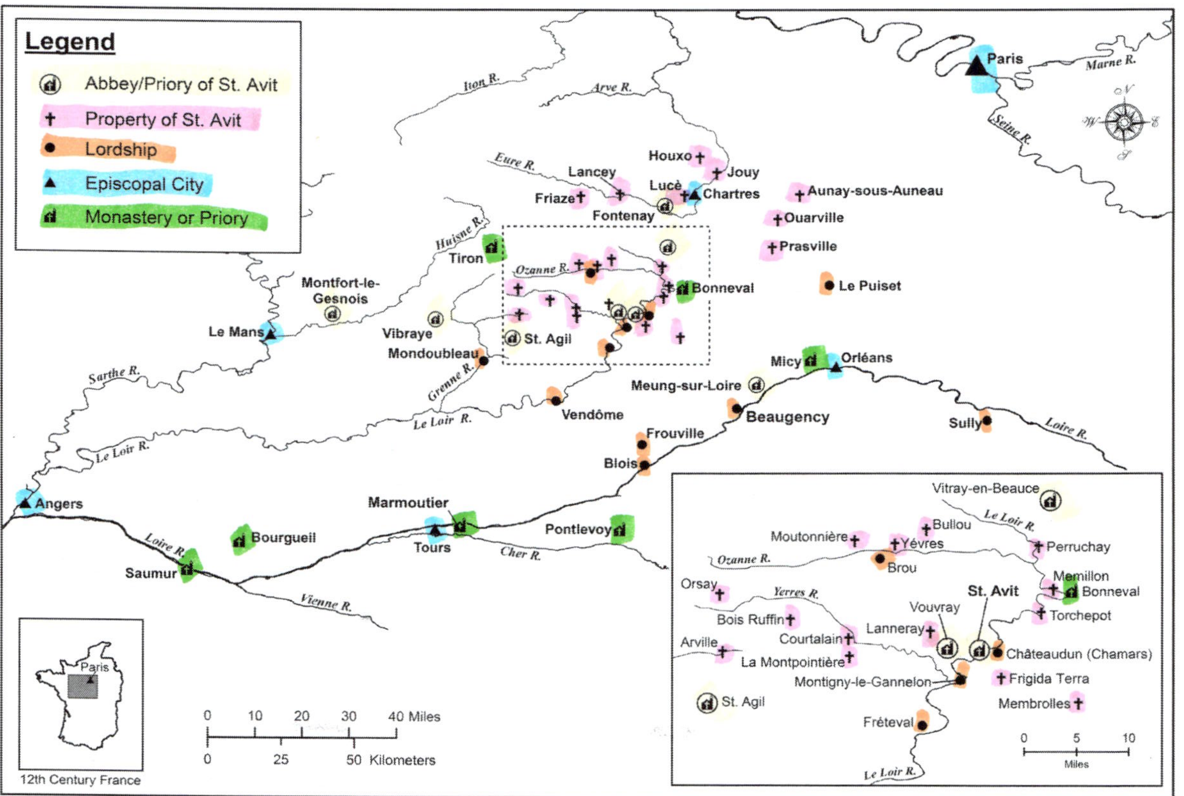

Map 6 The Patrimony of St. Avit of Châteaudun

Genealogical charts

The Lords of Beaugency, c. 1020-1300

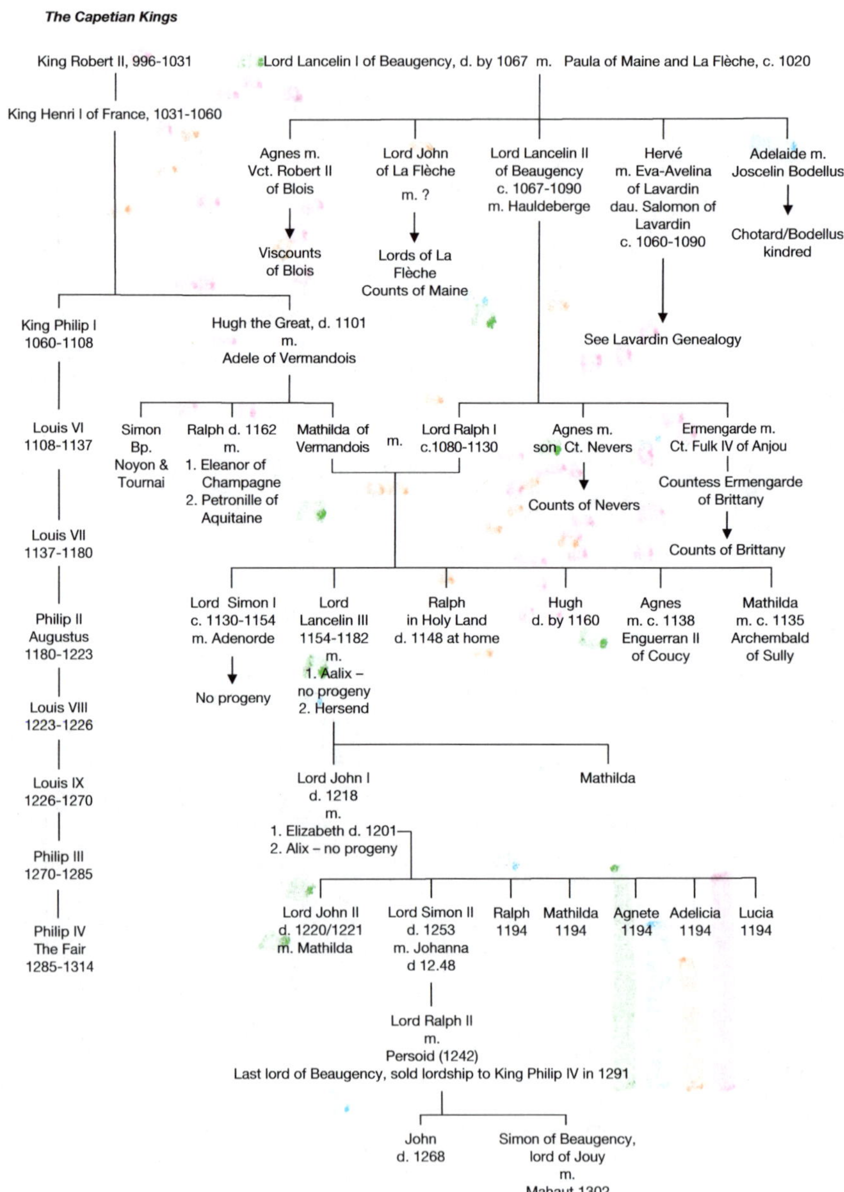

Genealogy 1 The lords of Beaugency

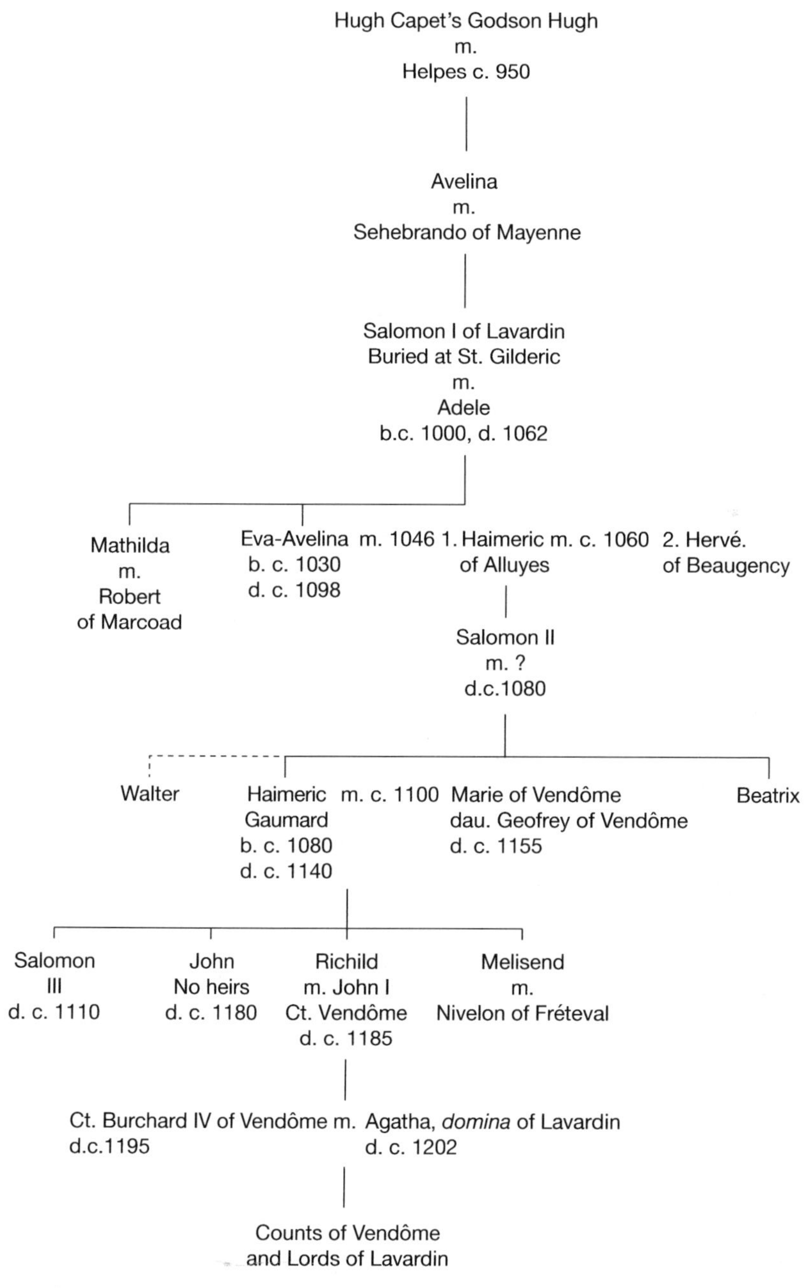

Genealogy 2 The lords of Larvardin

Acknowledgments

This book has grown directly from my experiences in the classroom. Several years ago, I assigned *A Medieval Life: Cecilia Penifader of Brigstock, 1295–1344* by Judith Bennett in my introductory medieval history course. I found telling the history of an era through the life of an "ordinary" individual, someone who might not otherwise be known, compelling. Perhaps more importantly, my students found this an engaging approach. So began *Medieval Lives: The World of the Beaugencys c. 1000–1292*, my attempt to use one noble family to relate the history of the Central Middle Ages. My Wittenberg students have informed this book through the questions they have asked, their enthusiasm for history and their feedback on various excerpts from the book. They have been with me at every step and this book was written with them in mind.

Like all historians, I rely on the help and good will of archivists and librarians. The evidentiary foundation for this book is the Cartulary of Notre Dame de Beaugency. The medieval manuscript of this cartulary is housed at the Archives départmentales du Loiret and I would like to thank Amandine Contet and her staff for all of their assistance during my time there in 2013. Similar thanks to Cécile Figliuzzi at the Archives départmentales d'Eure-et-Loir and Anne-Cécile Tizon-Germe of the Archives départmentales du Loir-et-Cher and their staffs who provided valuable assistance and access to charters involving the Beaugency family. These archives permitted reproductions of these manuscripts for this book, for which I am grateful. Olivier Morand at the Mediathèque d'Orléans was very helpful in tracking down the early modern transcriptions of the charters of the convent of St. Avit of Châteaudun. I spent a delightful day at the Centre de sigillographie et d'héraldique at the Archives nationales in Paris examining the seals of the Beaugency lords (one of them provides the cover of this book); my gratitude to Clement Blanc and Martine Lepany for their assistance in locating these seals. Closer to home, I would like to thank Suzanne Smailes of the Wittenberg Thomas Library for all of her help in tracking down obscure articles and other materials. Thanks to Eric Johnson, Curator of Rare Books and Manuscripts at The Ohio State University, for his knowledge of medieval Bibles and to The Ohio State University for permission to use the image of a glossed twelfth-century French Bible from their collection in this book. The staff of the Waldo Rare Book Room at Western Michigan University kindly allowed me to photograph the plan of the monastery of St. Trinité of Vendôme, which appears in these pages.

Several colleagues read versions or chapters of the book manuscript: Charlotte Newman Goldy read the entire book and Philp Adamo, Jonathan Lyon, Larry Marvin, Adam Matthews and Christian Raffensperger provided feedback on individual chapters. I would also like to thank the anonymous reviewers of the book manuscript. The book is better for all of the insights and suggestions provided by these colleagues. Judith Bennett was generous in sharing her experience with creating websites for classroom use. Rachel and Anders Tune, the Pastors at Wittenberg University, helped with scriptural passages and references. Thanks to Elizabeth A. R. Brown and Xavier Hélary for their help in tracking down information about the sale of Beaugency to King Philip IV. As the book progressed from idea to completion, several student faculty research aides have provided assistance and suggestions. Thanks to Gilbert Rutledge, Kristen Brady and Isabella Herman for their enthusiasm for the project and their hard work. I am fortunate to have exceptionally supportive history colleagues who have encouraged me over the years: Darlene Brooks Hedstrom, Christian Raffensperger, Scott Rosenberg, Thomas Taylor and Molly Wood. Wittenberg University has also been generous in supporting this project through various research and travel grants. Many friends have provided suggestions, criticisms and encouragement along the way and my thanks to them: Robert Berkhofer, Constance Berman, Constance Bouchard, Michael Burger, Adam Davis, Theodore Evergates, Theresa Earenfight, Valerie Garver, Charlotte Newman Goldy, Sally Hadden, Erin Jordan, Linda Mitchell, Tammy Proctor, Yvonne Seale, Miriam Shadis and Heather Wacha. My heartfelt gratitude to the Goda Gals, Laura Gathagan and Laura Wangerin, for their unflagging support and their perpetual good cheer. A big thanks also to my editors at Taylor & Francis, Laura Pilsworth and Morwenna Scott, for their assistance and patience in completing this project.

To Dominique Daury, a special appreciation for spending a day sharing his knowledge of the history Beaugency and providing access to many wonderful medieval sites relevant to the Beaugency family. He generously shared maps and images that have helped to inform this book, as well as providing invaluable insights and corrections to my interpretation of the Beaugency family. I am extremely grateful for the kind hospitality that he and Madame Daury showed me during my stay in April 2016. I am also appreciative of the warm welcome extended to me by the staff of the *Mairie* of Beaugency.

Writing the history of the Beaugency family has required several excursions into the French countryside. My dear friends and Paris family, Josef and Isa Konvitz, were my intrepid companions on these excursions. Many thanks for their appreciation of the medieval past and also their penetrating questions and delightful company over many a scrumptious meal and glass of wine.

Finally, this book is dedicated to my husband, Gordie Thompson , and my two sons, Sam and Will Thompson. Gordie, cartographer extraordinaire, created all of the maps for this book. I am always grateful for his attention to detail and cartographer's eye in rendering visual information. Sam and Will were, in many ways, the first audience for this book. Their suggestions, questions and enthusiasm for this project (not to mention their willingness to hear the story of "Wreck-It Ralph" yet again) are deeply appreciated. The support of the Thompson lads, expressed in so many ways – from the simple cup of coffee in the midst of an intense writing session to putting up with an absent spouse/mother while she rummaged through the archives – means more than I have words to express. You three are the lights of my life and this book is dedicated to you.

Introduction

History means more when it comes with a name

What is history? For some it is the story of Great Events and Significant People. For others, it is about the intersecting lives of people from all walks of life. Over the centuries, historians have tended to focus on long-term trends and important events. When they did turn their attention to individuals, they focused on the great men and (sometimes) women of the era. And for good reason: These are the events and figures that are best documented. More recently, however, scholars of the past have started asking different questions of the sources and assembling the evidence to explore the experiences of people more distant from the centers of power. This book draws from that tradition. Its goal is to craft a narrative of the lives of the men and women of one family of medieval lords: The Beaugencys.

The underlying premise of this study is that to truly understand the past, you have to focus on the lives of people. To invoke a well-worn cliché, you need to walk in their shoes – or perhaps more accurately for the subject of this book, their chainmail. To bring the medieval centuries to life, this book will center on the lives of a family of nobles who took their name from the castle of Beaugency and who resided there during the Central Middle Ages (c. 1000–1300 AD). Located in central France and nestled into a bend in the Loire River, Beaugency lays 90 miles almost due south of Paris (see Map 2 on page xv at the start of this book). The Beaugency family, while **noble**, only rose as far to attain the rank of regional **lord**. They were never counts or kings or princes. Nor did they ever hold any office from the king. Nevertheless, their experiences can illuminate a notoriously challenging historical period to decipher. Like their peers, the lords of Beaugency controlled considerable properties and owed allegiance to some of the most powerful individuals in medieval France, including several counts. They were also the lords of other elites. They granted fiefs from their property to **vassals** (definition of bolded words can be found in the glossary) who would owe them military service and loyalty, thus creating an extensive system of clientage. The Beaugencys also used marriage to extend their power and boost their social or political standing. Their political and family ties thus drew the Beaugencys into some of the headline events of the eleventh, twelfth and thirteenth centuries. The Beaugency family was also deeply enmeshed in the church. These men and women were generous ecclesiastical patrons, supported reform of the church, participated in crusades and some joined the church as **monks** or nuns. As well as ties to the highest levels of medieval society, as lords the Beaugencys were also connected to the humblest members of society: The peasants, **serfs** and village dwellers who worked the extensive properties that this family controlled. Populating the villages and towns of the Beaugency domain were people who bought, sold and made goods for a living. As their lords, the Beaugency family influenced how these people lived their lives and, in turn, were affected by the life experiences of the peasants, tradesmen and merchants.

The Central Middle Ages were transformational centuries for medieval Europe. The Beaugency family is uniquely placed to explore these events, trends and developments, but also to understand how such transformations shaped the course of the lives of medieval people. Between 1000 and 1300 the population in Europe tripled. Related to this growth was economic transformation as the economy of Western Europe developed from subsistence into a commercial economy fueled by trade and coin (a transformation often referred to as the **commercial revolution**). Many opted to move to cities, which were centers of trade and flourishing as a result of commerce. Kings centralized their kingdoms and created peace, making it safe to travel – which helped to spur on long-distance trade. The church underwent a significant period of reform and erected spectacular cathedrals throughout Western Europe, often in urban areas. Crusaders "took the cross" and voyaged across oceans to "liberate" the Holy Land. Universities and law codes developed that would provide the foundations for their modern counterparts. In short, the eleventh through the thirteenth centuries saw profound changes that transformed Europe and planted the seeds of attributes that would come to characterize the modern period.

While we can list and describe these crucial events, can we really understand them without factoring in the human experience? The Beaugency family will act as our entreé into these centuries. Through analysis of the lords and ladies of Beaugency, we are able to get a snapshot of what it was like to live as a mid-rank aristocrat in medieval France. Questions that need to be answered before proceeding are: Why this family? And why should we care about them? The answers are relatively simple. The lives of these men and women intersected with events such as royal centralization, the crusades, economic shifts, cultural revitalization and church reform. Understanding their individual experiences will provide a deeper appreciation of the impact of these larger, anonymous, events. Moreover, the eleventh through the thirteenth centuries saw profound changes that transformed Europe and put in place characteristics that would shape the modern period. These events, good and bad, were in large part directed by nobles just like the Beaugencys. Through charting of the ebb and flow of the lives of the Beaugency men and women, we can appreciate the complexities that made up the political, social, economic, religious and cultural landscape of the Central Middle Ages. This family was emblematic of an age.

The website, The Portal to the Past, has been developed to supplement this book with information about the people with whom the Beaugencys interacted, images of their physical and material environment, how they understood the world around them and where they traveled (www.routledge.com/cw/livingstone).

To reconstruct and recover past lives, historians of all periods and places are at the mercy of sources. Centuries of wars, rats, fires, neglect and general wear and tear have taken their toll on those from the Middle Ages. Furthermore, the great majority of documents created reflected or recorded the experiences of elites, secular and religious. What we are left with is only a small fraction of what was likely recorded or, in the case of material culture, existed. If we envision the history of the Middle Ages as an onion, with the skin of the onion representing all that happened in these centuries, all that we are left with is the tiny center core. Since history consists of many layers, how do we go about reconstructing the layers between the skin and the center of the onion?

Attempting to recover the lives of any medieval person is challenging, as the experiences of even the most prominent individuals were often undocumented. Even the most rudimentary information, such as dates of birth or death, often remains obscure and requires deductive reconstruction. Unlike modern historical figures who leave behind personal accounts, or who appear in a plethora of official documents, there are very few such sources for the medieval period, particularly before the thirteenth century. Because most medieval people, including the Beaugencys, did not leave behind accounts of their own lives, historians are dependent on what other people thought or recorded about them. The authors of these accounts were nearly always members of the clergy. As a consequence, much of what we know about medieval society in general, and the Beaugencys in particular, is filtered through this clerical lens. Fortunately, however, a handful of letters written by a lord and lady of Beaugency are extant.

Medieval clerics and scribes penned all sorts of sources. As the literate professionals, they were often tasked by kings and lords to keep records. They noted the events of their time in chronicles and maintained extensive records of what property the church held. Clerics also produced "biographies" of noteworthy people such as kings and **saints** (often called **hagiographies**). But their emphasis on a saint's sanctity or a king's piety renders these sources more of a didactic treatise than a day-to-day account of individual lives. Members of the Beaugency family appear briefly in the chronicles and royal acts concerning justice or the distribution of property. Unfortunately these references tend to be terse and do not tell us what we often want to know – Why was Lord Ralph I at court? What did he think about the king?

The queen? The **bishop**? The **count**? While they provide information on the political realm, they are less useful in weaving together the personal interactions. Chronicle entries can be colorful, but may also be subject to exaggeration or bias since medieval chroniclers recorded events with a purpose or point in mind. For example, when Abbot Suger recounted the events of the life of King Louis VI, he tended to depict anyone who was a threat to the king's power as excessively violent or power-hungry. This does not mean the information extant in such documents is necessarily toxic. Rather, caution needs to be exercised before taking these accounts at face value.

Fortunately, the lords and ladies of Beaugency lived through a literary blossoming that spread throughout Europe. Much like moderns, medieval people loved to be entertained by stories. In the eleventh and early twelfth centuries the plot line of these stories revolved around war and the deeds of brave warriors. As the twelfth century unfolded, however, tastes changed. Literature came to focus on the personal dramas that spurred on a warrior's actions, such as his relationship with other knights, his king or his lady. While these **romances** and songs of deeds are rich in evocative details, they belong to the realm of the imagination. Literature, however, can be used to buttress and expand upon what documents of practice (or those sources concerned with the mundane aspects of life) record. Literary sources can also provide access into what medieval elites thought, felt and valued, for members of the aristocracy, including the Châtelain of Coucy who was a distant relative of the Beaugencys, did put quill to parchment to compose romances.

Providing the backbone for this study will be documents known as **charters** (several of which can be found in the Documents section of this book). Charters at their most basic are property deeds: They record the alienation

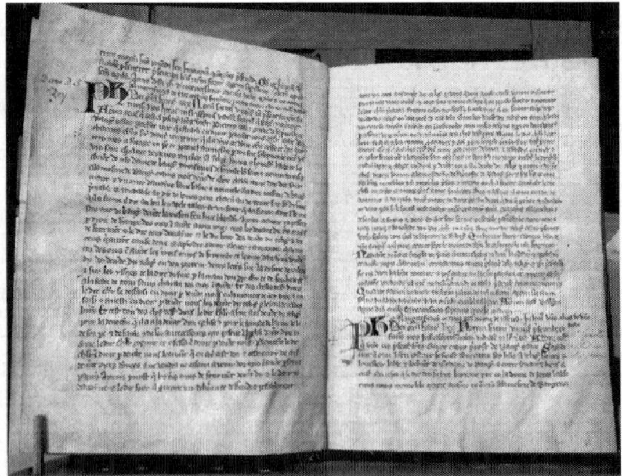

Figures 0.1a and 0.1b Title page and charters of the cartulary of Notre Dame de Beaugency. Archives départmentales du Loiret, H 10, folios 1v and 2r. Author photos.

of property from one person (or institution) to another. In most cases the recipient of the property was the church, which is why such documents survive. Single charters were often collected or copied into a **cartulary**. For example, the charters of Notre Dame of Beaugency were codified into a cartulary in the early fourteenth century (see Figures 0.1a and 0.1b)

Most of the acts recorded in the cartulary date before 1300, indicating that the scribe had access to the original charters which he then copied into the cartulary. Sometimes the original charter is extant, but sometimes the only charter we have is from a later cartulary. Cartulary copies raise certain questions about the information recorded. Specifically did the monk redact the document, meaning did he leave out information or recast events in a certain way? While it is difficult to tell sometimes, this is an issue that historians must consider in evaluating the information from these sources.

Because charters record the mundane aspects of day-to-day living, reflecting more of real actions, they are considered "documents of practice." The church kept careful records of the gifts made to them by pious donors. Each charter was written in a certain way and with standard information of who gave the property, to whom it was given, a description of the property, the consent of those who had a right or claim to the property and a list of witnesses to the transaction. But these documents can transcend the formulaic and provide nuggets of information useful to understanding life in the Middle Ages. Intriguingly, some charters record the emotional responses or motivations of the donors. One of the limitations of these sources is that they provide a frozen moment in time. What came before and what happened after the events recorded in the charter frequently go unaddressed in the document. Yet some individuals – like the members of the Beaugency family – appear in many charters during the course of their life. As a result, the charters make it possible to piece together who individuals married, how many children they had, where they lived, who their lords were, where they traveled, how they died and so on.

Material culture can prove useful for understanding the physical and natural environment in which a wide variety of medieval people lived. Remains of material culture, however, are by definition impersonal and anonymous. Although we cannot know that a certain article belonged to the lords and ladies of Beaugency, we can reasonably extrapolate that they may have possessed one like it. Surviving physical spaces can also help us to understand medieval life. The organization and decoration of space tells us much about the society that produced it – just as it does today. For example, the frescoes, stained-glass windows and sculpture extant from churches were not meant to be realistic but nevertheless provide insight into medieval attitudes toward the sacred and divine. Similarly, the layout of a castle out can reveal medieval notions of privacy or family life. The fields, ponds, mills, ovens, wine presses and other features of the agricultural landscape are described in the documents and a surprisingly large number still survive. So, too, do medieval castles, parish churches and cathedrals. Although the dwellings of the humble have long since vanished, archeology has proved vital to rescuing the material culture of the peasants. Excavations have yielded enough information that peasant homes and communities can be reconstructed. Recent archeological research even provides insight into the diet and health of medieval people of all classes.

The limitations of the sources thus pose a challenge in examining the lives of even a typical aristocratic family. When faced with a lack of sources sufficient to reconstruct one life, historians have developed an approach called prosopography, or collective biography. Instead of writing the biography of one individual, historians take bits of information about particular kinds of individuals – children, knights, merchants, women, the elderly – and put them together to create a mosaic of a life, or, put another way, a biography of a group. There are obvious limitations and flaws to this approach. Clearly not all life experiences were the same, but by being attentive to their sources and getting to know their subjects, historians are able to extrapolate the life experience of one from the experiences of the many. This methodology is far from perfect or foolproof, but it is one way to give voice to people in the past whose lives would otherwise remain silent.

What else can historians use to bring the past to life? Historical speculation and imagination can also be useful tools – if used judiciously. History, after all, is interpretation. Facts play a critical role in interpretation, but they are not the sum total of history. Rather history is the assemblage and interpretation of those facts. Historians literally immerse themselves in the sources of the past. This expertise allows them to make informed suppositions about how their subjects behaved, where they lived, what they felt. As long as their reconstructions and assertions are, as the noted historian Natalie Zemon Davis stated "held tightly in check by the voices of the past," speculations, visualizations and informed hypothesizing are a legitimate means of adding flesh to the factual barebones of the past.[1] Not all interpretations are created equal, however. The very best are founded upon an intimate knowledge of the sources and do not go to places where their sources do not take them.

What is offered here is my interpretation of the Beaugencys' past and their world. As such it is informed by my authorial choices in interpreting the evidence, events and personalities, as well as how I interpret the larger trends that defined the Middle Ages. These interpretative choices are based upon my years of reading and analyzing hundreds of medieval documents, as well as my intimate knowledge of the Beaugency family, their physical environment, the medieval aristocracy and the general history of the Middle Ages. Others may read the documents with a different eye,

1 Natalie Zemon Davis, *The Return of Martin Guerre* (Cambridge, MA: Harvard University Press, 1983) p. 5.

influenced by their own context and understanding of the past and come up with a completely different interpretation. And they are welcome, indeed encouraged, to do so. At key points in the narrative, I will be intentional in explaining my interpretation of the evidence and in discussing the methodology or thinking behind it. "Doing" history is an active process, done in dialogue with other historians, to debate the evidence and develop interpretation. Such differences of interpretation and historiographical debates will also be signposted throughout the narrative. In order for you to determine if the following interpretation of medieval aristocratic life is "held tightly in check by the voices of the past," translations of some of the documents used to inform the narrative can be found in the last section of the book (see pages 221–256). Readers, moreover, should use these documents to develop their own interpretation of the lives of the Beaugency family.

This examination of medieval life will be organized into concentric, overlapping, circles. We will start at the widest point and move to the most immediate relationships in the lives of the Beaugencys and then move out once again to other circles of affinity. The book begins by considering the physical environment in which the Beaugencys lived. What did their world look like? Focus will then shift from a general description of the wider world to the people who were closest to them: Their family. The next section moves the discussion from the family back to the wider world. First, the political landscape of the world of the Beaugencys will be considered. Specifically, these chapters examine the relationship between the lords of Beaugency and the men and women to whom they owed allegiance – including the king – and those who owed allegiance to them. The lives of particular lords of Beaugency will be highlighted to provide a more intimate or individual glimpse into how large political forces shaped their experience. Next to follow will be discussion of those who were essential to the lives of the Beaugencys: The peasants. Individual relationships between the Beaugency family and their local peasantry will be explored to get an on-the-ground sense of how these two classes interacted. Another vitally important force in the lives of these men and women was religion. Discussion will begin with a general consideration of religion in the lives of the Beaugency family and their neighbors. Focus will then move inside the walls of the monastery to consider the life of the medieval clergy by examining the experiences of a local **abbess** and one of the Beaugencys' distant kinsmen who was the **abbot** of a local monastery. Underlying the discussion of the lives of the Beaugencys will be forces – economic, political, familial and cultural – that shaped their world and ultimately resulted in changing their reality to the point that a new era began.

So what did the world of the Beaugencys look like? Where did they live? What would they have encountered as they traversed the countryside? Let us now begin our exploration of the world of the Beaugencys.

Suggested reading

For a general overview of how the discipline of history has evolved, see Norman J. Wilson, *History in Crisis? Recent Directions in Historiography*, 3rd edition. New York: Pearson Education, 2013; John Tosh, *The Pursuit of History: Aims, Methods and New Directions in the Study of History*, 6th edition. London: Routledge, 2015; and Martha Howell and Walter Prevenier, *From Reliable Sources: An Introduction to Historical Methods*. Ithaca and London: Cornell University Press, 2001. Although different in approach, each offers an easily accessible analysis of **historiography**, the challenges that historians face and how historians have reconstructed the past.

Primary sources are the lifeblood of studying the past. Joel Rosenthal offers an excellent analysis of the various genres of medieval sources, their particular strengths and challenges: Joel T. Rosenthal, *Understanding Medieval Primary Sources: Using Historical Sources to Discover Medieval Europe*. London: Routledge, 2011.

This study of the Beaugency family is a microhistory of the Central Middle Ages. Microhistories can be fascinating ways of learning about the past. There is none better than *The Return of Martin Guerre*. Cambridge, MA: Harvard University Press, 1983, by Natalie Zemon Davis. Her methodology for telling the story of Martin Guerre generated considerable discussion and debate at the time of its publication and continues to do so. See the forum on this book in the *American Historical Review,* 93 (June 1988): 553–603. More recently, Steven Bednarski offers a compelling analysis of the life of the trials of a medieval peasant woman in, *A Poisoned Past: The Life and Times of Margarida de Portu, A Fourteenth-Century Accused Poisoner*. Toronto: University of Toronto Press, 2014. He also welcomes the reader into the authorial choices he made in crafting his analysis of Margarida's life.

1 The Beaugencys and the world around them

The medieval world is endlessly fascinating to modern audiences. These centuries have been alternately romanticized as times of chivalry and elevated spirituality and excoriated as an era of darkness and superstition. People seem to either want to relive the Middle Ages – as evidenced by the popularity of medieval festivals and role-playing games (RPGs) set in the period – or they characterize everything and anything they see as backward or barbaric as "medieval." The Beaugencys would have found either of these dichotomies perplexing and far removed from their own lived reality. This chapter will try to animate the world in which the Beaugencys lived. Examination will start with the more intimate spaces these lords and ladies inhabited and then move out to consider the wider world around them.

Let us begin with the physical setting of the village of Beaugency. Consider the aerial photo (Figure 1.1). At the heart of Beaugency we see three very important structures and spaces that lie almost on top of the other: A castle, (1), two churches (2 and 3) and large squares (4 and 5) that served as a market place. This was the heart of Beaugency. Each of these spaces represents an important slice of medieval society. Their proximity also illustrates how each social sector depended upon the others.

In the tenth and eleventh centuries, medieval clerics developed a social schema consisting of "three orders." At the top were "those who pray," or the clergy (perhaps not surprisingly since medieval clerics were the ones to come up with this paradigm!). Next came "those who fight," which referred to the knights and lords. At the bottom were "those who work," meaning those who tilled the fields, essentially agricultural laborers. Each of these three orders was present in the heart of Beaugency.

Because of its height and mass, the structure that dominates the view is the tower or ***donjon*** (the root word for the modern "dungeon"). Clearly this tower was designed for defense and consonant with the lord's function of defending. It also sent a clear message of intimidation, perhaps necessary when less than 10 percent of the population holds 85 percent in thrall. Separated by a distance of only a 100 feet, lies the church of Notre Dame de Beaugency (see Figures 6.1 and 6.2). Like the adjacent structures themselves,

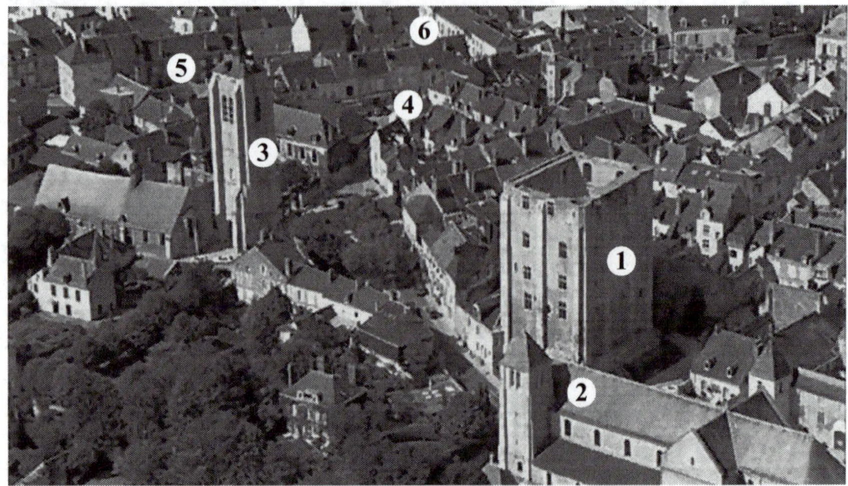

Figure 1.1 An aerial view of the heart of Beaugency: (1) The castle *donjon*; (2) The abbey church of Notre Dame de Beaugency; (3) The remaining tower of the parish church of St. Firmin and the Hôtel Dieu; (4) The little market; (5) The new market; (6) St. Sepulcher. Hemis / Alamy stock photo.

the people who populated these spaces were also close to one another. In fact, they were often blood relatives, as most clergy were members of noble families, thus frequently the brothers, sons and even fathers of local lords. While the church itself is not as tall as the tower, it is imposing nevertheless. Other structures for the clerics' use stretched down toward the river, resulting in the church occupying much of the space at the center of town. Across from both the *donjon* and **abbey** church was the parish church of St. Firmin (all that remains today is the tower). Just up from the castle precincts was the "little market" (number 4), where peasants from the surrounding countryside came to sell the produce they had grown (eventually expanded to the larger market place on the Square of the Martyrs, number 5). Stalls were placed around the market place in Middle Ages. The proximity of the market place to the castle and church reinforces the critical role that peasants' labor played in the lives of the elite. Exploitation of peasants was perhaps not a surprising result of this social ordering. The manuscript image in Figure 1.2 depicts the three orders with a member of the aristocracy treading on the foot of the peasant – a literal rendering of how the peasants were under the heel of the elites. However, each order recognized they could not survive without the others and all would mix regularly in these spaces, all of which were within the twelfth-century walls of Beaugency (see Map 1).

Glaringly absent from this tripartite configuration and accompanying illustration were people who did work other than agricultural labor. Where would the butcher, the baker and the candlestick maker fit into the three orders? Though there were certainly craftsmen and merchants living in

Figure 1.2 The three orders (thirteenth century) © The British Library Board Royal 6 C.VI f79v.

Europe during the tenth and eleventh centuries, they made up a rather small percentage of the over all population. Even though the clergy and warriors were also statistically insignificant (each at around 10 percent or less of the population), they controlled all of the power. The same could not be said of the craftsmen and merchants. A rendering of the ordering of medieval society from the fourteenth century reveals dramatic changes that resulted from the commercial revolution of the twelfth century which caused the economy to transition from one of subsistence and barter to one based in commerce and cash (Figure 1.3).

Perhaps one of the most striking differences between these two depictions is the number of figures in each. Many more people populate the registers of the later rendition, an indication of the dramatic population growth that occurred between 1000 and 1300. The figures are dressed more richly and the landscape is orderly, suggesting economic prosperity and political stability. The inclusion of the king at the center of the top register, with the lords and clergy as satellites, indicates the growth in monarchical power. The adoption of a money economy is apparent in the merchants holding their bags of coins. The urban growth associated with economic transformation and population boom is also evident in the walled towns depicted in the lower sections. This depiction records a very different world than the one before it. Although the most modest of all of the spaces, the market square in the center of Beaugency was witness to these profound changes. Missing in the earlier rendering of

Figure 1.3 Later rendition of the three orders (fourteenth century): Le roi trônant, les marchands et les travaillers from *Le régime des princes* by Gilles de Rome, Bibliothèque nationale de France MS Francais 126, folio 7.

medieval society, the merchants – and the peasants – provide the literal and figural foundation upon which the monarch, the lords and the church rest in Figure 1.3. By the mid-twelfth century, merchants were essential to medieval society; so essential, in fact, that they shaped the physical world of the lords and ladies of Beaugency. Their presence in the twelfth-century village is attested to by the market place, but also the twelfth-century houses constructed close to the market place.

Castle, abbey, market and fields – each was important in some way to the members of the Beaugency family. We will begin a more in-depth investigation of their physical world with the environment that was most immediate to these men and women: The castle.

The castle

One glance at the castle of Beaugency is enough to know that it was built with an eye toward military defense (Figure 1.4). The eleventh century saw a flurry of castle construction in France, including the one at Beaugency. Castles served many functions. They were a tangible sign of a lord's power, but also where courts and banquets were held, justice provided and order implemented. Most castles started out constructed of wood. They were erected in tactical locations as military outposts. Beaugency's position on the Loire River made it strategically important and it had been a fortified site since the Carolingian era. The original wooden fort was replaced by a stone castle sometime between 1030 and 1050. Wooden castles had much to recommend them – they were fairly quickly and cheaply constructed since the materials were close at hand in nearby forests – but they had the obvious drawback of being susceptible to fire. The development of a fortress controlled by the Beaugency lord at Montfollet provides a glimpse into a castle's development from a rustic outpost to a community.

Figure 1.4 The eleventh-century tower of Beaugency. Author photo.

The Beaugencys held Montfollet as vassals of the counts of Chartres. Montfollet (today Vievy-le-Rayé) was located in the heart of what was called "The Long Forest." (The "long" forest was exactly what it sounds like: a large forest that extended 30 miles south from Châteaudun to just north of Blois.) Montfollet lay about 18 miles west of Beaugency or about a half of a day's ride (see Map 2). Medieval lords were keen to extend their influence and one way to do so was to support the creation of new communities that would fall under their dominion: The more land and people you controlled in the Middle Ages, the more powerful a lord you were. Combined with the increasing population of peasants, there was a need for new communities and to expand the amount of land under cultivation. Because forests tended to be more remote and under-developed, lords offered incentives for people to settle in them. Around 1070 a castle at Montfollet started out as a wood and earth castle with an earthen rampart, but it eventually developed into stone fortress with a surrounding community. A fortress at Montfollet made tactical sense for the Beaugency family. It was about half-way to their holdings in Châteaudun, but also only 5 miles from the Le Loir River (not to be confused with the larger Loire River located to its south) which would they would take to travel to their holdings in Vendôme and further west. This fortress also provided the lord of Beaugency with a military presence close to their possessions at Oucques, Rocé and Villarceau – all of which were some distance from Beaugency itself. Montfollet was built on the "motte and bailey" model. Imagine a tall earthen hill with a ditch (or moat) dug around it. On top of this motte sat the bailey or the *donjon*, a tower used for defense (Figure 1.5). The *donjon* complex of Montfollet occupied an area of 13.5 acres. The fortress itself had walls about 20 feet tall, but when combined with the motte, the total height was about 60 feet.[1] There was a second motte several feet away and both were encircled by a wall.

Charters from the twelfth century indicate that there was a thriving community developing at Montfollet a short distance from the castle. In 1085, Lord Ralph I of Beaugency granted the monks and the residents the right to hold markets[2] (see Document 1 on page 221). Developing villages and markets in forests made good economic sense since they were rich in resources and all sorts of trades and industry could be supported because of the ready supply of wood for fuel. An important part of any medieval community was the church. Hence, accompanying the creation of a castle was the establishment of a church situated in the settlement. Lord Ralph I was a generous patron to the church and ensured that the monks from the monastery of St. Trinité in Vendôme would enjoy a community that consisted of several buildings, as well as privileges such as the right to pasture their pigs in the

1 André Chédeville, *Chartres et ses campagnes* (Rennes: Presses Universitaires de Haute Bretagne, 1972), pp. 275–276, note 171.

2 *Cartulaire de l'abbaye cardinale de la Trinité de Vendôme*, éd. Charles Métais (Paris: Picard, 1893–1904), vol. 2, no. 324, pp. 32–35. Hereafter, *STV*.

Figure 1.5 A motte and bailey castle as depicted in the Bayeux Tapestry. Note the wooden palisades on top of the earthen motte. Art Collection 3 / Alamy stock photo.

forest. He also provided that the wooden chapel be rebuilt in stone. What had begun as an outpost in the forest developed into a thriving community. The story of Montfollet would be repeated throughout France and Western Europe in the eleventh and twelfth centuries.

The **château** at Beaugency likely started out as a structure of earth and wood, but sometime before the mid-eleventh century Lord Lancelin I constructed a massive stone *donjon*. Unlike other *donjons* in the region of the Loire, the one at Beaugency was square.[3] Although round towers were common because they more defensible – across the Beaucerain plain at Châteaudun, for example – they were also more expensive to construct (Figure 1.6). The exterior of the tower does not lead one to expect creature comfort and life in a medieval castle was not all that pleasant. These stone forts were built to repel invaders and not for comfort so windows were slits to allow arrows to be fired out but not get in. This made them dark but also cold, damp and drafty.

Most castles had three or four levels, each with large rooms (Figure 1.7). The ground floors served as storage facilities for the grain and foodstuffs necessary to castle life. The next floors were dedicated to housing the men who provided defense of the castle. An **aula**, or an open-air hall of two stories, was built adjacent to the tower and was used by the lord on public occasions,

3 Christian Corvisier, "La tour maîtresse du château de Beaugency, dite 'Tour de César,'" *Bulletin monumental: Beaugency, monuments du Moyen Age et de la Renaissiance*, vol. 165–1 (2007), pp. 5–30.

Figure 1.6 The round tower at the nearby castle at Châteaudun. Author photo.

such as holding court or **homage** ceremonies. The rooms on the first and second story of the castle are described as quite luxurious and would have been where the lord and his family resided. Included were spaces for hygiene and prayer. Indeed, the castle at Beaugency was likely very similar to the one constructed by Lord Arnold of Ardres:

> Then he built a three-storey structure . . . The first storey, where there were cellars and granaries, also great chests, kegs, and vats, and other implements of the house, was on the ground level.
>
> Then the common living and work spaces of the inhabitants were on the second floor, where there were workrooms . . . Over here was the great chamber of the lord and his wife, in which they slept; the side chamber was contiguous to this, that is the chamber or dormitory of the attendants and children. Here in a more private part of the great chamber there was a private alcove, where they used to make a fire at full dawn or at dusk during an illness, or for letting blood or for warming the attendants or the weaned children.

Figure 1.7 Nineteeth-century engraving of the interior of the castle of Beaugency. Sadly, the tower was in ruins by the nineteenth century. Munitions had been stored in the lower level of the tower and exploded, which resulted in blowing the roof of the castle off. This engraving does illustrate the three floors of the tower. © Aurelia, Bibliothèque numérique d'Orléans.

On the top storey of the house, the rooms of the uppermost chambers were constructed, in which the sons might lie when they wished over here, while the daughters might lie down over there; vigilant servants, positioned and appointed to take care of the house and the always ready guards might catch some sleep over yonder.

There were flights of stairs and passages from storey to storey, from the house into the kitchen, from room to room, and from the house into the loggia [likely similar to the aula at Beaugency] and again from the loggia into the oratory or the chapel.[4]

4 Lambert of Ardres, *The History of the Counts of Guines and the Lords of Ardres*, ed. and trans. Leah Shopkow (Philadelphia: The University of Pennsylvania Press, 2001), pp. 160–161.

An important obligation a vassal owed to his lord was to serve as castle guard – and, as Lambert's description indicates, space was provided for them in the castle. In the 1130s the lord of Beaugency had about twelve men as part of his castle guard.[5] The length of this obligation varied, but forty days was a fairly common term of service. Wives sometimes accompanied their warrior husbands on this duty. A list of those retainers currently residing at Beaugency and probably providing castle guard, includes the names of their wives who were with them. Lords were bound to provide hospitality to their vassals, but this hospitality was fairly rudimentary. Men would sleep communally in the Great Hall or in any other nook or cranny they could find. Medieval people had a very different concept of personal space and lived out

Figure 1.8 Garderobe. The waste was usually evacuated to a moat or water feature below. Author photo.

5 *Cartulaire de Notre-Dame de Josaphat,* ed. Charles Métais, 2 vols. (Chartres: Garnier, 1911–1912) vol. 1, no. 47, pp. 65–68; hereafter, *NDJ*. *STV*, vol. 1, no. 2, pp. 6–9 outlines the duties and schedule of castle guard for Count Bouchard of Vendôme. See Chapter 3 for discussion of this document.

even the most intimate aspects of their life in public.[6] Even so, one can imagine that being a woman living in what was, in essence, a military barracks must have been interesting. Eventually, a separate space for the lady of the castle and her attendants would be added to the upper floor as a room often known as a solarium. Garderobes, or privies, were installed on the outside of walls of the castle (Figure 1.8). The kitchens were located on the other side of the *aula*, providing servants easy access from the kitchen to the tables of the Great Hall.[7] Some of the cooking would take place over the central fire; but at Beaugency the massive fire places that had chimneys to evacuate the smoke were in place by the eleventh century.

Although no extensive excavation has been conducted at Beaugency, the castle at Blois just a few miles south has been comprehensively excavated.[8] While Blois was the residence of a count and therefore larger, it is possible to extrapolate from the archeological findings at this castle to what we might find in the castle at Beaugency. The furnishings of the castle would likely be spartan, but comfortable. Most of the furniture would have been made of wood from the nearby forest. The Great Hall was a multi-purpose space.[9] It was a place for leisure activities or entertainment such as a game of chess or dancing. But it could also house retainers and banquets. The Great Hall would have been furnished with tables (which would be put up for meals), chairs, stools and benches to accommodate the Beaugency family, their retainers and guests. The table would have been set with implements made of iron, wood and ceramic. Cups, serving and storage vessels were ceramic and probably made on the castle grounds or in the village. The dishes and spoons were wood and archeologists have found initials carved into the back of plates to denote ownership. Knives were carried as personal property and were used to cut off pieces of meat from the common dish. Because of the easy access to wood – as well as the fact that it does not break – it was apparently the preferred medium for plates. Some locally produced glass may also have graced the table as glass was made downriver at Blois and thus easily accessible. The food served at the table would have consisted of some meats, most commonly fowl such as chicken or duck. The meat might have been grilled or put in a stew. Yet meat was also preserved by smoking or sealing in a pot with fat (much like modern-day duck confit). But the diet

6 Georges Duby, "Communal Living," in Georges Duby, ed., *A History of Private Life*, vol. 2, *Revelations of the Medieval World*, trans. Arthur Goldhammer (Cambridge, MA: Harvard University Press, 1988), pp. 35–85.

7 For a description of a castle kitchen, see Lambert of Ardres, *The History of the Counts of Guines*, p. 160.

8 Corvisier, "La tour maîtresse," note 1, p. 5. *Blois, un château en l'an mil*, *Château de Blois* (Somogy éditions d'art, Italy, 2000) pp. 51–95.

9 Given little is known about the *aula* adjoining the castle, it is possible that these activities might have taken place there and that it was furnished similar to the Great Hall. However, it assumed that this was an open-air space, which would have dictated what took place there and how it was furnished.

of the residents of the castle was based predominantly on cereals and grains such as wheat, barley and rye. These products may have been stored on the first floor of the *donjon* or in subterranean chambers on the castle grounds.

The more private spaces or chambers would have been furnished with a bed and a trunk, or coffer. Indeed, archeologists at Blois found trunks to be the most common item of furniture, likely because of the itinerant lives of the nobility. Combs of wood and even ivory were also found. Jars filled with unguents or perfumes were part of the ladies of Beaugency's toilette. Ceramic lamps would have been used for light throughout the castle. Tapestries would have been hung on the walls to insulate the castle rooms, but also provide decoration. These tapestries may have been produced locally by women living and working in the castle compound. But as trade became more international and less regional in the twelfth century, these wall-hangings could have been imported.

As well as being a residence, a castle was a community unto itself. In addition to the lord's retainers, other people called the château at Beaugency home. It is clear from the excavations at Blois that a variety of craftsmen and women lived and worked within the castle precincts. Although Beaugency was a smaller settlement, most castles housed people making goods and providing services to the castle. These workshops would have been modest in size and constructed of wood, with few windows and a central hearth. The craftsman and his family also lived where they worked. Very likely a weaving house existed in Beaugency to provide cloth to the lordly family. The need for weapons and horse shoes, as well as their repair, would have ensured that there was a blacksmith or iron works on the premises as well. Leather, too, would have been used; both for personal items and military implements. Servants such as cooks, stable hands, bakers, servers and those responsible for animals would also have lived within the walls of a castle. Castles were a hive of all sorts of activity – from the mundane to the dramatic during times of war or siege.

As the seat of a **lordship**, courts were held regularly in or near the castle to hear complaints of Beaugency vassals and tenants. During the Middle Ages there were two systems of justice. Secular courts, like the one held at Beaugency castle, dealt with matters concerning property and crime. Ecclesiastical courts addressed what fell under the moral purview of the church. For example, cases concerning marriage and legitimacy were heard in these courts. The lord of Beaugency held court to sort out conflicts among his vassals and peasants inside the great hall. Charters are invaluable sources for reconstructing how medieval justice and resolution operated, for they often record details of these events. For example, charters document that courts of law were public, held in the lord's hall or outside "in front of the tower" to accommodate large crowds. One can easily imagine a court being convened in the adjoining *aula* at Beaugency with those making the complaint and those responding to it gathered about with their supporters and witnesses. Members of the lord's family and retinue were also present and often participated in arbitration. Abbots and monks from local houses would also be present since they, too, were often involved in disputes as both disputant and defendant. The facts were heard, witnesses called to clarify issues or provide testimony, the lord would consult with his family and retinue and then pronounce his finding. Judgment was made public so that all could hear the outcome of the case. Indeed, charters refer to legal resolutions as a "public act" of the castle. Often these judgments were the result of compromise as lords implemented many different strategies to get parties to come to peace. Even when a compromise was reached and a dispute settled, however, problems could arise. Lord Ralph I of Beaugency had such a situation arise at his court in the 1120s. At his castle at Beaugency, Ralph and the bishop of Orléans confirmed a resolution of a dispute between several of Beaugency vassals and the monks of the monastery of Tiron.[10] Things did not go smoothly, for one of the vassals went back on his word and claimed the property once again. But soon he regretted that he had broken his agreement with the church and his lord – no minor misdeed – and gave up his control of the property. Sometimes these courts drew important visitors to castles. The bishop of Orléans was present at Ralph's court as the head of the diocese to oversee this dispute between an ecclesiastical community and secular lords.

Castles were vitally important political tools. Controlling castles was the key to any lord's power – including the count and the king. To keep an eye on their extensive properties, lords of all rank were itinerant. Kings, counts, **dukes**, **viscounts** and even the lords of Beaugency had several residences and traveled among them (see Maps 2–4). Being itinerant suited the lords well for it allowed them to keep abreast of what was happening in their domain, as well as insuring that they and their extensive retinue (which consisted of family members, about a dozen armed retainers and at least that many servants) did not exhaust the resources of one community. Travel overland in medieval Europe could be difficult. Chrétien de Troyes described just such perils in one of his Arthurian romances of the twelfth century: "Rain, as heavy as God could make it, began to fall . . . The road was so bad that her horse was often up to its girth in mud."[11]After such a journey, kings and counts expected their vassals to provide them with hospitality, including lodging, food and even entertainment.

Since castles were military fortresses, kings and counts wanted to be sure they approved of the construction of a castle built by a vassal. The last thing either count or king needed was a potential political enemy with a castle in their territory which could be used as a challenge to their power. It was during the eleventh century that castle fortresses came to dot the French landscape. Historians of medieval France have referred to this proliferation as

10 *Cartulaire de l'abbaye de la Sainte-Trinité de Tiron,* ed. Lucien Merlet, 2 vols. (Chartres: Garnier, 1883), vol. 1, no. 41, p. 61. Hereafter, *Tiron.*

11 Chrétien de Troyes, *The Knight and the Lion*, in *The Complete Romances of Chrétien de Troyes*, trans. David Staines (Bloomington: Indiana University Press, 1990), p. 314.

the "feudal revolution," a time when powerful warriors came to control the countryside.[12] This "revolution," some historians believe, signaled a decline in the power of central authority and a rise in the power of local lords. The castle has come to be both symbolic of and synonymous with the violence and breakdown of central power. Historians continue to debate the appropriateness of the idea of a "feudal revolution" and question if the changes were so violent or revolutionary.[13] The evidence from the counts of Chartres and Anjou, however, suggests the construction of castles followed the strategy and dictates of the count. Moreover, one scholar has estimated that twenty castles per 2,300 square miles were constructed in the region around Beaugency during the eleventh century.[14] While there were more castles in the region than there had been in the previous century, this estimate does not support the idea of a dramatic proliferation of castles controlled by unruly lords. Further, many of these castles were constructed with the approval of the count, viscount or bishop, and not by a local lord attempting to topple the political order.[15] While kings were not as powerful as they would become in the thirteenth century, there was some order in the kingdom – albeit often in the hands of counts. The interpretation of a "feudal revolution" therefore does not apply to the region around Beaugency.

Castle communities – like the ones at Beaugency and Montfollet – were walled, demarking another line of defense but also a community boundary. These walls served to provide protection, particularly during turbulent times, but they were also a means of controlling who was able to enter the castle precincts. Three sets walls were built around the castle of Beaugency during the course of the Middle Ages[16] (Map 1). The earliest ramparts encompassed only the castle and the church next to it. In the eleventh century, the walls were extended to include the nascent marketplace, the church of St. Firmin

12 In his seminal work, *Feudal Society*, Marc Bloch argued for two "feudal ages." This idea was later taken up by other scholars who proposed a "feudal revolution" of the eleventh century where centralized power broke down to be assumed by local lords. The construction of castles was symptomatic of this decentralization of authority.

13 The question of the "feudal" revolution was debated in the journal *Past and Present*. For references, see the suggested reading section at the end of this chapter. For more recent discussions of political order, see Thomas N. Bisson, *The Crisis of the Twelfth Century: Power, Lordship and the Origins of European Government* (Princeton: Princeton University Press, 2008); and John Cotts, *Europe's Long Twelfth Century: Order, Anxiety, and Adaptation* (New York, Palgrave MacMillan, 2012).

14 Chédeville, *Chartres*, p. 271.

15 Bernard Bachrach has argued that the count of Anjou followed a specific policy in constructing fortresses. That the count oversaw the development of these castles also argues against a lack of order. Bernard Bachrach, "The Angevin Strategy of Castle Building in the Reign of Fulk Nerra, 987–1040," *The American Historical Review* 88 (1983): 533–560.

16 Jacques Asklund, *Histoire des rues de Beaugency* (Beaugency, Société archéologique et historique de Beaugency, 1984) pp. 10–16; André Bezard and Daniel Vannier, *Beaugency sur la Loire en Orléanais* (Paris, Les éditions nouvelles, 1977), pp. 19, 43–46; Corvisier, "La tour maîtresse," pp. 5–6.

Figure 1.9 Porte du Change, the northernmost entry into the community in the eleventh-century walls. Author photo.

and a few residences. The walls apparently did not extend as far as St. Sepulcher as it is described in the eleventh century as being outside of the walls. The gate house guarding the northern most entry into the eleventh-century walls (Porte du Change) still stands today, with the addition of a Renaissance clock (see Figure 1.9). As Beaugency grew in the twelfth century, new walls were built between 1118 and 1130 that nearly tripled the amount of enclosed space, a reflection of the population growth, and included three gates. Parts of the older walls were incorporated into the new. Sections of the earlier wall remained within the outer ring to protect the heart of Beaugency. With the development of effective gunpowder weapons, such fortifications became obsolete, and in 1772 Beaugency's walls were destroyed.

But the walls required upkeep. A charter from the abbey of Notre Dame de Beaugency provides some colorful details concerning the maintenance of the back fence between the castle and the religious community. In 1292 Lord Ralph II recognized that the canons of Notre Dame were inconvenienced when the gates to the castle were closed because they or goods could not get to their church or other buildings.[17] So the lord agreed that the canons and those serving them could build their own gate, and come and go

17 After about 1104, Augustinian canons replaced Benedictine monks at Notre Dame de Beaugency. The difference between monks and canons will be addressed later in this chapter and in Chapter 7.

in the castle precincts as they wished "as long as those people coming in do not do any malice toward me, my people or my guards."[18] There was also concern about the state of repair of the wall during this time. The wall closest to the Loire River abutting the precincts of Notre Dame de Beaugency needed reinforcing and the lord of Beaugency granted the brothers license to reinforce the wall with iron and he agreed to restore the crenellations. This document tells us much not only about wall up keep but also how the community of Beaugency changed over the ages (the break in the wall is by the Abbey Gate on Map 1). By 1292 the likelihood of invasion seemed remote as kings established strong, centralized monarchies. The lords of Beaugency evidently thought assault was unlikely and became lax in their maintenance of their wall and comfortable granting access to their castle compound. But this charter also demonstrates just how closely the spaces of the lords and the clergy overlapped.

The church

The other prominent structure in Figure 1.1 (see page 10) is the abbey of Notre Dame de Beaugency.[19] Like the castle, the church played a central role in the lives of the Beaugency family. The physical proximity of the church to the castle, illustrated in Map 1, shows just how intertwined the nobles and the church could be. Indeed, the north entrance to the church provided easy and private access for the lords to the sanctuary. The importance that lords placed in the church is evident in that once their fortress had been completed, they turned next to erecting chapels and churches nearby. The first church the Beaugencys constructed was that of St. Sepulcher, which was built sometime in the mid eleventh century. Successive twelfth-century lords of Beaugency also planned and oversaw the construction of the new abbey church depicted in Figures 6.1 and 6.2.

For the lords and ladies of Beaugency "the church" consisted of many layers. Practically, it was an institution that was a neighbor and in which their friends and family served as clergy. Recall that the function of the church was to pray. There were two kinds of clergy in the Middle Ages to fulfill this obligation: regular and secular. **Regular clergy** denotes those clergy who followed a rule, or *regula*, such as the monastic rule crafted by St. Benedict in the sixth century. The monks' rule was based on the assertion that they live apart from the world in cloistered communities to be removed from the vanities and distractions of secular society. Nuns similarly lived by a rule and apart from the laity. Medieval people believed the monks and nuns

18 AD Loiret, H 10, fol. XXII; *Cartulaire de l'abbaye de Notre-Dame de Baugency*, ed. G. Vignat (Orléans, Herluison, 1879), no. 77, pp. 89–90. Hereafter, *NDB*.

19 Elaine Vergnolle, "L'ancienne collégiale Notre-Dame de Beaugency: Les campagnes romanes," *Bulletin monumental: Beaugency, monuments du Moyen Age et de la Renaissiance*, vol. 165–1 (2007), pp. 71–90.

had a direct link to God and that their prayers would be particularly efficacious in securing their salvation. For this reason, aristocrats were generous patrons of the church and many, but not all, were fierce protectors of their local ecclesiastical communities. In contrast, **secular clergy**, which included priests, secular canons, chaplains, deacons, bishops and archbishops, lived in the world and interacted with secular society. Starting in the early twelfth century, the neighboring church of Notre Dame was home to a community of canons. Canons were something of a hybrid between monks and secular clergy. There were two types of canons. Like monks, the canons of Notre Dame of Beaugency followed a rule, that of St. Augustine, making them regular canons. Although they too were expected to adhere to the vows of poverty, celibacy and obedience, as well as spending much of their time in prayer, they interacted with their secular neighbors. Canons preached, administered to the needs of the laity and taught. Some regular canons were cloistered; others were not. Secular canons lived in their own houses within the precincts of their religious community; they consumed meat, retained their personal property and collected their own revenues. The cathedral canons at nearby Chartres cathedral, for example, were secular canons and bishops could also be secular canons. As they were "secular," these canons were often engaged with the secular world. For instance, Count Henry I of Champagne employed canons to staff his chancery and one went on to become chancellor.[20] As evident in the events described in the charter earlier (see page 21), the Beaugencys would have also known their local bishops. They visited each other's courts and Lord Ralph I even corresponded with the bishop of Chartres (see Document 2 on page 223). Medieval nobles would have been close to their parish priest or have had their own personal chaplain. The presence of a chapel in the castle indicates that the Beaugency family had a private place to worship and by the mid twelfth century had a chaplain in their household for instruction or administering the sacrament.[21] But the Beaugency family would also have attended mass in the abbey church next to their castle through their own entrance in the north side of the church. There they would have heard fiery sermons about hell, damnation and how to avoid imperiling their soul. Like the modern bully pulpit, its medieval equivalent was used to reinforce community values. During the course of a lord or lady's life, he or she would have encountered many different sorts of clergy, each of which was vital to their spiritual life and eternal salvation.

Christianity arrived in Beaugency (then a Gallo-Roman settlement called *Balgentiacus*, from which the modern name of Beaugency derives) in the

20 Theodore Evergates, *Henry the Liberal, Count of Champagne, 1127–1181* (Philadelphia: University of Pennsylvania Press, 2016) pp. 48–49; 62–65.

21 A later lord of Beaugency, John I (d.1218) built a chapel within the castle compound over the eastern gate and installed a chaplain. Given his wife's tomb was located in this chapel, this space was likely intended as a family necropolis. The chapel located in the castle itself probably continued to be used for private devotions.

fourth century. Two large Early Christian cemeteries have been found in Beaugency that date to this time, indicating a significant Christian population. These Christians erected churches in Beaugency. The current abbey church of Notre Dame de Beaugency dates predominantly from the mid-twelfth century but it replaced an earlier structure.[22] Not only was the church itself rebuilt, but so was the community that inhabited the abbey. Around 1104 the lord of Beaugency and bishop of Chartres collaborated to create a reformed community by replacing the monks of Notre Dame with Augustinian canons. Periodically throughout its history, the Catholic Church has undergone periods of reform. The sixteenth-century Protestant Reformation is perhaps the best known of these movements, but another phase of reform occurred in the eleventh century. Named the Gregorian Reform after Pope Gregory VII by modern scholars, this movement had, at its heart, an attempt to expunge secular influences from the church. These reformers believed that kings, counts and lords, had far too much influence in the church, which had corrupted it. The church thus needed to be purified of secular influence. The lords and ladies of Beaugency were affected by these teachings and the establishment of regular canons at Notre Dame de Beaugency was undertaken to create a devout and circumspect community of canons – in contrast to unreformed monks who were seen as too worldly.

At the same time that castles were coming to populate the medieval landscape, churches were being built all across medieval Europe, which caused one eleventh-century monk to remark:

> But it seemed as though each Christian community were aiming to surpass all others in the splendor of construction. It was as if the whole world were shaking itself free, shrugging off the burden of the past and cladding itself in a white mantel of churches.[23]

As well as being a prominent feature of the physical landscape, the church also dominated the mental landscape of the Beaugencys. Medieval people believed that supernatural forces directed the course of their own lives, as well as those of their family, friends, neighbors, lords and enemies. Saints were crucially important not only to individuals but also for the health and well-being of communities. These were men and women who had once walked the earth whose devotion to God and piety made them extraordinary and allowed them to perform miracles while living and after their death. Because of their favor with God, their earthly and material remains, known as **relics**, were sought after as a physical link to the divine and to serve as the site of **pilgrimage**. Men and women, old and young, rich and poor, would travel to

22 The abbey church has undergone considerable rebuilding over the centuries due to damage inflicted mostly by war, both medieval and modern.

23 Raoul Glaber, *Opera*, ed. John France, Neithard Bulst and Paul Reynolds (Oxford: Oxford University Press, 1989) p. 117.

saints' shrines to ask for a saint's intervention or grace. Even the most humble and smallest churches could house relics. The church of Rhodon, which lays just about 25 miles west of Beaugency, housed several relics of local saints (see Figures 1.10 a and b). Although saints were dead, medieval people saw them as very much a part of the living. They believed that the saints could posthumously work miracles and could shape the course of their lives by granting miracles or intervention with God. For the medieval lay person, being a Christian involved active and physical piety as opposed to contemplation of texts, which most could not read. Pilgrimage thus became a way for medieval people of all status to express their dedication to God and the Holy and pilgrimage routes developed all over Europe.

Collections of saints' lives and miracles demonstrate just how much a part of the world medieval people thought them to be. St. Foy of Conques, a young Gallo-Roman girl who was martyred for her faith, was believed to be particularly fond of rings. When pilgrims visited her shrine, they brought rings to give to her while asking for her intercession. The saint was famous for making sure even the most reluctant donor gave her the jewelry she desired, for even when the wily pilgrim tried to keep their jewelry, the saint would find a way to ensure the rings and broaches were given in her honor. St. Foy performed miracles resurrecting dead animals, particularly donkeys and birds, but she also raised people from the dead. When a nobleman was left so bereft at the death of his wife, he prayed to St. Foy to restore her to life and the saint complied.[24]

Saints also played an important role in community life and identity. Chartres, for example, was home to the tunic that Mary wore during Jesus'

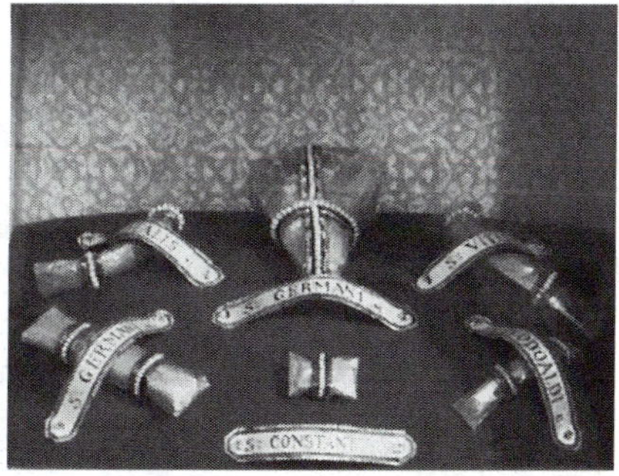

Figures 1.10a and b The parish church of Rhodon with the relics of Sts. Germain (to whom the church was dedicated), Vitalis, Constantine and Grimoald. The crusaders, Hugh Guernonatus and his son, donated property at Rhodon before going on crusade. It is possible they may have brought these relics home from the Holy Land. See Document 10 on page 231 for details. Author photos.

24 *The Book of St. Foy*, ed. and trans. Pamela Sheingorn (Philadelphia: University of Pennsylvania Press, 1995).

birth and it was central to the resident's community identity and well-being. When the town of Chartres was threatened by invasion by the Northmen, legend has it that the bishop of Chartres took the relic and circled the walls of the city to prevent its destruction. Whether due to the invocation of the protection of the Virgin or other more mundane factors, the Vikings who were poised to invade the city in 911, converted to Christianity. In 1192 when the cathedral where this relic was housed burned to the ground, the people of Chartres went into mourning. They took the destruction of the cathedral as a sign that they had earned the Virgin Mary's displeasure and that she would no longer act as the protector of their community. When the relic, carried by two of the cathedral canons, emerged from the ashes of the burned out cathedral, the townspeople were exultant.[25]

The abbey church of Beaugency was somewhat unusual in that it was dedicated to several saints: Mary or Notre Dame, St. Firmin, St. Fulcian, St. Victor and St. Gentian. This is an interesting combination of the holy. Mary is likely the only familiar one of the group and for good reason; the other four were rather obscure regional saints. Veneration of particular saints or types of saints varied throughout the Middle Ages. In the Early Middle Ages, for example, the saints that were most popular were those who closely connected to Christ. Relics of the apostles and holy people who lived in the early centuries of Christianity, therefore, were deemed especially significant. For example, the cult of St. Martin, the Roman soldier turned missionary, battler of **heretics** and eventually first bishop of Tours in the 370s, was popular. The monastery of Marmoutier founded by and named for Martin became one of the most powerful monasteries in France and one which the Beaugencys patronized. But as medieval Europe looked inward from the ninth to the twelfth centuries during the ravages of the Vikings and internecine fighting, local saints became especially popular. Perhaps it was hoped that a local saint would be more apt to protect the community that nurtured him or her. As medieval society became more cosmopolitan and international from the twelfth to the fourteenth century, saints that transcended national or regional boundaries such as Jesus, Mary and the Apostles, became the focus of medieval piety.

So what can the four saints to whom the abbey church in Beaugency was dedicated tell us about medieval religious practice or belief? The answer suggests much about the Beaugencys' understanding of the world. St. Firmin was an early bishop of Amiens which lay far to the north of Beaugency in Picardy (about 185 miles). Sts. Fulcian, Victor and Gentian were his companions and were martyred by the fourth-century Roman governor for refusing to recant their faith.[26] Two accounts of the founding of this church

25 See Robert Branner, ed., *Chartres* (New York: Norton), pp. 95–98.

26 To account for this association with martyrs from Picardy, J.-N. Pellieux, who wrote a history of Beaugency in the eighteenth century, attributed this connection to the fact that Beaugency had been settled by people from northern France in what is today Belgium. Because Beaugency

have been passed down and are so closely related that one likely used the first account as the basis for its narrative, but then added new details and embellishments. Both are fraught with historical anachronisms and neither explain events as the result of human action; rather, they rely on the divine and the miraculous. One would assume they would be of little use to historians, but scattered within these apocryphal accounts are kernels of historical reality. But let us start with the stories.

In both accounts, the abbey was founded by Lord Simon of Beaugency who was afflicted with leprosy.[27] Although each relates the story differently, both coincide in the interrelationship between the lord and the church. One account, which places Simon in the sixth century, says that he was convinced to convert to Christianity through the intercession of Firmin and was cured once he became Christian. Out of gratitude, he built the abbey church at Beaugency and dedicated it to St. Firmin and his companions, Sts. Fulcian, Victor and Gentian. Building upon this rather bare-bones account, another narrative adds a few more flourishes and places Simon in the Central Middle Ages rather than the sixth century. It recounts that during the bitter winter months, a mortally ill Simon was resting in his castle at Beaugency. He opened a window to let in some fresh air and found, much to his amazement, that the trees and flowers in his courtyard were in bloom and bearing fruit. In this midst of this rejuvenation, Simon was cured. Some time later he heard that a similar miracle had taken place outside of the city of Amiens, where the bones of the ancient martyrs Firmian, Fulcian, Victor and Gentian were buried.[28] This led Simon to build his church next to his castle wall and dedicate it to these saints as well as Mary out of gratitude.

was often spelled with *Belgen* or *Balgen*, he asserted that this was proof that there was a connection between Beaugency and those populating the Roman region of *Belgico*. Jacques-Nicolas Pellieux, *Essais historiques sur la ville et le canton de Beaugency, avec continuation en 1856 par M. Lorin de Chaffin*, 2 vols (Beaugency: J. Gatineau, 1856) vol. 1, p. 6. This is a highly dubious assertion and reflects early modern use of linguistic coincidence to establish a connection to the classical world. Also of note is a twelfth-century charter recording a gift and confirmation by two lords of Beaugency to the cathedral of Amiens, which was dedicated to St. Firmin. The charter attempts to establish that the cathedral had an "ancient" right to revenues collected at Beaugency. I read these documents as an attempt of the cathedral to expand its rights in the twelfth century, rather than proof of an "ancient" connection between Beaugency and Amiens or St. Firmin. Moreover, this grant would more likely be a gift by Lord Ralph I before or after his marriage to Mathilda of Vermandois, as her family had long been associated with this foundation. *Cartulaire du Chapitre de la cathedrale d'Amiens*, ed. Jacques Roux (Paris: Picard et Fils, 1897) no. 13, p. 19; no. 30, pp. 41–42. This is confirmed in a thirteenth-century confirmation of Lord John I of Beaugency of what Eleanor of Vermandois gave to King Philippe IV. Eleanor would have been John's cousin and, as such, he exercised a right to this property through his grandmother, Mathilda of Vermandois. *Catalogue des actes de Philippe-Auguste*, ed. and trans. Léopold Delisle (Paris: Auguste Durand, Libraire-Editeur, 1856) no. 1587, p. 305.

27 Bezard and Vannier, *Beaugency*, p. 22 and 67; Pellieux, *Beaugency*, vol. 1, pp. 7–15.

28 *The Golden Legend or Lives of the Saints as Englished by William Caxton*, 2 vols., (London: J.M. Dent, 1900), vol. 2, pp. 129–130.

How does the historian sort the fact from the fiction in these accounts? One could dismiss the miraculous recovery of Simon. The climatic change also seems dubious, but this detail could be a memory of a very early spring or of an unusually warm winter. Dendrochronology (the study of tree rings) and examination of ice bores from the polar ice caps demonstrate that the climate shifted dramatically in the Central Middle Ages. The extant documents reveal that there were two Lord Simons of Beaugency who lived in the twelfth and thirteenth centuries, so the accounts do ring of some historical accuracy. Indeed, Lord Simon II was credited with bringing the relics of Firmin, Gentian and Victor to Notre Dame de Beaugency in 1259.[29] Furthermore, it was during the twelfth century that the disease of leprosy spread throughout Western Europe. Could the sick Simon have been suffering from leprosy? Perhaps.

But the legends' explanation of the foundation of this church does capture the reality that medieval people yearned to be close to those who witnessed the early centuries of Christianity and were martyred for their faith. The region around Beaugency was home to churches dedicated to these earliest Christians and martyrs. In particular, many bear the name of some of the first bishops in France, like Firmin, but also local bishops such as Bishop Sulpice of Bourges, Bishop Martin of Tours, Bishops Lubin and Genoul of Chartres, Bishop Anian of Orléans. The dedication of the church in Beaugency to these early Christian Picard saints is thus in keeping with local hagiographical traditions and the desire that people of this later age had to capture something of the glory of the early centuries of Christianity by associating with these saints and their relics.

These legends also reveal other religious realities of the twelfth century. Although St. Firmin became the bishop of Amiens, he was born in Pamplona, Spain. His relics, along with those of the Virgin Mary, are housed in the cathedral there. Pamplona is on the popular pilgrimage route to Santiago de Compostella and many from Beaugency went on pilgrimage. Lord Lancelin II himself went on at least one pilgrimage in the eleventh century, as did his successors Simon I and Lancelin III in the twelfth. Ralph I, Lancelin II's son, was a famous twelfth-century crusader (see Genealogy 1 on page xx at the start of this book). It is possible that knowledge of St. Firmin came to the lords of Beaugency through travel to holy places – be it on crusade or pilgrimage. Perhaps a lord of Beaugency stopped at Pamplona because he was taken ill and when he prayed to St. Firmin, he was cured.[30]

While these legends add colorful detail and insight into medieval religious mentality, the historical record indicates that Lord Ralph I of Beaugency worked with Bishop Ivo of Chartres, one of the great reformers of his

29 Pellieux, *Beaugency*, vol. 1, pp. 124–125.

30 As well as the abbey church of Notre Dame de Beaugency, the parish church at Beaugency, located next to the castle, was also dedicated to St. Firmin.

generation, to found a community of Augustinian canons at Notre Dame de Beaugency around 1104.[31] Ralph also started the process and planning of a new abbey church. Significantly, parts of the church were built in what scholars call a "Paleo-Christian" style in an attempt to harken back to the earliest centuries of Christianity when reformers believed the church was in its purest state. Thus architecturally Notre Dame de Beaugency reinforced the values of the newly established canons. One of the first orders of business was to find an abbot for this newly reformed community. The ideal candidate needed to be someone who was dedicated to the tenants of the **Gregorian reform movement** and would work actively to keep the canons free of secular influence. A monk named Rainard was selected. He was from St. Quentin in Picardy, a house that had already been reformed by Ivo when he had been abbot there. Ivo knew Rainard and felt he had the background necessary to guide a fledgling community. Coincidentally, the first abbot of this newly reinvigorated ecclesiastical community came from a house named for the teacher of St. Firmin's companions and from the same region where these saints had been martyred. Another connection came through Lord Ralph I's wife, Mathilda. She was of the Vermandois family, one of the most powerful in the north of France and prominent patrons of the Picard church. The selection of Rainard as abbot likely stemmed from both Mathilda and Bishop Ivo's connections to the clergy of Picardy.

The line between legend and fact in the Middle Ages is sometimes indistinguishable. Fictionalized or imaginative accounts can often tell us as much about the past as fact. Association with the earliest martyrs of France was important to the medieval lord, abbot and bishop responsible for the founding of this religious community. This connection remains important to the people of Beaugency today. A modern rendering of a list of the abbots of Notre Dame de Beaugency adorns the wall of the church and states that the abbey was founded in 580 by Simon, lord of Beaugency. The eighteenth-century historian of Beaugency, J.-N. Pellieux, recorded that each year on St. Firmin's day (January 13), the canons of Notre Dame de Beaugency would dress in their summer robes, carry a candle and process to the parish church of St. Firmin. This procession was in remembrance of St. Firmin's miracle of the blossoming garden in January that caused Lord Simon to become his patron.[32] This tradition lasted until 1791. Clearly connection to a distant

31 Coincidentally, a church council was held in Beaugency this very same year. The council was called to determine if King Philip I's marriage to Bertrade of Montfort was in fact legitimate. Bishops from all over France came to Beaugency and it is likely the family of the lords of Beaugency hosted some of these prelates. The choice of Beaugency as a place of reform also likely informed the decision to have the council there as the church was in the midst of instituting reforms around marriage and the council was called to get King Philip and Queen Bertrade to abide by these practices. Hosting this council, moreover, signaled the Beaugencys' dedication and compliance with church reform. Ralph seems to have had a particularly close relationship with Bishop Ivo of Chartres, a committed reformer.

32 Pellieux, *Beaugency*, vol. 1, p. 11

past is as important to the modern people of village of Beaugency as it was to their medieval predecessors.

The foundation of Notre Dame and Sts. Firmin, Fulcian, Victor and Gentian, forged a relationship between the Beaugency family and this ecclesiastical community that would last centuries.[33] But this was not the only church that this family supported. **Patronage** was an important tool for aristocratic families. Not only did it help provide for their salvation, but also donations cultivated important ties to religious communities as well as other patrons. As a consequence, the Beaugencys favored a variety of religious houses. Early in their history, the members of this family made many donations to the abbey of St. Trinité in Vendôme. This patronage was an artifact of the family's origins to the west of Beaugency, in western France. St. Trinité was in the orbit of the counts of Anjou and Vendôme. To express their loyalty to the count, to whom some of the early Beaugencys owed allegiance, members of the family were benefactors of this monastery. The lords of Beaugency and their family members also made many gifts to the abbey of Marmoutier, located down the Loire near Tours. The comital family of Chartres had long been protectors and patrons of Marmoutier. Donating to this house allowed the Beaugencys to cultivate ties with this comital house and to associate with comital clients who were themselves powerful men. Both of these monasteries were traditional **Benedictine** houses (meaning they followed the rule of St. Benedict). The twelfth century, however, saw a flourishing of new foundations and new houses popped up all over Central France. For example, a community of monks grew up around the ascetic Bernard of Tiron in the woods of the west of France, which eventually became the monastery of St. Trinité of Tiron. Like Notre Dame de Beaugency, other monastic communities that were perceived as corrupt, such as thoseof St. Jean-en-Vallée and Notre Dame de Josaphat, both in the environs of Chartres, were replaced with reformed communities of monks or canons. The Benedictine monks of St. Avit of Châteaudun were similarly disbanded, but in this case a community of nuns was installed. Houses dedicated to caring for the poor and unfortunate were also established. Leprosaria, or houses dedicated to the care of lepers, appeared in towns both large and small, the largest of these communities in the region being that of Grand Beaulieu on the outskirts of Chartres. Even modest Beaugency housed a leprosarium and a **Hôtel Dieu** to help the poor and the stricken.

Religion was the lens through which the medieval residents of Beaugency understood the world around them. It was also a dominant feature of their physical world, as parish churches, chapels, priories, monasteries and cathedrals were prominent features of the medieval landscape. Nobles made gifts to the monks to be included in their prayers, to be buried near the saints and to be

33 For sake of simplicity, this church will simply be referred to as Notre Dame de Beaugency throughout.

part of the spiritual life of the monastery. Fear of the torments of Hell artfully rendered in stone, glass and paint in these many churches motivated medieval people to give generously to the church, to go on pilgrimage and partake in other good works, like feeding and clothing the poor. Religious expression for the laity of the Central Middle Ages consisted of doing things, rather than spiritual contemplation or individual reading of the Scripture. Although education for most nobles was rudimentary, many were educated. The chronicler Raoul Glaber remarked about a nobleman: "As is the custom amongst those of high birth, he was educated as a noble and then sent to schools of the liberal arts."[34] All noble sons – and likely daughters – were given the rudiments of an education. Those showing promise went on to be schooled in the **liberal arts**. Some noble born had private tutors, others were schooled in monasteries, but all were educated by the clergy. The existence of a *scola* at Notre Dame de Beaugency suggests that the lords of Beaugency may have been educated next door to their castle. The cathedral school at Chartres was probably the best known – and highest caliber – of such institutions. It was in these schools and cultural centers that a blossoming of medieval culture began in the twelfth century. In a society where virtually everyone was Christian, the church wielded tremendous influence over the hearts, minds and souls of medieval people.

As well as fulfilling spiritual and cultural roles, the church was one of the major land-holders of the Middle Ages. As such, the church often held property next to the fields of the medieval aristocracy. Hence the property interests of monasteries and bishops often intersected with those of their secular neighbors. Like the lords and ladies of Beaugency, the abbeys around them took part in the economic life of the region. Along with rights to land, the church also held rights to markets and enjoyed economic relationships with local merchants and craftsmen, which brings us to our final space in the center of Beaugency: The market place.

The market place

Inside both the eleventh- and twelfth-century walls of Beaugency were two market places. The first was tucked in between the castle precincts and the church of St. Firmin. Another market place was outside of the eleventh-century walls, just in front of St. Sepulcher and next to the cemetery of St. Firmin (hence its current name "Square of the Martyrs"). When a new set of walls was erected in the twelfth century, this market place was included and as trade blossomed it became the largest market. In this space the three orders of medieval society frequently overlapped. Merchants and peasants came to the market to sell their goods and make business deals. Lords, ladies and clergy – or their agents – visited these markets to obtain what they wanted or needed, as well as taking an economic interest in the commerce itself.

34 Glaber, *Opera*, p. 117.

Situated on one of the major tributaries of medieval France, the Loire River, Beaugency was ideally suited as a site for exchange and a source of revenue. Indeed, rights to markets were so desirable by the twelfth century that the lords of Beaugency gave them as pious gifts. The market places at Beaugency hosted two types of economic exchange: Weekly markets and regional fairs. Fairs were held all over Northern Europe in the Central Middle Ages, the most famous being the Champagne Fairs that took place to the north of Beaugency in the county of Champagne. During the twelfth century, these fairs attracted merchants from the corners of Europe – like those depicted earlier in Figure 1.3 (page 12). At Beaugency there were four larger seasonal fairs that took place throughout the year: Quasimodo (the week after Easter), Madeleine (May), St. Loup (October) and just before St. Nicholas Day (December 6).[35] While these fairs were more modest in scope than those to the north, they did attract merchants from outside of the region and even from abroad. Local markets were held weekly and provided residents with their necessities. The merchandise here would have been produced locally and sold by local merchants (Figure 1.11).

Figure 1.11 A bishop blessing a medieval Easter fair, much like the fairs and markets held at Beaugency. Note the stalls the merchants have set up and the livestock being brought to market. See Document 18 at the end of this book for the sorts of products and stalls at the Quasimodo Fair at Beaugency. Sonia Halliday Photo Library / Alamy stock photo.

35 Pellieux, *Beaugency*, vol. 2, p. 384.

In the fourteenth century, the abbey of Notre Dame de Beaugency compiled a list of rents and dues owed to it, including those from markets and fairs (see Document 18 on page 236). The cartulary is, hence, indispensable for reconstructing the economy of Beaugency and its environs.[36] The canons charged rent for the stalls that merchants and craftsmen used in the market place at weekly markets and seasonal fairs, as well as levying a toll on merchandise that was brought into the market. This accounting proves to be a treasure trove of information on the economic life of the village of Beaugency as well as the surrounding countryside. There are no fewer than thirty-one different kinds of merchants or merchandise listed in this compilation, an indication that residents of the castle, abbey and villages enjoyed access to a plethora of goods produced by the butcher, smith, draper, tapestry weaver, ragman, apothecary, sword maker, iron monger, furniture maker, mercer, leather worker, rope maker, boot maker, bow and shield maker, including: Bed clothes, cooked meat, reliquaries, caskets, chests, glassware, knives, olive oil, hemp, linen, spun wool (yarn or thread), horses, asses, sheep, cows, pigs, shovels, ploughs, salt and cheese. Let us visit one of the seasonal market fairs of Beaugency.

The larger seasonal fairs would have been a festive and exciting event. A holiday atmosphere would have permeated with the air filled with the aromas of cooking food, spices, perfumes, animals and the unwashed medieval masses. Throngs of people from all over the region would have flocked to Beaugency to purchase goods, but also to sell their own wares and surplus goods. The presence of the money-changers' stall indicates that those traveling to the Beaugency fairs – either to purchase or sell – would need to convert their money into the local currency. Money-changers also indicate that transactions were based on coin rather than barter or trade – a sign of the new monetary economy. Imagine the market square filled with dozens of colorful market stalls each hawking their own particular specialty – as illustrated in Figure 1.11. There would have been the more mundane stalls of the butchers, bakers, cheese-vendors and the ragman – who were probably local. But intermingled with such ordinary fare would have been exotic items such as spices, ointments, elegant cloth, sword and shield makers, glassware and relics offered by entrepreneurs whom the documents label "foreign" merchants (see Document 18 on page 236). Determining what was meant by "foreign" is difficult. Were these people simply "foreign" to Beaugency, meaning that they came from another region in France? Or were these merchants truly foreign and coming from distant lands? One way to determine this is by looking at the merchandise they were selling. Those foreign merchants who sold cloth, reliquaries, ointments and perfumes – items more for luxury than necessity – likely did come from some distance away. Products such as cloth and perfume conjure up images of the East. The variety of goods available to the residents of

36 AD Loiret, H 10, fol. XLVI; *NDB*, pp. 176–184.

Beaugency was rather staggering and truly any need could have been met – physical or spiritual – by one of these seasonal fairs. In addition to goods, labor, too, could have been purchased. In the spring markets, men looking to sell their skill behind a plow could have been secured for the planting seasons. In the summer, extra hands for help with harvesting were also available.

Weekly or regular markets would have more practical, locally produced, goods on offer (see Figure 5.2 for a peasant transporting their goods to a nearby market). While less tantalizing than the products available at the larger fairs, these markets provided the populace in and around Beaugency with what they needed to survive and fulfill their function in society. If a farmer broke his hoe, for example, he could go to a weekly market and purchase a new one. Cloth, although not as luxurious or well finished as foreign made, was also available for purchase. Seasonal fruits and vegetables, as well as fish from the Loire River, could be found in these stalls. Women who brewed a surplus of beer or made butter or cheese could also sell their products at the weekly market. These markets, too, would have been lively as people congregated, gossiped and enjoyed each other's company. Peasants selling their vegetables would rub shoulders with merchants hawking their cloth, with ladies shopping for shoes, with lords looking for a new knife and a monk looking to buy a cow to provide milk for his community.

The market place at Beaugency thus bore witness to one of the most important transitions of the Central Middle Ages: The birth of a profit economy. While those who exchanged goods for much of the eleventh century bartered for exchanges in kind, money came to be common in the purchase of goods starting in the twelfth century. This shift to a monetary economy also came with a change in social structure and mentalité, as represented by the discussion of Figures 1.2 and 1.3 earlier in this chapter. Instead of an economy based on sustenance, the underlying principal became to make a profit. The social, religious and cultural changes triggered by this subtle transformation were profound indeed and rippled out of the market place to touch virtually every aspect of medieval life.

Outside of the walls

The countryside surrounding Beaugency was fecund and provided the lords, ladies, peasants, merchants and clergy with a rich bounty of produce. The canons of Notre Dame de Beaugency also inventoried the types of property they possessed, making it possible to reconstruct the landscape around Beaugency.

Much of the land was dedicated to cereal production with fields of wheat, rye and barley covering the countryside. Like their contemporaries elsewhere, those living in the lands of the Loire rotated the kinds of crops grown in their fields or supplemented their grains with legumes to help restore nutrients to the land and ensure the continued fertility of the fields. Settlement patterns in the lands of the Loire were dictated by the predominance of cereal production. Instead of the American model of farm houses set amid fields of waving grain miles apart from each other, the open field system of medieval Europe meant that farmers clustered together in villages and farmed their fields collectively. To process the grain harvested from these cereal crops, medieval people needed to develop technologies to convert the raw kernels into a finished product that could be used in cooking and baking. Mills were used to grind the grain into various kinds of flour and were a valued resource to medieval agriculturalists. Just north of Beaugency on the plains of the Beauce, windmills were constructed to harness the wind that continuously blows across the plains. Today, giant modern windmills have been built alongside their medieval counterparts as modern society searches for alternatives to fossil fuel (Figures 1.12a and b).

Water mills were also built on the Loire River itself, but also on the many tributary rivers feeding into it. Indeed, there were six water mills located in Beaugency itself (Map 1). Lords (secular and ecclesiastical) used mills to better exploit the bounty of the land and jealously guarded their rights to them. Ovens, like mills, were needed to turn the milled flour into bread. Mills of wind and water, and ovens, became a source of revenue for lords, as villagers would often have to pay their lord (first in kind and then in coin) to mill their grain and bake their bread. For instance, a lord might demand one bag of flour for every ten processed as payment for using the mill. This payment in kind was eventually replaced by payment in coin. Grain was also used for another staple of the medieval diet: Beer. Medieval people consumed an immense quantity of beer for breakfast, lunch and dinner – in varying potencies. A great deal of their daily caloric intake came from beer. It was not unusual for an adult to consume a gallon of ale or beer a day, but the alcohol content was low.

Figures 1.12a and b A modern windmill stands side by side with a medieval one on the Beaucerain plain, just north of Beaugency. Author photo.

In addition to grain, wine was also an important staple of the medieval diet and economy. The canons of Notre Dame de Beaugency depended upon viniculture for their support. This community possessed vines in different locales for a total of 2,600 acres of vineyards. Like grain, wine needs to be processed and the canons of Beaugency had the right to a portion of the wine pressed from at least six different wine presses. As well as needing bread and wine for sustenance, the canons also had another need for it: Communion. Today the valley of the Loire is home to many important wineries, a tradition that literally has its "roots" in the Middle Ages. Other fruits were harvested from the orchards associated with peasant dwellings. Vegetables were also grown both inside Beaugency and without and are mentioned in the sources as contributing to the canons' upkeep.

Other natural resources provided sustenance for the lives of both the religious and secular. Although the landscape was covered with large fields devoted to cereal production, large and dense forests still covered much of France. While much energy and effort was devoted to clearing the countryside and adding to the arable land (remember the settlement at Montfollet), forests were also rich in resources that could be exploited. For the residents of Beaugency, access to arborial resources like the Long Forest was particularly useful. Wood, both dead and alive, was used in a variety of ways and charging for the collection of dead wood provided revenue to lords. Forests were also used to turn out pigs to root for food, otherwise known as pannaging pigs. Nuts and honey could also be collected from the woods and were two important ingredients in medieval cuisine; one as a source of protein, the other as a sweetener. The canons of Notre Dame, for example, held the right to half of the nuts that fell to the ground in various places located within the Long Forest. Rights to water were also important to the lords of Beaugency and their neighbors. Fishing rights to ponds, streams and rivers were energetically supervised and guarded. Gifts of such privileges were welcomed by the monks and nuns, for whom fish was the only animal flesh they consumed. The lords of Beaugency also enjoyed control of another major water resource that few in their position could claim: The Loire River. Not only could the lords claim a portion of fish caught from the Loire, they were also able to levy tolls on ships going down the Loire and on the bridge spanning the river. Two lords of Beaugency – one in the twelfth century, the other in the thirteenth – gave the tolls that they collected on ships traveling the Loire to the community of Notre Dame de Beaugency. The total amount of these tolls recorded in the charters was about two hundred shillings, or ten pounds, not an inconsequential sum.[37] As well as tolls, the lords of

37 In the Middle Ages, only silver coins were produced. There was no paper money. The most common coin was the silver penny or *denarius* (pl. *denarii*) and is designated by a "d," meaning "denarius." The lords of Beaugency did strike their own coinage, as is evident by the survival of the denarius struck by Ralph I. Twelve pennies, or *denarii*, equaled one shilling, or *solidus* (pl. *solidi*), and is noted as "s." A pound, or *libra*, consisted of 20 *solidi* and was designated as £, which is why British pounds today are designated by a £. So 2 £ 10 s 5d equates to 2 *libra*/pounds, 10 *solidi*/shillings and 5 *denarii*/ pennies.

Figure 1.13 Early modern engraving of the bridge and tower at Beaugency. The bridge had towers for defense, as well as a drawbridge that could be elevated in case of attack from the river. There was also a chapel on the bridge, where travellers could pray. The central portions of the bridge were bombed by the Allies in World War II and subsequently rebuilt. © Aurelia, Bibliothèque numérique d'Orléans.

Beaugency garnished a portion of the goods that were being shipped by their lordship: Specifically salt. Salt was an extremely valuable commodity in the pre-modern world not only for its use as a spice but also, in the era before refrigeration, for preserving food. Tolls were also collected from the bridge spanning the Loire River (see Figure 1.13). The medieval bridge at Beaugency still stands today and was one of a handful of bridges over the Loire for much of the Middle Ages. As a consequence, it was both strategically important and economically profitable for its lords. As recently as World War II, this bridge served as a major artery between eastern and western France. In 1944 it was bombed by the Allies to prevent the Germans from crossing the Loire (tragically sixty-three residents of Beaugency died in this attack). Control of the river thus gave the lords of Beaugency access to both resources and revenues, which were equally important to their daily existence and to their acquisition of money as the economy changed.

The lords and ladies who called the castle of Beaugency home interacted with peasants, village people, craftsmen, merchants and clergy throughout their lives in a variety of ways and in a variety of settings. Now that we understand their immediate environment, it is time to consider the intimate dimensions of their family life before moving on to their interactions with neighbors, other lords, vassals, peasants, kings and the church.

Suggested reading

Ellen F. Arnold, *Negotiating the Landscape: Environment and Monastic Identity in the Medieval Ardennes*. Philadelphia: University of Pennsylvania Press, 2012.

See the essays by Dominique Barthélemy and Stephen D. White, Thomas Bisson, Timothy Reuter and Chris Wickham debating the Feudal Revolution in *Past and Present* 142 (1994) and 152 (1996).

Marc Bloch, *Feudal Society*, 2 vols, trans. Louis Manyon. Chicago: University of Chicago Press, 1961.

Constance B. Bouchard, *Rewriting Saints and Ancestors: Memory and Forgetting in France, 500–1200*. Philadelphia: University of Pennsylvania Press, 2014; and *Sword, Miter and Cloister: Nobility and the Church in Burgundy, 980–1198*. Ithaca: Cornell University Press, 1987.

Georges Duby, *The Three Orders: Feudal Society Imagined*, trans. Arthur Goldhammer. Chicago: University of Chicago Press, 1982. See also Theodore Evergates' critique of Duby's work: "The Feudal Imaginary of Georges Duby," *Journal of Medieval and Early Modern Studies* 27 (1997): 641–660.

Sharon Farmer, *Communities of Saint Martin: Legend and Ritual in Medieval Tours*. Ithaca: Cornell University Press, 1991.

Patrick Geary, *Furta Sacra: Thefts of Relics in the Central Middle Ages*. Princeton: Princeton University Press, 1991.

David Nicholas, *Urban Europe, 1100–1700*. New York: Palgrave Macmillan, 2003.

2 Beaugency family life

Having sketched out a broad picture of the landscape in which the Beaugency family members lived their lives, let us now turn from the center of the village, go through the castle compound, climb the stairs and enter the castle of Beaugency (see Map 1). Within the confines of these castle walls, the lords of Beaugency and their family were bound together by the most important relationship that defined their lives: That of family. From birth to death, family ties shaped the life experience of medieval aristocrats. These relationships determined an individual's place in the social hierarchy, if they would marry or enter the church, whom they would marry, what resources or lordships they might control, their political allies and enemies and their relationship with clergy. But how did medieval elites like the Beaugencys experience family life?

Like modern families, it is impossible to say there was one singular family experience for medieval people – even people in the same class. Much depended on individual circumstance and personalities. Scholars have debated how to best characterize family life in the Middle Ages. As the study of history shifted from Great Men and Big Events to an interest in history from the ground up, understanding how family operated in former times became a subject of interest among historians. Influenced by a large dose of anthropology, social historians of the 1970s developed a paradigm of family life that went something like this:

The modern family, bound and guided by affection, did not emerge until the modern era. Pre-modern families, in contrast, were characterized by detachment. Husbands and wives did not marry for love (although affection could develop) and, because of a high mortality rate, parents remained emotionally distant from their children. Some scholars went as far to assert that pre-modern people viewed children as disposable and subject to the sometimes violent will of their elders. Moreover, families were run by men. Women were powerless, unimportant and even viewed as a disadvantage to the family. Family resources were invested in the male offspring, oftentimes only in the line of the first born male. Indeed one scholar remarked:

> The history of childhood is a nightmare from which we have only recently begun to awaken. The further back in history one goes, the lower the

level of child care, and the more likely children are to be killed, abandoned, beaten, terrorized, and sexually abused.[1]

Recent scholarship, however, challenges this interpretation and thoroughly debunks this harsh view of family life.[2] In spite of a mortality rate much higher than ours, medievalists have demonstrated that children were valued – both boys and girls – and that most parents cared deeply about them. While not based on modern notions of "love," medieval husbands and wives did care for each other. John Gillingham even argues that as the idea of romantic love was developed by the poets of the twelfth century, men and women came to expect that they would love their spouse.[3] Women were important members of their family, vested with considerable influence and power. Although some families did prefer to distribute the majority of their resources to one or two children, others were still received support or training.

The evidence from the Beaugency family, I will argue, supports the more recent interpretation of family life. The Beaugencys cared about each other, mourned the loss of their kin and provided material support for their members. However, their family life differed significantly from those living in cities or the peasants living on their estates. Indeed, discussion here is of the family life of one small segment of the population and their experiences cannot be extrapolated to other sectors of society. Investigating medieval family life is challenging for all social classes. Documents recording the intimate aspects of life, such as letters and diaries, are not extant for this period. Childhood, in particular, remains oblique because children did not leave behind their own accounts of their experiences. But by weaving together evidence from charters, chronicles, saints' lives and material culture, it is possible to develop a sense of the family life of one noble family. Medieval aristocrats were profoundly concerned about the state of their souls and the souls of their loved ones. By making pious gifts to the church, they sought the intercession of the clergy and saints. Analyzing for whom lords and ladies made such pious gifts can allow us to determine who was important to them and sometimes their emotional attachment to particular relatives or people. Charters that record such gifts, as well as how noble families distributed their resources, are a valuable tool for reconstructing Beaugency family life. Although charters were not penned to specifically address family life, they do allow for the occasional glimpse into aristocratic private life and will provide the foundation for my interpretation of Beaugency family life.

1 Lloyd DeMause, *The History of Childhood* (New York: Harper and Row, 1974) p. 1. While not so extreme, other scholars felt that a family life defined by affection did not develop until the modern era. See the suggested reading section at the end of this chapter.

2 Barbara Hanawalt provides an extensive analysis of the historiography of childhood in her article "Medievalists and the Study of Childhood," *Speculum* 77 (2002), pp. 440–460.

3 John Gillingham, "Love, Marriage and Politics in the Twelfth Century," *Forum for Modern Language Studies* 25 (1989): 292–302. Reprinted in John Gillingham, *Richard Coeur de Lion: Kingship, Chivalry and War in Twelfth Century* (London: Hambledon, 1994).

In order to understand how family life shaped the lives of the Beaugencys, this chapter will trace the role that family played over the course of life, from birth to death. Family life was experienced differently by different members of the Beaugency family. For example, gender played a role in determining how family shaped the lives of men and women. Furthermore, whether or not a person stayed in the world or joined the church affected how they experienced family. With an eye to these distinctions, let us now enter the castle tower at Beaugency to observe family dynamics.

Birth and childhood

When a child was born into the Beaugency family, he or she joined a family that exercised considerable influence and had accumulated significant wealth. Most of the Beaugency children born after c. 1050 likely made their entrance into the world in the lord's chamber located on the second floor of the castle from which the family took its name. Gathered in the birthing chamber would have been the women of the castle, and probably a midwife, to assist the mother in birth. As vividly brought to life in medieval painting and illuminations, childbirth was the exclusive provenance of women (Figure 2.1). So when a Beaugency child took his first breath, he or she was surrounded

Figure 2.1 Childbirth among the medieval elite (*Geburt Maria* by Meister des Marienlebens – *Mary's Birth* by Master of the Life of the Virgin 1460–90 German Koln Cologne Germany). Peter Horree / Alamy stock photo.

by women likely ranging in status from his/her highly born mother to the village woman experienced in healing. Later child-birthing manuals indicate that the room would have been warm and that his or her mother likely gave birth laying down – although birthing stools were also used. Once the baby was born, he or she was bathed, wrapped snuggly in swaddling and given to his/her mother to nurse. Much of the first year was spent swaddled and in a crib to keep bones straight and keep babies from the dangers of a medieval castle. Modern analysis of medieval children's accidental deaths reveals that fire and falls seem to be some of the most common causes of fatality. Medieval parents, including peasants and those living in cities, thus immobilized their children for their own protection.

As a Beaugency baby began to creep and then walk she, like modern children, might have mastered her feet by using a walking toy. Manuscripts contain images of wooden structures with a frame and wheels that children could use to help them learn to walk (Figure 2.2). Leading strings, which were something of a harness, might also have been put on the toddler to confine or manage movement as she first learned how to walk and after she had mastered the skill and was likely to dart off without warning. A medieval castle would have been fraught with many with possible dangers for a small child: Stone stairs, high galleries, open windows, large dogs, weapons, a massive fireplace complete with open pots containing boiling liquid, wells, horses, cobblestones – not to mention the microscopic inhabitants of the castle that posed a threat to a small child's developing immune system. Medieval chroniclers recorded many outbreaks of epidemics. In 1106,

> an infection of a phlegmatic kind, spread all over the west, afflicting everyone with catarrh [the build-up of excessive mucus and phlegm] and streaming eyes . . . [In the fall] burning fevers of different kinds and other infections caused great human suffering, and stretching many people on beds of sickness.[4]

Undoubtedly many children were among those to succumb to such outbreaks.

Mothers and nurses looked after babies and toddlers. Nursemaids would have been indispensable to the itinerant noblewoman as she moved her family from castle to castle, as well as a constant presence in the life of the child. There has been much debate over whether pre-modern women nursed their own children. While it is fairly clear that elite women in the Renaissance preferred not to (in spite of recommendations made in Renaissance child advice manuals), the situation is less clear for medieval women. Indeed, one charter from the region indicates that at least one noblewoman chose to nurse

4 Orderic Vitalis, *The Ecclesiastical History*, ed. and trans. Marjorie Chibnall, 6 vols. (Oxford, Clarendon Press, 1969–1980), vol. 6, p. 75. Hereafter, OV.

Figure 2.2 A medieval child learning to walk. Note also the child playing on the stick horse. Contrary to modern assertions, medieval children did have a childhood and were not simply "little adults." *Seven Ages of Man*, 1485. / Woodcut. Granger Historical Picture Archive / Alamy stock photo.

her child and others likely did too: "Hildeburg, the young daughter of Amelina . . . was still in a cradle and her mother was nursing her" when her name was listed in a transaction recorded in a charter.[5] Given the popularity of images of the lactating Virgin, many of which are extant from the region of the Loire, it seems likely that medieval women were encouraged by the clergy and perhaps other women to nurse their own children rather than engaging a wet nurse.

In spite of Beaugency parents' best efforts, some of their children did die young. Sadly, due to the high rate of child mortality (which could run as high as one in three children), parents experienced the loss of their children and grieved deeply when they died.

> So great, so astounding were the grief and sorrow that struck his father, his mother and the leading men of the kingdom that Homer himself would have lacked the skill to express it . . . His wise father grieved mournfully and cursed his wretched life because he was the one who survived . . .[6]

5 *Cartulaire de Marmoutier pour le Vendômois*, ed. Charles Auguste de Trémault (Paris: Picard, 1893), no. 36, pp. 331–332. Hereafter, *CMV*.

6 Abbot Suger, *The Deeds of Louis the Fat*, ed. and trans. Richard Cusimano and John Moorhead (Washington D.C.: Catholic University of America Press, 1992) p. 150.

Abbot Suger, biographer of the King Louis VI who was a contemporary of the Beaugencys, records the profound sense of loss that the king and queen felt at the death of their son. Children of the Beaugency family also died young and their parents expressed similar emotions. In the early twelfth century, a monk recorded that Lady Marie of Lavardin (cousin to the Beaugencys) lost her son, Salomon, when he was a small child (see Genealogy 2).

> We wish it to be known that lord of the castle of Lavardin, named Haimeric, **cognomen** Gaumard, and his wife Marie give and concede to the monks of the holy Church of God and St. Martin, the dues paid for market stalls on bread which . . . they hold freely and absolutely, [so the monks] will also hold them freely and absolutely for all time. Because their son, named Salomon, was on the brink of death, it appeared to both parents, and those who joined with them, that the boy was in greater need of divine favor than tears . . . so humbly entreating they asked that the same boy be received by the monks; therefore, as a result of their asking, the monks received him as a monk [the boy later died].[7]

My interpretation of this document is that these were grieving parents, moved to tears, by the plight of their child. Of paramount concern to medieval parents was that their child died in a state of grace to avoid the perils of Hell. To ensure their child did not suffer in the afterlife, this couple donated property to the church. Moreover, realizing that their son was nearing death, Marie and her husband took the further step of arranging him to die as a monk. Being "received as a monk" meant that the child numbered among the most holy in society who dedicated their lives to prayer. This would provide further assurance that the child would go to heaven. Others might interpret this document as an attempt by the parents to be rid of a sickly child. To me, however, this document suggests a degree of care and emotional attachment to Salomon. The description of the parents doing what was the "greater need" for the child I read as an indication of care and trying to do what was best for the boy. Although this charter is somewhat unusual in providing such a graphic description of parental grief and caring for a mortally ill child, others record similar reactions.[8] Another noblewoman, contemporary with Lord Lancelin II, traveled to a monastery just three weeks after the death of her child, where she, like Haimeric and Marie, made a gift for her child's soul. The charter tells us that she was "groaning and weeping" with such grief that one of her sons had to help her walk down to the altar of the church to make her gift. Tragically, the death of children was a reality with which medieval parents had to cope. Expressions of parental affection, however,

7 AD Loir-et-Cher, 16 H 83, no. 10; *CMV*, no. 31, pp. 323–324.

8 *STV*, vol. 2, no. 326, pp. 37–38.

were not reserved for children who died. Indeed, when Lord John I of Beaugency made a donation to the church, he did so for his "beloved family."[9] Chronicle and literary sources are full of instances of mothers and fathers proclaiming affection for their children. Queen Mathilda, the wife of William the Conqueror, for instance, had this to say about her feelings for her son, Robert:

> Do not wonder that I love my first-born child with tender affection. By the power of the Most High, if my son Robert were dead and buried seven feet deep in the earth, hid from the eyes of the living, and I could bring him back to life with my own blood, I would shed my life-blood for him and suffer more anguish for his sake.[10]

Not only were medieval children loved, they were also very much underfoot. As the life of a different Queen Mathilda records: "As the venerable Mathilda seated herself at the royal banquet table next to Queen Adelheid, the young ones ran about nearby, absorbed in their childish games."[11] The dinner table would have been a place where children would have interacted with the adult members of their household and the description of Queen Mathilda's hall suggests that children were both seen and heard. This quote also indicates that medieval children spent time in play. Archeological excavations have uncovered all sorts of toys from children of all classes: Spinning tops, blocks, stick horses, dolls and even hockey sticks. Manuscript illuminations also depict children at play – from swinging on swings, having mock jousts and playing with hoops – which indicates that medieval children played much as modern children do.

With what other children might a Beaugency child expect to share dinner or play? The progeny of aristocrats were often raised with cousins or children of other nobles who were being fostered by the family. Siblings would often have been a presence in a child's life (but not always). In some cases, illegitimate siblings may also have been part of the nursery. It was not unusual for aristocratic men to father children outside of marriage. Illegitimacy, at least in the eleventh and twelfth century, did not carry with it the stigma of later eras. No Beaugency bastards are mentioned in the records, but their Lavardin cousins did produce one child outside of marriage. When Haimeric Gaumard of Lavardin made a gift to the monks, he had his sister and his illegitimate brother consent to it.[12] Whether Haimeric included his illegitimate brother because he felt some familial attachment or because all children – even bastards – had a right to property, it is difficult to determine. What the

9 *NDB*, no. 124, pp. 143–144.

10 OV, vol. III, pp. 103–105.

11 *Queenship and Sanctity: The Lives of Mathilda and the Epitaph of Adelheid*, trans. Sean Gilsdorf (Washington D.C.: Catholic University of America Press, 2004), p. 115.

12 *CMV*, no. 32, pp. 325–326

charters do demonstrate is that bastards were included in transactions and, in some cases, their right to property recognized or upheld.[13] Intriguingly, the only illegitimate progeny recorded in the charters were male – although why this was the case remains unclear. Given that bastards both possessed and had a claim to property, they were likely educated in running estates

suarū: et preualuit in uanitate sua.
Ego autem sicut oliua fructifera in domo
dei: speraui in misericordia dei in eternū
et in seculum seculi.
Confitebor tibi in seculum quia fecisti:
et expectabo nomen tuum quoniam
bonū est in conspectu sanctorū tuorū.
ixit insipiens in cor
de suo: non est deus.
Corrupti sunt et
abominabiles facti
sunt in iniquitatibus:
non est qui faciat bo
num.
eus de celo pspexit
super filios hominum: ut uideat si est
intelligens aut requirens deum.
Omnes declinauerunt simul inutiles
facti sunt: non est qui faciat bonum.
non est usq; ad unum.
Nonne scient omnes qui opantur iniq̄

Figure 2.3 Page from a medieval psalter. The enlarged initials could be used to teach a child the alphabet. This one shows David battling Goliath. Photo © RMN-Grand Palais (domaine de Chantilly) / René-Gabriel Ojéda. David and Goliath Folio 84 verso. Psalter of Ingeburge of Denmark, Queen of France (beginning of XIIIth century) Ms9 folio84-sided. Anonymous. Location: Chantilly, Musée Condé.

13 For a discussion of the property rights of bastards, see Amy Livingstone, *Out of Love for My Kin* (Ithaca: Cornell University Press, 2010), pp. 51–52. For the illegitimate progeny of royalty, see Sara McDougall, *Royal Bastards: The Birth of Illegitimacy, 800–1200* (Oxford: Oxford University Press, 2017).

alongside their legitimate siblings. Indeed, bastard sons were also fostered and trained as knights. So an aristocratic son or daughter might share their dinner with an illegitimate half-sibling – although probably an illegitimate half-brother.

As a toddler grew into a child, his mother would likely have been the one who taught him the rudiments of reading and first exposed him to the tenets of Christianity. Recent scholarship has highlighted the role that mothers had in the upbringing of their children and rebuts earlier interpretations that dismissed them.[14] In neighboring Chartres, for example, a charter recorded that a nobleman's grandmother (who was his surrogate mother) taught him Scripture when he was a young boy. Because sons were usually destined for knighthood, scholars assumed mothers were not present in their lives. But, it does appear that women were primarily responsible for the education of their children before sons entered military training or before sons and daughters entered the church. Medieval aristocratic women were often literate, as evident by the books they owned and by the frequent depictions of women with books in medieval art. Mathilda of Beaugency, the wife of Ralph I, was literate and she likely played some role in educating her young children. The Central Middle Ages was a time of increased literacy. Psalters or books of Psalms were particularly popular among elite and were often illustrated. The letter of the first word of the first line of the Psalm was usually larger and elaborately illustrated (see Figure 2.3). One could imagine a Beaugency mother – like Mathilda – with a child snuggled on her lap, using these books to teach her young child the rudiments of the alphabet; much as mothers today use alphabet books to school their children in the letters of the alphabet. As a child developed, numerical literacy could also have been taught from the Psalter, as well as the names of the months, for many Psalters contain a calendar of prayers for specific saints' days.

Growing up and adolescence

After mastering the basics of learning at home, both sons and daughters could have been sent to a monastery, nunnery or parish school to continue their education. In this regard, aristocratic childhood differed from that of peasants or most children in the cities. Peasant children would have started helping their parents with tasks in the house and fields. Urban male children entered into apprenticeship to be trained in a trade around the age of seven and moved away from home. Beaugency sons who would become knights were educated. As the theologian Peter Abelard remarked:

14 See Pamela Sheingorn, "'The Wise Mother:' The Image of St. Anne Teaching the Virgin Mary," *Gesta* 32 (1993), 69–80; Michael Clanchy, "Did Mothers Teach Their Children to Read?" in *Motherhood, Religion, and Society in Medieval Europe: Essays Presented to Henrietta Leyser*, ed. Conrad Leyser and Lesley Smith (Routledge: Farnham, UK, 2011) pp. 129–153.

> I had a father who had won some smattering of letters before he had girded on the soldier's belt. And so it came about that long afterwards his love thereof was so strong that he saw to it that each son of his should be taught in letters even earlier than in the management of arms.[15]

The existence of a *scola* at Notre Dame de Beaugency, located just yards from the castle, suggests that the Beaugency children might have been taught by the canons. Beaugency daughters may also have been sent to the nearby convent of St. Avit or its **priory** in neighboring Meung-sur-Loire for instruction. Other aristocratic households preferred to hire tutors for their children. In keeping with their role in the early education of their children, mothers were often responsible for finding learned men – likely clerics – as tutors for their sons. The countess of Chartres, for example, engaged tutors for her children. Neighboring families followed this educational path for their sons. In the twelfth century, the vicecomital family of Châteaudun had a tutor for their children who witnessed charters for his patron.[16] Guibert of Nogent, who penned his memoirs in the twelfth century, remembered his tutor fondly – even though he was a harsh taskmaster. He also recalled the powerful role that his mother played in both his education and clerical vocation.[17] Noblewomen also had female tutors to educate them.[18] So it is also possible that the Beaugency children were educated in the castle.

Children destined for both the secular world and religious life were often not raised within the family. Starting around the age of ten, a child might join a religious community or be sent to a relative to be fostered. Guibert of Nogent, mentioned above, was pledged by his parents to the church. The chronicler Raoul Glaber records the entry of a young boy into the monastery:

> And there, according to the custom of the monastic rule, [his parents] presented him to the abbot of that place, who, receiving him very devotedly, clothed him with the habit of holy monasticism, and thereafter passed on to him his first rudiments of learning.[19]

Child **oblates**, or children who were "given" to the church by their parents, have often been held up as evidence of parental detachment. While donating

15 Peter Abelard, *Historia Calamitatem*, trans. Henry Adams Bellows (Mineola, New York: Dover Publications, 1992) p. 1.

16 *Tiron*, vol. 1, nos. 152 and 153, p. 176.

17 *Self and Society in Medieval France: The Memoirs of Abbot Guibert of Nogent*, ed. and trans. John F. Benton, *Medieval Academy Reprints for Teaching*, 2nd edition (Toronto: University of Toronto Press, 1984).

18 Theodore Evergates has found that Countess Marie of Champagne had Alice of Mareuil as her tutor for several years. Alice also travelled with Marie, indicating that she did more than just teach the young countess the rudiments of Latin. See Theodore Evergates, *Countess Marie of Champagne* (Philadelphia: University of Pennsylvania Press, forthcoming), chapter 1.

19 Glaber, *Opera*, p. 259.

a child to the church might seem heartless to modern audiences, medieval people had a different view and took steps to ensure all a young child's needs were met (see Document 3, page 224). For example, in addition to being provided with a tutor, the young boy mentioned above was also provided with a local woman who acted as his surrogate mother. Families had several valid reasons for placing their children into the church. First, entrance into an ecclesiastical community secured a future for a child. Second, he or she would be further educated. Finally, the child would be provided with opportunities for advancement and might even attain high ecclesiastical office. Aristocratic children had very little say over their future; rather, they trusted their parents and family to decide what was best for them – Guibert of Nogent clearly did not view his parents' vow to make him a cleric as a sign of disaffection. If anything, Guibert's path to the monastery drew him even closer to his mother (his father died when he was quite young) and the abiding affection that they felt for one another is apparent in his memoir.

Family played an important part in shaping the life of the young monk or nun – although in a different way than it did for their siblings who stayed in the secular world. Aristocratic families developed close ties to particular ecclesiastical houses, usually through patronage, and often placed their children in these same communities. Chances were rather good that the young oblate would find that an uncle, aunt, cousin, or even brother or sister, might already be in residence. These relatives would be instrumental in providing the child with emotional support and helping with the transition to the religious life. We should not assume that children were coerced to enter the church or not valued by their family. One young nobleman living near the Beaugencys decided to become a monk and ran away to the monastery. His mother followed and after some negotiation agreed to let him become a monk. While some nobles were not suited for the church (there were some infamous cases of bishops not being able to read), there were some who clearly were. Saints' lives and chronicles portray a young aristocrat's struggle against his or her family to become a **religious**, but monastic authors may have exaggerated family hostility to emphasize the saint's dedication or piety. In recounting the life of a young nobleman who went on to attain a high ecclesiastical office, for instance, Raoul Glaber says that when the young man's father heard he wanted to become a monk, he "was transported with rage, came to the monastery, and dragged his son thence, pouring reproaches upon this child who only sought the higher good."[20] The father arranged for his son to be sent to the royal court in hopes of dissuading him from his religious vocation. But to no end, as the king recognized the young man's zeal and made him the treasurer of one of the most important monasteries in France.

To place a child in an ecclesiastical house, families had to endow a son or daughter with property to provide support for the span of their lifetime.

20 Glaber, *Opera*, p. 119.

Noble families were eager to invest these resources because children who became nuns and monks performed a valuable service for their family: They interceded with God. A vassal of the Beaugency cousins at Lavardin gave one of his sons "so that the child may so greatly entreat for the salvation of hís relatives."[21] The monks accepted the boy out of "friendship for his father." To ensure his son's entrance, he gave land and its rents to the monastery (see Document 3, page 224). About a century later, another nobleman gave his **fief** so that his sister could join the **Cistercian** nuns of Clairets.[22] Although nuns and monks lived apart from their natal family, they maintained contact with their kin. Clergy participated in family transactions, even consenting to donations despite having taken a vow of poverty. Family members often visited local houses on pilgrimage, to rest, or stay, or ensure transfers of property to the church. Monks and nuns were reunited with their relatives on these occasions. Moreover, any offices or honors that clerical family members achieved would reflect well on the family by bringing power and influence. These brothers and sisters in Christ would also be expected to help their kin secure entrance to their house and adjust to the religious life, or win an ecclesiastical office. Nuns and monks also attained a higher level of learning, would have been further schooled in Scripture and could likely read several languages in addition to Latin.

Although they did not receive the same schooling as their clerical siblings, sons and daughters destined for the secular life also increasingly needed to be able to read and perhaps write so that they could render judgments, read charters and letters. Over the course of the twelfth century, knights became far more lettered and some of them became distinguished authors themselves. Ralph I of Beaugency exchanged letters with both Bishop Ivo of Chartres (see Document 2, page 223) and Abbot Geoffrey of Vendôme early in the twelfth century. He could presumably read the letters he received and may have written – or dictated – the responses he sent.[23] A little later in the twelfth century, tales of love and daring centering on King Arthur's court written in the vernacular became popularized throughout Europe. Indeed, the French author who penned this literature resided at the court of the countess of Champagne, about 100 miles to the north of Beaugency, where traveling bards likely brought these tales. These Arthurian tales focused on relationships between men and women, as opposed to earlier lay literature that had celebrated the deeds of warriors (for an example, see a quote from *The Song of Roland*, page 96). This new emphasis on courtly manners shaped the way the aristocracy interacted. By the end of the twelfth century, being a noble meant more than swinging a sword. Knights were expected to abide by a

21 *CMV*, no. 29, pp. 321–322.

22 *Chartres vendômoises*, ed. Charles Métais (Vendôme: Société Archéologique, Scientifique et Littéraire du Vendômois, 1905) no. 208, pp. 244–245. Hereafter, *ChV*.

23 Martin Aurell, *Le chevalier lettré: Savoir et conduit de l'aristocratie aux XIIeme-XIIIeme siècles* (Paris: Fayard, 2011) pp. 63–109.

code of behavior that demonstrated their honor, their respect of the church, their defense of the poor and unfortunate and their proper conduct toward women. The impetus for this new social consciousness is apparent in aristocratic literature and behavior. This cultural flowering also resulted in more lords becoming literate; some even went on to pen romances themselves. A distant cousin of the lord of Beaugency, for example, wrote a romance in the thirteenth century.[24] Noblewomen, too, were educated. They are portrayed in the literature of the twelfth and thirteenth centuries as knowing Scripture, classical literature and being able to read Latin (particularly after the cultural revival known as the Twelfth-Century Renaissance). These women needed to be educated so they could run their households and co-rule lordships. Mathilda of Beaugency wrote a letter to King Louis VII, demonstrating both her education but also her management of property (see Document 4, page 225). By the late thirteenth century the charters of Notre Dame de Beaugency started to be written in the vernacular; a language which the laity could easily read. A century later, it was common for these documents to be issued in French, which represents an important cultural shift.

After attaining a basic literacy, gender and career track would shape what more education Beaugency sons and daughters required. Boys destined to be warriors began to learn and hone their military skills by the age of ten. Their sisters who remained in the world were trained to become the lady of their own castle. Arthurian romances of the twelfth century provide a glimpse into what the ladies of the castle were expected to do. In addition to managing the resources of the estate, noblewomen were also to provide hospitality. Sometimes hospitality could be as simple as welcoming guests and preparing their room, and one can imagine that after a long, difficult journey travelers were grateful to have the lady of the castle to provide creature comforts. We know from the household accounts of thirteenth-century noblewomen that they oversaw every facet of the household. Their purchase of food stuffs, beverages, candles and table linens indicates they were intimately involved in both providing hospitality and provisioning the household.[25] Such hospitality could be quite elaborate and is recorded in the literature of the time. When Lancelot accompanied a lady back to her castle they found

> [a] table covered with a long wide tablecloth. Candles were already lit in the candlesticks, and dishes had been placed on the table along with gilded silver goblets and two pitchers, one filled with red wine and the

24 For a translation of *The Romance of the Châtelain of Coucy*, see *The Ways of Love: Eleven Romances of Medieval France*, ed. Norma Lorre Goodrich (Toronto: Beacon Press, 1964) pp. 159–199. Alain Lerond provided a critical edition of the poems of the Châtelain of Coucy: *Chansons attribuée au Chastelain de Couci* (Paris: Presses Universitaires de France, 1964).

25 For noblewomen managing households, see Louise J. Wilkinson, *Eleanor of Montfort: A Rebel Countess* and Linda M. Mitchell, *Joan de Valence* in the suggested reading section at the end of this chapter.

> other filled with a heavy white wine. On the end of a bench beside the table they noticed two basins full of warm water for washing their hands, and on the other saw a richly patterned towel, clean and white, for drying them.[26]

Like the modern corporate entertainments, banquets served as an expression of power, wealth and position and Chrétien de Troyes describes one consisting of "five hundred tables and more."[27] Allowing for some literary license as the romances were imaginative tales, organizing and preparing for such events must have taken considerable planning and skill. But a daughter's training extended beyond household comfort. From a very early age, as early as seven, noble children appeared with their parents in making donations and settling disputes. These experiences exposed sons and daughters alike to the responsibilities of lordship. Given that women tended to outlive their husbands, unless they died in child-birth, and that husbands were often away for long stretches of time waging war, a woman could expect to be left in charge of the family lands, vassals and castle. To prepare daughters for just such a reality, aristocratic families included them in all sorts of family transactions: Mortgaging property, making pious gifts, and protecting family property in court by participating in legal and proprietary disputes and contestations. In short, they received the education and training they would need to be valued members of their family and society, as the example of Mathilda of Beaugency demonstrates. Daughters could be prepared at home to undertake these duties or they could be sent to a relative to be fostered, much as their brothers would have been. While not evident in the documents of practice, the lady in the poem, *Guigemar,* has her niece living with her. The niece takes care of the lady and waits on her, suggesting the girl is being raised and trained by her aunt.[28] So an aristocratic girl could expect to spend her days at her mother or foster-mother's side learning household management as well as how to oversee property – which would require the ability to read, write and figure. She would also acquire other skills such as needlework, music and dancing.

Aristocratic boys' serious training as a knight began in their early teens and lasted well into their late teens. The dangers of such training is evident in a charter that records a gift made by a father whose son had been killed while training to be a knight. Although this youth had been training at home, many of his peers would have been fostered out to receive their training. This meant that a child or adolescent was sent to another household to be trained as a warrior and in the other skills he would need as a lord, such as manners, deportment, strategy and diplomacy. Fostering with other young

26 Chrétien de Troyes, *The Knight of the Cart* in *The Complete Romances of Chrétien de Troyes*, p. 182.

27 Chrétien de Troyes, *Erec and Enide* in *The Complete Romances of Chrétien de Troyes*, p. 86.

28 Marie de France, *Guigemar,* in *The Lais of Marie de France*, ed. and trans. Robert Hanning and Joan Ferrante (Durham, NC: Labyrinth Press, 1978), pp. 225–252.

warriors also created crucial ties among a military cohort. The romances of Chrétien de Troyes, written in the mid-twelfth century, prove useful in describing the sort of training a noble youth would receive. Although these were stories developed to entertain, the details about aristocratic life can be assumed to be accurate since these romances were performed for aristocrats and their entourage so the author would need to get these details right or risk losing his audience. The experiences of the Arthurian heroes can thus be used to extract details about the lives of medieval lords and ladies. Young Perceval, the protagonist of the Grail legend, for example, was taught by a worthy knight to "hold a lance, and spur and check a horse."[29] He also received instruction in "how to defend himself with the sword if anyone attacked him or to attack with it when the occasion demanded."[30] Additionally, fostering involved teaching young men appropriate behavior and etiquette. When Perceval demonstrates his military prowess, he is rewarded by being seated next to his mentor and sharing food from the same platter.[31] Manners, especially those recognizing or reinforcing social hierarchies, were also important for warriors, as the knight Erec demonstrated when he showed he "knew proper manners and rose" to meet the count.[32]

Medieval literature suggests that boys were frequently sent to their maternal uncles and exemplifies the close bonds that often developed between these kinsmen. Indeed, fostering is evidence of the care and concern that the entire family took in preparing their children for adulthood. Aunts, uncles, cousins, as well as the nuclear family, were involved in ensuring that children had the skills necessary to succeed in medieval society. With whom might the Beaugency sons have been fostered? Let us consider the possibilities for young Lord Ralph I (c. 1060–1130). He might have been fostered with his lord, the count of Chartres, or Ralph could have joined the household of one of his kin. Unfortunately nothing is known about Ralph's mother beyond her first name, so it is difficult to determine if Ralph could have been fostered with maternal kin. Given he had several well-placed paternal aunts and uncles, it seems likely that Ralph was fostered by one of his father's siblings. It was not unheard of for young men to be fostered at the home of an aunt, particularly if that aunt had married well and Ralph's Aunt Agnes had married the viscount of Blois. Placement in this household would have been politically strategic as the viscounts of Blois had long been loyal supporters of the counts of Chartres. Fostering Ralph with Agnes and her husband would have secured his family's ties to this comital house. Equally attractive would have been to foster Ralph in the household of his Uncle John, who was the lord of La Fléche and married to a daughter of the count of Maine. If Ralph's parents wanted to strengthen their ties to Anjou or the Vendômois,

29 Chrétien de Troyes, *The Story of the Grail* in *The Complete Romances of Chrétien de Troyes,* p. 357.

30 *The Story of the Grail*, p. 359.

31 *The Story of the Grail*, p. 359.

32 *Erec and Enide*, p. 42.

having him train with his Uncle Hervé, who was lord of Lavardin, would also have been a possibility. Ralph's family was fortunate to have several household choices for fostering young Ralph – if he was fostered away from home. Ralph's cousins, specifically the children of his Aunt Adelaide, appear to have been fostered with his own father. Adelaide married a lord by the name Joscelin Bodellus. While Joscelin appears as a witness for many important men, he seems a modest lord in his own right. So it would have benefited the Bodellus family to foster their children with Adelaide's well-connected brother. The probability that her son, Joscelin II, was fostered in the Beaugency household is supported by the fact that he appears as a young man as a witness to a gift by his uncle and in two later charters with Ralph.[33]

Fostering trained Ralph in the art of war and lordship; it also forged bonds that could last a lifetime. Ralph was particularly close to one of his vassals, Landric Malesherbes. Indeed, Ralph took special care to have Landric, his dear friend, buried with the monks and have his death commemorated annually[34] (see Document 9, p. 230). Joscelin Bodellus II's presence at the gift Ralph made for Landric lends further evidence to the assumption that these two cousins were fostered together and testifies to the strength of that bond. The experience of two cousins who were peers of Ralph and Joscelin, illuminates the depth of friendship that could exist between foster brothers.

Pagan of Mondoubleau was sent to be fostered with his maternal aunt's family, some distance from his natal home. His cousin, Herluin, was Pagan's age and they were brought up and fostered together. The relationship they developed as brothers-in-arms was put to the test when they became mature warriors. During a heated battle, Herluin gave his life to protect his cousin Pagan. Pagan was profoundly moved by the loss of his cousin and made a gift for him so that his soul could reap the benefits of his sacrifice.[35] The real life experience of Herluin and Pagan reads like the tale of two of King Arthur's most stalwart knights, Yvain and Gawain, who were cousins. Their deep affection for each other as comrades-in-arms and kinsmen is evident when the two engage in hand-to-hand combat without knowing the identity of their opponent:

> The two fighters did not recognize each other, though they had loved each other always . . . Sir Gawain did love Yvain and called him his companion, and wherever he was, Yvain referred to Gawain in the same way. Even here, had he recognized him, he would have had a celebration for him and would have laid down his life for him. Each would have acted that way rather than permit harm to befall the other.[36]

33 *STV*, no. 279, vol. 1, p. 431.

34 *STV*, no. 329, vol. 2, pp. 43–45.

35 *Cartulaire de l'abbaye de Saint Vincent du Mans (ordre de Saint-Benoît)*, ed. Robert Charles and Vicomte Menjot d'Elbenne (Le Mans: Fleury, 1886–1913), no. 179, p. 109.

36 *Knight with the Lion*, p. 328.

Like Pagan and Herluin, Yvain and Gawain, Ralph and his cousin Joscelin also came to care about one another. The lords of Beaugency forged deep and personal relationships with many of the men with whom they served, including some with whom they were fostered.

What did young men do during fostering? While they spent much of their time training, it is clear that they also had time for fun. One such activity would have been hunting, which served two purposes for medieval male youths: An enjoyable pursuit open only to nobles; and a place where they could practice and hone their skill with weapons. Hunting could be quite dangerous, however. William the Conqueror lost two sons to hunting accidents, one when he was an adolescent:

> For his son Richard . . . who was a youth who had not yet received the belt of knighthood, had gone hunting in the New Forest near to Winchester; and whilst he was galloping in pursuit of a wild beast he had been badly crushed between a strong hazel branch and the pommel of his saddle, and mortally injured. [He died later in the week.][37]

Young men also engaged in tamer pursuits, such as playing board games like backgammon and chess.

"Receiving the belt of knighthood" granted at the end of knightly training separated the boys from the men – and the girls. Once a noble born youth had completed his military training, he would have literally earned his spurs. To mark the end of a military apprenticeship and the beginning of a young man's life as a knight, he went through a dubbing ceremony. It is difficult to gauge at what age this took place for Ralph or his peers, but if we use the example of Richard above, who was a "youth who had not yet received the belt of knighthood," it would seem most were formally invested with their weapons around the age of twenty. This ceremony evolved over the course of the Middle Ages, becoming more elaborate and infused with religious overtones. Many of the specifics of the knighting ceremony remain somewhat murky for the eleventh century and are complicated by the fact that what sources we do have come from the church, which provides a religious overlay. Since Ralph became a knight around the mid-eleventh century, his dubbing likely consisted of being vested with his sword and making an oath to his lord. Yet by the early twelfth century, Ralph's son Simon's entry into knighthood would have been more elaborate and probably went something like this:

The night before the ceremony, Simon would have taken a ritual bath. The next day he would have been donned his finest (and presumably clean) clothes and have been led in front of his lord. His lord may have been in a church – perhaps the one next to the castle of Beaugency or one near his lord's holding

37 OV, vol. 3, p. 115.

– or in his own hall surrounded by his entourage. Simon would have then been girded with his sword and belt and have spurs attached to his feet. He would also have been given his shield, which might have born an insignia of his family (see Figure 4.1), and perhaps a lance. These weapons may have been blessed by a priest, who would have charged Simon to protect the weak and defenseless, as well as the church. His lord would then have delivered a slap or blow, probably on his hand, to signify that Simon was now a knight and to fix the event in the memory of all those watching or participating. Simon may have been knighted with other young men along with him. These men would have been the same age, probably fostered together, were from families who undoubtedly knew each other and were all vassals of the same lord.[38] This ceremony marked a youth's transition into the next stage of their life and solidified relationships between lord and vassal, and among vassals – the very men with whom Simon would be fighting. Simon would likely also have done homage to his lord as part of this ceremony (Figure 2.4).

Secular writers celebrated the bravery, civility and selflessness of the knight which came to be known as "chivalry." Chivalry takes its name for the French word for "horse," for it designated those who spent their lives fighting on

Figure 2.4 Vassal swearing homage to his lord, with a scribe recording the event (Hommage au Moyen Age miniature). ART Collection / Alamy stock photo.

38 Maurice Keen, *Chivalry* (New Haven: Yale University Press, 1986) pp. 18ff.

horseback. While poetry, stories and songs celebrated the attributes of chivalry, they also integrated strong Christian overtones. The Arthurian romances demonstrate that manners and a certain code of conduct became important to being a knight and young aristocratic men were well schooled in them. For example, it was considered unknightly to attack a defenseless or wounded man: "Damn you for attacking a man alone and powerless, a man in pain and almost dead from his wounds . . .Your reputation will not increase for capturing or killing a knight who . . . has not the strength to stand again."[39] Similarly it was deemed important that the fight be fair and warriors not gang up on a single knight: "In those days it was not the custom or practice for two knights to assault one. Had they also attacked, their behavior would have been considered a treacherous offense."[40] It is difficult to gauge the reality of the behaviors celebrated in these tales, however. Did the lords of Beaugency think of themselves as chivalrous? While they may not have gone on quests to find the Holy Grail, they did serve their lords. They were also certainly brave, with Ralph I earning praise for his courage both on crusade and in battles at home. These lords also saw themselves as protectors of the church. Traditionally, the lords of Beaugency had been the defenders of the priory of Villeberfol, located about 18 miles from their castle. In addition to fighting to defend the church, defense of women became part of the "chivalric code," which sought to regulate knights' conduct toward women. In the Arthurian romance *Erec and Enide*, when Enide is slapped across the face by a count, "The barons round the count reproached him for his act. 'Stop, sir!' they told the count. You should be ashamed for hitting this lady!"[41]

Often paired with chivalry is the concept of courtly love. Unlike chivalry, which seems to have some basis in historical reality, scholars now assume that courtly love was a fiction. In the mid-twelfth century, a chaplain named André penned his guide to courtly love, which purportedly outlined the appropriate amorous relationships for a knight.[42] Central to the treatise was the worship of a knight's lady, who was not his wife. Thus it was postulated that if a medieval aristocratic man found love it was not with his wife but in adulterous relationships. Dismissed as a work of fiction, the idea that medieval marriages were loveless has continued to dominate modern characterizations of marriage in the Middle Ages. While the idea of service and dedication to one's lady is apparent in the romances of the central Middle Ages, conjugal love was also celebrated. The romance *Erec and Enide* explores the complexity of marriage – particularly in balancing a knight's duty as a warrior with his responsibilities as a husband.

39 *Erec and Enide*, p. 63.
40 *Erec and Enide*, p. 36.
41 *Erec and Enide*, p. 60.
42 For discussion of the possible identifications of André the Chaplain, see Evergates, *Countess Marie of Champagne*, chapter 3.

Adulthood: Arranging marriage

Noblemen and noblewomen came of age and entered adulthood at different points in their lives. In this regard, their life experience was similar to peasants and urban dwellers. For noblewomen, it was more clearly delineated: Either marriage to a man or marriage to God as a nun. Marriage signaled adulthood for peasant and urban women, too. In contrast, an aristocratic male's entrance into adulthood could be signaled by several events. Gaining knighthood could indicate that the noble had left boyhood behind and was a full-fledged warrior. Depending on individual circumstance, this could mean that the knight inherited a portion of his parents' holding and set up a household. This seems to have been how Ralph I and his sons, Simon I and Lancelin III, transitioned into knighthood – and may have been how most Beaugency sons came of age. For other men, marriage was the event that led to their independence from their parents. For still others, particularly those who were not as well endowed with land or who came from a very large family, they had to win resources either through their service to a lord or in tournaments. Sometimes young noblemen – and not so young noblemen – could cause disruption by their unruly behavior. Stealing cattle seems to have been a way for those aristocratic sons who had yet to inherit property to act up or even gain precious resources. But it was not just unruly or rebellious youths. The son of the Lord of Montigny, who was married and had two young children, got in trouble for just such activities. The charter calls him a "*juvenis*," or youth, when this was a man probably in his thirties. Perhaps the monk was making an ironic statement about his presumed level of maturity. Peasant and urban men also had to wait to accrue resources before they could marry. For urban males, however, the end of apprenticeship indicated their transition to adulthood.

Although what would come to be known as romantic love came to flourish in the twelfth century, historians have been hesitant to apply the term "love" to medieval marriage – and for good reason. The creation of a marriage in the Middle Ages was not an affair of the heart, but rather was motivated by family considerations. Would the future spouse bring connections or alliances to powerful people? Would he or she enrich family coffers through gifts or control of other property –real estate or commercial? Sons and daughters had little control over whom they would marry. They were to marry to benefit their family, not for their emotional satisfaction. As a consequence, this decision rested firmly in the hands of their parents and kin. The marriages of Lord Lancelin I's children provide illustration as each of the matches benefited the family in some way (see Genealogy 1).

Agnes, who seems to have been the eldest daughter, married the viscount of Blois, which was quite a social coup for her family. As mentioned earlier, her younger sister, Adelaide, also married. Joscelin Bodellus was a lord who held his lands in the region around Vendôme, thus providing the family with an important ally in their lands in the Vendômois. Ironically, we do not know who the man who became lord of Beaugency, Lancelin II, married. She remains unrecorded in the sources. John, another son, married the daughter of the count of Maine, which was another prestigious match for the Beaugency family. Finally, Hervé married Eva-Avelina, the heiress to the lordship of Lavardin. As with the alliances between John and the count of Maine's daughter and Adelaide and Joscelin, Hervé's marriage to Eva-Avelina reflects the family's interest in maintaining and developing relationships with other powerful families holding land to the west. Lavardin was located just to the west of Vendôme and easily accessible via the Le Loir River from the Beaugency holdings in the Chartrain.

Although political and social motivations guided the selection of a spouse, I believe that affection did develop among many husbands and wives. Charters record donations made for "beloved" spouses. As such clauses do not appear in every donation made for a husband or wife, I interpret such statements as actual statements of affection between spouses.[43] The donors themselves may have insisted that such demonstrative statements be included or the monks recording the gift perceived the relationship to be affectionate. Boellus of Beaugency, who was Lord Ralph's nephew, made a gift for his wife so that she could be buried with the monks. Burial with the monks was a unique privilege, which I think indicates Boellus' concern for his wife's soul and affection for her. The somewhat unusual fact that a large portion of aristocratic couples in the region around Beaugency married only once and stayed married may be the root of this marital affection. Unlike the marital discord of the Angevin counts or the kings of France, none of the lords of Beaugency divorced or repudiated their wives. In spite of the assumption that divorce is a modern invention, medieval men and women could and did divorce. Indeed Notre Dame de Beaugency was the site of perhaps the most famous divorce (although technically an annulment) of the Middle Ages: That of King Louis VII and Eleanor of Aquitaine (who went on to marry his rival, King Henry II of England, shortly after). While the Beaugencys did not divorce, this is not to say that all of their marriages were happy; although some – perhaps most – certainly were.

Unlike the modern era where couples are required to get a marriage license or register births, figuring out how old men and women were when they married in the Middle Ages rests on deduction. For example, we know that Ralph I of Beaugency married after he had gone on crusade. Because he seems to have been a knight when he left and had appeared in documents in the mid- to late 1080s before his departure, we can assume he was an adult by 1096, the year of his departure, meaning he was probably in his early twenties at this time. When he married around 1100, he was likely in his late twenties.

43 *NDB*, no. 17, pp. 29030; *Cartulaire de Saint-Père de Chartres*, ed., Benjamin Guérard, 2 vols. (Paris: Crapelet, 1840), vol. 1 no. 16, p. 241; hereafter, *Père*. *Cartulaire de Marmoutier pour le Dunois*, ed. Emile Mabille (Châteaudun: Lecesne, 1874) no. 97, pp. 90–91; hereafter, *CMPD*.

This estimate is supported by the date of Ralph's death around 1130, which would mean he was about sixty when he died. The age of his wife Mathilda is more difficult to approximate. We know she was married in 1100 and still acting in documents in the 1130s (she joined a nunnery sometime after 1115). Wives were usually younger than their husbands. Women had to wait until they were well past when they began menstruation before they married. Securing heirs was paramount to aristocratic couples, so they wanted to be sure that wives had a long period of fertility, which accounts for why women married younger than men. In contrast, men usually had to wait until they completed their military training and secured property – either through inheritance or service – before they could marry. Some wives were quite a bit younger than their spouses (particularly in the case of second marriages); others were closer to being contemporaries. In Ralph and Mathilda's case, they would seem to have been separated by about a decade, making Ralph twenty-eight at their marriage and Mathilda probably around eighteen – if her age at marriage was consistent with other women in the region. In the lands of the Loire, this couple would have been fairly typical in terms of age at marriage. Because betrothals between princes and princesses occurred quite young, and some royal daughters did marry very young, the inclination has been to assume all medieval people – particularly women – married at a very young age and too much older men. But, as part of the Gregorian Reform contemporary with Ralph and Mathilda in the early twelfth century, **canon law** (the law of the church) came to insist upon two very important points concerning marriage: That the couple be at least twelve years of age; and that they provide their consent to the marriage. While there were certainly some daughters who married as early as twelve and may have been coerced into marrying their selected spouse, this sort of experience seems to be the exception rather than the rule.[44] Although many women may have been younger than their husbands, the age gap tended to be years rather than decades. Others married their contemporaries; some even married younger men. Moreover, even though medieval children may have been betrothed at an early age, the actual marriage did not take place until both children had at least reached the canonical age of consent – if not later.

The medieval lords and ladies of Beaugency lived through something of a sea change in marriage. In addition to a more assertive stance on consent, the church proclaimed that men and women could not marry their kin who were related to them within seven degrees. If they did so, these marriages were considered "consanguineous" or incestuous. This meant that if a man and

44 The perception that medieval women married at a very young age is compounded by confusion between betrothal and marriage. Royal and noble children were betrothed as toddlers and infants, but the marriage itself was not celebrated until the children were at the age of consent. Physical consummation of the marriage was further postponed until the girl had begun menstruating.

woman shared the same great-great-great-great-great grandparent[45] or if their intended was related to one of their godparents or had married one of their relatives, they could not marry. Given that the aristocracy made up perhaps 10 percent of society, these strictures made it virtually impossible for nobles of the same region to intermarry. While the church was able to impose its vision of appropriate kinship relations (that is, **consanguinity**) on kings and counts to a limited degree, it is difficult to assess its impact on the lower nobility. Bishop Ivo of Chartres, for instance, wrote to the count of Vendôme warning him not to go through with his intended marriage because of an issue of consanguinity on the part of the bride.[46] The count, however, ignored this reprimand and went through with the marriage. Moreover, the upper echelons were able to obtain waivers or dispensations in order to marry relatives that would otherwise be considered too closely related. The evidence suggests that those of the lower ranks of the aristocracy avoided blatantly consanguineous marriages, such as marrying first or second cousins. The Beaugency family apparently abided by these strictures, however, and sought marriages for its members with families to whom they were not related – or so distantly related it was difficult to calculate. Ecclesiastical provisions also insisted that once a person married into another family, that person shared the same relationship to those family members as did his or her spouse. For example, sisters of the spouse were seen as the actual sister of the bride or groom.

The church's dedication to being sure both parties consented to the marriage meant that both had to verbally express their consent both at betrothal and in the marriage ceremony. As a consequence, it became more common for marriages to take place in church and in the presence of clergy. Before the eleventh century, weddings had been pretty much a secular affair. The Beaugencys likely would have secured clerical witnesses to their marriages by having the couple speak their consent in front of the abbey or parish church door. The recitation of consent came to be accompanied by the exchange of a gift, most commonly a ring, which was also done in the presence of clergy. Indeed, the celebration of marriage at the door of a church became so popular that by the thirteenth century the south porch of many churches was designated as the space for marriages. Architecturally, these porches came to have rather elaborate roofs over them to provide a protected space for the

45 To complicate matters, there was disagreement on how to reckon kinship. Some advocated simply going up the family tree (hence the prohibition against descendants of a common great-great-great-great-great grandparent). Others went up the family tree to the common ancestor and then back down to the prospective bride or groom. This method would mean that first cousins were related in four degrees rather than just two. In this system those descended from great-great grandparents could wed – a dramatic increase in the number of prospective spouses.

46 Bishop Ivo also wrote to the count's intended bride, Countess Mathilda of Blois, who was related to the Beaugencys. *Lettres de Saint Ives*, ed. and trans. Lucien Merlet, Mémoires de la société archéologque d'Eure-et-Loir, 8 (1885), pp. 241–243.

exchange of vows. A wedding feast would follow this ceremony. These feasts could last several days. During some point in the revelry, the couple would excuse themselves to the bridal chamber. In order for a marriage to be considered official, it had to be consummated, for a lack of consummation would have provided grounds for the dissolution of the marriage.

From the medieval woman's perspective – aristocratic, peasant or urban – one of the key elements of marriage was the property settlements made for her by her natal and affinal family. The women of the Beaugency family, like their peers in other parts of Europe, received two sorts of marriage portions: A **dowry** given by her birth family and a **dower** provided by her husband. These grants could consist of all types of property, rights and revenues. Eva-Avelina of Lavardin (see Genealogy 2), who married into the Beaugency family, was granted a dowry of a fief by her father when she married for the first time. Hersend, the wife of Gradulf Albus, who was a vassal of Lancelin II of Beaugency, was provided with a dowry by her father: "The . . . property which Fulcher of Vendôme gave to Hersend, his daughter, when she married."[47] Husbands also endowed wives. Mathilda, Ralph I's wife, received rights to a forest near Beaugency as her dower. For the women of the later Middle Ages, cash awards would come to replace other types of property. The Beaugencys' neighbor, Margaret of *Montispelli*, for example, was granted an annuity of 20 shillings from Paris.[48] The motive for providing these endowments was to ensure a woman's support as both wife and widow but also to contribute to the family coffers. While scholars used to think that a dowry was a one-time-buy-out for daughters of their family inheritance, recent research has shown that many women continued to exercise a right to family property – and indeed inherit – after receiving their dowry. In 1079, when Lord Lancelin II donated his church of the Holy Sepulcher to the abbey of St. Trinité, his daughter Agnes, who was married to the count of Nevers, witnessed and approved the gift. Even though she had married, she remained in contact with her birth family and continued to exercise a claim to the family **patrimony**.[49]

Not only did women have a right to their family land after marriage, but also they controlled their dowers and dowries as wives and widows. Adelaide, the daughter of Lancelin I, used her dowry or dower as a gift to ensure she was buried with the monks.[50] Both dower and dowry property belonged to noblewomen as they were able to determine its use independently or jointly with their spouse. Eva-Avelina, along with her husband, sold her dowry to the countess of Vendôme. The right of women to this property was grounded in the fact that their consent was needed to alienate or transfer the property. In 1067, Lord Lancelin I traveled to the monastery of St. Trinité in Vendôme,

47 *MV*, no. 126, pp. 215–216.

48 AD Loiret H 10, fol. XLIII verso; *NDB*, no. 147, pp. 168–169.

49 *STV*, vol. 1, no. 279, pp. 431–436.

50 *STV*, vol. 1, no. 182, pp. 313–312.

where he consented to a gift made by one of his vassals and his wife. The charter states specifically that the woman consented because the property in question came from her dowry.[51] Dowers also stayed in a woman's control, as several lords of Beaugency encountered. Mathilda, Ralph I's wife, did not wish her rights to gather firewood to be given to the monks as part of a gift made by her husband. Her wishes were respected and she kept these dower rights.[52] Similarly, Ralph's son Simon found that his wife, Adenorde, would not allow a portion of her dower to be included in a grant to the monks. However, Adenorde fell seriously ill shortly after refusing these properties to transfer and "becoming aware that she was embarking on the journey of all flesh [i.e. she was dying]," freely consented to the transference of her dower rights[53] (see Document 5, page 226). About a century later, around 1220, Mathilda, the widow of Lord John II of Beaugency, was entangled in a case concerning her dower from her marriage to John. Once the matter was settled, Mathilda sent a letter of patent to the court (a letter with her seal) saying she approved of the alienation of her property to the monks.[54] Dowers stayed with women throughout their lives, even if they remarried after the death of their spouse as exemplified by Mathilda who maintained control of her dower from her marriage to Lord John even when she married again. The rights to dower property could become unclear as children sometimes tried to claim dowers from their mothers' previous marriages as inheritance. A woman's right to her dower was always upheld, however, at least in the extant documents.

What was marriage like for the men and women who lived in the castle at Beaugency? While there is much that we are simply unable to know because there are no sources to tell us, I will use evidence from the charters to tease out some information by focusing on what we know about three Beaugency couples who lived in the eleventh, twelfth and thirteenth centuries.

Married life

When Hervé of Beaugency and Eva-Avelina of Lavardin married, he secured an important lordship for himself and both gained a strategic ally for their respective family. Because Eva-Avelina had no brothers, she was her father's heir to the lordship. Sometime around 1060 this couple was wed. Although this was Hervé's first marriage, it was Eva-Avelina's second and she had a son, Salomon, from this previous alliance. Shortly after their marriage, her father died, making Eva-Avelina and Hervé the lords of Lavardin. In order to identify himself more fully as lord, Hervé came to adopt the cognomen "of Lavardin," replacing his former appellation "of Beaugency." The charters indicate that this couple ruled their lordship together for they appear in acts

51 *STV*, vol. 1, no. 185, pp. 320–321.
52 *STV*, vol. 2, no. 410, pp. 169–170.
53 *STV*, vol. 2, no. 526, pp. 364–365.
54 AD Loiret H 10, fol. VI verso; *NDB*, no. 15, pp. 25–27.

confirming donations made by their vassals. Eva-Avelina also acted on her own as lord of Lavardin. She held a court to determine rights among her vassals to certain property. The charter indicates that she was in control of the court and that the matter was settled, "in front of [Eva-]Avelina, daughter of Salomon."[55] The couple also successfully defended their holdings in wars with neighboring lords and together raised Eva-Avelina's son from her first marriage, Salomon. Sadly, Salomon disappears from the sources, but he did leave behind a son, Haimeric Gaumard, who would succeed Eva-Avelina and Hervé as lord of Lavardin in the early 1090s.

Hervé's marriage illustrates some key points about aristocratic marriage. I would argue that the charters indicate that his relationship with Eva-Avelina was a partnership as they clearly ruled Lavardin together. When one of them was absent, however, the other was able to rule independently – a practice that they held in common with many other noble couples. Their marriage reflects the effective training that aristocratic daughters were given so that they could take on the responsibility of the lordship and make judgments. It does not appear that Hervé was away for any extended time, unlike, for example, the count of Vendôme who was imprisoned by Hervé's father for three years. The count's wife, Euphronia, stepped in to take over management of the county. One can appreciate that imprisonment might have caused the count to try to solicit the favor of the monks. To secure their support, Euphronia followed through on a donation her husband had intended to make to St. Trinité of Vendôme and traveled herself to the monastery to ensure the gift was made.[56] Like this comital couple, Hervé and Eva-Avelina acted in concert to decide which churches and ecclesiastical foundations would benefit from their largesse. They also raised the next lord of Lavardin together as both his parents died before he came of age. Eva-Avelina likely taught her grandson Haimeric his letters and exposed him to the teachings of the church, while Hervé would have been responsible for his early military training. Although it is not clear if Haimeric was fostered out, perhaps to his mother's family, it is clear that he was well prepared to assume the responsibilities of lordship when his grandmother passed away. Hervé and Eva-Avelina were married for about thirty years (c.1060–c.1090). Although the personal dimensions of their relationship are not recoverable, the charters depict a husband and wife acting jointly to rule their lands and ensure a prosperous lordship for the next generation of lords.

But not all aristocratic marriages worked out quite so smoothly. While marrying-up could benefit families, there could also be unexpected

55 *CMV*, no. 53, pp. 85–87. This noblewoman appears as both Eva and Avelina in the charters, so I have used both names for her. As to why she changed her name, see Amy Livingstone, "Piecing Together the Fragments: Telling the Lives of the Ladies of Lavardin through Image and Text," in *Writing Medieval Women's Lives*, ed. Charlotte Newman Goldy and Amy Livingstone (New York: Palgrave, 2012), p. 136.

56 *STV*, vol. 2, no. 334, pp. 52–54.

consequences. Hervé's nephew, Lord Ralph I, married Mathilda of Vermandois, who was the niece of the king and extremely well connected politically. Unfortunately for Ralph, his loyalties to the count of Chartres put him on the other side of the political fence from his in-laws and the king (for the details of this conflict, see Chapter 4). While the charters unfortunately do not record Mathilda's response to this situation, I would argue they are revealing in another way: She ceases to appear in the Beaugency documents after around 1112, the very time when Ralph fought against the king and her uncle in the battles that raged in the Loire Valley. Up to about 1112, Mathilda and Ralph had acted together in donations until Ralph chose the side of his comital lord over that of the king and Mathilda's kin. It would appear they were a functional couple to the point where political intrigue poisoned their relationship. Charters extant from her own family indicate that Mathilda returned to her family and joined the church. Mathilda's departure coincided with her children (at least her three eldest) reaching the age when they would have been fostered out or placed in the church for education. The consequences of Ralph's actions would leave a long legacy for his heirs, as both the Vermandois family and the **Capetian** kings attempted to undermine the Beaugency family.[57] In spite of the initially successful alliance, Ralph's marriage appears to have been unsuccessful on many levels.

As far as I am able to tell, Ralph and Mathilda's marital experience seems the exception and not the rule for the Beaugency family. Evidence from later lords of Beaugency demonstrates both partnership and affection. John I was the grandson of Ralph and Mathilda and lord of Beaugency between approximately 1182 and 1218. During her lifetime, his wife, Elizabeth, appears in every extant document with him. In the year 1194, Elizabeth approved two gifts made to Notre Dame de Beaugency for the souls of John's parents.[58] John also made several gifts for her soul and calls her his "most beloved wife" in each one of these donation charters (see Document 6, page 226). In anticipation of her death, John arranged that rents from some of his land would go toward prayers for Elizabeth's soul. Elizabeth herself arranged that revenues, likely provided as part of her dower, be given to the monks so that a silver lamp could be lit eternally on her tomb. Shortly after Elizabeth's death, John arranged for masses to be sung on the day of the anniversary of her death; he also provided food, drink and clothing for the chaplain who would be saying the prayers.[59] John stated he was building a chapel where his family would be buried. Elizabeth, with the eternal light on her tomb and prayers provided by the chaplain, was to be the first occupant. About a year later, John made another gift for *dilectissima* (most beloved) Elizabeth to another ecclesiastical community. He again provided sustenance for the monks

57 Amy Livingstone, "Climbing the Tree of Jesse: Aristocratic Marriage in the Lands of the Loire," in *Les stratégies matrimoniale*, ed. Martin Aurell (Turnhout: Brepols, 2013) pp. 101–118.

58 AD Loiret H 10, fol. V; *NDB*, nos. 10 and 11, pp. 18–20.

59 AD Loiret H 10, fol. XXX; *NDB*, no. 102, pp. 117–119.

by giving a portion of the wheat and grains grown annually in Beaugency.[60] John cared deeply about his wife and expressed his affection by insuring her soul was properly tended for by two different communities of monks. By the time of Elizabeth and John, the idea of love that had been celebrated in romances was making its way into actual medieval marriages. Here we see a couple who lived together, worked together and came to know each other intimately. Love, as expressed in John's charters and actions, was the result.

Parenting and inheriting

Raising and providing for their children was one of the chief responsibilities of a married couple. Both parents played a role in the life of a child and young adult, as well as when they became adults. Because the families of the lands of the Loire recognized the claim of all children to their holdings, property served as a tie to their natal family for the duration of their lifetime. A mid-twelfth-century dispute by the descendants of Adelaide of Beaugency, who died in c. 1069, demonstrates the longevity of claims to family property as these grandchildren believed they were entitled to what their grandparents had held. Consequently, as charters record such property transactions and claims, I am able to use this evidence to trace Beaugency family interactions and chart inheritance patterns. Other scholars have asserted that French aristocratic families changed their mode of inheritance in the eleventh century from providing all progeny with a share of the property to restricting inheritance to only the line of the eldest born male, often called primogeniture.[61] My interpretation differs as evidence from the Beaugency family demonstrates that this family divided the patrimony among their children. The division may not have always been equal, but each child was provided with something for their support. Two generations of lords of Beaugency that span the late eleventh and twelfth centuries provide illustration.

Around 1020, Lord Lancelin I of Beaugency controlled considerable properties stretching from Anjou to Orléans, which he had inherited from both his mother and father. Along with Beaugency, Lancelin also received the lordship of La Flèche situated just northeast of Angers (see Map 2). He and his wife had five children. Two of his sons each inherited one of these lordships, while the daughters were vested with family property as their dowry. The third, Hervé, married the heiress to the lordship of Lavardin and became its lord. Yet even after marriage, these children continued to exercise a right to the Beaugency patrimony as they appeared with their father in donating property to the church. If siblings or children did not consent, gifts were subject to contestation. One of Adelaide of Beaugency's stepsons, for

60 *STV*, vol. 3, no. 643, pp. 13–14.

61 Georges Duby is the most recognized proponent of this model, but he based much of argument of aristocratic family dynamics on the work of Karl Schmid. See the suggested reading section at the end of this chapter.

instance, disputed what his father had given because he had not consented to the donation.[62] I interpret the Beaugency siblings/children consent to the alienation of family property as indicative of the claim they had to each other's property. Throughout the eleventh century, the Beaugencys used their considerable resources to provide for all of their children. Each received a portion of the patrimony and had a right to family property.

Inheritance was simpler in the next generation of Beaugency lords as Ralph was the only son of Lancelin II. His two sisters, however, were well provided for through their marriages to counts and their dowry from their natal lands. They also continued to have a claim to Beaugency land, as had their predecessors. Inheritance in the generation of Ralph's sons conformed once again to the earlier pattern of Lancelin II's generation. Ralph I and Mathilda had six children: Simon I, Lancelin III, Ralph, Hugh, Mathilda and Agnes. When Ralph died around 1130, their son Simon succeeded him as lord. Two of their other sons, Lancelin III and Ralph, both inherited a portion of the family holdings. Lancelin eventually became lord and Ralph followed in his crusading father's footsteps and went to the Holy Land as he appears in a charter around 1124 recording a gift to the Holy Sepulcher in Jerusalem. He returned home sometime after and died in 1148. As Ralph was approaching death, he made a substantial gift of land he had inherited to the abbey of Notre Dame de Josaphat in Chartres so that "his eternal rest be softened by the praying of prayers."[63] It is not clear what Hugh, another son, inherited. He may have joined the church, gone to the Holy Land, or resided with one of his brothers. The only information extant on him is a post-mortem gift made on his behalf by his brother.[64] One interpretation of this evidence could be that Hugh's brother made this gift because Hugh himself did not have the resources to do so. But based on what I know about aristocratic family dynamics in this region and the Beaugency family practice, I would argue that this brotherly concern with Hugh's afterlife makes it likely that the family would have provided for him while he was alive. Moreover, gifts made for the souls of relatives were a common expression of concern and affection among the aristocracy. The daughters of Ralph I and Mathilda both married and received dowries. The property provisions for these children were much the same as those arranged by the younger Ralph's grandparents in the eleventh century and hence argue against a transformation in inheritance modes that favored the line of the eldest male and restricted the rights of other progeny. While one son came to hold the lordship of Beaugency, his brothers and sisters were not disinherited. Nor were claims to the lordship reduced by preventing these men and women to marry, for at least four of the six did marry.

62 *CMV*, no. 115, pp. 176–179.

63 *Cartulaire de Notre-Dame de Josaphat*, ed. Charles Métais, 2 vols. (Chartres: Garnier, 1911–1912), vol. 1, no 149, pp. 199–200.

64 AD Loiret H 10, fol. XXXI verso; *NDB*, no. 108, pp. 124–125.

As an adult, the family ties forged in childhood bound aristocrats tightly together and determined their life course. These ties, furthermore, could be depended upon in times of strife. For example, when Lancelin II's sister Agnes' husband, the viscount of Blois, was embroiled in a dispute with the abbey of Marmoutier and in trouble with those same monks, Lancelin intervened on his behalf by presiding over the court that resolved this dispute. (For further details, see pages 140–143.) Property and affection connected offspring to their parents, their siblings and their affinal families. The Beaugencys used their considerable holdings to provide for all of their offspring – a demonstration of their concern for their children and their literal investment in their future. Aristocratic life was truly a family affair. Marriage alliances were undoubtedly facilitated by brothers and sisters seeking to promote the social and economic prestige of their family. Families gathered to make donations for their ancestors to ensure they were properly memorialized, and to be sure that the souls of the people they cared about would attain salvation. As adults aged, these family ties continued to be a major factor in their lives.

Disability and death

Suffering from an illness or approaching old age can be frightening prospects even in the modern era. In the Middle Ages, where hospitals were few and far between and retirement communities had yet to develop, medieval people from peasant to lord depended on their family and friends for assistance when they grew old or infirmed – although, starting in the twelfth century, those living in cities did have the advantage of seeking care and support from hospitals as they became infirmed. Most medieval people, however, had to make different arrangements for the elderly, sick or disabled. For example, when the younger brother of one of the Beaugency's vassals became severely ill, his brother arranged for him to go to the abbey of Marmoutier to receive nursing. Sadly, the young man never regained his health and died as a monk. The charters tell us that while he was ill, his older brother and other family members visited him. When he passed away, his brother was so bereaved that he undertook construction of a stone chapel next to the family's holdings to commemorate his dead brother. Similarly, when visiting Chartres, young Simon Turre fell ill at his sister's house. He remained with her during his illness and she probably provided nursing care. Simon likewise did not recover from his illness. His family made a gift to the local church in Simon's memory and to ensure his soul would be received in heaven.

Life as a professional warrior was dangerous and many knights fell in battle. Some time around 1050, Hervé of Lavardin's father-in-law, fought a battle against his neighbors at Montoire. One of his war-band was gravely wounded trying to storm the castle. This knight made a gift on the battlefield with the assistance of one of the monks; his main concern was ensuring that his soul was in good standing just in case he did not recover from his wounds. Unfortunately, the charter does not tell us if he ever recovered. About a century later, Lord Simon I of Beaugency made a gift for one of his knights who had been wounded in his service. This knight recovered for a bit, since he spent some time in the monks' hospital, but eventually he succumbed to his wounds.[65] If a warrior was lucky enough to survive his injury, what sort of future was in store for a knight who could no longer fight? When one of the Beaugencys' vassals named Ascelin was "wounded nearly to death," he petitioned a local abbot to join his monastery. But when the abbot consulted with the monks, they were reticent to add him to their number. To demonstrate his piety, but also to perhaps sway the brothers to let him in, Ascelin gave all that he had in property to the monks, including a quarter of a church. Ascelin must have been a distinguished warrior, as he was held in such high regard among the nobles of the region that many made gifts on his behalf. One of his vassals gave his quarter of this church and Ascelin's wife and daughter stepped forward to give the other half. Thanks to Ascelin's generosity, as well as his friends and family, the monks found themselves with a new priory in the Vendômois. In return, Brother Ascelin became part of their community and spent the rest of his days as a monk.[66] It is difficult to ascertain if this was a path taken by many injured warriors. The anecdotal evidence does suggest than many found at least comfort, if not a new home, inside the walls of a monastery.

For those fortunate enough to live to old age, what options did they have for "retirement?" Many noblewomen and men opted to join the church. Some did so as widows and widowers; others joined before their spouse had died. If they pursued this option, a noble had to have the consent of his or her spouse. Some found retirement to the monastery comfortable – for example, the nobleman from Vendôme who retired to a small chamber in the monastery with his books and his servant. Others found the rigor of monastic life a bit too much. Ermengarde of Brittany, the niece of Lord Ralph I, decided to join a Cistercian women's house. But she found the ascetic lifestyle not to her liking and left. Other women, however, found retirement in a nunnery satisfying. The local convent of St. Avit in Châteaudun was a women's religious community. The charters reveal that many neighboring noble born women made donations so that they could pass the last years of their lives in this community. Other women elected to simply become associated with a religious foundation. For example, one noblewoman became affiliated with the monastery of St. Père of Chartres as a lay sister, meaning that while she may not have been cloistered or taken vows, she did dedicate her last years to serving God by doing good works. Women of the urban elite also had the opportunity to join a religious community. This was not an option open to peasant women, however, as only members of the upper classes could join the church. They retired by moving in with one of their children or perhaps having a small dwelling on the family property.

65 *STV*, vol. 2, no. 526, pp. 364–365.
66 *ChV*, no. 57, pp. 78–80.

Joining a monastery or convent did not mean that the nobleman or woman necessarily left the world behind, however. Often they joined communities that had a long association with their family and where some of their relatives might already have been serving God. Nuns and monks would also encounter family members as they came to the monastery to make donations or attend monastic court. Property, too, was a thread to the outside world. Although many gave generously to the church to join its ranks, they still retained an interest in and claim to other family property. We know some lords and ladies who joined the religious life remained engaged in the secular world and provided advice to their heirs. Countess Adela of Chartres retired to the convent of Marcigny, but she stayed abreast of politics in Blois-Chartres and provided advice to her son. Similarly, when Ralph I's niece Ermengarde of Brittany's husband, the count of Brittany, became a monk at the monastery of Redon he continued to be consulted and active in comital politics.

Death, too, was a family affair. Medieval people were deeply pious and concerned about the afterlife. To ensure that souls were "healthy" enough for entrance into heaven, medieval men and women made gifts to the clergy to garner prayers for those who mattered to them. These gifts were expressions of the care that family members had for one another. Nothing was more important than ensuring their loved ones were able to be among the elect and escape the torments of hell. Lord Lancelin III, for example, gave property to Notre Dame de Beaugency on behalf of his father, his mother, his brother, his sister-in-law and his two wives.[67] In 1185, Eva-Avelina of Lavardin's great-great grandson, Burchard, lost his father, the count of Vendôme, to illness. His father was returning from pilgrimage when he succumbed to sickness at the monastery of La Charité-sur-Loire. Realizing that he was dying, Burchard's father petitioned to take the monastic habit on his death bed. He also made a generous donation to the monks. Evidently, his illness was somewhat protracted since he was able to send word to his son. Burchard approved his father's benefaction by letter with his personal seal. Some might suggest that sending a letter rather than traveling to the monastery himself indicates a lack of care on Burchard's part but I would disagree. Burchard acted to ensure his father a place in heaven, which is what caring children did for their parents in the Middle Ages. Moreover, this son's concern for his father's soul and arrangements for his afterlife did not stop here as Burchard expanded his father's gift by providing additional revenues. The charter also suggests that at the very least Burchard respected his father, as it states: "Truly always from the law of the son to obey and hold fast to the father, and to adhere to their good works and example."[68] Although the count of Vendôme did not die surrounded by his family, he did leave the world knowing his soul was provided for and that his family approved what was essentially his last will and testament.

67 AD Loiret H 10, fol. XXI verso; *NDB*, no. 75, pp. 86–88.
68 *ChV*, no. 112, pp. 145–146.

Donations were also made to have names recorded in the memory books or **martyrology** (sometimes also called **necrology**) of ecclesiastical communities to ensure that these people were prayed for each year on the anniversary of their death or on the appropriate saints' day.

> During the illness that led to his death, Joscelin Bodellus gave half of the church of Danzé on behalf of himself and also authorized that the half of the church of Thoré, which was from his fief, and five shillings which the monks paid him each year for the pasture, [be given to the monks]. At his death another fifty shillings was given to us . . . by his wife and son Helias . . . The lord abbot also secured that a thousand prayers would be sung for Joscelin. And we wrote his name in our Martyrology, at the request of his sons.[69]

Adelaide of Beaugency, Joscelin's wife, and their children confirmed his gift, but also added to it so that his death would be observed by the monks and a "thousand prayers" sung on his behalf. Virtually every lord of Beaugency from Lancelin I (d. 1069) to Lord John I (d. 1220) was recorded in the necrology of at least one of the important houses of the region; a demonstration of the care that families provided for one another.

Ensuring a proper place of burial for relatives was also a family concern. Medieval elites sought burial in churches because they wanted association with pious men and women, but also to be buried in close proximity to the saints. The sons of one of Hervé of Lavardin's vassals, for example, made a gift so that their father could be buried with the monks at Marmoutier.[70] Nobles hoped that by making gifts they and their kin might merit such burial. Indeed, the charter recording the Lavardin vassal's gift states explicitly that the monks of St. Martin granted this request "by the grace of the great and long standing familiarity which was a result of giving substantial property." Burial also became a family concern as families began to establish a family necropolis. Eva-Avelina's father founded a priory of Marmoutier at Lavardin and was entombed there, as were several succeeding generations of lords.[71] The Beaugency family may have been buried at their family chapel of St. Sepulcher, which was a priory of St. Trinité of Vendôme. But at the turn of the thirteenth century, Lord John I of Beaugency undertook construction of a chapel in the castle precincts.[72] He did so with the hope that he and his family would be buried there.

69 *STV*, vol. 1, no. 123, pp. 222–223.

70 *MV*, no. 18, pp. 300–301.

71 To find out where the women of the family were buried, see Livingstone, "Piecing Together the Fragments," pp. 131–151.

72 Recall there was also a chapel located in the *donjon* as well. But this chapel was for prayer and did not house tombs.

Conclusion

The lords and ladies of Beaugency started life in the castle tower, where they learned to walk, play, read, fight, rule and pray. They spent eternity just a few steps from where they began life in the chapel located next to their home. From birth to death, family guided the course of their lives. Their family determined their social standing, whom they would marry and their political alliances. Over the years, from childhood to adulthood, their lives would intersect with their parents, children, siblings, aunts, cousins, uncles, nieces and nephews. Yet it is important to keep in mind that the Beaugency family experience is representative of a small slice of medieval society and that family life differed among the peasants and urban classes. But, as I hope to have shown, Beaugency family life was based on affection, inclusion and support. They could only hope that their death would be met by the same outpouring of affection evident in the following charter (see Figure 2.5):

> With weeping pen, we [the monks] wish those in the present and future to know that Agatha, lady of the village and mother of the whole community [has died]. On the day of exaltation of the holy crucifix, the debt of her worldly body paid, for the redemption of her soul, her husband Burchard [the same Burchard discussed earlier] . . . gave to the monks who live in the same place, all of his land among Varenne . . . At the conclusion of the funeral, knights of the court attended and [those] of the court of Hubert the prior and the other monks, as well as many other men and women, were all attending . . . For this pious gift the monks of

Figure 2.5 A thirteenth-century charter recording Lady Agatha's death and the gifts made for her. Archives départmentales du Loir-et Cher, 16 H 85, no. 20. Gift of land by Burchard to the Abbey of Marmoutier for the benefit of the soul of his wife, Agatha, of land at Varenne.

that same place will appoint each day one mass for the soul of Agatha and for her ancestors.[73]

Now that we have a sense of the more private aspects of aristocratic life, it is time to consider the relationships the lords and ladies of Beaugency forged with other medieval people, specifically those who fought, those who worked and those who prayed.

Suggested reading

Philippe Ariès, *Centuries of Childhood: A Social History of Family Life*, trans. Robert Baldick. New York: Vintage, 1965.

John W. Baldwin, *Aristocratic Life in Medieval France: The Romances of Jean Renart and Gerbert de Montreuil, 1190–1230*. Baltimore: Johns Hopkins University Press, 2000; and *The Language of Sex: Five Voices from Northern France around 1200*. Chicago: University of Chicago Press, 1996.

Mary Dockray-Miller, *The Books and Life of Judith of Flanders.* Farningham, UK: Ashgate, 2015.

Georges. Duby, *Medieval Marriage: Two Models from Twelfth-Century France*, trans. Elbourg Forster. Baltimore: Johns Hopkins University Press, 1978; *The Knight the Lady and the Priest: The Making of Modern Marriage in Medieval France*, trans. Barbara Bray. New York: Pantheon Books, 1983; *The Chivalrous Society*, trans. Cynthia Postan. Berkeley: University of California Press, 1977; and *Love and Marriage in the Middle Ages*, trans. Janet Dunnett. Chicago: University of Chicago Press, 1996.

Kathryn Dutton, "*Ad erudiendum tradidit*: The Upbringing of Angevin Comital Children," *Anglo-Norman Studies* 32 (2010): 24–39.

Theodore Evergates, *The Aristocracy in the County of Champagne, 1100–1300*. Philadelphia: University of Pennsylvania Press, 2007.

Theodore Evergates, ed., *Aristocratic Women in Medieval France.* Philadelphia: Pennsylvania University Press, 1999.

Barbara A. Hanawalt, "Medievalists and the Study of Childhood," *Speculum* 22 (2002): 440–460; and *Growing Up in Medieval London*. Oxford: Oxford University Press, 1993.

David Herlihy, *Medieval Households.* Cambridge, MA: Harvard University Press, 1985.

Amy Livingstone, *Out of Love for My Kin: Aristocratic Family Life in the Lands of the Loire, 1000–1200.* London and Ithaca: Cornell University Press, 2010.

Kimberly A. LoPrete, *Adela of Blois, Countess and Lord.* Dublin: Four Courts Press, 2007.

Linda E. Mitchell, *Joan de Valance: The Life and Influence of a Thirteenth-Century Noblewoman*. New York: Palgrave Macmillan, 2016.

Nicholas Orme, *Medieval Children.* New Haven: Yale University Press, 2003.

Karl Schmid, "The Structure of the Nobility in the Earlier Middle Ages." In *The Medieval Nobility: Studies on the Ruling Classes of France and Germany from the Sixth to the Twelfth Century*, ed., Timothy Reuter, pp. 37–59. Amsterdam: Elsevier Science Ltd., 1978.

Louise Wilkinson, *Eleanor de Montfort: A Rebel Countess in Medieval England.* London: Bloomsbury Academic, 2012.

73 *MV*, no. 38, pp. 334–335.

3 "Those who fought": Medieval lordship

The Beaugency family attained their power, lands and offices through their status as lords. At its heart, lordship was a relationship between a client and patron. Powerful people had been using wealth to gain supporters for centuries. In the Roman world, patrons might provide wealth or offices to clients to gain their political support. In contrast, medieval lords accumulated power through their control of land, which they would then grant out to their followers who became their clients or vassals. The more land a lord held, the more power she or he could wield. The Beaugencys were part of this political system as both lords and vassals. They received fiefs, or grants of land, from the counts of Anjou, Chartres and Vendôme for which they were expected to provide military service and to serve at their lord's court (see Maps 2–4) for how the Beaugency lordship evolved). In addition to military authority, lords also had juridical and legal power that they wielded by holding courts and enforcing the peace. Medieval lords exercised a constellation of powers known as the **ban**, which gave them the power to provide justice and adjudicate disputes. Economic privileges were part of these powers as well, as lords had authority over certain resources such as a mill or wine press. In essence, the ban meant that lords exercised dominion over people – both peasants and warriors. Yet exercise of the ban was grounded in control of land.

This chapter will examine the development of Beaugency lordship. How did the Beaugencys come to be lords? Why and how had control of land become the means to power and how did this shape political hierarchy? To explore these questions, we must understand the political context in which this hierarchy emerged: The history of the late Carolingian world.

When the Beaugency family came to power in the eleventh century, France was under the leadership of the Capetian kings. In 986, this royal dynasty had ousted the Carolingian family who had ruled much of what would become France since the mid-eighth century. The apex of the Carolingian Empire had been under Charlemagne, but after the death of his son, Louis the Pious, the empire broke into three separate kingdoms, each ruled by one of Charlemagne's three surviving grandsons. Although many of Charlemagne's descendants were capable kings, in the western part of his empire, called *Francia*, royal power had been undercut by the aristocracy that the Carolingians depended upon for political and military support. Thus by the time of the later Carolingians, whose sobriquets like "the Simple" and "the Child" perhaps best epitomize their abilities, power was decentralized. There were still Carolingian, and later Capetian, kings, but much of the power rested in the hands of prominent, regional families, especially those of counts and dukes. At the same time that power was becoming internally decentralized, *Francia* was beset with invasions by the Vikings. The cities of Chartres and Orléans, for example, were attacked by Vikings in the ninth and tenth centuries. Medieval people turned to local lords and counts for protection from these marauders.

The vastness of the Carolingian empire, stretching from the Pyrenees to the dense forests of Saxony, required the Carolingians to develop an administrative delegation of power to rule uniformly. Derived from the old Roman system of governance, the Carolingians divided their lands into units called *pagi* (plural) or *pagus* (singular). These areas varied in size, but most were modest in geographic scope. A ruler for each *pagus*, called a *comes*, was selected to appear as the Carolingian king's representative in enacting royal justice and laws, collecting taxes and defense. "Count" and "county" derive from *comes* and eventually *comitus/comitatus* (county) would come to replace *pagus*. The organization of count and county continued into the time of the Beaugency family. But an important change had occurred. When a Carolingian count died, he was replaced by the royal government. But by the eleventh century the title of count – and control of the relevant county – had become hereditary, which meant the land and title passed from generation to generation within a noble family. Dukes controlled slightly larger areas, often made up of one or more counties, called duchies. Counts and dukes often divided their lands and appointed men to help them rule, defend and administrate. *Vicecomes*, literally vice-count, was just such an office developed to help administer lands. By the eleventh century, some counts came to control more than one county. This was true for the region of the Loire where the Beaugencys lived as one family came to control the counties of both Chartres and Blois. (This family controlled both counties until the thirteenth century. Although they possessed both counties in the eleventh and twelfth centuries, they will be referred to as simply the counts of Chartres. It is only in the thirteenth century that the counties had separate counts and will be designated individually as the count of Chartres or the count of Blois.) As the tenth and eleventh centuries progressed, counts, dukes and viscounts subdivided their lands into lordships and granted them to men who would become their followers.

Yet, counts, dukes, kings and even lords did not just want power; they wanted *legitimate* power. Power in the Middle Ages was vested in two often complementary sources: Secular and sacred. Each type of power had its own rights and responsibilities and both were thought to flow from God. Bishops and abbots of the Beaugencys' time commanded ecclesiastical power founded on the legacy of St. Peter as the bishop of Rome. Kings and their chroniclers drew heavily from the Old Testament for models of just and legitimate rule. For instance, when writing to Lord Ralph I, Bishop Ivo of Chartres referenced the Old Testament Kings David and Saul (see Document 2, page 223). Thus within the medieval world there were two forces of power: The church and the secular leaders. Ideally, these two forms of governance and law operated cooperatively, each with its own jurisdictions. In a single county, therefore, it was possible to have overlapping jurisdictions between the local bishop and the count – as well as those among counts, viscounts, lords and abbots.

But as the Carolingian empire disintegrated over the course of the ninth and tenth centuries, many comital families turned the office of count into a hereditary principality. Though the political authority of kings became ever fainter during the tenth century, the delegated responsibilities of the Carolingian political system were retained by the counts in what historians call lordship. Although the underlying ideology remained unchanged, the origin of power shifted from a downward flow of power from the king to the control of proprietary privileges held by a count/lord and his family.

These were the political realities in which the Beaugency family first emerged. Their rise to power was by no means unique; rather it was a journey shared by many of their order. Hence, in tracing out the story of this family, we are relating the story of many such lordly families.

The rise to power

Tracing the origins of ordinary lordly families is difficult. But the charters, once again, prove useful in determining both how the Beaugencys acquired land and gained political power. While direct evidence for the progenitors of the Beaugency family is not extant, those for a later branch of the family are: The lords of Lavardin (see Genealogy 2). A twelfth-century charter from the abbey of Marmoutier relates the establishment of the lordship of Lavardin and the lineage of its lords. Nobles of the mid-twelfth century – secular and monastic – were preoccupied with establishing or tracing the roots of contemporary aristocrats to an earlier age. Coincidently, at the time of this charter a monk from the same abbey was writing the *Gesta Ambaziensium Dominorum* (*The Deeds of the Lords of Amboise*), a chronicle celebrating the history of the lords of Amboise who were distantly related to those at Lavardin. Both documents relate that the seigneurial family of Lavardin was established when Hugh Capet, founder of the Capetian dynasty, gave his godson, also named Hugh (likely after his godfather), the newly created lordship and its heiress as wife.[1] The Lavardin family was established through the marriage of one of the "new men," or powerful lords of lesser fortune rising in prominence in the early eleventh century, with a woman from an established landed family. How might a monk know of the origins of this family? While the scribe of both accounts (perhaps the charter was drawn from the *Gesta* or vice versa) may well have creatively filled in the blanks, he may have learned about the early history of the family from the family members themselves. Indeed the Lavardin women may have provided the information, as Elisabeth

1 *ChV*, no. 32, p. 38 and Louis Halphen and René Poupardin, eds., *Chroniques des Comtes d'Anjou et des Seigneurs d'Amboise* (Paris: Auguste Picard, 1913), p. 75.

van Houts has demonstrated that monks consulted women's memories of events.[2] Even if this account had been embellished (remember from our earlier discussion of the account of the miracles at Beaugency in Chapter 1 that embellished sources can be useful to the historian), the fact that a monk believed the appropriate origins of a lordly family came from the match between a man given his position by his lord with a woman from an older, wealthy and well-established family, is significant. Not only would such a description have resonated well with the intended aristocratic audience of this chronicle, but this pattern of an up-and-coming warrior marrying a woman from a more prestigious family is one that modern scholarship has also confirmed throughout tenth and eleventh-century France.[3]

The description provided in the monastic sources above – and buttressed by modern scholars – indicates that the lords of the eleventh century were often descended from women of powerful families who were married to men of lesser fortunes. While these "new men" were beholden to their lords and their wives for the position and property, this did not prevent them from flexing their muscles, so to speak, and causing difficulties for the men who had originally granted them their title and holdings. Indeed the chronicler Raoul Glaber commented that this was a particular problem for one of the early Capetian kings, King Robert I the Pious (d. 1031):

> At that time Robert was king of the Franks. He had to suffer many insults and much abuse from his own men, particularly those whom he himself, or . . . his father and grandfather, had raised to great honour, although they came from middle or humble stock.[4]

The counts of Chartres – at least according to Raoul – were particularly difficult clients of the king:

> Chief amongst these rebels was Odo, son of Theobald the Deceiver, count of Chartres, with very many of lesser rank, who rebelled against the king from positions that should have made them humble. Of [a similar disposition] was Odo II, son of Odo I, who was more cunning as well as more powerful than the others. When Stephen, count of Troyes and Meaux and the son of Herbert died, Odo, contrary to the royal will, seized all the estates which ought by law to have reverted to the royal demesne [land controlled directly by the king], for Stephen had died without heir and he was a cousin of the king.[5]

2 Elisabeth van Houts, *Memory and Gender in Medieval Europe, 900–1200* (Toronto: University of Toronto Press, 1999).

3 See the articles by Constance B. Bouchard and Jane Martindale in the suggested reading section at the end of this chapter.

4 Glaber, *Opera*, p. 105.

5 Glaber, *Opera*, p. 105.

In Raoul's opinion, the men who came to challenge the power of the king were upstarts from inconsequential families. The story of Odo and King Robert could have been written about nearly every other count of the realm. These were men who gained power because of their ability to fight and scrap and not their table manners.

Once elevated to a title and given lands, a lord still had much to do to secure his or her place in the power hierarchy. A sure means to gaining more power and influence was to create bonds with still other lords – either through swearing fealty to a lord in return for additional holdings called fiefs or in granting out what the lord already held to other men who would become his vassals. A fief usually consisted of landed property (although later in the Middle Ages money fiefs would develop). In return for a fief, a warrior would vow his fealty or faith to his lord and provide homage. Homage was a ceremony where a vassal would pledge his or her fealty to a lord (see Figure 2.4).

Because of the military nature of lordship and vassalage, scholars assumed women could not hold fiefs or take part in homage. Georges Duby, an eminent French scholar, stated unequivocally that:

> By nature, because she was a woman, the woman could not exercise public power. She was incapable of exercising it. *Potestas*, the power to command and punish, the duty of preserving peace and justice, was exercised by the sword . . . . A woman could not take sword in hand.[6]

Kimberly LoPrete, in her essay "Women, Gender and Lordship in France, c. 1050–1250," dismantles Duby's argument by showing that women could and did exercise the power to judge and command.[7] LoPrete argues that their gender was not an effective barrier for women to exercise ***potestas***. Based largely on charter evidence in contrast to Duby's prescriptive sources mostly taken from ecclesiastical writers who tended to view women with suspicion if not downright hostility, LoPrete establishes that ruling women were routine in medieval France. It is clear from documents from the Beaugencys' time that women were both lords and vassals. In the family of the lords of Fréteval, women controlled fiefs and did homage for them – one to the countess of Champagne, the other to the count of Blois[8] (see Document 7, page 227). One of these lords, who were ladies, also used her own seal to verify the charter at hand. Moreover, as has already been noted, marriage to women who

6 Georges Duby, "Women and Power," in *Cultures of Power*, ed. Thomas Bisson (Philadelphia: University of Pennsylvania Press, 1995) p. 73.

7 Kimberly A. LoPrete, "Women, Gender and Lordship in France, c. 1050–1250," *History Compass* 5 (2007): 1–21. See also the articles in *The Medieval Feminist Forum* and the essays in *Aristocratic Women in Medieval France*, in the suggested reading section for this chapter.

8 *ChV*, no. 269, p. 296. By this point the patrimony of the counts of Chartres, which had consisted of both counties of Blois and Chartres, had been divided into two counties under two different counts.

controlled extensive lands or inherited offices was another way that noblemen gained power. As discussed in the previous chapter, husbands and wives often ruled their lordships together. Recent scholarship, like that of LoPrete, has proven that noblewomen were integral to vassalage, lordship and the exercise of power.

While the Carolingians had also used land to secure alliances, by the eleventh century a new relationship between lords and their clients was emerging. This is evident in a letter written by the duke of Aquitaine in 1021 to Bishop Fulbert of Chartres. In this missive, the duke asks for clarification as to what the mutual duties are between those who grant out lands and those who receive them. If we were able to eavesdrop on how Fulbert and William might have conversed if they had met in person instead of exchanging letters, what might they have said?

DUKE WILLIAM: Esteemed Bishop, I have some questions concerning the oath of fidelity that my vassals swear. What is it that they owe me?

BISHOP FULBERT: What is owed by a vassal who swears loyalty to a lord consists of six key concepts: Safe and sound, secure, honest, useful, easy, possible. In other words, a vassal should never conspire to do any harm to his lord. He should keep his lord secure by not betraying his secrets or giving away information about his castle defenses. In addition to these, a vassal should also not interfere with or impede his lord's rights to justice or any of his other prerogatives. Nor should a vassal do anything that would cause the lord to lose his possessions. Finally, he who swears this oath should never prevent a lord from doing what the lord thinks is best or what the lord is accustomed to doing.

DUKE WILLIAM: So if a vassal abides by these six conditions, he is deserving of a fief? Is there nothing else he needs to do?

BISHOP FULBERT: To the contrary my good duke, following these precepts is not all that should qualify a vassal for a fief. In addition to abstaining from evil deeds against his lord, a vassal must also serve his lord faithfully by giving him counsel and aid as the lord requires. Only if he does this, is he qualified to receive a fief.

DUKE WILLIAM: That is well, because I rely on my vassals to help guide my deliberations. Since their safety and good fortune rest upon my actions, I depend upon them to provide wise counsel. I wonder, good Bishop, what my obligations are toward my vassals?

BISHOP FULBERT: You are wise to ask, for in doing so you demonstrate that you understand that the bond of fealty also ties lord to vassal, as well as vassal to lord. A lord should be faithful to his vassal in the same six ways. A lord should not betray his vassal, rather he should protect. A lord should also refrain from impeding his vassal's customary rights and obligations in any way. Similarly, a lord should do nothing that would cause his vassal to lose his possessions. Finally, like a vassal, a lord should not prevent a vassal in doing what he thinks is best, right or customary.

Thus, in essence when swearing the oath of fidelity, lord and vassal both swear to protect and behave with honor toward one another.

DUKE WILLIAM: What if, as a lord, I choose not to abide by these guidelines?

BISHOP FULBERT: If you are not faithful to your vassal in all of these matters, you will be considered unfaithful and treacherous. This is a contract of mutual responsibility and behavior, and if either lord or vassal goes back on their word, they have perjured themselves and broken the contract.

DUKE WILLIAM: Many thanks for these clarifications. I now better comprehend what is owed through the oath of fealty. I will endeavor to be a good lord and abide by these principals.

BISHOP FULBERT: I would expect nothing less of you, honorable duke. I fear I must bid you adieu.[9]

One way a vassal fulfilled the obligation of loyalty and protection, as set out by Bishop Fulbert, was through castle guard. This meant that a vassal would take up residence at his lord's castle, usually for a period of forty days, each year. While we do not have direct documentation of how castle guard worked for the lords of Beaugency, the neighboring count of Vendôme (from whom the Beaugency lords received fiefs) did issue a charter in the eleventh century that set out the parameters for guarding his castle.

> These are the customs which Count Burchard held in his time in the castle and county of Vendôme. First within the castle ward, just as he himself commanded it to be done . . . [in] namely the five months of March, April, June, July and August [castle guard] was done in this way. The first two months were to be served in the hall of the count, and the other three guarding [the count's] person, as it had been before in the settlement of Vendôme. Otrad, father of Salomon, was doing [castle guard for] September for which he was holding [the fiefs of] *Septo*[10] and Artins. Hervé of *Sancto-Marcello* was doing [castle guard in] October, for which he was holding [the fiefs of] La Chaise and Villaria and Lulme. Hubert of La Ferté was doing [castle guard for] November, for which he was holding [the fiefs of] La Cigogne and the church of Crucheray and also Couture. December [castle guard] was being done by Gislebert Dives, for which he was holding [the fiefs of] *Monte-Henricum* and Pezou and Lignières. Viscount Hubert was doing [castle guard in] January, for

9 This dialogue is a retelling of on an actual letter between Bishop Fulbert and Duke William V of Aquitaine. A translation of this letter is available in *The Letters and Poems of Fulbert of Chartres*, trans. Frederick Behrends (Oxford: Oxford University Press, 1976), letter 51, pp. 90–93.

10 Reconstructing medieval place names can be challenging as names of places have changed and been modified over the centuries. While some places are confidently and easily identifiable, such as Vendôme (Vindocinum), Chartres (Carnotum) and even Beaugency (Balgentiacum); other, more obscure, places can be more difficulty to determine, like *Septo.* Place names in italics indicate they are in the original Latin and that I have not been able to track down a modern equivalent.

> which he was holding the great benefice in Corbonnière. Gundriacus was doing [castle guard in] February, for which he was holding the **alods** of Saint-Amand. [Castle guard for] May was being done by Fulcher, for which he was holding the church of Nourray and the church of Lancé. These are all who guard the castle and the count, so that each night [the count] has within the castle five guard positions: one above the gate below the castle, another above the gate next to the house of Salomon, the third above the wall next to the house of Gislebert, and another two patrol the castle precincts the entire night.[11]

According to this document, castle guard entailed essentially two duties: Guarding the castle and also guarding the person of the count. Vassals were assigned castle guard by the month or a period of approximately thirty days. The other ten days of the customary forty days of service were spent engaged in other duties, such as advising the count at his court or providing protection as he traveled. When guarding the castle both specific strategic positions were assigned for the gates, as well as simply surveilling the castle grounds. For their service, these men were invested with fiefs.

While the nature of the relationship between lord and vassal remained much the same through the history of the Beaugency family, the organization of a lord's retinue developed over time. At the outset of the eleventh century, the men gathered around the lord of Beaugency had one essential function: To fight. But during the course of the Central Middle Ages, specific offices and functions emerged as the onus of lordship came to include managing as well as fighting. While early officers were preoccupied with providing the support necessary for waging war, later offices involved more specialized skills, like reading and writing. By the end of the twelfth century some individual lords – but definitely counts and kings – would have their own chanceries or offices in charge of making and keeping records. First mention of a Beaugency chancery comes under Simon I around 1150.[12] Simon also appears to have been the first lord of Beaugency to use a seal (see Figure 8.1a), further indication of the increased importance that was being placed on keeping and verifying documents.[13]

11 *STV*, vol. 1, no. 2, pp. 6–9.

12 Mediathéque d'Orléans, MS 489.

13 The seal identified as that of Simon I of Beaugency in Figure 8.1a (see Conclusion, Chapter 8 in this book) is considered by the Centre sigillographie as being that of John I, who was lord c. 1182–1218. However, close examination of the seal suggests it belongs to the twelfth century rather than the thirteenth. The rendering of the image is more in keeping with twelfth-century practices and represents a rather rudimentary execution of a knight on a horse – particularly when compared with the seal of Ralph II, which dates from the second half of the thirteenth century. It seems unlikely that a thirteenth-century seal would be so undeveloped, particularly when compared a seal that is quite complicated, elegant and well-executed a mere thirty years later. Moreover, in J.-N. Pellieux's history of Beaugency (vol. 1, p. 111) he provides a sketch of Simon I's seal, which is nearly identical to seal BM 157 in the Archives nationales. Hence, I believe this seal to be more accurately identified as Simon I's seal, rather than John I's.

During the eleventh century, however, certain of the Beaugency retinue began to be referred to as holding specific offices or functions. The earliest such reference comes in 1079 when Walter was designated as the marshal of Lord Lancelin II.[14] Medieval lordship was itinerant as most lords held several lordships and traveled among them to keep abreast of what was going on, but also as to avoid taxing the resources of one place for too long. For a lord who held lands all over western France, having an officer in charge of the lord's stable would have been doubly important as horses were the main means of transportation but also vital to the military duties of lordship. The next office to evolve within the Beaugency retinue was that of steward. A steward's duties were various, but he was essentially charged with overseeing his lord's household. This meant not only the itinerant household, but also the lord's chief residence of Beaugency. While in residence, the steward would help the lord and lady manage various household accounts and who owed what to them. The steward would also be responsible for overseeing other officers and servants within the castle, ranging from the dairy maid to the marshal. A lord's retinue often intersected with the household. The chamberlain, for example, was responsible for the lord and lady's chamber. This officer would have also traveled with the family and been tasked with keeping track of the lord's personal possessions – which could also include the lord and lady's treasury. While not so challenging when sedentary, being sure the proper linens, candles, bed clothes, clothing and other personal items were transferred from place to place required considerable organizational ability. In addition to these secular officers, lords frequently had personal chaplains or clerics as part of their retinue. This would provide them with a person who could perform religious offices when the lords were at various residences and while they traveled. This is confirmed architecturally by the existence of a small chapel with fresco of Christ in the ceiling vault on the second floor of the castle of Beaugency.[15] These clergymen also likely helped to record the lord's acts and donations. Like a lord's retinue, a king's also combined the responsibilities of lordship (i.e. fighting) with that of a household. Many of the offices described here would have been found in a royal household and provided the basis (as well as the name) for more formal governmental positions.

This discussion of fiefs, lords and vassals raises the question of what medievalists have come to regard as the "f-word:" Feudalism. Historians of yore developed the concept of feudalism (based on the Latin word for fief, *feodum*) to conceptualize relationships between lords and vassals into a tidy pyramid. Complicating matters further, Karl Marx used the term "feudalism" as an economic state that was part of his communist dialectic. Because the

14 *STV*, vol. 1, no. 279, pp. 431–436.

15 Corvisier, "Château de Beaugency," p. 17. A chapel outside the castle, but still in the castle precincts, was built in the thirteenth century.

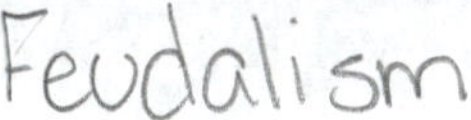

term "feudalism" was never used by medieval people, historians have become reluctant to employ it in describing the socio-political system that bound lords to vassals. In her seminal article of 1974, Elizabeth A.R. Brown famously labeled the use of the term "feudalism" as the "tyranny of a construct" rather than an accurate depiction of how this exchange of fiefs actually worked. Following up in 1996, Susan Reynolds went so far as to argue that the term fief was not used in the Middle Ages and advocated abandoning this term.[16] Most medievalists recognize the problems inherent with the term "feudalism" and use other terms, i.e. lordship, to describe the relationship between lords and vassals. For example, they might characterize the eleventh century as "feudal" but not as governed by "feudalism." Similarly, the bonds between vassal and lord may be described as "feudal tenure" to avoid the pitfalls inherent in "feudalism." Considering this issue from the perspective of the Beaugencys, they would have recognized the term for fief (*feodum* and its derivations), but would not have understood their world to be organized in a neat pyramidal hierarchy. Moreover, there was no one system of lordship in medieval Western Europe as lordship was exercised in different ways in different places. The Beaugencys would have likely acknowledged Bishop Fulbert's discussion of the obligations owed by both lord and vassal and perhaps tried to abide by them. But as Captain Barbossa of *Pirates of the Caribbean* fame pointed out about the "Pirate Code," when speaking of the bonds of feudal tenure, "What we have here are more 'guidelines' than rules." However, medieval literature did provide cautionary tales as to what could go awry if these precepts were not followed. But how did the Beaugency lords gain property and experience lordship?

The earliest lords of Beaugency: Lords, fiefs and vassals

Determining the origins of Beaugency power is challenging as the documents are not plentiful. Because the possession of land and its resources (both material and human) was key to the establishment of both lordship and family, charters can be used to flesh out how the lords of Beaugency came to power through their relationships with powerful individuals or families.

The first trace of a lord of Beaugency occurs in the first quarter of the eleventh century when a certain Lancelin of Beaugency is referred to as holding a fief from Count Fulk Nerra of Anjou.[17] Analysis of Map 2 indicates that the seedbed for Beaugency power lay around Vendôme and the earliest acts of the Beaugency family come from this region. This seems at odds for a family who took their name from a lordship located two days' ride to the west (approximately 37 miles) of Vendôme. Yet Vendôme was strategically located as well as the seat of the count and countess of Vendôme (who were

16 See the suggested reading section at the end of this chapter.

17 *STV*, vol. 1, no. 44, pp. 95–97.

related to the counts of Anjou) and it was from them that the lords of Beaugency received much of their property. How then did they come to control a lordship in a different county?

The first Beaugency to emerge in the records was a man by the name of Lancelin[18] (see Genealogy 1). While it is difficult to determine where he might have been born, the extant sources suggest he was intimately involved in the politics of western France – particularly in the counties of Maine, Anjou and Normandy. Lancelin had accrued considerable standing in the region as he was able to marry a daughter of the count of Maine, which also gave him control of the important lordship of La Flèche, located between Maine and Anjou and of strategic value to both counts. Nothing in the record suggests that distinguished blood ran in Lancelin's veins. Rather it seems he, like most of his peers, gained his position because of his abilities as a warrior. Indeed, in an early charter Lancelin describes himself as "I, Lancelin, a man with warriors' weapons," and indication of how he gained his status: As a warrior.[19] Like the lords of Lavardin and many rising families, Lancelin would arrange marriages for his children with families – specifically the counts of Maine and viscounts of Blois – who could trace their families back into the Carolingian past.

Lancelin ascended the ranks because of his service to the count of Anjou. One of the important responsibilities of a vassal was to attend his lord's court, which could include witnessing or affirming donations or transfer of property. Extant charters indicate that Lancelin witnessed several acts for Count Fulk Nerra in the early eleventh century. Vassals could also travel as part of their lord's retinue to another location when he made a gift. While Lancelin got his start in the center of the county of Anjou, by the 1030s his center of orbit had shifted to Vendôme. What would have motivated Lancelin to move further east? Fulk Nerra had ambitions up the Loire River. As he extended his reach to the east, he placed men he could trust in strategic lordships. As the fortress furthest to the east on a major tributary, Vendôme was militarily important. But Fulk had other reasons to be concerned about his dominion over Vendôme.

18 Pellieux believed that there had been a previous lord of Beaugency called Landric Sore. He asserted Landric was given Beaugency by King Hugh I Capet as "missus dominicus de castro de Balgenticensi" or as the missi dominici (servant of the lord) of the castle of Beaugency. This assertion seems highly dubious and I have not been able to find any record of this Landric in the acts of Hugh Capet and Pellieux did not provide a citation. Moreover, Pellieux believed that the Beaugency family was related to several comital families and the Bourbon dynasty. He also relies on a letter from Bishop Ivo of Chartres outlining the genealogy of a descendant of the Beaugencys. See, Pellieux, *Beaugency*, pp. 91–96. Modern scholars have demonstrated just how unreliable Ivo's genealogical reconstructions were. Pellieux's interpretation seems more an eighteenth-century attempt to establish a glorious past for a local family. The first Beaugency I am able to find in the sources is Lancelin I, vassal of Fulk Nerra and the count and countess of Vendôme.

19 AD Maine-et-Loire 40 H 1.

The county of Vendôme was controlled by Bishop Fulbert of Chartres, who was an ally of Fulk's rival, the count of Chartres. As Fulk Nerra of Anjou stretched his control eastward, those living under the authority of the counts of Chartres were drawn into battles between these two comital powers. The eleventh-century historian, Raoul Glaber, commented: "There were perpetual quarrels and frequent wars between this Odo [count of Chartres] and Fulk count of Anjou, because both were swollen with pride and so little disposed towards peace."[20] These wars, however, provided opportunities for men such as Lancelin. To help secure his control of Vendôme, Fulk married the heiress to the county and they had one daughter together. In 1016, his wife died, making his control of the Vendômois more tenuous and the county fell back under the political umbrella of the counts of Chartres. Between 1016 and 1031, Fulk strategized to wrest Vendôme from the house of Chartres. To do so, he needed a presence in this region. So he placed his daughter, Adele, in residence in Vendôme. Lancelin, a capable and trusted vassal, was entrusted with lands in this region. By 1033 Fulk's son Geoffrey Martel and his wife Agnes were in control of Vendôme and Lancelin appears in many of their acts as their faithful supporter.

Lancelin was called "the lord of Beaugency" for the first time just before 1040 in an act involving Countess Agnes of Vendôme.[21] Determining which count invested him with this lordship is difficult. Count Fulk Nerra also had aspirations to control Château-Landon located above the Loire to the northeast in the region of the Gatinais. Vital to maintaining contact with this fortress would have been having men situated strategically along the Loire River. Lancelin may have received Beaugency from Fulk as part of this count's strategy of pushing his control far to the east, right to the doorstep of the Capetian kings' royal domain.

At the same time, however – that is, the 1030s and early 1040s – Lancelin also held property from the count of Chartres. Lancelin would have been a welcome ally to the Chartrain count. Fulk Nerra, though, likely looked askance at Lancelin's ties to Chartres. Lancelin controlled diverse properties at Chamars, a suburb of Châteaudun, in the very heartlands of the county of Chartres (see Figure 3.1). Lancelin, moreover, also made alliances with the counts of Chartres. His daughter, Agnes, was married to the viscount of Blois

20 Glaber, *Opera*, p. 105.

21 This charter, often cited as evidence that the Beaugencys were invested with their lands by Hugh Capet for Lancelin I, is called "dominico vasso," indicating he was a royal vassal. This is the only charter where this entitulation is used, which brings this assertion into question. Moreover, instead of being a royal vassal, I would interpret this as an indication that Lancelin, rather, was the direct vassal of the counts of Vendôme or Anjou. *STV*, vol. 1, no. 22, pp. 42–44. Counts, however, did hold their lands and office from the king. So the lords of Beaugency could be considered indirect vassals of the king, meaning that they held fiefs from men who owed allegiance to the king. In my view, the Beaugencys' primary allegiance was to the counts they served rather than the king.

Figure 3.1 The church of St. John of Chamars. One of the Beaugency lords' earliest holdings. Eventually this church would be given to the abbey of Marmoutier and become one of its priories. Author photo.

– a staunch supporter of the Chartrain count. Beaugency itself was located in the county of Blois, which was part of the patrimony of the counts of Chartres. So it is equally possible that Lancelin received this lordship originally from the Chartrain count. Or the count of Chartres may have wrested lands that Fulk Nerra was claiming as part of his campaign to move northeast and invested Lancelin with this fortress. Perhaps in an attempt to woo him back from the count of Chartres or to secure his allegiance, Fulk invested Lancelin with the fortress of Mazé, located a day's ride to the south of La Fléche. Like many men of his generation, Lancelin was able to gain prominence due to his ability as a warrior and skill in navigating the turbulent political waters of the early eleventh century. But regardless of how Lancelin was originally invested with Beaugency, or by whom, the lords of Beaugency came to owe their loyalty and allegiance to the counts of Chartres.

Holding lands that covered such geo-political breadth was a challenge. The distance between Beaugency and La Fléche is approximately 100 miles. On a good day, a person traveling by horse could cover about 30 miles a day. Thus, by land the trip would have taken at least three days. Water travel would have been easier and faster. One could cover up to 60 miles a day by water, depending if the journey were up or down stream. Many of the

Beaugency holdings were located close to rivers: The Le Loir in the area of the Vendômois and the Chartrain; the Loire in the regions around Beaugency and the county of Blois. For example, Chamars could have been an embarkation point for travel to the Beaugency holdings in Vendôme, Anjou and even Maine. But there would still be a day's trip by land from Chamars to Beaugency (or virtually any other stop on the Le Loir). Chamars to La Fléche would be about 90 miles or a day and a half by water (with a day's ride between Chamars and Beaugency) or three to four days by horse. Lancelin solved this problem of overseeing the geographically dispersed holdings by investing two of his sons each with a lordship: John became the lord of La Fléche and Lancelin II the lord of Beaugency (see Genealogy 1).

The challenge of overseeing such a disparate constellation of lands was compounded by maintaining the delicate balance of being a vassal of two warring counts. This political calculus is evident in the resolution of a series of disputes to a hamlet located to the south of Vendôme sometime between 1040 and 1043. The complaint was heard at a location equidistant from Vendôme and Blois, the respective seats of both counts. Count Thibaut III of Chartres and Count Geoffrey Martel of Anjou were meeting to try to make peace. Lancelin I was present at the dispute; brought there by the responsibility of advising his lords who were set to go to war but also as the lord who held the disputed property as part of his fief. After considerable deliberation and rehearsal of who had held the property and its revenues for the last thirty years, a resolution was reached. Lancelin agreed to its terms and, along with both counts, signed the charter. While this matter was easily dispatched, the larger problem of peace between two belligerent counts was not. In spite of the attempts by the counts and their men to make peace, war would ensue a few short months later. Count Thibaut would be captured by the count of Anjou as the latter wrested Tours, perhaps the jewel in Thibaut's territorial crown, away from the house of Chartres once and for all.[22] Although the efforts at peace failed, the record of this council affords a glimpse into a vassal serving his lord(s) by providing advice, a duty that was at the heart of the lord–vassal relationship.

A further indication of Lancelin of Beaugency's (as well as later lords of Beaugency) prominent place among the ranks of the nobility was that he/they participated in royal acts – as well as those of counts, viscounts and other lords. When King Henri I confirmed pious donations made by Lancelin's lords to churches from Angers to Orléans, Lancelin was present.[23] In 1104, Ralph I of Beaugency even hosted a church council aimed at resolving the marital conflicts of King Philip I. But one royal act of the eleventh century

22 *CMPD*, no. 102, pp. 94–95.

23 *Catalogue des Actes de Henri Ier, roi de France (1031–1060)*, ed. Frédéric Soehnée (Paris: Champion, 1907) no. 38, p. 85; no. 58, pp. 56–57; no. 69, pp. 69–70; *Recueil des actes de Philippe Ier, roi de France (1059–1108)*, ed. Maurice Prou (Paris: Académie des Inscriptions et Belles-Lettres, 1908) no. 77, pp. 193–196; no. 97, pp. 250–252.

suggests that the lords of Beaugency may have even over-reached their power. Sometime in the early summer months of 1075, King Philip I was holding court at Orléans where he issued a proclamation:

> Philip I, at the request of Christian the abbot of St. Mesmin of Micy, placed his officers – the knights and sergeants of Beaugency and Sully – under interdict [meaning they could not receive the church sacraments], because they went against a ruling of King Robert I [King Philip's grandfather] and levied certain unjust customs on the lands and men of the abbey of Micy.[24]

The abbot also complained that these knights were hunting their falcons on his land – which could cause a certain amount of chaos if not damage. This was not the end of the abbot's grievances: He was also concerned that the lords of Beaugency did not recognize that the abbey's boats were free from tolls on the Loire and other rivers. Furthermore the abbot also insisted that the abbey have right to collect fines for legal cases concerning the shedding of blood, rape, murder, or fire.

This royal diploma of 1075 encapsulates many of the issues affecting lordship and politics in the mid-eleventh century. Philip I was neither the strongest nor the weakest eleventh-century king. Indeed, this diploma demonstrates that he commanded considerable influence given that the abbot of Micy appealed directly to him for aid against these unruly lords. That the lords were punished shows an attempt on the part of both king and church to provide order. This diploma also illustrates the tensions between secular and ecclesiastical lords over what rights each exercised to property, but also justice. Bound up in lordship was the obligation to provide justice and order. Hence, the right to try and to punish those for what we would deem capital crimes was central to a lord's exercise of authority – as well as collecting any fines associated with such infractions. Even as late as the thirteenth century, the lord of Beaugency would assert his right to the "tools" of justice, such as the gallows, and only at the very end of the Beaugencys' tenure as lord did they finally abandon the right of justice.

Securing alliances and making friends: Beaugency vassals

Forging alliances with men more powerful than themselves – like kings and counts – was one way the Beaugencys gained influence and position.[25] But

24 *Actes de Philippe Ier*, no. 77, pp. 193–196; For Robert I's original charge, see *Catalogue des actes de Robert II, roi de France*, ed. William M. Newman (Librarie du Recueil Sirey, Paris, 1937) no. 96, pp. 121-–122.

25 By the end of their tenure as lords, the Beaugency family also held fiefs from the archbishop of Bourges and the bishop of Orléans. P. Bouvier, "L'acquisition de la seigneurie de Beaugency par Philip le Bel," *Le Môyen Age* 26 (1913), p. 261.

part of their power stemmed from creating relationships with other warriors by granting out their lands as fiefs. This is a process scholars call "subinfeudation." As we have seen, Lancelin I was invested with extensive lands by the counts of Anjou and Chartres. Given the length and breadth of these holdings, it would not be possible for Lancelin I to rule them all individually – even with the help of his children. To ensure the defense of his lands and the maintenance of order, he granted out lordships that made up his larger patrimony to vassals, who then themselves became lords. This created a web of ties that bound Lancelin to men and women from the edge of the county of Maine up to Beaugency. The geographic placement of these vassals is significant as many were clustered in the area around Vendôme, thus providing clues as to where the Beaugencys' power originated. The lord of Moncontour, located on the Loire River just east of Tours, seems to have been one of the earliest Beaugency vassals. Moncontour became a fief of Lord Lancelin I as a result of a battle that occurred here in 1033 between the count of Anjou and the count of Poitiers where Lancelin provided valorous military service to the Angevin count.[26] As the Angevin count attempted to extend his power up the Loire toward eastern *Francia*, the control of a fortress perched high above the Loire River would have been important.

While the Beaugency family originated in the west and owed their allegiance to the comital houses of Anjou and Vendôme, during the second half of the eleventh century the family began to actively accumulate vassals and property in the heart of the Chartrain (see Map 2). These acquisitions were strategic and implemented to strengthen the Beaugency bond with the counts of the Chartrain. The church of St. John at Chamars and its surrounding property was one of the early Beaugency possessions in the Chartrain (early 1040s). The geographic sweep of the Beaugencys' holdings meant that they needed to secure routes that would allow them to travel between their family seat at Beaugency and their territories in the west. As early as 1067, the Beaugencys exercised authority over Rocé, located 4 miles due east of Vendôme. In the same year, Lancelin II approved a gift given by his vassals Ingebald Brito and Domitilla to the abbey of St. Trinité of property in Villarceau, just a few miles south of Rocé.[27] These two holdings served as a bridge between the Beaugency holdings in Vendôme and the west with their Chartrain possessions. Around 1080, Lancelin II confirmed a gift made by another vassal, Hersend, the wife of Gradulf Albus of Montigny. Montigny's situation on the Le Loir River just north of Vendôme meant that the Beaugencys had vassals on whom they could depend for hospitality.[28] The Beaugencys also became lords of Ouzouer-le-Marché, located in the plain of the Beauce. This would have been an attractive acquisition for the Beaugencys

26 *Annales de St. Aubin*, in *Recueil d'Annales Angevines et Vendômoises*, ed. Louis Halphen (Paris: Alphonse Picard et Fils, 1903) p. 3.

27 *STV*, vol. 1, no. 185, pp. 320–321.

28 *CMV*, no. 126, pp. 215–217.

as it was located in the agriculturally rich Beaucerain plain, but Ouzouer-le-Marché would also have provided a stopping point on the way west toward Chamars or Montigny.[29] Another means by which the Beaugency family anchored themselves in the Chartrain was by becoming the protectors of the priory of Villeberfol (modern day Conan).[30]

By the end of the eleventh century, the Beaugency family had established a presence in the Chartrain and had secured properties that were arrayed strategically to allow them to travel to Vendôme and points west. The shift in their allegiance from the counts of Anjou and toward the count of Chartres was further reinforced by the Beaugencys' gift of a church near Courville to the abbey of Marmoutier, which the Chartrain counts had long patronized, in 1092.[31] The Beaugencys had been rewarded with fiefs in the northern part of the county and close to the count's seat of Chartres, as well as land in the town of Chartres itself. Appearing with the lord of Beaugency in this charter were men designated as "of Beaugency," indicating that they were vassals who held property from this lord near or around their seat of power. While the Beaugency rise to power began in the west, by the twelfth century they had focused their allegiance on the count of Chartres (who called the lord of Beaugency one of his "best men" in 1114) and their lordship of Beaugency.

Relationships with vassals: Conflict and devotion

Now that we understand how the lords of Beaugency accumulated fiefs and vassals, how did they interact with their vassals?

Like the counts of Vendôme, the lords of Beaugency also had vassals who guarded their castle and person. One can easily imagine men placed about the castle walls charged with protecting its inhabitants. Medieval warfare was, by and large, based in defense rather than offense and was characterized by "wasting" where non-military possessions were targeted, which presented an easy gain at a low risk. The aim was to harass the enemy, but also deplete their resources. Castle guard was part of this defensive strategy and crucial to a lord's power and defense of his lands. Starting as early as the 1040s, the lords of Beaugency were exercising the juridical authority of lordship by holding *placita* or hearings to adjudicate disputes. The charters recording these courts indicate that their vassals took part as witnesses, confirmers and plaintiffs. For example, when individuals claimed **tithes** from the monks of Tiron then recognized that their claim was invalid and abandoned it, the resolution was brokered in "the tower of the castle" of Beaugency and Lord Ralph I presided because the disputed property belonged to his fief.[32]

29 *STV*, vol. 2, no. 324, pp. 32–35.
30 AD Loir-et-Cher 16 H 118 no. 5.
31 *CMPD*, no. 60, pp. 52–53.
32 *Tiron*, vol. 1, no. 41, p. 61.

Part of the obligation of the lord was not only to protect his vassal, but also his vassal's rights. As Bishop Fulbert advised, a lord should not impede, but rather protect what the vassal sees as what belongs to him customarily. Medieval literature reflects this same preoccupation with justice, as King Arthur is often depicted as holding courts and adjudicating disputes between his knights. Old Testament Kings, particularly King Salomon, additionally provided medieval lords with model for dispensing justice. King David was also invoked as the ideal warrior king. Historian David Crouch has argued that a "Davidic Ethic" was developed to create a "moral justification" for the medieval ruler's exercise of power.[33] The clergy were essential in developing and disseminating these ideals – recall that Bishop Ivo referenced King David in his letter to Lord Ralph I (Document 2, page 223–224). In the abbey church at Beaugency, there is a carving depicting David's battle with Goliath. Here, in stone, the idea of a leader using might to protect his kingdom was visualized. Significantly, this carving was rendered on a pillar on the northside of the church where the lords of Beaugency entered the sanctuary through their private entrance. Each time they would go to worship, they would be reminded of their role as just leaders and the appropriate use of force[34]

Figure 3.2 Capital with David with his slingshot (left) slaying the giant, Goliath (right). Located in the north transept of Notre Dame de Beaugency. Author photo.

33 See the suggested reading section at the end of this chapter.

34 This is the only historiated capital in the sanctuary (meaning it tells a story). Other capitals are carved with vegetative motifs. Vergnolle, "Notre-Dame de Beaugency," pp. 80–81.

(see Figure 3.2). Depictions of David would also have populated the pages of Psalters as medieval people thought King David composed the Psalms. Indeed, the image from the Psalter in Figure 2.3 shows David confronting Goliath. As mothers used Psalters to teach their children to read, sons and daughters were inculcated with the Davidic ethic from a young age.

Because both lords and vassals had rights to the fief, each had to secure the other's consent to alienate it. In 1067, for example, Lord Lancelin II traveled to the chapter house of the monastery of St. Trinité of Vendôme to approve the gift made by his vassals, Ingelbaud Brito and Domitilla. Not securing the consent of one's lord (or vassal) could be risky. The gift might be challenged since lord and vassal depended on the property for their support; and they did not alienate such holdings lightly. But even more violent consequences could result if lords were not kept apprised, and approved, their vassals' alienations. Twenty years earlier, another charter records that a couple who also held fiefs from Lancelin donated property to the same monks. In this case, Lancelin was not this couple's direct lord; rather, they held the fief from his vassal, Odo of Mondoubleau. Hearing that this land had been given to the church without their approval, Lancelin and Odo reacted quickly and violently by sending their armed supporters to these lands. When the countess of Vendôme, from whom Lancelin and Odo held these fiefs, was made aware of the havoc being caused by these men, she was outraged. She intervened at once and demanded her vassals cease and desist "out of love of God and herself." Lancelin complied at once and conceded the land to the monastery. Clearly the countess was a woman who did have the power to command.

This was not the sole incident of the lords of Beaugency reacting violently when they believed their vassals had acted without their approval. Indeed, Lancelin II and his son Ralph I, went even further in exacting retribution against one of their vassals. In 1081, Robert of Moncontour donated his holdings at Coulommiers-la-Tour so that he could retire from life and become a monk. He made this gift with the approval of his lords, Lancelin and Ralph, and they were present in the monks' chapterhouse when Robert made the gift (see Document 8, page 228). All should have gone smoothly, except that Robert did not secure the consent of his son to this gift. The monk documenting this incident wrote that: "unjustness allowed Bertran the son of the aforementioned Robert to make a false claim to the same gift of his father . . . [and] he inflicted many injuries on us."[35] Bertan sought the support of Count Geoffrey Jordan, who took up his cause. Lord Lancelin II was doubly insulted. First, his vassal's son, who would have done homage to Lancelin for this fief and become his vassal, had the temerity to dispute the gift and then harass the monks. To add insult to injury, Lancelin saw Geoffrey Jordan as an upstart to the office of count of Vendôme who had no authority to find in Bertran's favor. This was apparently too much for Lancelin to bear, so he

35 AD Loir-et-Cher, 21 H 69, nos. 4 and 5; *STV*, vol. 2, no. 361, pp. 105–106.

simply imprisoned this count. Given that the Beaugencys had been stalwart supporters of the counts of Vendôme and Anjou, there was clearly more to Lancelin's imprisoning of the count than a dispute over a vassal securing his approval for a gift. Indeed, Vendôme was split in something close to a civil war over who was the rightful count and Lancelin had clearly chosen sides. Regrettably, the situation did not improve.

Bertran did finally see the error of his ways and made a deal with the monks. But there was one small oversight: The lord of Beaugency was not consulted. This time it was Ralph, having succeeded his father, who was insulted and deeply angry. The charter records, "Ralph angered by the false claim for the same reason that because it was his property and from himself [that] Robert held [the property] earlier, and so too did his son Bertran." As lord, Ralph had every expectation that he would be consulted in any agreements concerning this fief. In response, he violently seized Coulommiers-la-Tour. But motivated "partly from fear of God creeping over him, partly from advice of counsel," he allowed the land to revert to the monks. Ralph signed the charter by making the mark of the cross to demonstrate his approval of the resolution.[36]

The conflicts between the Beaugency lords and their vassals demonstrate the contractual character of their bond. Lords expected certain behavior from their vassals, and when vassals behaved badly in their eyes, they reacted with swift – and often violent – justice. For reasons that are not entirely clear, Bertran of Moncontour was reluctant to recognize the suzerainty of either Lancelin or Ralph over his patrimonial lands. Yet his lords were equally dedicated to exercising their power over him and demonstrating their supremacy. In the end, they won. Bound up in this struggle over fiefs and lordly rights was also honor. The literature of the day emphasized the importance of a lord's honor, which was intimately connected to lordship. An honorable lord served his king well through his counsel, was an accomplished (often undefeated) warrior and treated his vassals fairly. Vassals, in return, fought valiantly for their lords, did not conspire against them and obeyed them nearly unconditionally. Given that these were the standards of the day, Lancelin and Ralph clearly felt that Bertran had violated this code of conduct – and Bishop Fulbert of Chartres would have likely agreed.

Even while relations between lord and vassal could deteriorate to violence or disrespect, strong bonds of affection also could develop between them. Indeed, given the emphasis placed on the close and abiding relationship between lord and vassal, I would argue that these relationships were more of the norm than the violence and backstabbing captured in the account above. While Ralph I of Beaugency was waging war against one disrespectful vassal, he was also profoundly grieved by the death of another. For his "very familiar friend and vassal," Landric of Malesherbes, who died at Beaugency, Ralph

36 AD Loir-et-Cher, 21 H 69, nos. 4 and 5; *STV*, vol. 2, no. 340, pp. 63–66.

arranged to have him buried in the cemetery of St. Trinité – an honor shared by few for proximity to the holy helped to improve one's spiritual status. Not only that, but Ralph himself and his entourage conveyed the body to the monastery and humbly asked that Landric be buried there (see Document 9, page 230). That a lord went to these lengths for his vassal to be buried with the monks bespeaks a close bond between the two. Ralph also stipulated that he would provide clothing and materiel necessary to clothe one pauper annually in Landric's memory. Thus each year, Landric would be remembered by his lord, the monks, his fellow vassals, as well as the entire community. The gift was made in front of Ralph's court, in addition to anyone else who was gathered at the chapterhouse of the monastery; a public testament of Ralph's esteem for Landric. The charter also indicates the size, as well as the individual men, who were part of Ralph's entourage, for they witnessed the agreement: Odo the brother of Landric, Fulcher of Turre, Vulgrin the son of Ingelbald Brito (one of Ralph's vassals), Gervase son of Lancelin, Peter Chotard and his brother Bodellus, who were Ralph's cousins, Tetbald son of Leterius and Hugh son of Salomon.

Ralph's son, Lord Simon I, also showed concern and affection for one of his vassals. Hugh of Rilly-sur-Loire was admitted into the monks' hospital for care.[37] Most monasteries had hospitals attached to them – although these were not hospitals in any modern sense, but rather places where people could receive nursing. What caused Hugh to be in need of such care is not clear, but an injury resulting from his warrior occupation is likely. The literary and chronicle accounts depict the ferociousness of medieval battles, as these excerpts from *The Song of Roland* depict:

> Down through his coif and his fell of hair, Betwixt his eyes came the falchion [sword] bare, Down through his plated harness fine, Down through the Saracen's chest and chine, Down through the saddle with gold inlaid, Till sank in the living horse the blade, Severed the spine where no joint was found . . . Out of the head both the two eyes have burst, And all the brains are fallen in the dust.[38]

Even the border of the *Bayeux Tapestry*, which narrates the Battle of Hastings of 1066, has some fairly graphic images of limbs severed and heads crushed in battle (see Figure 3.3). Wounds could be quite serious and even put an end to a career. Indeed, Simon's own uncle, Ralph of Vermandois, lost an eye in battle. Given that Hugh was a vassal of the lord of Beaugency, it is likely he was injured while fighting for Lord Simon. Simon felt a duty toward Hugh, as the charter makes clear that he had already arranged for Hugh to be admitted to the monks' care to finish out his life.

37 *STV*, vol. 2, no. 508, pp. 329–330.

38 *The Song of Roland,* trans. Charles Moncrieff (New York: E.P. Dutton, 1920) pp. 44–45.

Figure 3.3 Carnage from the Battle of Hastings as illustrated in the Bayeux Tapestry. These images demonstrate the ferocity of battle, but also the severity of injuries. Granger Historical Picture Archive / Alamy stock photo.

Fighting together in battle forged bonds that lasted a life time and that allowed warriors to literally lay down their lives for one another – recall the Yvain and Galahad story, but also the cousin of the lord of Semblançay who sacrificed his life for his kinsmen. The lords of Beaugency clearly felt both compassion and affection for the men who they depended upon to defend their person and their property. But these bonds also transcended the battlefield. Some scholars have even speculated that such protestations of affection were not merely for a comrade, but indicative of a homosexual relationship. Intriguingly, in parallel to charters recording grief felt at the death of a spouse or child, the charter indicates that Ralph was deeply bereaved by Landric's death. Moreover, the charter says Landric died at Beaugency. Does this suggest they were lovers? Possibly. In other places and times, Ancient Greece for example, warriors developed emotional and sexual relationships with their brothers-in-arms. So this charter could be read in this way. Regrettably, the sources do not get much more specific than this about such relationships – which is not surprising given the church's pronouncements against homosexuality. Considering the nature of the evidence, one can say with surety that there was a bond of affection between Ralph and Landric – as well as other men. But I do not think we can push this evidence any further; it just is not conclusive enough.

The lord is a lady

The lords of Beaugency encountered female lords and several women were their vassals throughout the eleventh, twelfth and thirteenth centuries – as the preceding examples have indicated. Women did exercise public power and, on admittedly rare occasions, led men into battle. Nor were they afraid to use violence to achieve their ends. Countess Euphronia of Vendôme led an armed group of her soldiers in an attack on a church. She and her men rode up to the church, broke down the doors, seized the tithes collected in the church and distributed the wealth amongst themselves. The evidence from the region around Beaugency is also rich with examples of women as both vassals and lords. For example, a neighboring noblewoman named Rosecelina was lord to three knights, who owed her military service. Eustachia of Gouet held law courts and distributed justice among her vassals. The office of *vicedominus* of Chartres was held by two women, a mother and daughter, for much of the twelfth century. These examples challenge Duby's assertion that noblewomen were powerless and demonstrate that women did enjoy *potestas* and that some were even able to wield a sword.

While the letter that Mathilda of Beaugency wrote to her kinsman the king indicates that she took an active part in managing and developing her lands (see Document 4, page 225), the sources do not allow us to trace Mathilda's experience – or that of one of the other ladies of Beaugency – more completely. But their kinswoman, Countess Ermengarde of Brittany (c. 1070–1147), is well documented and exemplifies the kind of power that women of the aristocracy could command. Ermengarde led an intriguing and complicated life that merits a biography in its own right. Here we will focus on a short description of her exercise of lordly power.

"Powerful in eloquence, shrewd in counsel" was how Bishop Marbode of Rennes described Countess Ermengarde of Brittany in a poem he dedicated to her around 1096.[39] Ermengarde's mother, also named Ermengarde, was Ralph I's sister and daughter of Lancelin II. Her father was Count Fulk IV of Anjou and Ermengarde was raised at his court. Count Fulk IV was one of the most powerful men of his day and established a thriving intellectual center at his court in Angers. It was here that Ermengarde learned the rudiments of lordship, but also encountered many of the important intellectuals and clergy of the time. She married Count Alan IV of Brittany around 1093. Three years later, she found herself solely in charge of the county as he departed on crusade (likely in the company of Ermengarde's uncle, Ralph). Ermengarde ruled Brittany in his absence and did an admirable job of maintaining political stability of a county which was often plagued with internal fighting. Once Alan returned in 1101, they ruled the county together. Ermengarde appears in virtually every comital act from the period

39 For a translation of Marbode's poem, see http://epistolae.ccnmtl.columbia.edu/woman/31.html#letterslist.

1101 to 1112. Like countesses in other regions, she was present at law courts, settled disputes, oversaw vassals and made gifts to the church. Nor was Ermengarde a mere spectator to these events. The verbs used to describe these rulings and actions are *plural* verbs indicating that Ermengarde and Alan ruled together. In particular, Ermengarde was valuable in helping Alan maintain cordial relationships with the church. As we know from the Beaugency lords, counts and lords alike depended upon the church to help them provide stability but also to support their authority.

In 1112, Ermengarde's life changed dramatically, for in this year her husband decided to become a monk at the Breton abbey of Redon. The charter recording Alan's entry into Redon indicates that he had been seriously ill. His retirement had significant repercussions for the county. As Ermengarde and Alan's son Conan was not quite ready to rule the county alone, Ermengarde and Conan assumed joint rule for Brittany, a responsibility that they would share until Ermengarde's death in 1147. In the extant acts from the period 1112–1147 (with exception of the years between c. 1129 and 1135 when she traveled to the Holy Land), Ermengarde again appears in virtually every act with Count Conan. These charters also employ plural verbs and often say that Conan was "persuaded by his mother" to take action. As co-ruler, Ermengarde acted with Conan in making gifts to monasteries and overseeing the comital lands. In several documents, she is referred to as the "venerable" countess. The documents also indicate that Ermengarde advised her son on several matters, ranging from dealing with disruptive vassals to his relationship with the church. Marbode's description of Ermengarde being "shrewd in counsel," served her son and Brittany well.

As had been the case with her husband, Ermengarde spent considerable energy helping her son to manage his relationship with the church. Medieval people did not separate the power of church and state, as is espoused in modern America. In the Middle Ages, religious and secular power were connected and often tightly interwoven. Indeed both secular and sacred rulers founded their legitimate right to rule on Biblical precedents. Moreover, lords, counts and kings depended upon the church to help them legitimatize their rule as "Christian" leaders. Unfortunately for Conan, he had a serious falling out with the church between 1117 and 1119. Because he and a group of his vassals had violated church property, he was placed under anathema of excommunication by the papal legate. Ermengarde had not been privy to this action and spent the next two years working actively to restore Conan to the church's good graces. This included writing letters to the pope's representative in France and using her relationship with several prominent clergy. In the end, Ermengarde's intercession was successful. Conan repented his actions and became a favored son of the church once again. Ermengarde's eloquence in pleading her son's case worked to his benefit and that of the county.

Ermengarde is not unusual in her role as intermediary between her son and the church. Indeed, the role of intercessor was one that aristocratic women commonly assumed. Like noblemen, women were also encouraged to follow

Figure 3.4 The Virgin Mary as the Throne of Salomon, painted capital sculpture, from the parish church of St. Genest at Lavardin. Author photo.

the example of Old Testament rulers. Queen Esther of the Old Testament, who similarly interceded for her people (the Hebrews) with the King of Persia, was often held up as a role model for female rulers. Moreover, women as judges were also celebrated in medieval art in the image of the Virgin as the Throne of Salomon. Here the Virgin sits in judgement in a throne, embodying the just ruler informed by Christian law, holding the Christ-child on her lap. Significantly, there was just such a depiction in the church at Lavardin where Eva-Avelina governed with her husband and raised her grandson to be the next lord[40] (see Figure 3.4).

As well as being politically adept, Ermengarde was a deeply pious woman. Throughout her life, she was attracted to various new forms of monasticism and medieval piety. She became an advocate for these communities and used

40 For a discussion of this image in the context of female lordship in the Lavardin family, see Livingstone, "Piecing Together the Fragments: Telling the Lives of the Ladies of Lavardin through Image and Text."

her eloquence to persuade her son and other male kin to support these new monastic communities. St. Bernard of Clairvaux was one of the most influential churchmen of his time, who could count the king of France among his admirers. He was a dynamic figure who drew many to his new vision of Cistercian monasticism, much to the displeasure of the traditional Benedictine monastery of **Cluny** which saw the reformed monasticism of the Cistercians as a threat.[41] Many aristocrats were attracted to the piety of the Cistercian brothers and became ardent patrons of this order, compounding the rivalry between the two monasteries of Cluny and Cîteaux. Ermengarde was one of them. She was instrumental in founding one of the earliest Cistercian monasteries in Brittany. Ermengarde was a woman of considerable status and respect. She was friends with many of the important people of her day and used these relationships, along with her shrewdness and personal charisma, to buttress the power of the comital family. Patronizing monasteries was one way to solidify friendships and demonstrate influence.

Like the men of her class, Ermengarde could also depend on her ties to her natal kin to extend and highlight her influence. She enjoyed a close relationship with her father, the count of Anjou, and her half-brother who succeeded her father as count, but was also count of Maine and eventually king of Jerusalem. She appeared in donations with these men, traveled to their courts, had friends and enemies in common, and shared an interest in developing close relations with clergy and religious communities. Ermengarde left an indelible imprint on Brittany. Hers must have been a stabilizing hand, for after her death, her son managed to weaken the county to the point that Brittany was never again an autonomous polity.

Conclusion

The eleventh century witnessed the establishment and rise of the Beaugency family. Through their relationships with powerful men such as the counts of Anjou, Vendôme and Chartres they were able to garner significant influence and territory. These lords, in turn, used this territory to create a network of clients that buttressed and extended their power. Perhaps the most tangible symbol and expression of their status and power was the *donjon* they constructed at Beaugency during this century. Intriguingly this castle shares many of the same architectural characteristics, as well as visual impact, with many castles built along the Loire by Count Fulk Nerra of Anjou. Given the Beaugency families close ties to Anjou, as well as to the lords of La Flèche in Maine, it is perhaps not surprising that they would have imported castle design from these regions. Now that the basic contours of lordship have been drawn, let us continue by exploring the lives of the Beaugency lords who called this fortress home.

41 "Cistercian" is derived from the religious house at Cîteaux, from which the Cistercians took their name. Similarly, monks from Cluny are often referred to as "Cluniac."

Suggested reading

Bernard S. Bachrach, *Fulk Nerra: The Neo-Roman Consul, 987–1040*. Berkeley: University of California Press, 1993.

Constance Britain Bouchard, "The Origins of the French Nobility: A Reassessment." *American Historical Review* 86 (1981): 501–532.

Elizabeth A.R. Brown, "The Tyranny of a Construct: Feudalism and Historians of Medieval Europe." *The American Historical Review* 79 (1974): 1063–1088.

David Crouch, *The Birth of Nobility: Constructing Aristocracy in England and France, 900–1300*. London: Routledge, 2005.

Theodore Evergates, ed., *Aristocratic Women in Medieval France.* Philadelphia: The University of Pennsylvania Press, 1999; *Henry the Liberal, Count of Champagne*. Philadelphia: The University of Pennsylvania Press, 2016; and *Marie, Countess of Champagne*. Philadelphia: The University of Pennsylvania Press, forthcoming.

Lois Huneycutt, "Intercession and the High-Medieval Queen: The Esther Topos." In *The Power of the Weak*, eds. Jennifer Carpenter and Sally MacLean, pp. 126–146. Urbana: University of Illinois Press, 1995.

Amy Livingstone, "Pious Women in a 'Den of Scorpions:' The Piety and Patronage of the Countesses of Brittany, c. 1050–1150." *Historical Reflections/Réflexions historiques* 43 (2017): 45–61; and "'You Will Dwell with Barbarous and Uneducated Men:' Countess Ermengarde and Political Culture in Twelfth-Century Brittany." *History: The Journal of the Historical Association* 102 (2017): 858–873.

Jane Martindale, "The French Aristocracy in the Early Middle Ages: A Reappraisal." *Past and Present* 75 (1977): 5–45.

Susan Reynolds, *Fiefs and Vassals: The Medieval Evidence Reinterpreted.* Oxford: The Clarendon Press, second edition, 1996.

A special edition of the *Medieval Feminist Form* was dedicated to exploring medieval women and power: *Beyond Women and Power: Looking Backward, Moving Forward, Medieval Feminist Forum*, vol. 51, no. 2 (2016). http://ir.uiowa.edu/mff/vol51/iss2/. Several articles argue that aristocratic women controlling fiefs and holding *potestas* was the norm in medieval society.

4 Ralph I, lord of Beaugency, c. 1080–c. 1130

In many ways the lordship of Ralph I of Beaugency was the apex of Beaugency power and influence, and pivotal for this family. He was the quintessential warrior and his life would even lend itself to Hollywood adaptation. Ralph went on crusade and earned accolades for both his bravery and piety; he ruled over holdings that spanned at least two counties; he married into one of the most prominent aristocratic families in France; he was lauded by the royal chronicler of his time; he was fervently loyal to his lords; and he even corresponded with a bishop. Ralph represents the pinnacle of Beaugency power and influence for, as far as we can tell, no other Beaugency lord held the respect or the ear of so many powerful figures. Recovering the life of even a prominent local lord can be challenging as many of the details of their lives go unrecorded. Fortunately, a run of charters, references in contemporary chronicles and letters, have survived that allows me to reconstruct how Ralph ruled and his relationship with his clients and peers. This chapter will focus on Ralph of Beaugency to explore how a medieval lord lived his life.

The young Ralph of Beaugency, c. 1065–c. 1096

Ralph first emerges in the documents as the young lord of Beaugency around 1080. We know from the charters that his father Lancelin II went on pilgrimage to Rome about this time. That Lancelin left the lordship in Ralph's hands for a significant span of months suggests he had confidence that his son was sufficiently able and mature to run the lordship. Given these facts, it would seem that Ralph was about 15 years of age when his father left on pilgrimage. Unfortunately, upon his return Lancelin found that there was a dispute over the property he had given for the construction of a chapel. He and Ralph worked together to find a solution to the problem and resolved that the canons of Notre Dame de Beaugency gave up some of their land so that the chapel of St. Sepulcher could be refurbished. The brothers of St. Trinité were so grateful to them that they granted their bodies, as well as those of their wives and children, burial in the monks' own cemetery.[1]

1 *STV*, vol. 2, no. 301, pp. 3–6.

Visit the companion website: www.routledge.com/cw/livingstone

Ralph's father left quite an impression on his son. Lancelin was an active participant in the politics of the day and conveyed that political ambition to his son. As the examples from the previous chapter show, neither Lancelin nor Ralph were shy about exercising their authority. Recall that Lancelin imprisoned the count of Vendôme at Beaugency after he ruled against Lancelin's right to certain property but also as part of the wars between the counts of Vendôme and Anjou. Ralph, like his father, did not tolerate questions to his authority as lord – as his response to Bertran of Moncontour indicates. Just as Ralph was coming of age, a notice in a charter from St. Trinité Vendôme says that Lancelin of Beaugency, along with the Count of Nevers, had joined the king in besieging the fortress of Viscount of Hugh of Chartres.[2] Things did not go well for Lancelin, however, as he and William of Nevers, were imprisoned by the viscount. What was it like for young Ralph to have his father imprisoned? This interval may have been the young lord's introduction to command as it is likely he would have played some role in overseeing the Beaugency patrimony while his father was imprisoned. Lancelin may have gone on pilgrimage and undertaken construction of the chapel of St. Sepulcher in thanksgiving for his release from prison. Similar political turbulence would shape the life of his son.

Between 1080 and 1090, Ralph co-ruled the Beaugency lands and personnel with his father. The 1086 charter recording Ralph's gift for Landric Malesherbes, his friend and companion-in-arms (Document 9, page 230), reads that he gave "all of that from his lordship which he held from the church of St. Bienheuré." This indicates that Lancelin invested his son with certain property over which Ralph would have sole control, indicating both a shared governance of Beaugency lands and that Ralph was given property in advance of his father's demise – a practice consistent among many noble families.[3] Given that Ralph was Lancelin's only son, it was strategic for Ralph to serve an apprenticeship of learning how to rule while at the same time receiving a share of the patrimony for his own support. Much of the property over which Ralph held sway was located in the Vendômois and Chartrain. The once extended Beaugency lordship that stretched from the county of Maine to Orléans had, by Ralph's time, come to be focused on the lands in to the east and those closest to what had become their home base of Beaugency. As Map 3 illustrates, from Ralph's rule forward the Beaugencys' power was rooted in the Chartrain. This realignment began under Lancelin, but was solidified by the political choices and alliances of Ralph.

2 *STV*, vol. 1, no. 290, pp. 444–446. Scholars have asserted that Lancelin's participation in this battle against the viscount of Chartres indicates that he was a royal vassal. However, it seems more plausible that Lancelin entered the fray because of his allegiance to the count, his own interest in local affairs, or to support the count of Nevers who was married to his daughter, Agnes.

3 *STV*, vol. 2, no. 329, pp. 43–45.

Ralph on crusade, 1096–1100

The single event that most defined Ralph's life was the calling of what became known as the First Crusade.[4] Like many of his generation, Ralph was inspired to take up the cross and seize Jerusalem from the Muslims. In 1095 Pope Urban II received a request for help from the Byzantine Emperor, Alexius II. Over the recent decades, Byzantium had lost many of its holdings in the Holy Land to the Seljuk Turks and the emperor was concerned by the threat that the Turks' control of Asia Minor presented. What Alexius had expected was a small group of crack military operatives. What he got was a rag tag army numbering in the tens of thousands made up of people ranging from those had no idea how to fight to some of the most celebrated warriors of the age.

In late 1095 and early 1096, word spread north from the Council of Clermont (held in the south of France) where Urban II had originally called for crusade. Preachers, including the pope, traveled throughout Western Europe to gain followers for the expedition. Urban II himself journeyed to the heart of the Loire. One of the highpoints of his visit was his consecration of the abbey church of Marmoutier. Many aristocrats who were devoted patrons of this monastery came to hear the pope bless the sanctuary and preach holy war. Ralph was likely in the audience. Men and women from the region were moved to go to the East and many made donations in preparation for the journey (see Document 10, page 231). One of the most famous was Count Stephen of Chartres. Being a loyal vassal of the count and devoted Christian, Ralph became part of Stephen's entourage. The count and his followers joined the army led by Duke Robert of Normandy, Count Robert of Flanders and Hugh the Great of Vermandois, the brother to the king of France. To follow Ralph's experience on crusade, we are fortunate that one of the several narrative accounts of the crusade was penned by a man from the region, Fulcher of Chartres. Fulcher was probably a **canon** from the cathedral chapter at Chartres, who accompanied Count Stephen on his trek east – perhaps as his personal chaplain. So Fulcher was well placed to record what men like Ralph would have experienced on the journey.

Departure was wrenching for both those going and those staying behind. As Fulcher described: "Oh, how much grief there was! How many sighs! How much sorrow! How much weeping among loved ones when the husband left his wife so dear to him, as well as his children, father and mother, brothers and grandparents!"[5] One can easily imagine Ralph's family saddened by his

4 Contemporaries did not call it the First Crusade, as they would have been unaware of future crusades. This is a terminology employed by modern historians. The term "crusader" designated someone who had taken the cross, meaning that they had agreed to travel to the Holy Land to fight the Muslims.

5 Fulcher of Chartres, *History of the Expedition to Jerusalem*, trans. Rita Ryan, ed. Harold Fink (New York: W.W. Norton and Co, 1969) p. 37.

departure, but also their pride in his dedication to serve God and the church. But their pride would have been tempered with anxiety as Ralph was the only son and unmarried, which meant he left no heir. If he failed to return, succession to the Beaugency lordship was uncertain. All realized that the participants might never come home. According to Fulcher, some women were so distraught by the prospect that they fainted as their "beloveds" left for the crusade. The crusaders struggled with their fear of death and loss of the homeland, but Fulcher reassures us that they behaved as manly men and kept a stiff upper lip. Like others, Ralph kissed his family good-bye, reassured them he would return, and departed. To follow Ralph's journey on crusade, see Map 5.

Count Stephen, Count Robert and Duke Robert and their armies departed in October 1096. They spent the fall traveling through Italy, where they visited Pope Urban II in Rome and traveled to the shrine of St. Nicholas of Bari to pray (see Map 5). As winter loomed, the group decided to stay in Italy before traveling by sea to the Holy Land the following spring. Resuming their journey east, they trekked to Brindisi, hoping to catch a ship heading to the East. Tragedy struck when a ship carrying crusaders sunk in the bay. Appalled witnesses watched as crusaders and their horses drowned. Some were frightened into giving up the quest, confident that God had abandoned their cause. Ralph and his group remained stalwart and forged ahead:

> Relying implicitly on Almighty God, [we] put out to sea in a very gentle breeze with sails hoisted and to the sound of many trumpets. For three days we were detained at sea by the lack of wind. On the fourth day, we reached land near the city of Durazzo.[6]

From Durazzo, the crusaders continued east through the lands of the Bulgars. This was an extremely difficult journey as Ralph and his companions were forced to climb treacherous mountains and ford dangerous rivers. After a journey of several weeks, the crusaders finally arrived at Constantinople in early May 1097. There they rested for two weeks outside of the city walls before visiting the metropolis.

While Fulcher does not say so in his account, the Emperor of Byzantium prevented westerners from entering the city since he feared what this foreign invasion force might do to his capitol. Count Stephen and Duke Robert's party was eventually allowed to enter. Visiting the city where Constantine ruled, a city so steeped in history, encompassed by massive walls and populated with wondrous churches, must have been a nearly indescribable experience for men coming from Western Europe where the largest urban center could have easily fit inside the city center of Constantinople. Fulcher's own enthusiasm is apparent: "O what a noble and beautiful city is Constantinople!

6 Fulcher, *History*, p. 77.

How many monasteries and palaces it contains, constructed with wonderful skill! How many remarkable things may be seen in the principal avenues and even in the lesser streets!"[7] The visit was not without tension, however. Anna Commena, the daughter of the Byzantine emperor, had a less than favorable reaction to the crusaders. She found them uncouth, unwashed and uncivilized. The emperor himself regarded the crusading forces with understandable concern. He insisted that the leaders of the crusade swear an oath that any land they seized from the Muslims was part of his dominion. Other crusaders, with the exception of Count Raymond of Toulouse, had already sworn this oath and Ralph's superiors did the same. The crusaders were now poised to enter the land of the Turks.

Ralph's party's first destination was Nicaea. The capture of this city was necessary so the crusade army could advance east. After crossing the Bosporus, they headed southeast, arriving early in June to help to secure the city. On their way, they passed through Nicomedia, where they viewed the remains of the hapless **Popular Crusade** led by Peter the Hermit, whose participants had been slaughtered the year before by the Turks. Such a sight must have struck fear into Ralph's heart as he pondered the dangers of the journey ahead. After about ten days of fighting, the crusaders captured Nicaea on June 19, 1097. However, the Byzantine Emperor's agents moved in quickly to claim the city. Ralph and his companions' next destination was Antioch. To reach this city, the crusaders made a long and dangerous trek across enemy territory.

The crusading army was organized into two divisions. Ralph was in the first division led by Bohemond of Taranto which included the Normans, as well as the followers of the Count of Flanders and the Count of Chartres. The terrain was harsh and the weather beastly hot –they were crossing a desert in mid-summer. Fulcher records that: "One day we suffered such extreme thirst that some men and women died from its torments."[8] While the knights like Ralph got to ride their horses, those who had lost their mount and the foot soldiers had an especially difficult time as they were outfitted in heavy chain mail, were wearing a wool or linen padded garment underneath the chainmail, a metal helmet and carrying about 40 pounds of gear – including swords and spears. Although he likely had at least two horses with him, Ralph probably elected to walk for part of the journey to save his horses. Compounding the fierce physical demands of the journey, the crusaders were in constant fear of attack by the Muslims; a fear that was almost immediately realized after the crusaders left Nicaea.

For reasons that Fulcher himself did not understand or explain, the two divisions of the crusading army became separated, which undercut the power of the crusaders. Indeed, just outside of Dorylaeum, the first division came

7 Fulcher, *History*, p. 79.

8 Fulcher, *History*, p. 87.

under Muslim attack. Fulcher relates Ralph and his companions' suffering: "We were all indeed huddled together like sheep in a fold, trembling and frightened surrounded on all sides by enemies so that we could not turn in any direction."[9] Ralph, who stayed with his lord, Count Stephen, continued to fight valiantly against the oncoming Muslims. This branch of the army was clearly in great peril.

The return of Hugh of Vermandois and Raymond of Toulouse greatly assisted the trapped division. But Fulcher believed that it was their prayers and the divine intervention that saved the day:

> The Lord does not give victory to splendor of nobility nor brilliance in arms but lovingly helps in their need the pure in heart and those who are fortified with divine strength. Therefore He, perhaps appeased by our supplications, gradually restored our strength and more and more weakened the Turks.[10]

The expedition to Jerusalem was equally a demonstration of faith and holy war. As such, medieval people believed their piety – or lack of it – could directly affect the outcome. Having prayed and purified themselves, Fulcher records that the rest of the journey to Antioch was free from attack – but not thirst, hunger and heat exhaustion. Hunger was a constant companion of the crusaders. It was a scruffy army that finally arrived at Antioch in October of 1097 after 105 days of marching and averaging 8 miles a day. Ralph himself may have been one of the

> many of our people who lacked beasts of burden since many of their own had died, loaded wethers [male goats], she-goats, sows and dogs with their possessions, namely clothing, food, or whatever baggage was necessary for pilgrims . . . And sometimes even armed knights used oxen as mounts.[11]

While the army was relieved and overjoyed to have finally reached Antioch, no one anticipated the long, gruesome siege that was to come.

The winter of 1097–1098 was a difficult experience for Ralph. Antioch was an old city with formidable fortifications that would not be easily taken. Now down to about forty thousand, debilitated by hunger and exhaustion, the army simply could not take a city of Antioch's size or fortifications. Thus the crusaders settled in for what would be a long and tortuous siege. Feeding a force that large was difficult in the Middle Ages under the best of circumstances and the conditions at Antioch were far from ideal. Food was

9 Fulcher, *History*, p. 85.
10 Fulcher, *History*, p. 86.
11 Fulcher, *History*, p. 88.

so difficult to obtain that crusaders resorted to eating their horses, the undigested grain found in animal manure and even cannibalism. Morale, understandably, was at an all-time low. Antioch either made or broke a crusader.

After months of siege, it was clear that Antioch would not fall to the crusaders by traditional means. Bohemond of Taranto, one of the most prominent and accomplished military leaders, came up with a plan to win Antioch by subterfuge. He bribed a Muslim resident inside the walls of the city to let him in with several others, who then opened the gates up for their brothers-in-arms waiting outside the city walls. Ralph of Beaugency was one of the men with Bohemond. He was tasked, along with his kinsman Hugh of Chaumont, with guarding one of the main gates of the city.[12] Ralph acquitted himself valiantly in the assault and earned the admiration of several of the most powerful commanders, among them Bohemond and Hugh of Vermandois. Ralph's distinction in battle had profound consequences for the rest of his life. Indeed, memory of Ralph's bravery at Antioch would live on into the thirteenth-century account of the battle in *Chanson d'Antioche* (*The Song of Antioch*). The army's success was well timed, for a Muslim force was on its way to relieve Antioch. What they did not know was that Antioch was now in crusader control. This victory on June 3, 1098 assured the crusaders' belief that God was with them and that they were on a holy mission. This was reaffirmed shortly after the conquest of Antioch when the Holy Lance, the lance that pierced Christ's side whilst he was on the cross, was "discovered" there. Medieval people believed passionately in the miraculous. The possession of such a wondrous relic undoubtedly strengthened Ralph and his companions' resolve and their sense that their travails were in fact blessed by God. They needed this resolve as the besiegers of Antioch quickly became the besieged.

While Ralph earned distinction for his valor at Antioch, the same could not be said for his lord. Count Stephen was not at Antioch when it was taken, but he was privy to the information that a large Muslim force was on the way to lay siege to the city. Assuming that all was lost, he quit the expedition and returned to France.[13] This was a significant blow because Stephen had been a respected – indeed beloved – leader. His decision to abandon the cause must have been particularly difficult for men like Ralph to bear. Ralph had joined his lord to demonstrate his support for the church but also as an expression of knightly solidarity. To have Stephen leave when his leadership was needed most must have demoralized and angered those who elected to stay. In spite of the odds against them, and compounded by the fact that Stephen's dire report of the situation resulted in an army of the Byzantine

12 *Gesta Ambaziensium Dominorum*, p. 101.

13 Stephen did return to the crusade in 1101, at the urging of Countess Adela, when another wave of crusaders went to the Holy Land after the fall of Jerusalem. He died in 1102 at the Battle of Ramla.

Emperor abandoning a relief mission to help out the crusaders at Antioch, those remaining repelled the Muslim force and succeeded in turning back their relief army.[14]

The victory at Antioch in June 1098 meant that the army could continue the journey south to Jerusalem, although due to a lack of leadership they did not begin to depart until November 1098. Hugh of Vermandois had left the crusade in August.[15] Unlike Stephen's departure, Hugh's was not seen as an act of cowardice. Rather he was sent to the Byzantine Emperor to offer him Antioch if he would send additional forces. But the emperor declined and Hugh sailed on to France.

Determining Ralph's whereabouts after Antioch provides a challenge because the charter recording the 1098 resolution to Bertran of Moncontour's dispute with Beaugencys places Ralph in Poitiers at the general time of the agreement. The document says Ralph gave his assent at Bertran's request and in his presence, which implies Bertran had traveled to Poitiers. How do we reconcile this evidence with Ralph's crusading experience? Did he return home after Antioch fell in in June 1098 and before the fall of Jerusalem in 1099? Some scholars suggest he accompanied Hugh of Vermandois back to France and then returned to the Holy Land, but I disagree. Although the charter is dated 1098, it also suggests that Bertran probably joined the French crusaders who left for the Holy Land in 1100 led by Duke William of Aquitaine. Ralph was likely on his way home at that point since most crusaders left for Europe in the fall of 1099 and met up with Bertran at Poitiers.[16] There is no other evidence that Ralph was in France before 1100. Moreover, the several pious donations he made in 1101/1102 indicate he was recently returned from crusade.

Ralph, I believe, was among the crusaders battling city after city in their quest to reach Jerusalem between November 1098 and July 1099. The conditions of the crusade did not improve and, at Marra, Fulcher reports that the men were so hungry they ate the buttocks of dead Muslims.[17] Bohemond returned to Antioch and remained there while the other leaders of the crusade continued toward the Holy City. One of the highpoints of the trip, according to Fulcher, was the crusaders' visit to Bethlehem, where they were able to pray at the basilica dedicated to Mary.[18] What was it like for Ralph to witness the place of his savior's birth? He must have been profoundly moved to worship there. Experiencing the sights, sounds and smells of the Holy Land were at once strange but also deeply meaningful to people who thought of Jerusalem as the center of their world.

14 Fulcher, *History*, p. 105.

15 Along with Stephen of Chartres, Hugh of Vermandois returned to the Holy Land in 1101. He died from his wounds at Tarsus.

16 AD Loir-et-Cher 21 H 69, no. 4; *STV*, vol. 2, no. 361, pp. 105–107.

17 Fulcher, *History*, p. 112.

18 Fulcher, *History*, p. 116.

From Bethlehem, the crusaders were poised to launch their attack of Jerusalem, which started in June 1099. This was a difficult siege as Jerusalem was a well-fortified city and the crusading army did not have the siege machines necessary to take on its walls. This problem was soon remedied by the arrival of Genoese ships carrying these very devices. By early July the siege weapons were in place and the assault on Jerusalem began in earnest. It was a long, difficult and bloody struggle. But on July 15, Godfrey of Lorraine got inside the city, opened one of its main gates and let in the crusading army. According to Fulcher, the streets ran with blood for days as the crusaders massacred the garrison, then prisoners and then finally the general Muslim population of Jerusalem: "If you had been there your feet would have been stained to the ankles in the blood of the slain. What shall I say? None of them were left alive. Neither women nor children were spared."[19] While Fulcher may be forgiven a bit of exaggeration, his description nonetheless points to the carnage that resulted in the loss of life on both sides. Where was Ralph of Beaugency during this epic siege and bloody aftermath? He probably fought with the contingents of Robert of Normandy and Robert of Flanders, whom he had accompanied on the crusade. The two Roberts were stationed, according to Fulcher, across Jerusalem from Godfrey of Lorraine, who was on the side of Mount Zion. Ralph stormed the walls and was in the thick of the fighting once the crusaders made their way into the city. While the capture of Jerusalem was heralded as the ultimate triumph of Christianity, it was horrific. Crusaders who participated in it, as well as the other terrors of the crusade, were profoundly affected by these events. Some must have returned home as haunted men who would never completely recover from all that they did and saw while on crusade. Was Ralph similarly tormented? The records do not say. But witnessing the battle of Jerusalem must have affected him deeply, as both a believer and warrior.

The fall of Jerusalem did not go unanswered by the Muslims. The Fatamid Caliph of Cairo brought his army north to face the crusaders. They met at Ascalon, approximately 50 miles southwest of Jerusalem. The crusaders were victorious and this last battle gave enough assurance that several of the leaders of the crusade made plans to return home, among them Count Robert of Normandy and Count Robert of Flanders. Before embarking for the journey west, however, most took time out to visit some of the important Biblical sites. For example, they went to bathe in the River Jordan where Jesus had been baptized by St. John the Baptist. They also collected palm fronds near Jericho from a place they thought to be the Garden of Abraham. After over two years in the Holy Land and nearly three years from home, Ralph embarked for Constantinople and, from there, home to France. The crusaders would return home heroes as their role in freeing Jerusalem from the Muslims gave them celebrity status in medieval Europe. For Ralph, participation in this crusade and the bonds he forged with fellow crusaders would shape his life for years to come.

19 Fulcher, *History*, p. 122.

Ralph at home: The immediate aftermath of crusade

What must it have been like for Ralph to return from crusade? He had been through an experience that only its participants could truly comprehend. Some, like Gui Trousseau of Montlhéry, found the physical and mental stresses of the crusade too much and came home broken men. Ralph's companion and kinsman with whom he had fought at Antioch, Hugh of Chaumont, was also debilitated. Others were exhausted and sought the solace of the monastery to recover their health. Sadly, some never did. Those who had been part of the liberation of Jerusalem received an enthusiastic welcome upon their return. Crowds gathered and triumphs were held for the liberators of the Holy City. Some crusaders returned home with souvenirs. One nobleman was even reported to have brought home a tame lion! Others were satisfied with more traditional reminders of their time. The East was rich in the relics of the Christian past and many came home with such relics, which they installed in their local churches (see Figure 1.10b). While the crusade involved warfare, for the participants it was an expression of their faith. Consequently, it is not surprising that the first act in which Ralph appears after his return from crusade was the donation to the chapel of St. Sepulcher in Beaugency (see Document 11, page 232). This gift to a church dedicated to the Holy Sepulcher in Jerusalem is itself symbolic of Ralph's time on crusade. The charter describes Ralph's humility and that he gave the gift "with great devotion, on bended knee." He made the gift for himself, his parents and "all of his friends," which given the timing of the charter would have been to commemorate his brothers-in-arms who had sacrificed their lives to reclaim Jerusalem. Many of those witnessing the benefaction for Ralph carried names that associated them with the Holy Land, such as "of the Holy Sepulcher" and "of Jerusalem."[20] The benefaction of tithes also reflected his adherence to church rulings. Tithes were payments to the church made either in kind or revenue and were used to support church personnel. As part of a greater attempt to wrest ecclesiastical property away from secular lords, the church had come to insist that tithes could not and should not be held or collected by laymen. The preamble to the charter reflects this concern and encourages restoration of these tithes into church hands. Ralph recognized the importance of restoring tithes and being grateful for a safe return home, gave all of the tithes on wheat and wine that he held at Beaugency to the monks. Donating the tithes on these goods also had additional meaning because these products provided the monks with the wine and bread that sustained them or that they could have used in the Eucharist.

During the crusaders' absence, some took advantage of a lord's absence to make trouble. So when some lords returned, they had to reassert their power. Bertran of Moncontour appears to have been one such mischief maker and

20 *STV*, vol. 2, no. 362, pp. 108–109.

usurped land from the absent Beaugency lord. But when Bertran himself wanted to go on crusade, he reconciled with his lord by abandoning his claim and giving Ralph monetary compensation (see Document 8, page 230).

As well as making gifts and sorting out any disputes that had arisen during his absence, Ralph also needed to get married. His sisters had married well, both to prominent counts (Agnes to the count of Nevers and Ermengarde to the count of Anjou). By the time he returned Ralph must have been nearly 30 and ready to find a wife. It seems that Ralph's bravery at Antioch earned him the respect of Hugh the Great of Vermandois (the brother of the king), for Ralph soon married his daughter, Mathilda. I believe it was Ralph's participation on crusade that provided him with the opportunity to marry into such a prominent family. As bonds between crusaders were forged in blood and suffering, the experience of crusading created bonds that lasted a lifetime.

A marriage between Ralph and Mathilda benefitted both families. Marriage to one of the heroes of Antioch would have likely delighted Mathilda. For the Beaugencys, this was quite a social coup as Mathilda had the blood of two royal houses running in her veins: Her father was a Capetian and her mother was descended from Charlemagne. Through his marriage to Mathilda, Ralph was related to some of the most powerful men in France. Not only was King Philip I Ralph's uncle-in-law, his father-in-law and brother-in-law were extremely influential at court. Indeed, Mathilda's brother, Ralph of Vermandois, became the close adviser to both Louis VI and Louis VII and held the office of **seneschal** of France. The profound impact of the Vermandois alliance on the Beaugency family is even evident in Beaugencys' development

Figure 4.1 The Beaugency Coat of Arms, likely influenced by the Vermandois family coat of arms. The checkerboard pattern of the design was rendered in blue and yellow with the horizontal bar in red. Based on a drawing from J-N Pellieux, *Essais historiques sur la ville et le canton de Beaugency*, vol. 1, p. 111.

of a coat of arms. The Beaugencys borrowed the blue and yellow checkerboard effect of the Vermandois insignia and added a bar of red placed halfway down the shield (see Figure 4.1). It seems that Ralph was the first to employ such a symbol, indicating his family's alliance with the prominent Vermandois.[21] This symbol was a literal, material representation of the merger of these two families. The prominence of the Vermandois pattern reflects how critical identification with this family was to the Beaugencys. These family connections drew the Beaugencys further into royal politics and power plays, but also came with hidden complications.

Ralph and the politics of the realm: 1101–1115

Like many a medieval lord, Ralph harmonized his obligations to his immediate lord(s) with the loyalty he owed the king. Sometimes this was a bit of a balancing act as comital and royal interests did not always coincide and Ralph's alliance with the Vermandois clan made this balance even more delicate. His marriage to Hugh the Great's daughter drew Ralph deeper into the circle of royal politics, as he was called upon to attend the king at court to provide advice. Recall that a church council was held at Beaugency in 1104 to help reconcile King Philip I, Ralph's uncle by marriage, with the church. Ralph was also witness to some of Louis VI's earliest transactions. Indeed, in 1108 Ralph traveled with the king to the abbey of Longpont to confirm one of Louis' gifts, and to Bourges, where he appeared with some of the most powerful men of the kingdom.[22] Although the relationship between the counts of Chartres and the Capetian kings had been relatively cordial, the situation changed dramatically about a decade after Ralph returned from the East.

Between 950 and 1100, royal power had become something of an abstraction for those living in *Francia*. Although counts, viscounts and lords recognized the authority of the Capetian kings, these kings did struggle to assert their sovereignty over them. With the ascension of King Louis VI, the situation altered as Louis began to make these lords submit to his authority. While lords had always recognized that the king held special rights given to him by God, they had come to operate independently. Some, according to Louis VI's biographer Abbot Suger, had become downright tyrannical. But caution needs to be exercised when interpreting Suger. Since the abbot very clearly wanted to show King Louis as a just and Christian king, he tended to paint royal opponents as irrational and overly savage. While the details may have been exaggerated, it is clear that Louis VI did have to battle some lords – several times in some cases– in order to pull them more fully into the royal orbit.

To bring these men and women to heel, Louis VI needed allies. The death of Count Stephen of Chartres in 1102 in the Holy Land, where he had

21 William Smith Ellis, *The Antiquities of Heraldry* (London: John Russell Smith, 1869) pp. 175–179.

22 *Louis VI le Gros: Annales de sa vie et de son règne (1081–1137)*, ed. and trans. Achille Luchaire (Paris: Picard, 1890), no. 53, p. 28 and no. 58, pp. 31–32.

returned to try to restore his reputation after his earlier desertion, meant his wife Countess Adela and his son Thibaut IV assumed control of the county. Thibaut was still in need of guidance, so his mother retained a firm hand on the reins of power. Abbot Suger states that Adela and Thibaut enlisted the help of the king when the viscount of Chartres, Hugh du Puiset, "ravaged their land all the way to Chartres, delivering it over to plunder and fires."[23] While Suger portrays the counts of Chartres as weak, ineffectual and begging for Louis' aid, the reality was more nuanced. Both the counts and the king recognized the need for cooperation to subdue such a disruptive force. Adela, Thibaut and Louis joined forces, captured Hugh and razed his mighty fortress at Le Puiset. As a faithful vassal of the count, Ralph of Beaugency was in the thick of the battle against the viscount.[24] The bond forged on crusade between Count Stephen and Ralph was exceptionally strong and Ralph would dedicate his life to aiding Stephen's widow and son. In fact, Countess Adele would come to rely on Ralph as one of her most trusted vassals. Unfortunately, after the success of the first battle at Le Puiset, the alliance between the king of France and the house of Chartres began to unravel.

In the aftermath of the siege, Thibaut requested to construct a castle at Allaines, close to Le Puiset, in the lands that he held in fief from the king.[25] Fearing comital power, Louis VI denied the request, which deeply angered Thibaut. Thibaut then broke with Louis and began actively assisting his uncle, King Henry I of England, in attacking the Capetian king's lands. This situation put Ralph in a very difficult spot, as both vassal and kinsman. Suger recounts that Thibaut was successful in bringing many of his vassals with him, which he casts as treacherous. More realistically, these men supported the count because of their sense of duty, the strength of their bond, or their own best interest. For Ralph, his close ties to the comital family and his loyalty to the son of the man with whom he crusaded caused him to cast his lot with Thibaut and Adela. Suger relates that Ralph was instrumental in cutting the king off from the strategically important city of Orléans by leading the men of Chartres and Châteaudun to mount resistance.

Ralph also fought bravely for the count in resisting the king. Although Suger clearly saw Ralph as a royal traitor, during the second battle of Toury he could not help but be impressed with Ralph's military acumen earned as a crusader. Not only was he a brave fighter, he was also strategic:

> But Ralph of Beaugency, a man of great shrewdness and valor, had earlier been afraid of the very thing that was taking place. So he had concealed

23 Abbot Suger, *The Deeds of Louis the Fat*, ed. and trans. Ricard C. Cusimano and John Moorhead (Washington D.C.: The Catholic University Press of America, 1992) p. 84.

24 Ralph's father, Lancelin II, had also fought against the Le Puiset family and had ended up imprisoned by the viscount. So there was no love lost between the Beaugencys and Le Puiset families.

25 Suger, *Deeds*, p. 90.

> his host in a part of the castle where the height of a church and shadows cast by neighboring houses would allow it to go unnoticed. Now, when he saw the men of his part going out through the gate, he sent forth his fresh forces against then exhausted knights of the king and attacked them harshly. Our men began fleeing in droves. Being on foot they were burdened by heavy hauberks [tunics of chain mail] and weapons, and could hardly withstand the ordered attack of knights on horse. After countless blows and lengthy fighting back and forth, they retreated through the moat they had taken.[26]

As a veteran of the crusade, Ralph used his considerable battle experience to his lord's advantage. Countess Adela viewed Ralph as one of her most valued men who she deployed when trouble arose in her lands. His loyalty and service earned him the distinction of *optimates* or one of the best men of the count. For the rest of his life, Ralph actively supported the count and countess wherever they needed his services. He fought battles, helped broker peace and resolved disputes.

Yet all did not go smoothly between Count Thibaut and Ralph. Around 1115, they had some sort of falling out. Evidence for this estrangement comes from a letter of Bishop Ivo of Chartres in which he counsels Ralph to repair relations with his lord (see Document 2, page 223). In his letter, Ivo reminded Ralph of the importance of honor and used the example of David from the Old Testament as a model. He told Ralph to follow the example of David, who, when mistreated by his lord and king, behaved honorably and did not act against him. Ralph would have been familiar with the story of David and reminded of it when he saw the capital carving each time he entered the sanctuary at Notre Dame de Beaugency. Ivo's advice follows that given by his predecessor, Bishop Fulbert of Chartres, a century earlier to Duke William of Aquitaine. Like Fulbert, Ivo clearly was involved in the world of lords and vassals. As a close adviser and ally of the comital family, he had a vested interest in restoring peace between the count and one of his most valued and dependable lords. One can imagine that Ralph would not react well if he believed he had been slighted by the count as he had sacrificed a lot to support Thibaut: His place at the royal court, his relationship with the king, his relationship with his powerful in-laws and his marriage to Mathilda. For Mathilda disappears from Beaugency family charters about 1112–1115, the time of Ralph's decision to support his count over his king (for the details, see pages 66–67).

Ralph's final years: 1115–c. 1130

Although Ralph remained a faithful vassal to the house of Chartres for the rest of his life, he seems to have spent from about 1115 until his death around

26 Suger, *Deeds*, p. 99.

1130 attending to his own lordship.[27] If Ralph were born around 1065, he would have been in his late forties by the time of the battle of Toury. After acquitting himself so well in the service of his lord and given the tension that had arisen between Ralph and Thibaut, Ralph may have opted to focus his energies on matters at home.[28] Moreover, Ralph had sons at home who he needed to be schooled in the ways of lordship and estate management. And with Mathilda's return to her natal family, Ralph was the only parent able to oversee their education and training. Tension between the count of Chartres and the king, however, did not diminish. In 1129 Louis VI set torch to the town of Bonneval located in the heart of the count's lands, burning it down. In the next generation, King Louis VII destroyed Vitry, one of Thibaut IV's most important holdings and residences. Ralph, nor his sons, were drawn into these conflicts. In the 1120s, Ralph spent his time holding court and settling disputes. When a group of his vassals seized property from the monastery of Tiron's priory of Cintry, Ralph held a court in the tower of his castle to resolve the matter.[29] Although Ralph may no longer have been as central to the comital court of Chartres as he once was, he did patronize and protect the abbey to which Countess Adela herself had been a generous patron. Two building projects also demanded Ralph's attention: The construction of a new set of walls around Beaugency between 1118 and 1130, and planning for a new church to replace Notre Dame de Beaugency. While the focus of the Beaugencys' holdings and political aspirations had moved from west to east, Ralph still had ties to Anjou and the Vendômois. In 1124, Ralph and two of his officers witnessed a gift by the count of Anjou to St. Trinité of Vendôme. Although Ralph had spent his life in the service of the counts of Chartres – and had sacrificed much to do so – ties to the Angevins had not been severed completely.

In the final years of his life, Ralph turned his attention to providing for his immortal soul. In the early 1120s, he abandoned his right to property at Limoron, which he had previously contested. Judith of Breteuil had donated this property to a new ecclesiastical foundation in the region, that of Notre Dame de Josaphat. Why did Ralph contest this woman's pious gift? Perhaps Ralph believed his rights had been overlooked; perhaps he wanted the land. But since Judith was a member of the vicecomital family of Chartres, the

27 In 1118, Ralph traveled with Count Thibaut to Provins, where the count, his mother, Countess Adela and his vassals discussed the worsening situation between Thibaut's uncle, King Henry I of England, and Louis VI of France.

28 The *Ex historiae Andegavensis Fragmento* says that in 1118 Louis VI asked Amaury of Montfort, Abbot Geoffrey of Vendôme and Ralph of Beaugency to intervene on his behalf with Count Fulk V, who was refusing to do homage to him. While the chronicle discusses Amaury of Montfort's efforts to reconcile his nephew, Count Fulk, with the king, no further mention is made of either Ralph or Geoffrey. Given the state of their relationship, Ralph either did not go or may have refused the king's request. *Recueil des historians des Gaules et de la France*, vol. 12, nouvelle edition, ed. Léopold Délisle (Paris: Victor Palme: 1877), p. 493. Hereafter, *RHF*.

29 *Tiron*, vol. 1, no. 41, p. 61.

very family that he had fought against on behalf of his lord and who had imprisoned his father, I would speculate that Ralph obstructed the gift because of animus toward the Le Puiset kindred. While in the end Ralph did abandon his right to the land, he insisted that his name and those of his family members be written in the monks' martyrology and their souls prayed for on the day of their death. A similar element of piety is evident in Ralph's abandonment of all things that pertained to the abbey located next to his castle and his confirmation that they would be in the possession of the canons. He recognized that he and some of his ancestors had wrongly held ecclesiastical prerogatives but he assured the canons that this would no longer be the case. Ralph made restitution for previous wrongs, perhaps in preparation for his death. While we do not know the precise year of Ralph's death, the **obituary** of the abbey of Pontlevoy records that he died on July 18, mostly likely before 1130 because the documents record no further trace of Ralph after this point. Interestingly, Pontlevoy was located neither in the Chartrain or Vendômois, but lay about 37 miles southwest of Beaugency. Pontlevoy was a prestigious abbey and supported by many of the noble houses of the region. Unfortunately, its cartulary (collection of charters) is not extant so we cannot tell if Ralph or the Beaugency family were generous patrons. That Ralph's passing was noted by these monks, however, attests to his stature as one of the most powerful – and well-connected – lords of the region.

The aftermath: Life of the lords of Beaugency, c. 1130–1180

Ralph's life demonstrates both the successes and failures of medieval lords. The notoriety that he achieved on crusade served him well. This experience created strong bonds between him and his lord, the counts of Chartres, and made him one of the most trusted men of Countess Adela and Thibaut IV (for an example, see note 27 above). Ralph's bravery in the East also attracted the attention of the powerful and well placed Vermandois family. As late as 1111/1112, Ralph was present at the king's court just before Count Thibaut defected from the royal camp. In considering the later history of the Beaugency family, I believe that the decision to support his count was a watershed moment not only in the life of Ralph, but also his family. Throughout the eleventh century, the Beaugency lords had been gaining prominence. Ralph's marriage into the Vermandois was designed to promote their political and territorial interests even further. But the history of the twelfth and thirteenth-century France reveals no Beaugencys in positions of political prominence or involvement in the major political events of the realm. How do we account for this rather abrupt shift in this family's fortunes? My interpretation is that up until 1112, Ralph's alliance accomplished what it should have: Power and prominence. But Ralph's betrayal of his king, and by association his powerful in-laws, meant that the Beaugency family would never again attain the sort of prestige that Ralph enjoyed. In fact, the family was barred from royal politics and consigned to a fate of being local lords who were never again drawn into national politics. Yet this does not mean that the Beaugencys were without power. Indeed, their castle became the locus of local power and home to a family that commanded the respect of their peers and vassals and continued to shape the world around them.

Incurring the ire of the king and a family as influential as the Vermandois, nevertheless, had consequences for Ralph's successors. Ralph and Mathilda had six children: Four sons and two daughters. Simon I succeeded his father. His brother, Lancelin III, became lord around 1154 upon Simon's death. Their brother, Ralph, followed in their father's crusading footsteps and went to the Holy Land in the 1120s, but eventually returned home, where he died around 1148/1149. Unfortunately, their son Hugh's life experience is not recoverable from the documents. It is possible, however, that he entered the church. The two daughters, Mathilda and Agnes, married into local lordly families and their marriages would have significant ramifications for the family.

Simon's time as lord was spent overseeing his lands and making pious gifts. Unlike Ralph, Simon never attended the royal court. Even when King Louis VII had business in the area, Simon was not present at his court. Even more telling is when Louis VII confirmed a gift made from Beaugency land, none of the Beaugencys were present even though the act was confirmed in Orléans, which was just a few miles away. As far as we can tell, the only time Simon was involved in any military actions while he was lord came as he had just attained the lordship. In 1132, he joined some of the other powerful men in the region in a campaign against the count of Anjou on behalf of Sulpice of Chaumont. The lords of Chaumont were distant cousins to the Beaugencys, and Simon and Sulpice's fathers had crusaded together.[30] Simon was following family precedent in his participation in this military venture in a couple of ways. Around 1110, Ralph had also helped Hugh of Chaumont gain his holdings back from the Angevins. While he was helping out his former comrade in arms, he also assisted Countess Adela in her effort to curb Angevin power so close to her territories. The difference between Simon and Ralph's participation is that the call to arms here did not come from the count of Chartres. Rather Simon helped Sulpice of Chaumont because of the ties between them and the reality that it was best for all lords in the Chartrain if the Angevin threat was contained.

Unfortunately for the Beaugency family, they did not simply experience the Capetians' benign neglect. Ralph's children and grandchildren had to cope with the lingering effects of their predecessor's defection. Ralph's loyalty to the counts of Chartres was not limited to the battlefield for his daughter, Mathilda, married Archembald of Sully, the grandson of Countess Adela and the nephew of Count Thibaut IV of Chartres. This match drew the attention of the king around 1138 when Louis VII, Louis VI's son and

30 *Gesta Ambaziensium Dominorum*, p. 119: *Tiron,* vol. I, no. 41, pp. 67–68.

successor, had his loyal prelate, the archbishop of Sens, contest the marriage on the grounds that the couple was too closely related. What could have motivated the king to interfere in a marriage between two lordly families? The animus that Ralph incurred by deserting Louis VII's father and the Vermandois family had continued into the next generation. To complicate matters further, there was no love lost between Count Thibaut IV and Ralph of Vermandois (Ralph of Beaugency's powerful brother-in-law) as both jockeyed for power in the late 1130s and 1140s. Ralph, furthermore, only increased royal and Vermandois ire with the marriage of his other daughter, Agnes, to Enguerraud of Coucy. Like the Le Puiset family, the Coucys had been a thorn in the royal side and Louis VI besieged their holdings many times before bringing the family in line. Furthermore, the Vermandois and the Coucys held their principal holdings in the north of France and had competed against each other for power for generations. Ralph's political choices and marriage alliances of his daughters contributed further to the rift with the royal family. Unlike others who had fought against the king and had been forgiven for their transgression, the Beaugency family remained without royal favor. Although not involved in royal circles, the Beaugency lords did remain powerful and effective regional lords.

Conclusion

Ralph of Beaugency was emblematic of his age. He owed his power and position to his family, service to his lords, control of extensive properties and a network of clients. Like many of his generation, he traveled to the Holy Land on crusade – an experience that would shape the rest of his life and the lives of his descendants. Ralph enjoyed close friendships and amicable relationships with his lords. Unfortunately, the conflict between the king and powerful French counts meant that Ralph faced the unenviable position of having to choose sides between his most direct lord (the count of Chartres) and the king to whom all lords and vassals owed allegiance (at least in theory). Ralph chose the counts, a decision that would shape the Beaugency family for generations to come.

During his lifetime, Ralph witnessed certain transformations that changed the inherent nature of lordship. While men of his era were preoccupied by war (battles, service to their lords, maintaining defenses), Ralph's children, grandchildren and great grandchildren were preoccupied by peace. As will be explored in the chapters to come, lordship for these men and women meant exploiting their resources and searching for new sources of income and influence. They still held courts and granted out fiefs, and expected loyalty from their vassals, but the fiefs they granted out might consist of cash payments rather than land in return for service. Their vassals were responsible for not only protecting the land but also insuring it was run properly and developed to its full advantage. Like the lords depicted in Figure 1.3, the Beaugencys still wore armor and fulfilled a military obligation, but other matters also came to demand their attention and contribute to their status.

The prosperity that generations of the Beaugency family and their peers enjoyed as lords rested firmly on the shoulders of the peasants to who tilled the soil, who tended their vineyards and mills. How were the lives of lords and peasants interrelated? The next chapter explores the lives of the men and women who populated the villages surrounding Beaugency and who worked the rich plains of the Loire Valley.

Suggested reading

Marcus Bull, *Knightly Piety and the Lay Response to the First Crusade: The Limousin and Gascony c. 970–c. 1130.* Oxford: Oxford University Press, 1993.

Jean Dunbabin, *France in the Making*. Oxford: Oxford University Press, second edition, 2000.

Elizabeth Hallam, *Capetian France 986–1328*. London: Routledge, second edition 2001.

Thomas F. Madden, *A Concise History of the Crusades*. Lanham, MD: Rowan and Littlefield, third edition 2013.

Nicholas L. Paul, *To Follow in their Footsteps: The Crusades and Family Memory in the High Middle Ages*. Ithaca and London: Cornell University Press, 2012.

Jonathan Riley-Smith, *The First Crusaders 1095–1131*. Cambridge, Cambridge University Press, 1998 and *The First Crusade and the Idea of Crusading*. Philadelphia, PA: University of Pennsylvania Press, reprinted 2009.

Jay Rubenstein, "Cannibals and Crusaders," *French Historical Studies* 31 (2008): 525–552.

5 "Those who worked": The Beaugencys and the peasants

Just as the Beaugency lords depended on their family and vassals, they also needed those who worked their land for food and income. Bonds of mutual obligation tied the Beaugency lords to these peasants. The objectives of this chapter are to sketch out the Beaugencys' relationships with those who tilled the soil of their lordship, as well as life experience of those working the Beaugency lands.

Trying to reconstruct the lived experience of medieval peasants can be an arduous, although not impossible, task. Particularly challenging are the limitations of the remaining primary sources. Since peasants were illiterate, we have to depend on the observations of monks and nobles, whose perspective was skewed by their assumptions and biases. Often the medieval peasant was ignored in the sources unless lords – monastic and lay – needed to record what peasants owed or if there was a dispute over their status or property. Documents of practice do contain nuggets of detail into the lived realities of peasants and their interactions with the lords of Beaugency. Combining the written evidence with material culture allows us to enter the world of the medieval peasant. Although rife with challenges and struggle, the lot of the Beaugency peasant was not as grim as modern audiences often presume. Some peasants living on Beaugency lands were quite humble, but others, through their control of certain offices and skills, were able to raise themselves high up in the social hierarchy of the medieval peasantry – to the point where they could make the jump into the land-holding class.

Lords and their peasants

As the lord and lady of Beaugency travelled across the lands of the Loire, the people they saw working in the fields and living in the villages they passed through belonged to the third order, "those who worked" (see Figure 5.1). Some of those in the village or field might also specialize in baking or smithing, but their primary obligation was to work the land. Like the aristocracy, the peasantry was not monolithic but made up of many different economic and social strata. Of those working in the Beaugency fields, some

Figure 5.1 A Book of Hours, from which this illustration comes, contains images of the labors of the months. This is the month of June and shows peasants harvesting hay. Note that both men and women worked in the fields. Ms 65/1284 f.6v June: Haymaking, from the *Tres riches heures du duc de Berry* (vellum) (for fascimile copy see 65831), Limbourg Brothers (fl. 1400–1416) / Musée Condé, Chantilly, France / Bridgeman Images.

would have been serfs or unfree and others free peasants who were landholders. Determining what percentage were serfs versus free peasants is difficult. Stereotypical representations depict all peasants as serfs. More recent estimations, however, suggest a greater number of free peasants. So what made a serf a serf and a free peasant free?

All who lived by farming the land were bound to the Beaugency lords through an economic and labor relationship called manorialism. "Manorialism" was derived by historians from the word "manor" to describe an agricultural community that centered around the residence of a lord; it was not a term used by medieval people. A variety of obligations and dues bound all of those

Figure 5.2 This is another representation of the labors of the months from a Book of Hours. The month is February, when peasants spent time by the fire. Note the interior of the dwelling but also farmyard around it, which contains barrels holding food stuffs, a sheepfold, an apiary and a smokehouse. Compare the woman in the farmyard at the far right dressed in rags to her more comfortable neighbors sitting by the fire. Clearly the order of "those who work" was made up of people of different socio-economic and legal status. See also the peasant with his mule above taking his goods to the market in the neighboring village. Ms 65/1284 f.2v February: Farmyard scene with peasants, from the *Tres riches heures du duc de Berry* (vellum) (for fascimile copy see 65824), Limbourg Brothers (fl.1400–1416) / Musée Condé, Chantilly, France / Bridgeman Images.

living in the villages of the Beaugency patrimony to the lord, but their status ran along a broad spectrum. Those at the very top owed little to the Beaugencys and were fairly prosperous. Those at the very bottom rung of the peasantry were poor. The illustration from the *Tres riches heures du duc de Berry* (see Figure 5.2) illustrates the breadth of peasant experience. Serfs spent much of their time working on the lord's land, owed the Beaugency lord part of their harvest and were subject to certain fees to marry or pass along their inheritance. "Serf" designated a particular legal status. These villagers were "unfree," meaning they were bound to the land by legal obligation and unable to leave it. A serf from a medieval romance described his position as "a serf must refuse nothing his rightful lord demands of him. I do not even belong to myself and I have nothing except that what he grants me."[1] Such was the lot of a serf. As serfdom was passed through the mother, it was possible for a free peasant to have children who were serfs if he married a woman who was not free. Yet some of the Beaugency serfs could be better off than a free peasant if the peasant did not have sufficient resources. Serf and free peasant lived side by side in Beaugency and the surrounding villages. They were neighbors, friends and sometimes inter-married.

Starting in the thirteenth century, custumals or texts describing the legal customs of a certain region were compiled. From these records, certain services and fees designated servile or serf status. For example, serfs had to pay a fee if they wanted to marry their daughter to a person from a different lordship (***foremariage***), when they passed their property from generation to generation they owed a portion of what they held to their lord (***mainmorte***) and they were liable for a head tax (***chevage***). Moreover, serfs were subject to the ***corvée***, which required their labor on the Beaugencys' land on certain days of the year, and ***taillage***, a due owed by the serf to his lord to help aid in the defense of the lordship. Unfortunately, terms describing these fees often do not appear in the Beaugency documents from the earlier periods, which begs the question of whether historians are transposing practices which were articulated in a later century onto previous centuries.[2] While the specific terms do not appear in the documents of the eleventh and twelfth centuries, descriptions of such dues are extant although they had yet to be given a formal name. What is clear from the documents is that serfs and free peasants living on the Beaugency lands were subject to the will of their lords, much as the serf from the medieval romance described earlier. In turn, fear of rebellion or murder limited what the Beaugency lords demanded of their peasants.

While the Beaugency serfs were personally unfree, they were not slaves. Slaves of the antebellum American south and the ancient world were property: They could be bought and sold. Legally, the same did not hold true for serfs. The land to which they were attached could be transferred, and the serfs along with it, but they were not supposed to be bought and sold individually – although this did happen in practice. Slaves also could not own property; everything they possessed belonged to their owner. Serfs, in contrast, could inherit possession of property as part of their servile status. But serfs were legally "attached" to property and unable to leave it. While these may seem

1 *Cliges*, p. 166.
2 Chédeville, *Chartres et ses campagnes*, p. 364.

minor distinctions to modern observers who value personal freedom above all else, they were extremely important to medieval society.

The Beaugency lords also required those who lived on the lands – both free peasant and serf – to pay for using their assets. For example, villagers would have to pay a portion of their bread or milled grain for using his mill or bake house. The use of a winepress also required a payment, usually a portion of the wine pressed. Through the *corvée* the Beaugencys could demand peasant labor in their fields, in repairing their residence, or in keeping up the roads or bridges. The amount of labor required, along with the various servile fees, combined to determine a villager's place in the social hierarchy. Serfs might work anywhere from a few days a week for their lord to giving all of their labor. In return for protection and justice, free peasants also had to provide the lord of Beaugency with labor. Thus all rural dwellers would be bound to the Beaugency lord in some way, either legally or economically. By around 1150, technological advancements in agriculture had triggered significant social and economic transformations, which resulted in changes in the relationship between lord and peasant.

Throughout Europe – including Beaugency lands – the yield from peasant fields increased dramatically as more land was brought under cultivation through the use of the **three field system** and the cultivation of previously untilled lands. Similar to the Beaugencys, other lords started settlements like Montfollet as a means of extending their influence and bringing more land under cultivation. The planting of legumes, such as lentils and beans, meant that the peasant diet was enriched with more protein and the land was fertilized through these nitrogen rich crops. These changes mean that peasants ate well, but also that they were healthier and thus lived longer and were more fertile. As a consequence, the population began to increase, which contributed to the rise of towns. Beaugency itself grew in the twelfth century and new walls had to be built to surround the new footprint of the village (see Map 1). Towns like nearby Blois and Orléans provided Beaugency peasants with an option to leave the farm as there was an abundance of labor in the rural sector and new opportunities for them in the towns. A money economy soon replaced subsistence and barter. In response, the bonds between the Beaugency lords and their peasants underwent modification. As the economy changed to one based on profit and coin, lords and kings needed cash rather than labor. Instead of providing labor or produce to their lord, Beaugency peasants were now asked to pay with coin. Servitude thus began to change from one of personal service to a financial agreement. This change significantly altered the lord-peasant relationship so that it came to resemble a tenant-landlord agreement. Thus, as the thirteenth and fourteenth centuries unfolded, peasants became more independent. The thirteenth-century lords of Beaugency had different expectations from their peasants than their ancestors had in the previous centuries.[3]

3 Chédeville, *Chartres et ses campagnes*, pp. 374–380.

Geographical and chronological factors also played a part in determining the severity and character of serfdom throughout the Beaugency lands. By the twelfth century, much of the Beaugencys' holdings were in the area known as the Beauce (see Maps 3 and 4). This area was extremely fertile and hence organized into large, open fields (see Figures 1.12a and b). Labor was needed to work these fields, which resulted in stronger lordship for the Beaugencys, which, in turn, promoted stronger serfdom for those who worked the land for them. In contrast, for those peasants who settled in the regions south of the Loire in the area known as the Sologne, serfdom was not as severe because this area was not as fertile. Hence, large-scale farming was not an option. This correlation between open field farming and stronger lordship holds true throughout much of Europe. Lordship and strong serfdom were not as firmly established in more remote regions where open fields did not predominate.[4] The Beaugency peasants enjoyed different levels of autonomy because agricultural needs varied. Although the bonds of serfdom might have been lighter in some areas, the serf's possibility of gaining freedom was diminished for the agricultural bounty that served to enserf those bound to the Beaugencys in the Beauce also furnished a means for them to escape these bonds. This region was renowned for its abundant wheat harvests (and still is today), which provided local serfs with a richer lifestyle thus making it more likely that they would be able to buy their freedom.[5]

Explaining and justifying serfdom

For the medieval lord, serfs were literally part of the landscape. One of the Beaugencys' vassals, for instance, saw serfs not as individuals, but as an integral part of the agricultural world:

> The men now living will know, as well as those living in the world in the future, that Robert of Moncontour, at the request of Lord Abbot Oderic of Vendôme, gave to St. Trinité and the monastery of Vendôme, for the redemption of his soul as well as his parents, all of his property and which land he held from Coulommiers-la-Tour, namely in houses, vines, in woods, in water [i.e. streams or ponds], mills, in servants and serfs, in fiefs, in fields and all and whatever he holds there from Lancelin of Beaugency.[6]

For this lord and the Beaugencys as well, serfs and other servants were not distinguishable, but were bundled with other property. This attitude toward

4 Chédeville, *Chartres et ses campagnes*, p. 370.

5 Chédeville, *Chartres et ses campagnes*, p. 369.

6 AD Loir-et-Cher, 21 H 69; *STV*, vol. I, no. 361, pp. 105–107.

"those who work" is also apparent in medieval literature where peasants were depicted as stupid, slow, almost beast-like. There was no greater insult for a lord than to be mistaken for a peasant. In the Arthurian romance, *Erec and Enide*, the hero Erec complained, "You took me for a peasant, and that was a dreadful insult on your part," when a fellow knight did not recognize him.[7] Perhaps not surprisingly, "when all [peasants] saw their lord, they trembled in fear."[8]

Those clergy who described the tripartite organization of medieval society understood that the warrior aristocracy and they themselves needed peasant labor to provide them with sustenance. Abbo of Fleury, a monk who lived just up the Loire from Beaugency at the abbey of Fleury, argued that all of society rested firmly on the backs of peasants and were supported by the sweat of their collective brow. Other clergy even worried about the treatment of the peasants and the quality of their lives. One of the twelfth-century bishops of Brittany was concerned that the best products harvested by the peasants went to the lords, which resulted in peasants having to settle for food of a lesser quality.

Implicit in this social system was the exploitation and repression of the peasantry, particularly the serfs. Intellectuals living in the medieval centuries comprehended these social inequities and sought to explain why serfs and peasants could be so subjugated. As this was a society deeply rooted in Christianity, a Biblical explanation was developed by medieval scholars. When Noah and his progeny were settled after the flood, Noah got drunk. Ham happened upon his father, who was passed out naked from too much drink. He went and got his brothers, who, instead of gawking at their unconscious father, covered him up. A fully awake and angry Noah cursed Ham for his insult and said that the children of Ham's son, Canaan, would be bound in servitude to the offspring of his brothers. Medieval serfs who had the misfortune of being bound in servitude owed their position to being descended from Ham. Cain, who committed fratricide, similarly served as a Biblical explanation for the subjugation of free peasants by lords.[9] Because they were descended from Cain, peasants were destined to labor for the rest of society to make up for Cain's crime. These ideas also made their way from the pens of scholastics into popular sermons and informed some aristocrats' understanding of the peasantry.

Although the use of Ham for the justification of serfdom was particularly popular in England and Germany, the Beaugencys' understanding of the origins of serfdom was explained by a national myth rather than a Biblical foundation. As Paul Freedman asserts, Charlemagne was the "father of subjugation" for the French.[10] The text known as the *Pseudo Turpin Chronicle*

7 *Erec and Enide*, p. 14.

8 *The Story of the Grail*, p. 343.

9 Paul Freedman, *Images of the Medieval Peasant* (Palo Alto, CA: Stanford University Press,1999) pp. 86–87.

10 Freedman, *Images of the Medieval Peasant*, p. 107.

is an example how of myths and stories were created to explicate serfdom and social exploitation. This chronicle dates from the early twelfth century and is based on the action and characters memorialized and fictionalized in the epic poem, *The Song of Roland*. Although Charlemagne was a great warrior who had many military successes, one of the low points of his career came in 778 when the rear of his troops were ambushed in the Pyrenees by a cohort of Basque soldiers (although the poem relates that Muslims actually attacked Charlemagne's rearguard). *The Song of Roland* tells the tale of this eighth-century defeat, but does so in a twelfth-century context by infusing the poem with the values of the day. Given the chivalric ideals that permeated society, it is perhaps not surprising that the issue of bravery is at the heart of the *Pseudo Turpin Chronicle*'s explanation of serfdom. Peasants, it posits, were cowardly and would not fight with Charlemagne. Thus, they deserved their fate of being bound to the land and inferior to those who were brave enough to fight, i.e. the aristocracy. In contrast, bravery and freedom were epitomized by the warrior lords. Such a message would certainly have resonated with the lords and ladies of Beaugency. Using this bravery-cowardice dichotomy, a later redaction of the chronicle mythologized the foundation of Provins (earlier known as Apremont), a prosperous trade town in Champagne. "The cowards of Apremont," the legend goes, were 16,000 individuals who refused to follow Charlemagne on his Spanish campaign. An incensed Charlemagne responded that they would remain in Apremont and be forced to pay a fine known as the ***taille*** (the root for *taillage*), which became a payment owed by those bound in servitude.[11] In a society that valued the warrior, that the justification for the repression of the peasants would be based on the fact they were cowardly and would not fight made sense.

Why become a serf?

Modern people have generally assumed that serfdom was something that peasants would not choose unless they were coerced or in desperate straits. The traditional explanation of why peasants would enserf themselves to lords like the Beaugencys goes something like this. During the ninth and tenth centuries, France was beset by Viking invasions and local wars. In exchange for the defense that a lord's strong sword arm could provide, peasants willingly gave themselves and their property over to the authority of a lord and became serfs. Remember that strong central governments did not exist in this period. If a defense was to be mounted against an aggressive lord or a Viking named Sven, medieval peasants, town-dwellers and monks turned to local men like the lords of Beaugency who were skilled warriors. These men of action were supplied with land for their support – as the Beaugency lords received their fiefs from the count of Anjou and the count of Chartres for their service to

11 Freedman, *Images of the Medieval Peasant*, p. 112.

them. Peasants provided their labor on the lord's land and were compelled to give a portion of the agricultural goods they produced.

A new view of serfdom has been developing over the course of the last forty years. While recognizing that free peasants and serfs were dominated by their lords – sacred and secular – scholars have come to point out the fluidity of the status of serfdom and to posit that serfs enjoyed more freedom and privileges than originally thought.[12] Recent research even suggests that some peasants actively sought to become the serfs of monastic communities. The distinguished French historian, Dominique Barthélemy, argues that peasants wanted to become the serfs of the monks of the abbey of Marmoutier to gain spiritual association.[13] He also contends that becoming a serf of Marmoutier did not dramatically change the lives of peasants. Barthélemy's argument has direct bearing on the Beaugencys because they held property in the region surrounding this abbey and Marmoutier held land in and around Beaugency. Hence, what Barthélemy concludes about the behavior and motivation of Marmoutier serfs likely was true for the serfs and peasants who owed their labor or land to the Beaugency family.

What Barthélemy labels "self-oblation" was the act of a serf giving himself or herself to a monastery. The extant documents suggest a religious motivation for becoming a serf of the abbey of Marmoutier. In the eleventh and early twelfth centuries, the monks of the abbey of Marmoutier kept an accounting of the serfs and peasants that were bound to them or who owed them service which has come to be known as "the Book of the Serfs." Based on my own reading of these sources, I agree with Barthélemy's interpretation that these self-oblations had a religious dimension and would argue further that free peasants were motivated by factors other than religious in becoming serfs. These documents, which number over one hundred, provide clues into the life and times of the medieval peasantry, both serf and free: In other words, the very people on whom the Beaugencys depended to work their patrimony. What these sources reveal, I believe, is that peasants living in this region of France had more agency than previously recognized.

For instance, Christian, a man from Brittany, had moved close to the community of Marmoutier around the year 1080. After some time observing the brothers, Christian was evidently taken with their way of life and asked to "become a serf of Saint Martin and of his monks and to be considered one of their servants."[14] Seemingly out of his own free will, Christian, who was

12 For example, Chédeville, *Chartres et ses campagnes*, pp. 387–390; Guy Bois, *The Transformation of the Year One Thousand: The Village of Lournand from Antiquity to Feudalism*, trans. Jean Birrell (Manchester: Manchester University Press, 1992).

13 Dominique Barthélemy, "Voluntary Serfdom at Marmoutier in Touraine," in *The Serf, the Knight and the Historian*, trans. Graham Robert Edwards (Ithaca: Cornell University Press, 2009) pp. 36–46. See also "Serfdom and Its Rites" in the same volume, pp. 68–136.

14 *Le Livre des Serfs de Marmoutier*, ed. André Salmon (Tours : Imprimerie Ladevèze, 1864) no. 124, pp. 115–116. Hereafter, *LDSM*. See Barthélemy's translation on p. 48 in "Voluntary Serfdom at Marmoutier in the Touraine."

not designated as a serf in the charter *before* his self-oblation to Marmoutier, became a servant of the monastery. A ceremony accompanied this change in status. Christian placed four coins on his head and stated that he gave himself to the service of the monks. This ceremony would be repeated annually to remind both serf and community alike of the relationship between the two. What is interesting about self-donations like Christian's is the clearly religious component. He was impressed by the piety of the monks and by giving himself to them, his labor served a greater good: The support of God's representatives, and intercessors, here on earth. Clearly Christian hoped that working in the fields of the holy would earn him God's favor and the monks' intercession. Bernoin the Miller was similarly motivated:

> Let it be known by all of our successors that a certain miller, named Bernoin. . . with his wife Erimingarde and children, Constantio, Richild, Fredeburg, for love of God, [and] St. Martin of Marmoutier, in the presence of Lord Abbot Albert, as he was free, he surrendered himself to servitude; namely with the agreement that not only himself but truly all progeny born from him, will be in the condition of serfdom [to]the abbot of Marmoutier and the brothers of the same place all the days of their lives. And therefore so that this surrendering [of freedom] was manifestly and certainly in order, [Bernoin] putting four denarii [pennies] on his own head in recognition of servitude, offered himself in such a way to omnipotent God. These are the names of the witnesses who saw this, inserted below. Landric the serf, Ulger the serf of St. Lomer, Alcher the carpenter. Martin the serf, Girald the serf, Joseph the carpenter, Fulco the monk, Berenger the monk.[15]

When Bernoin appeared in front of the abbot, he bowed his head and placed four coins on it (which the abbot presumably collected). This act demonstrated his submission to the abbot and St. Martin and was a visible demonstration of his new status as a serf, one who bowed before his superiors. The grant of these four coins has been suggested to be the *chevage* or head tax that serfs owed to their lords and Barthélemy believes that it was an act carried out each year when serfs paid this tax.

There are other oblations that do not contain this religious overtone and seem to be motivated by other forces. A young man named Adam also gave up his free status to become the monks' serf.[16] For Adam, being the serf of Marmoutier was preferable than being a free miller or carpenter. Several factors may have made this the case for Adam and others. Perhaps they felt they were more likely to improve their livelihood if they became associated with the monks as monastic serfs may have had been guaranteed more work.

15 *LDSM*, no. 64, p. 62.
16 *LDSM*, no. 125, p. 116.

The monks may not have been as exacting or heavy-handed in demanding payment in kind or their labor as secular lords. These serfs may also have hoped to gain spiritual protection from the monks and St. Martin, but also physical protection of the monks' patrons and vassals.

Other self-oblations indicate that Adam's peers were motivated by economic opportunities that could come with being a serf of St. Martin. In 1095 Raher the fisherman gave up his freedom to marry one of the Marmoutier serfs (see Document 12, page 233). The monks, in return, helped to set him up in a new business. For a payment of 60 shillings, Raher was given a house from which he could sell food and wine. Raher was also able to ensure that his wife retain the business even after his death as her dower. Like Raher, Bertran Agnellus was able to negotiate with Marmoutier once he became one of their serfs. The monks allowed him to buy a house in their settlement from another of their serfs (see Document 13, page 233). That both Raher and Bertran had money to underwrite their futures is also significant and that they were able to negotiate their entrance into serfdom casts becoming a serf in a different light. These do not appear to be desperate peasants seeking serfdom as a last resort. Rather, they were able to come to terms with the monks and received certain benefits in doing so – both material and spiritual. Modern scholars' view of such actions has likely been colored by the value they themselves place on personal freedom; they could not conceive of giving up personal liberty except in the most dire of circumstances. Hence, they may have underestimated or overlooked that the serfs had agency.

Given the number of different professions in the documents extant from Marmoutier's book of serfs, the monks seemed to be interested in attracting serfs who had a skill or who could enrich their community in some way: Millers, carpenters, smiths, bakers, cooks, tailors, pelterers, masons, goatherds, swineherds, cowherds, shepherds, fishermen, foresters and stablemen populate the Marmoutier documents. Some of these peasants-turned-serfs were involved in tending animals as well as other agricultural work, but others had a more specialized trade, such as mason, smith or a carpenter. These trades indicate the dynamism of this community, but also the monks' commitment to developing the local economy. Monastic communities and secular lords were vested in expanding the lands under their control. Clearing the forest and establishing a new settlement was one way of doing this – as in the Beaugencys' foundation of the community of Montfollet. The monks of Marmoutier appear to be trying to attract peasants to newly developed areas and offered "incentives" for these peasants to become their serfs. Did some peasants give themselves to secular lords like the Beaugencys? It is certainly possible, although no record of it is extant. Becoming a serf of Marmoutier certainly carried certain spiritual and even economic benefits, but so too would becoming a serf of a powerful lord. The serf would gain protection – something which cannot be undervalued in a time of violence and turbulence.

However, one must also recognize that these records of self-oblation were written by the monks, who may have emphasized the spiritual elements given their particular world view. Regrettably, we do not have the account of peasants who gave themselves as serfs to the monks; they probably would have had a slightly different version of their self-oblation.

Peasants and village life

So what can we discern from the documents about the actual life of a Beaugency peasant or serf? Although we know a significant amount about peasants, most sources were not concerned with the life details of those acting in the document. As a consequence, sources for peasant life are not as personalized as those for the lives of lords. Material culture, retrieved through archeology, can provide some information about how the Beaugency peasants lived. How and where their peasants lived mattered to the Beaugency lords because they depended upon them for their livelihood. Indeed, all of medieval society rested upon the labor and contributions of serf and free peasant. How and where "those who worked" lived could affect what the Beaugencys had to eat, what was available at the local markets and their suzerainty over their lordship. A peasant's status was also important to the Beaugency lords, since marriage could affect the status of the next generation of peasants or serfs as well as which peasants fell under Beaugency jurisdiction. Indeed, early in the thirteenth century, Lord John I held a court to sort out the status of the serf Berion and her children (see Document 17, page 235).

Archeologists believe that the twelfth century was an important turning point in the rural landscape of Western Europe. By this point in time, medieval Europe was populated by many villages and the wastelands were in the process of being cleared and settled. This was certainly the case for the region surrounding Beaugency. In fact, many of the villages that were established in the 1100s and under the dominion of the Beaugency lords continue to this day. Castles and churches often acted as hubs for the settlement of villages.[17] Over the course of the twelfth century, some villages might also have come to specialize in certain forms of agrarian production, such as viniculture.

The village was central to the life of a medieval peasant. Let us consider the neighboring village of Ouzouer-le-Marché, located just to the north of Beaugency (about 12 miles) and part of these lords' patrimony. If we were able to walk down the main street of medieval Ouzouer-le-Marché, we would see buildings large and small. This village, like most, was a nucleated village organized along a central street or road and surrounded by fields. Even today, the fields run right up to the boundary of the village. This would have been convenient for its medieval residents who would have easy access to their fields. Villagers would voluntarily combine their labor and resources (such as

17 Jean Chapelot and Robert Fossier, *The Village and the House in the Middle Ages*, trans. Henry Cleere (Berkeley and Los Angeles: University of California Press, 1985).

plows and draft animals) to farm them. A variety of dwellings would be found along the road. The largest building we would encounter would be the parish church, the church of St. Martin. For other villages, however, a castle keep (like that at nearby Montfollet or Beaugency) would have competed with the church as the largest structure (see Figures 1.4, 1.10a and b, 6.1 and 6.2). Accompanying the church would be a cemetery, where generations of residents would spend eternity.

Medieval Ouzouer-le-Marché would have been made up of other structures as well, that would stretch along either side of the main thoroughfare, ranging in aspect from humble homes of one room to larger, multi-room dwellings (much as the village does today). The houses of twelfth-century Ouzouer-le-Marché would have been quite different from those built in the earlier centuries when larger hall-like houses had characterized domestic life. These measured about 164 × 65 feet in size and housed both people and animals. Starting in the eleventh century, smaller structures of about 65 × 33 feet would have come to replace them in the village.[18]

These houses were designed for single families, rather than the more communal style of habitation of previous centuries, and housed a nuclear family of parents and children. Moreover, in contrast to modern visions of medieval families, most peasant families of Ouzouer-le-Marché did not have more than three to four children. Indeed, the average household size for the Middle Ages was 3.5: Two parents, and between two and four children. Animals were moved out of the domestic space and given structures of their own, although "mixed houses" continued to be in use in other parts of France (Brittany, for example).[19] In addition to houses, areas for storage of animals, tools and agricultural goods would also have been part of the village of Ouzouer-le-Marché. The advent of the use of the horse collar, horse shoe and heavier ploughs in the eleventh century meant that draft horses were more in demand and required their own shelters which the villagers likely built and managed communally. The increase in production created an increased need for barns and the like to store grain and other produce. The residents of Ouzouer-le-Marché may have stored their grain and agricultural produce at a nearby grange or tithe barn. Changes to the peasant diet meant that peasants were healthier and lived longer. As a consequence, the population began to increase, causing the size of villages like Ouzouer-le-Marché to increase as well.

These transformations in agrarian life left their imprint upon the material lives of peasants on the Beaugency lands. As villages like Ouzouer-le-Marché grew, so too did the type of structures in the village. Most peasant houses were one room, but as the population increased in the twelfth century, so too

18 Robert Fossier, *The Axe and the Oath: Ordinary Life in the Middle Ages*, trans. Lydia Cochrane (Princeton: Princeton University Press, 2010) p. 110.

19 Chapelot and Fossier, *Village and House*, p. 211.

did the size and layout of peasant homes. One-room houses in the village grew into two rooms and lofts became converted into habitation spaces – although most peasant homes remained one-story throughout the Middle Ages. Inside the home, changes were made as well, as open hearths were replaced with wall chimneys and fireplaces. Homes were generally constructed out of what was available – wood, peat or stone – and roofs were either thatched or used stone or tile: Those in Ouzouer-le-Marché were made from a combination of wood and stone with a thatched roof. There were few windows in these peasant homes and usually only one door. Most of the interior furnishings were made from wood. If we were to open the door to one of these peasant dwellings in Ouzouer-le-Marché and enter, we would be in a dark house due to the dearth of windows. The main room might be somewhat smoky due to poor ventilation. Meats and other produce hung along the rafters to dry. At the center of the room might be a table, a few chairs or benches and several beds arranged along the walls. If the peasant family were prosperous enough to have a second room or loft, more beds would be found there. Peasants ate off of wooden plates as well, although some ceramic plates, cups and storage vessels might have been employed. Animal horn was also made into drinking and tableware. Some household objects of our peasant family of Ouzouer-le-Marché were created locally by craftsmen in the village; others purchased at the market in Beaugency or Montfollet. As we continue our walk through the village, we might find that areas within the village developed into specialty zones, such as market spaces and commercial zones. Water mills also became part of the landscape in the twelfth century and could come to dominate or shape a section of the village. For example, structures to house grain might be located close to the mill for convenience. Beaugency itself had several mills located within its walls. Villages like Ouzouer-le-Marché were tight-knit communities. Residents worked together, played together and depended upon each other for labor and support in times of hardship.

Although all peasants lived in villages, not all peasants in Ouzouer-le-Marché and other villages were the same. Of utmost importance to all rural dwellers was their status: Were they free or serf? Serfs appear in the documents at a very young age. "A certain youth," Adam, wished to become a serf of Marmoutier. Adam was not just an agricultural worker; he had training as a carpenter. That Adam had the ability to give himself as a serf suggests he had agency and had reached his majority, meaning he did not need his parents' or guardians' permission to determine his own future[20] (see Document 14, page 234). In contrast, Vitalis, the "minor" son of Letard the cowherd, was given by his father to the monks as a serf, with the approval and consent of his older brothers (see Document 15, page 234). Vitalis seems to have had little choice in the matter. The circumstances of his oblation are significant,

20 *LDSM*, no. 125, p. 116.

however, because Letard was critically ill at the time and approaching death. No mention was made of a mother, so presumably Vitalis would soon be an orphan. His father likely hoped that the monks would take care of his young son and perhaps Vitalis' prospects were better as a man of the monks rather than an orphan trying to make it on his own with only his bachelor brothers for support. Unlike Adam, Vitalis is not mentioned as having a skill, indicating he may have been too young to have started any training.[21]

Marriage was an important watershed in the life of a medieval peasant – and a decision that directly involved the Beaugency lords. Determining the age at which peasants married is difficult. But it seems that the peasants of Ouzouer-le-Marché and elsewhere on the Beaugency patrimony married later than members of the Beaugency family because they needed to accrue resources to support a household when they married. Many peasants married within the village or to neighboring villagers. As a consequence, the peasants of Ouzouer-le-Marché may have been more involved in deciding, as well as better acquainted with, their future spouse. As well as affection or compatibility, there were legal issues to be considered when marrying and approval had to be sought from their lord. If a serf from this village wished to marry a serf from another lord's manor, a *foremariage* payment had to be made. *Foremariage* and marriages between free and enserfed peasants could create complications – as will be discussed later in this chapter (see also Document 17, page 235). As status came from the mother, it would benefit a male serf of Ouzouer-le-Marché to marry a free woman since their children would be free. Conversely, a free woman of this village would have to think long and hard about marrying a serf. While she and her children would remain free, her children's status as free peasants might be challenged and they would not inherit their father's land unless they too were willing to become serfs. Although these anxieties would have lessened somewhat in the thirteenth century as serfdom became more about paying extra fees than a social handicap. Because of their legal standing and clear claim to property, the free peasant women of Ouzouer-le-Marché may have had an advantage over their serf counterparts in seeking out marital prospects. One peasant mother from the neighboring Touraine certainly believed so. What follows is a narrative based on a charter with some imaginative embellishments[22] (see Document 16, page 234).

On a chilly January day in 1069, Maria Conversa made her way to the chapterhouse of the monks of Marmoutier. This was a sad time for Maria. Her husband Otbert, who was the monks' mayor for their small village, had just died. As she made her way over the frozen ruts in the road with her clogs

21 *LDSM*, no. 98, p. 92.

22 *LDSM*, no. 76, p. 73. This charter provides the factual basis for this discussion. The imaginative "embellishments" are details like Maria wearing clogs or that it was cold in France in the winter.

crunching along in the snow, she thought of their life together. But while Maria mourned the loss of her mate, she had other matters preoccupying her. Specifically, she was concerned about the future of her two children, most particularly her daughter. As a woman who had once been free but who was now a serf, she was aware of the disadvantages such a station in life could bring and she was determined that her daughter not suffer from such legal disadvantages.[23] So she set off that morning for the cold walk to the monastery, leaving her children at home.

When she arrived at the gates of the monastery, she asked to see the lord abbot himself. She was granted an audience and one of the brothers led her through the grounds to the monks' chapterhouse where all abbey business (sacred and profane) was conducted. Arriving in the presence of the abbot, Maria bowed low as befitting her station and made her petition. She asked him to grant her daughter her freedom, so that she would be able to marry a man unencumbered by the bonds of serfdom. Motivated by a combination of Christian kindness and the realization such an agreement could benefit the monastic community, Abbot Bartholomew was disposed to grant her this request. He proposed a pact: If both of Maria's children would dismiss any claim that they had to their father's land, and if her son remained a serf, Maria's daughter would be free but only if she married a free man. If she married another serf, she would be a serf. Maria was content with the agreement and returned home to discuss it with her children.

Several days later, Maria, her daughter and son, plowed their way through the newly fallen snow to the monastery of St. Martin. As before, one of the monks escorted Maria and her family from the gate house to the chapter house, where all of the monks were assembled – with the exception of the abbot who was attending to monastery business elsewhere so the prior acted in his place. Cecelia and Gausbert, Maria's children, stood before the chapter and swore that they abandoned all claim to their father's property. With this concession, Cecelia was made free and Gausbert's status as a serf was reaffirmed. Several witnesses were gathered to attest to these events: Two clergy, Cecelia's half-brother from another father, several cooks and bakers and a freedman. The list of witnesses for Cecelia and Gausbert's renouncement of rights also holds important information about peasant life. Witnesses to legal transactions needed to have standing before the court. This suggests that although there

23 Maria's cognomen of "conversa" is unusual. Usually "conversa" refers to a woman who "converts" to the religious life, meaning she became a nun. "Conversa" can also describe a woman who has attached herself in some way to a religious community without taking vows. Maria, however, was clearly not a nun nor a member of a religious community. "Conversa" here might refer to her "converted" status from a free peasant to a serf. For a discussion of the term "conversa" in its religious context, see Constance Berman, "Distinguishing between the Humble Peasant Lay-Brother and-Sister and the Converted Knight in Medieval Southern France," *Religious and Laity in Northern Europe*, ed. Janet Burton and Emilia Jamroziak (Turnhout: Brepols, 2006), pp. 263–283.

were legal restrictions placed on serfs, they were still able to participate in matters of justice and property transactions.

The experience of Maria and Cecelia raise some interesting questions about marriage and status among medieval peasants – particularly for women. They were both personally acquainted with the legal and social inequities that were the lot of medieval serfs. That Maria's son, daughter and the monks agreed to her request indicates that they too recognized the benefits enjoyed by free peasants and the disparities suffered by the serfs. Indeed the entire family agreed to work together to secure Cecelia the possibility of marrying a free man. Her brother even gave up his prospect for freedom – as well as his claim to his father's holdings — so that his sister might marry well. Cecelia's potential marriage to a freeman was advantageous to the whole family and would ensure that her children were free. This shows a degree of strategizing and weighing of options often not associated with becoming a medieval serf. Peasants did not blithely enter into these relationships. Nor were they necessarily disadvantaged by them. A fascinating detail of this transaction is the fact that it was recorded as a *chirograph*. This means that two versions of this agreement were written on one piece of parchment, the word "chirograph" written in between them, and then the parchment was cut in a curvy line through "chirograph" between the two copies of the transaction (Figure 5.3). Each party was given a copy, so that if there was a dispute, the two records of the transaction could be matched up. While *chirographs* were commonly used among transactions between nobles and the church, the use here between the monks and peasants is rather unusual. This poses the intriguing possibility that Maria and her family recognized the importance of the written word, even if they could not read.[24]

The family of Maria indicates both agency on the part of peasants in determining their status and that a serf's status could be fluid. Maria's husband, Otbert, was the monks' mayor of their village. Mayors served an important function as a liaison between the village and the lord and it is sometimes difficult to determine their status. Some were certainly free, others appear to be serfs and still others may have been manumitted serfs. Mayors commanded considerable respect and frequently appeared in law courts and legal transactions, so much so that one French scholar has characterized them as the "roosters of the village." This office could be extremely lucrative and allowed certain individuals and families to advance far up the socio-economic ladder. However, most had to adopt a servile status to become mayor. As a consequence, free peasants who won the office of mayor of a village would take on the status of serf for the duration of the office.[25] Thus, serfdom did not always equate with abject poverty or repression. Significantly, males were

24 It also suggests that Maria and her family had access to someone who could read the document for them. I am grateful to Constance Bouchard for pointing this out to me.

25 Chédeville, *Chartres et ses campagnes*, pp. 387–390.

CYROGRAPHVM

Figure 5.3 An example of a *chirograph*. Although this is a *chirograph* between Odo Desredatus and the abbey of Marmoutier, it shows what the document between Maria Conversa and the monks of Marmoutier would have looked like. Archives départmentales d'Eure-et-Loir, H 2382, dated 1095. Author photo.

able to put on and off their servile status, but because mothers determined a child's status it was more difficult for women to vacillate between free and unfree, as it would confuse and alter their children's (or potential children's) status.

Fugitives and disputants: The quest for freedom

Peasants and serfs seemed to accept their status in medieval society, although there were doubtless instances of subtle resistance if not outright rebellion. But because no peasant left behind an account of his or her view of their lot in life, it is difficult to say this with any surety. Tensions certainly existed between lords and peasants. Lords had a vested interest in having peasants remain bound to them and that serfs remained unfree. The lords of Beaugency and their neighbors confronted the reality that serfs ran away and did all that they could to retrieve them. Just such a drama played out at the castle of Beaugency in the eleventh century when the lord received a letter from the abbot of Marmoutier inquiring about a fugitive serf.[26]

When his lord made the pronouncement that he was a serf, Hamelin fled and refused to return to this lord's dominion. The charter remains frustratingly silent as to the interactions between Hamelin and his lord, who was a vassal of the Beaugencys. Whatever the provocation, Hamelin left and spent many years in the fields, tending to the flocks and presumably avoiding human contact. In time, however, he made his way onto Marmoutier's lands and when the abbot found out about this fugitive from justice, he sent a letter of inquiry to the castle of Beaugency. How the abbot knew to reach out to Beaugency remains unclear, but it seems likely that Hamelin must have told them the identity of his lord or where he was born.

Hamelin's lord was, in fact, a lady: Hildeberg Malesherbes, the mother of Lord Ralph I's close companion, Landric Malesherbes. Hildeberg brokered a mutually acceptable arrangement, agreeing that she, along with her children, would give up their dominion over Hamelin, in return for the monks' prayers for her soul and that of her son, but also of their lord – who would have been Lancelin II of Beaugency. In return, Hamelin would stay with the monks. Ironically, Hamelin's fugitive status was reconciled by a pious benefaction for the lord who had spurred Hamelin's flight. Fugitive serfs were not something medieval lords, secular or sacred, could tolerate. Their dominion over these men and women was vital to the economic system, but also their own authority and sustenance.

Even when they manumitted their serfs, lords would still demand payments. In his examination of the Sénonais, a region to the northeast of Beaugency, William Chester Jordan finds that lords would demand that freed peasants continue to pay dues that were a marker of serfdom.[27] These freed serfs almost certainly resented being compelled to make a payment that signified their earlier status as a serf. This practice raises the question of just how free manumitted serfs really were. Imagine working your whole life to purchase your freedom, only to find that when you inherited from your parents you had to pay the same fine that your serf neighbors did. What is perhaps surprising is that more serfs and peasants did not openly rebel against their lords more violently or frequently. The complications, and frustrations, of both manumission and *foremariage* – that is, marrying a serf under the jurisdiction of a different lord – are evident in a long and tortured series of legal disputes that involved the Beaugency family.

26 *LDSM*, no. 65, pp. 62–63.

27 William Chester Jordan, *From Servitude to Freedom: Manumission in the Sénonais in the Thirteenth Century* (Philadelphia: University of Pennsylvania Press, 1986), pp. 88–90.

Late in the 1070s, the monks of Marmoutier issued a charter concerning a certain serf, Ascelin, the son of Ohlem and Hilducia. The monks were concerned that Ascelin's pending nuptials not result in disputes over his intended's status or property. To ensure this, the monks insisted that if Ascelin's wife remained free that neither she nor her children would have any claim on Ascelin's property, which he held from the monastery and worked as their serf.[28] If, however, his wife and children were to surrender their freedom and become serfs, they would have a right to Ascelin's land – but *only* if they became serfs.[29] The monks further stipulated that Ascelin had to watch the company he kept and not "associate with arrogant men and be a faithful servant to the monks."[30] Why did the monks react so aggressively, indeed hostilely, to Ascelin's pending marriage? Based on a collection of charters, the monks' response was a textbook case of the sins of the father, whom the scribe characterizes as rebellious and negligent, being visited upon the son (for a visual diagram of this complicated case, see Figure 5.4).

By 1060 the serf Ohlem (Ascelin's father) had been donated to Marmoutier by the count of Chartres and his mother.[31] At the time, Ohlem was married to Hilducia. She had been a serf of Viscount Robert I of Blois, but was transferred by him to one of his knights, Herbald, when the viscount invested him with property for his support. This would appear to be a classic instance of *foremariage*, when serfs from two different lordships married. Like the peasants of the neighboring Sénonais, Ohlem desired to secure the freedom of his wife to ensure that his children were free, but also to prevent Hilducia from being "subject to dispute by [her] lord."[32] To do this Ohlem gave Herbald "a moderate amount of money," had a charter of freedom drawn up and delivered to his wife, and he had the viscount and **viscountess** affirm the document. Intriguingly, Ohlem, like Maria Conversa, both illiterate serfs, comprehended the value of the written word. In spite of Ohlem's precautions, however, a dispute arose after Viscount Robert and Herbald had died. Their sons demanded back Hilducia's dowry, which they asserted belonged to them because she was a serf, and denied that their parents had granted her freedom.

This assertion would result in a long, protracted and tangled arbitration process, which lasted over ten years and required at least six different courts

28 With the exception of her dowry.

29 These stipulations are similar to those arranged between Maria Conversa and Marmoutier.

30 *CMPD*, no. 17, pp. 18–19.

31 It is difficult to know when exactly these events transpired. The charter is dated between 1060 and 1064, but some of these events took place sometime in the past. Given that Ohlem was dead by c. 1065, his donation to Marmoutier and manumission of Hilducia may have occurred years earlier, c. 1040–1045. Since Ascelin was considering marriage around 1070 and that peasant men married late, he might have been about 25 years old at this point, which would place his birth around 1045. However, Ascelin's status suggests he was born before his mother had gained her freedom.

32 *CMPD*, no. 14, pp. 14–15.

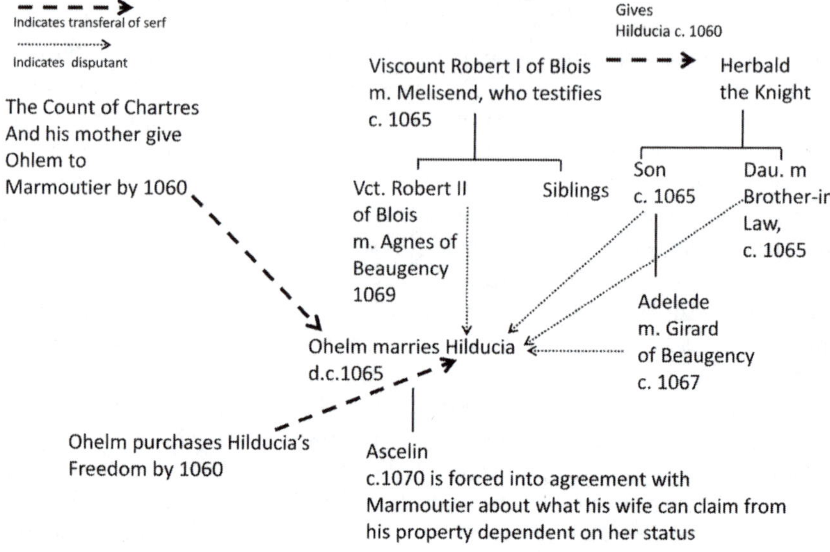

Figure 5.4 Charting the dispute over Ohlem and Hilducia. Provided by the author.

to air the various claims and counter claims. In response to the heirs of Viscount Robert I and Herbald's insistence that Hilducia and her dowry belonged to them, the monks held a court where they called witnesses and produced the charter recording the grant of freedom.[33] Yet "contrary to the clarity of the illustrious testimony and in light of all of the evidence," neither disputant was swayed and continued with their claim – even threatening to take the lands back by force.[34] There were many attempts to reach a compromise until another court was finally called. The monks produced the charter of freedom once again, but the disputant remained resolute. So the monks had one of their own men (likely a servant) undergo the **ordeal** of the hot iron. Ordeals were a feature of medieval justice, such as ordeal by battle, the hot iron and hot water. All were predicated on the belief that God would intervene on the side that was in the right. Recall that Lord Ralph I got an admonishing letter from Bishop Ivo for his participation in what may have been an ordeal by battle (see Document 2, page 223). Ordeals were employed in the region of the Loire, usually when litigation had been ongoing and the litigants unable to reach a resolution. In the case of ordeal by hot iron, a hot iron rod was placed in the hand of the person undergoing the ordeal. After the iron was removed (and the hand badly burned) the wound was bandaged and if the wound did not fester this was seen as divine endorsement of the

33 Viscountess Melisend, the wife of Robert I and mother to Robert II (who was making the claim), testified that her husband had manumitted Hilducia and that she was in fact free.
34 *CMPD*, no. 14, pp. 14–15.

ordeal-taker's position – in this case the monks. Luckily for the monks' servant, no infection set in and Herbald's claim was finally abandoned in front of many witnesses.[35]

The final phase of the dispute involved the Beaugency family directly because the court that was called to hear yet another claim was held at Beaugency in the tower of the castle with Lord Lancelin II presiding.[36] In 1069 Viscount Robert II, the son of Viscount Robert I, made a claim against the estates of Ohlem and Hilducia. He asserted that because they had belonged "his father, grandfather and great grandfather," Ohlem and Hilducia (and their property) belonged to him as well.[37] Once again the monks called witnesses who testified that they had seen Robert II witness his father's authorization of Hilducia's manumission. Robert responded that he had not consented to this concession by his father and that she and these properties belonged to him as part of his inheritance. Robert did have a change of heart, however, and begged the monks for their forgiveness. He abandoned his claim affirming that the monks would hold the property "completely and peacefully in perpetuity."[38]

Perhaps we can now better appreciate why the monks reacted so forcefully to the prospect that this drama over a female serf's status might be re-enacted with Ohlem and Hilducia's son Ascelin's marriage and why they would be so insistent that the status of Ascelin's wife be made explicit. Ironically, the monks held Ohlem and Ascelin responsible for all of these trials and tribulations when in fact they were clearly not the cause of the trouble – indeed Ohlem had even gone so far to secure written record of Hilducia's freedom. It was the lords who brought the many disputes over the property and Hilducia, which demonstrates just how valuable serfs were to them and how vulnerable a peasant's freedom could be. The monks could not control the aristocracy's claim to property, but they could hold

35 The assertions by Herbald's descendants to Hilducia had yet to be completely put to rest. In 1067 Girard of Beaugency, one of the vassals of the lords of Beaugency, brought a claim to the property of Ohlem and Ascelin based on the grounds that Hilducia had been a serf of his wife's grandfather, the eponymous Herbald. But Girard and the monks eventually "grew weary of the claim" and resolved to end it. Girard and his family were awarded coin in recognition of the abandonment of their claim to Hilducia's property, which they affirmed in public. Girard, however, was fearful that he had offended the monks – and God – and asked the abbot's pardon, which was granted. This reconciliation ended with Girard kissing the hand of the abbot as a sign of obedience and humility and being restored to the monks' good graces. This mini-drama was enacted on the lawn between the count's tower and hall in the château of Blois. *CMPD*, no. 16, pp. 17–18.

36 Viscount Robert II was married to Lancelin II's sister, Agnes. Hence, Robert's brother-in-law presided over the court that heard his claim.

37 AD Eure-et-Loir H 2770.

38 *CMPD*, no. 15, p. 16. Agnes, Robert's wife and Lancelin's sister, was also consulted in this matter. Robert journeyed to their home about 20 miles away in La Ferté-Villeneuil with the monks' representative to secure Agnes' consent to the resolution. Robert's brother and four sisters also agreed and were awarded cash countergifts for their cooperation.

the peasants accountable. Robert Berkhofer III has argued that lords, secular and ecclesiastical, used marriage as a tool to control their peasants and that certainly seems to be the case here.[39] While peasants might have some autonomy over who they could marry or if they decided to become serfs, they were still very much under the heel of their lords – as depicted earlier in Figure 1.2.

The tale of Ohlem and Hilducia attests to the Beaugencys' and their peers' interest in their peasants and serfs, as well as the complications of *foremariage*. It also underscores the domination that the Beaugencys and their class could exercise over peasants – both free and unfree. Poor Ohlem had done everything he could to secure and document his wife's freedom. He must have been extremely angry when her liberty was disputed. Perhaps it is surprising that this dispute was resolved through peaceful measures, rather than by force. We know that some did resort to violence for there are some tantalizing glimpses in what would seem to be peasant unrest. But these are rare. There were no major peasant revolutions until the fourteenth century – and significantly they were motivated by attempts to reinforce the service obligations of serfdom that had become lax. Some localized outbreaks of peasant violence occurred around 1000 AD in Normandy, for example. But clearly this "rebellion" was not enough to overthrow the social system in Normandy, or elsewhere, since serfdom continued for many more centuries. There was discontent because peasants sometimes killed their lords or carried out violence against them. Paul Freedman has estimated that there were twelve incidents of peasant killing their lords in northern France between 1050 and 1150.[40] While interesting, this statistic is hardly suggestive of wholesale peasant resistance.[41]

Although the social gap between "those who worked" and "those who fought" was immense, there were exceptions to the rules that blurred the lines that demarcated the three orders of medieval society and the boundary between free and unfree. In June of 1047 Lord Lancelin I approved when Hubert, his wife and her brother gave themselves and their children, along with their property, to St. Trinité of Vendôme, because "they truly loved" the monks of this place. While this would seem like a straightforward self-oblation, these were not ordinary serfs. Rather they were described as "servants of the fief." Serfs and servants were generally not associated with fiefs; these were the monopoly of fighting men. Hubert and his family belonged to a different category of serf: They were fighting serfs, sometimes called *ministeriales*, and they fought for the lord of Beaugency.[42] These were warriors

39 See the suggested reading section at the end of the chapter.

40 Freedman, *Images of a Medieval Peasant*, p. 183.

41 There were large, violent, peasant revolts in the late Middle Ages. English peasants revolted in 1381. Twenty-three years earlier, in 1358, the Jacquerie or the French peasant revolt occurred and, according to the account of Jean Froissart, specifically targeted lords and their families.

42 *STV,* vol. I, no. 74, pp. 135-137.

who served lords but who were bound to them as their serfs rather than their vassals. While *ministeriales* did exist in medieval France, they were never as prominent in the lands of the Loire as in other parts of Europe, particularly Germany where there was a class of *ministeriales.*[43] The monastery, like other communities, would certainly be interested in having fighting men in their service to provide protection. Geoffrey and his brother Richard were also fighting serfs who ended up as the servants of the abbey of St. Trinité. Their story, however, has a less than happy ending.

In the mid-eleventh century, wars between Count Geoffrey Martel of Anjou and Count Thibaut III of Chartres tore asunder the peace and prosperity of the region. Poverty, so a charter records, became a constant companion, even of the most wealthy, whose estates were ravaged and who became so impoverished they hardly had food for themselves or their animals. The lords of Beaugency were affected by these wars as they held fiefs from both counts and their lands likely suffered some deprivation. Many fled the region of their birth, among them Geoffrey and Richard, who were *ministeriales* of Count Geoffrey.[44] But unlike others who left, these men hoped to better themselves by offering their services to Count Geoffrey's political rival in return for their freedom. So Richard and Geoffrey made their way to the castle of Blois, where they were brought into Count Thibaut's service. Their knowledge of the countryside, as well as the count of Anjou's defenses, made them valuable indeed in ravaging of the lands of the region. Unfortunately, they did not enjoy their newly acquired status as "shrewd and sly" knights for long, for shortly after they began their work for the count of Chartres, they were captured by an agent of the count of Anjou. To punish them for their treachery, their eyes were put out. Geoffrey and Richard were in dire straits indeed, as they could no longer support themselves as fighting men or through manual labor. So Geoffrey and Richard offered themselves as serfs to the monks. In return for their support, they would act as servers for the monks' table. Moreover, they promised that their progeny would similarly be held in thrall by the abbey.

What had started out as a tale of derring-do ended in tragedy. These two brothers, who were clearly warriors fighting for one count and then another, tried to use their skills and knowledge to improve their station in life. Regrettably, they ended up trading their swords for serving-trays and suffering mightily. Their tale, however, holds some interesting insights into lives of serfs. While Geoffrey and Richard were ultimately unsuccessful, and ended up far worse than where they had started, the fact that they tried, that they had ambition, is significant. Too often it is assumed that peasants and serfs had few opportunities for improvement and simply suffered through their plight in life. Other serfs also tried to improve their status. Take Turbatus

43 Chédeville, *Chartres et ses campagnes,* pp. 374; 384-385.
44 *STV,* vol. I, no. 122, pp. 219-222

for instance. The monks of Marmoutier and Turbatus had a disagreement over whether or not Turbatus was the monks' serf or not. Turbatus asserted that he was free and demanded a court to hear his case. The monks obliged and a hearing was called. Unfortunately for Turbatus, the monks secured the testimony of one of his own kinsmen who testified that he was in fact a serf. Turbatus did not take the news well and demanded a judicial duel. The outcome was not in Turbatus' favor, since another court was called where he admitted that he was, in fact, a serf of the monks.[45] Unfortunately, the charter remains silent as to why Turbatus changed his story. As these examples suggest, not all serfs were complacent.

There were, however, safer ways of gaining freedom than becoming a traitor to your lord or fighting a judicial duel. Some were manumitted by their masters. At the end of the eleventh century Haimeric Gaumard, a kinsman of the lords of Beaugency, granted one of his serfs his freedom:

> Desiring to acquit himself from the domination of his sins and consequently wishing to absolve the chains of servitude, therefore out of love of the omnipotent God, I, Haimeric Gaumard, young lord of Lavardin, with the assent of my sister Beatrice, for the soul of my father Salomon, I concede liberty to my serf Bertran, so that in any four corners of the world he will be free and in peace, if anyone however wishes to quarrel or challenge this liberty, he will incur the anger of the Omnipotent God and the Holy Virgin Mary and all of the saints, and will pay one hundred pounds of gold.[46]

Manumitting their serfs was one way for aristocrats to expiate their sins and work towards a place in heaven. Although the fine and the curse that close this charter may be an indication that freed serfs, like Bertran and Hilducia, were likely to have their manumission challenged and their freedom questioned. Other lucky serfs were able to purchase their freedom or that of their spouse. Securing the free status of a wife was particularly important because a child's status was determined by that of his or her mother. Scholars have estimated that a serf's freedom cost 10 pounds in the eleventh century but the price had increased to 80 pounds by the twelfth.[47] These were not inconsequential sums. As we know from previous examples of serfs having the financial wherewithal to purchase homes from the monks once they came under their jurisdiction, "those who worked" were able to accrue money through their labors. As towns began to grow in the late eleventh and twelfth centuries, the adage "town air makes you free" meant that if a serf could escape to a town and remain there undetected for a year and a day, she or he

45 *LDSM*, no. 11, pp. 12–13.
46 *CMV*, no. 26, pp. 314–316.
47 Chédeville, *Chartres et ses campagnes*, p. 389.

would gain their freedom. Yet questions concerning status continued to be an issue even as serfs worked their way up the social ladder. In 1127, Count Charles the Good of Flanders was murdered as he was praying in church. Galbert of Bruges, who was eyewitness to the events before and after Charles' death, indicates that the murderer slayed Count Charles because of the suggestion that his family had servile origins.[48] Recall also the knight Erec's outrage when he was mistaken as a peasant at the start of this chapter. There was no worse insult for an aspiring knight or nobleman than to be identified as a peasant or the descendant of one.

Conclusion

The evidence from Marmoutier's book of serfs and the experiences of the Beaugency peasants, I would argue, indicates that our perception of serfdom and the interactions between lords and peasants needs some reconsideration. Free peasants became serfs for many different reasons and there were those who saw becoming a serf of Marmoutier as a way of improving their situation. Moreover, serfdom could be conditional and a serf's status could change from unfree to free and possibly back to unfree during the course of his or her life, indicating that the boundaries between free and unfree were not as fixed as might have been assumed. Nevertheless, it is clear from the case of Ohlem and Hilducia that peasants – free and serf – were very much under the control of the lords. The labor of "those who worked" was vital for the survival of the Beaugencys and their peers. As a consequence, they jealously guarded their rights to peasant labor and property.

Now that the general contours and characteristics of the interactions between the Beaugency lords and those who worked their lands have been outlined, let us consider the other major force that shaped the lives of the Beaugency family and their neighbors: "Those who prayed." As we shall examine in the next chapter, the church was a constant presence in shaping everything from the way both medieval lords and peasants viewed the world to determining the holidays that set the rhythm of life.

Suggested reading

Robert Bartlett, *Trial by Fire and Water: The Medieval Judicial Ordeal.* Echo Points Books and Media, second edition, 2014.

Judith M. Bennett, *A Medieval Life: Cecilia Penifader of Brigstock, c. 1295–1344*. New York: McGraw Hill Education, 1998; and *Women in the Medieval English Countryside: Gender and Household in Brigstock before the Plague*. Oxford: Oxford University Press, 1989.

48 Galbert of Bruges, *The Murder, Betrayal and Slaughter of the Glorious Charles, Count of Flanders*, ed. and trans. Jeff Rider (New Haven: Yale University Press, 2013).

Robert Berkhofer III, "Marriage, Lordship and the Greater Unfree in Twelfth-Century France," *Past and Present* 173 (2001): 3–27.

Georges Duby, *Rural Economy and Country Life in the Medieval West*, trans. Cynthia Postan. London: Edward Arnold, 1968.

Robert Fossier, *The Axe and the Oath: Ordinary Life in the Middle Ages,* trans. Lydia G. Cochrane. Princeton: Princeton University Press, 2010; and *The House and the Village in the Middle Ages*, with Jean Chapelot, trans. Henry Cleere. Berkeley: The University of California Press, 1986.

Paul Freedman, *Images of the Medieval Peasant*. Palo Alto: Stanford University Press, 1999.

Barbara A. Hanawalt, *The Ties that Bound: Peasant Families in Medieval England*. Oxford: Oxford University Press, 1988.

William Chester Jordan, *From Servitude to Freedom: Manumission in the Sénonais in the Thirteenth Century.* Philadelphia: University of Pennsylvania Press, 1986.

6 The Beaugencys and the community of believers

Let us now place ourselves in the shoes of the Beaugency family and examine the role that religion and the church played in their lives. How can we know what medieval people like the Beaugencys believed? Unfortunately, since they left behind no personalized accounts, it is difficult for us to ascertain. We can, however, reconstruct the norms of belief and what the Beaugency family did to express their faith. Medieval nobles would have encountered clergy on almost a daily basis and their Christian piety was central to their lives.

Religion and daily life

Walking outside of the precincts of the castle, a lord or lady would have immediately encountered the monastery of Notre Dame de Beaugency (Figures 6.1 and 6.2). Yet this was only one of several ecclesiastical foundations within the walls of Beaugency. The two parish churches of St. Nicholas and St. Firmin have since disappeared, but St. Firmin was located just across from the castle (its tower remains today – see Figure 1.1) and the Beaugencys may have worshiped there as well.[1] Just a short distance away from the castle was the chapel that Lancelin II had constructed in the mid-eleventh century which he eventually donated to the abbey of St. Trinité of Vendôme in 1079 (Figure 6.3). This church was named after the Holy Sepulcher in Jerusalem. Although destroyed by the Muslims in 1009 and rebuilt in the eleventh through the twelfth century, the Holy Sepulcher was a church built around what people believed was Jesus' tomb. During the eleventh century, western Europeans had begun constructing churches dedicated to the Holy Sepulcher, many using the same round plan, all over Europe. Lancelin's church, however, was not round, but rather built in the traditional cruciform plan. To do homage to Christ's tomb, there was probably a small round tomb constructed in front of the altar or under the crossing of the transcept and nave. This tomb may have contained relics that Lancelin brought back from his

1 Bezard and Vannier, *Beaugency*, p. 40.

Visit the companion website: www.routledge.com/cw/livingstone

pilgrimage to Rome – which he completed shortly before he gave the church to St. Trinité – as well as those Ralph might have brought back from crusade. Indeed, if Lancelin were anything like his contemporary, Archdeacon Hervé of St. Croix of Orléans, acquisition of relics would have encouraged him to build a tomb to house them. As Hervé related: "Returning then [from Jerusalem] I brought with me relics of the most Holy Sepulcher of our lord Jesus Christ, in veneration of which, inspired by God, I embarked on the construction of a worthy church for these relics."[2] Association with holy places and people was of the utmost importance to medieval believers. (Recall the church of Rhodon and its relics, Figures 1.10a and 1.10b.) Elites traveled to visit places where the earliest martyrs of the faith had lived their lives, collected their relics and built chapels to create this sense of immediacy with the holy.

Figure 6.1 Notre Dame de Beaugency and the castle at Beaugency. Note the proximity of the abbey church to the castle. Author photo.

2 "Un perlinage à Jérusalem," in *Bibliothéque d'école de chartes* 51 (1890): 204–206.

Figure 6.2 View of the abbey church of Notre Dame de Beaugency, western portal. Author photo.

Our lord or lady would have encountered both secular and regular clergy on their walk along the byways of Beaugency. Regular clergy followed a "rule" (*regula*), like that of St. Benedict, and lived separated from the secular world (at least in theory). In the sixth century, dedicating oneself to prayer and removing oneself from the world became a compelling expression of faith and piety. Those choosing this lifestyle needed guidance as to how to manage their faith, their interactions with other religious and their relationship with the secular. St. Benedict of Nursia developed a rule (the Benedictine Rule) for his own community of Monte Cassino that other religious communities adopted to provide organization. These clerics spent their lives in prayer and were removed from the laity in the sense that they did not minister to secular society. In contrast, secular clergy included canons, priests, chaplains, archdeacons (like Hervé discussed above) and bishops, whose duty it was to minister to their lay flock.[3] Parish priests resided within the walls of

3 Remember that some canons lived by a rule as well. The canons at Notre Dame de Beaugency followed the Augustinian rule. For additional information, see Chapter 1.

Figure 6.3 St. Sepulcher of Beaugency. Built by Lancelin II c. 1070 and later given to St. Trinité of Vendôme. It would become one of the abbey's priories. Author photo.

twelfth-century Beaugency, but so too did a small community of monks of St. Trinité at the church of St. Sepulcher and after c. 1104 canons inhabited the abbey of Notre Dame de Beaugency. By the mid-twelfth century the lords of Beaugency also had their own chaplain, who might have been a canon from the neighboring abbey.

Medieval life revolved around religious holidays, which ranged from the major church celebrations of Christmas and Easter to feast or fast days for local saints. The number of feast days varied from place to place in Europe, as all communities did not celebrate the same feast days. For example, in England, in the diocese of Canterbury, forty feast days were declared annually, so on average one could expect a feast day nearly once a week. I would estimate that those living in Beaugency, too, could expect to celebrate one saint's day or holy day every week or two. The feast days of St. Firmin and his companions, St. Fulcian, St. Victor and St. Gentian (September 25), and St. Nicholas (December 6) would have been observed in Beaugency since there were churches dedicated to these saints in the village. Additionally, festivals held in honor of other local saints occurred throughout the year: St. Bienheuré (May 9), St. Anian (November 17), St. Aubin (March 1) and St. Lubin (March 14). As well as local saints, there were some universal saint days observed throughout Europe, such as All Souls and All Saints days on the first two days of November, and those holidays centering on the Virgin Mary.

As Christianity spread throughout Western Europe, the church adopted pagan holidays into the calendar of Christian celebration. Christmas celebrated Jesus' birth, but people continued the old pagan traditions of Yule by burning a yule log during the twelve days of Christmas and ringing bells to drive away evil spirits – traditions that continue to the present day. Medieval people prepared elaborate feasts on these days and indulged in all sorts of revelry. Indeed, feasts served several social functions in medieval society. They provided a place to indulge and let off steam, but were also a stage for the powerful to showcase their largesse, to highlight their wealth and social station. But, at the same time, holding feasts redistributed wealth by allowing the less well-off an opportunity to partake in what the upper classes enjoyed. These feasts also gave lords a tangible means to thank and recognize their loyal followers.

For all of the residents of Beaugency, I would reconstruct their seasonal calendar along these lines. Autumn was an important time of year, for it was then that the harvest took place. Survival for the winter, as well as securing the next year's seed, depended on the fall harvest. Several saints' days were interspersed throughout the months of September, October and November that provided respite from harvest labor. In early September, the people of Beaugency would stop to celebrate the days of two local saints, Sts. Egidius and Lupus. The celebration of the Nativity of Mary would follow shortly after. At the end of the month, September 25, St. Firmin's day would have been of special significance since he was one of the patron saints of the abbey of Notre Dame de Beaugency and a parish church. As well as times of celebration, saints' days also signified when certain dues or labors were to be paid to lords. Warin of *Usello*, for example, had to pay the canons of Notre Dame an annual rent of 5 shillings on the feast of St. Firmin. Several people owed dues on St. Remigius' day in October. These rents were sometimes paid in kind in correspondence with the fall harvest. There would be celebrations on All Souls and All Saints day to commemorate the dead. In some places, children would go begging for cakes to feed the souls of the dead – a pagan holdover which influenced the start of the modern Halloween (All Hallows Eve) tradition. November 11, or Martinmas, represented the beginning of the slaughter of livestock that would not winter over. Meat would be cured, usually smoked, and provide protein for the winter months until the spring when animals could be butchered for the spring feast of Easter.

The holidays of Advent, Christmas and Candlemas dominated the winter season. Advent (which started on the fourth Sunday before Christmas) and the feast of the Epiphany on January 6 bookended the winter celebration of Christ's birth. In preparation for the feasting and merriment associated with Christmas, medieval people spent Advent in prayer and repenting their misdeeds. A high point for children during Advent was St. Nicholas Day, which would have been of particular significance to the children of Beaugency as St. Nicholas was the patron saint of one of the parish churches. Because St. Nicholas was thought to have restored three dead children to life, giving gifts to children became part of his holiday celebration and is still observed today in parts of Northern Europe. As commemorated in the modern Christmas carol of *The Twelve Days of Christmas*, the Feast of the Nativity (or Christmas) was twelve days of feasting and fun (although Christmas was not as important a holiday as Easter, at least until St. Francis made it so in the thirteenth century). Special dishes and foods were part of the celebration, as well as entertainment, such as dancing and games. Plays were also often put on, where men and women might exchange places. Amidst the fun, three masses were celebrated during these twelve days: On Christmas Eve, dawn of Christmas morning and at midday. New Year's Day saw the Feast of Fools, where things could get really out of hand. Even the clergy might join in the unruly behavior by disguising themselves with masks. Most medieval people, however, marked the new year with the arrival of spring in late March.[4] The holidays celebrating Christ's birth came to an end with Epiphany, or the visit of the Three Kings to the infant Jesus in Bethlehem, on January 6.

Candlemas was an important watershed in the medieval calendar. Although the official holiday was the Feast of the Presentation of Jesus at the Temple or the Feast of the Purification of the Virgin, this holiday came to be called Candlemas because it marked the midpoint of winter and the hope that spring was on the way. Winter in Northern Europe consists of short days and long nights. To celebrate light and the lengthening of the days, medieval people would gather for this mass with candles to create their own version of sunlight. Today people in the United States gather on February 2 not with candles but to see if the groundhog Puxatawny Phil has seen his shadow; both gatherings were motivated by the same desire to see winter pass and spring arrive. For the women of Beaugency, Candlemas was particularly significant. In Hebrew and then Christian tradition, after giving birth a woman had to undergo purification before returning to worship. The Feast of the Presentation or of the Purification commemorated when Mary had undergone purification after the birth of her son and was able to present him to her religious community. Medieval women who had given birth would take part in Candlemas to celebrate of the safe birth of their child and their restoration to the community. The Beaugency women would bring candles to be used throughout the year to be blessed by the priests.

Easter was the major focus of celebration of the spring – and the major holiday of the medieval Christian calendar. Fat Tuesday (Mardi Gras), the

4 The modern tradition of April Fools stems from when celebration of the new year changed from spring to January 1 in the sixteenth century when the Gregorian Calendar replaced the Julian calendar as part of the Catholic Church's post–Protesant Reformation reform. Those still celebrating the start of the year in the spring were designated as "foolish" for not knowing the proper date of the new year.

Tuesday before Lent, was the last chance for the Beaugencys and their neighbors to indulge before the start of the Easter observance, which began with Lent the next day. Lent was a period of forty days of fasting and repentance. Medieval people began the Lenten season by attending mass on Ash Wednesday where they repented their sins and their foreheads were marked with the sign of the cross with ashes. During Lent, meat and dairy were often given up as a sign of the penitent's faith. Fish and vegetables were the staples of the Beaugencys' Lenten diet – hence the celebration of "Fat" Tuesday where people could indulge their appetites before the onset of Lent. Unlike Christmas, Easter was a more somber time of celebration, with focus on piety and reflection rather than entertainment and fun. Palm Sunday began Easter week. On Maundy Thursday, Christians demonstrated their humility with certain rituals. The powerful washed the feet of the poor. King Louis IX of France went as far as to wash the feet of lepers. Perhaps the lords and ladies of Beaugency did so as well. This was also a time of charity, where the poor were hosted in the homes of the wealthy and given gifts of coin. Easter was also when paupers would receive a new shirt – a medieval precursor to the modern tradition of getting new clothes, and particularly hats, for the spring season. Lord Ralph I made a gift of clothing a pauper at Easter as part of his benefaction to commemorate his friend and vassal, Landric Malesherbes (see Document 9, page 230).

Good Friday Mass told the events of the crucifixion. In some places, tombs or **sepulchers** were built inside of churches representing the tomb of Christ. In Beaugency, the tomb in the chapel of the Holy Sepulcher would likely have played an important role in the Easter celebration. During the ceremony of *depositio* (or burial), a carved figure of Christ, perhaps detached from a crucifix, would be laid to rest in the tomb. Often this figure was life sized and was washed in wine and water, imitating contemporary burial practices. The Eucharist would also be placed in the burial chamber. The tomb was then closed and the clergy kept watch. Before dawn on Easter Sunday, a member of the clergy would remove the body from the tomb, leaving the bread and wine of the Eucharist behind. At daybreak bells were rung to call people to Easter Mass. This was a joyous celebration and the apex of the ecclesiastical year. The mass itself was an elaborate affair with music, but also dramatizations of the story of the visit to Christ's tomb. These dramatizations of the Easter story provided the foundation from which Western European drama would emerge. Significantly, the nearby monastery of St. Fleury-sur-Loire was one of the earliest sites for the Easter drama.[5] The Beaugencys may have traveled there to witness these liturgical plays. By the end of the Middle Ages, miracle plays were performed during the Easter season. The

5 I would like to thank my student, Lauren Instenes, for bringing these plays to my attention. For translations of the Easter plays of St. Fleury-sur-Loire, see Wyndham Thomas, ed. and trans., *The Fleury Playbook II: Plays for Christmas and Easter* (Newton Abbot, UK: Antico Edition, 2001).

Easter holiday ended with a great feast after forty days of fasting. Young lamb and mutton were often staples of the Beaugencys' feast, as well as eggs that had been hard boiled to preserve them during Lent. Lords also collected rents of eggs at this time, all of which filters into the modern tradition of Easter eggs.

In contrast to the holy holiday of Easter, spring and summer holidays were a combination of pagan and Christian observances (although Easter does often correspond with celebrations of the spring equinox, a tradition in many pagan cultures), as well as times of fun and times of serious veneration. May Day was a festival with roots in the pagan world and not embraced by the church. Villages like Beaugency would erect maypoles and hold dances and banquets where the norms of social behavior were often relaxed. In contrast, fifty days after Easter Sunday was the holiday of Pentecost, which was a three-day holiday and often associated with fairs.[6] Pagan and Christian tradition combined in late June with the celebration of the midsummer solstice and the celebration of the birth of St. John the Baptist. Bonfires were lit throughout Europe as part of their pagan traditions. For Beaugency tenants, rents were also rendered at the feast of St. John.[7] The month of June also became associated with weddings for those living in the Middle Ages (and the tradition of a "June Wedding" continues into our day). High summer saw the holidays of Peter and Paul, as well as the Assumption of the Virgin in August.

The rhythms of life for those living in Beaugency were dictated both by the seasons and the ecclesiastical calendar. Often the two merged. Courts were held at the holidays – such as St. Remigius' day, Christmas and the feast of St. John the Baptist – where disputes were heard and taxes paid. Indeed the seasonal fairs that took place close to the church of Notre Dame were held in coordination with ecclesiastical holidays: One was held in October on the feast day of St. Loup; followed by a fair on St. Nicholas's day on the sixth of December; the Quasimodo fair took place the week after Easter; and the fair of the Madeleine was held in May. Holidays also marked the beginning and end of agricultural seasons. Moreover, these were times when all the residents of Beaugency would gather and rub elbows in church, at feasts, in courts and at fairs. These celebrations certainly had religious significance, but they permeated the lives of medieval people in other, significant ways.

Education and culture

Like the calendar, the intellectual lives of the people of Beaugency were shaped by religion and the church. Peasants' understanding of religion was molded by the sermons they heard and the images they saw in the churches

6 Pentecost commemorated the descent of the holy spirit upon Christ's apostles fifty days after his death and resurrection.

7 *CMV*, no. 126, pp. 215–217.

where they attended mass. Nobles were influenced by sermons and sculptures, but they also began to collect religious books, an indication of how important their faith was to them. Eleventh-century lords had some form of functional literacy, but their twelfth-century descendants were better educated. Some of these men were taught in the school in the neighboring abbey of Notre Dame de Beaugency. Charters from this institution indicate there was a schoolmaster in residence in twelfth century and that Lord John I of Beaugency had made a gift to support the school at Notre Dame by the end of the century.[8] Poignantly, John had endowed the school in the name of his young son who had died recently and may have studied with the monks. We are fortunate to have an inventory of the books in the abbey's library extant in the early fourteenth-century copy of the original cartulary. Unfortunately it is not possible to determine if this was the entire list of books held at the monastery or what portion of its collections these works represented. Nevertheless, this collection, I would argue, provides important clues into how the Beaugency family was educated. Listed under the heading of "Books from our little cupboard" are the following titles:

A glossed Psalter in one part
A gloss over the Psalter in three great parts
A gloss that is in a small volume
Another similar gloss
A volume of glosses of the books of St. Luke and St. John
Another similar gloss for the book of St. John
Two glosses on the book of St. Mark
A gloss on the book of St. Matthew
The City of God by St. Augustine
Gloss on the five books of Moses
Similar glosses on the books from the Old Testament, including Joshua, Judges, Kings, Tobias, Ezekiel, Daniel, Esther, Judith, Nehmiah, Hester, Macabees
A large volume on the writing of the Evangelists and the Acts of the Apostles
The Moralia in Job by Gregory the Great in one great volume
Sentences by Peter Lombard, several volumes
Tract on Virtue by Guillaum Perrault [William of Auvergne]
The Summary by Raymond of Pennafort
The Letters of St. Paul with two glosses
A gloss on *The Song of Songs*
Small summary on rhetoric
Confessions by St. Augustine
Book of the Apocalypse

8 AD Loiret H 10, folio XXXVI verso; *NDB*, no. 124, pp. 143–144.

Huguccio, *Lexicon sue derivationes* or *Liber derivationum*
A glossed hymnal with sermons of the Lord
Collections of sermons, including those of Jean of Abbeville, Gautier of Château-Thierry, [chancellor then bishop of Paris], St. Bernard of Clairvaux
Liturgical and other works by John Beleth
Book of the Names of the Gems by Marbode of Rennes [Liber de lapidus]
Book of the Sparks [a collection of sayings by church fathers]
Treatise on Canon Law by Martin the Pole.
The works of Peter of Riga
Summary of the letters following Pope Innocent III and his commentary on the Evanglists
Book compiled of arts – collections
Book on Medicine
A florilegium [collection of various works]

One of the common texts found throughout this collection is something called "a gloss." What exactly was a gloss and how would the canons and their students have used it? A "glossed" book meant that a scribe had gone through and provided additional definitions of key words or passages (see Figure 6.4). Glosses could also supply the reader with additional information about the work, additional context, or elaborate on the argument made in the book – much as college textbooks do today. Indeed the practice of glossing is the origin for modern glossaries – like the one found in this book. Glosses would have been very useful texts for the monks for teaching, as a glossed text gave students (clerical and lay) additional information about the text and could have helped the teacher explain abstract or difficult contexts. The particular collection of glosses from the "little cupboard" is also significant since some of the foundational Biblical texts for training monks in theology were glossed. Books from the Old Testament, the *Song of Songs* and a Psalter (a collection of psalms – see Figure 2.3) had glosses to explain key concepts and passages. Similarly all four Gospels of the New Testament were also in glossed form.

In addition to the various glosses, several of the foundational works of medieval Christianity were part of the library of Notre Dame de Beaugency. St. Augustine (d. 430) was one of the most important Early Christian theologians and the library had copies of two of his most important works: *The City of God* and *Confessions.* Augustine was widely read by medieval theologians and his works were essential for teaching students about Christian theology. These texts would have had additional meaning to the canons, for as Augustinian canons, they followed the rule created by St. Augustine. Another influential author was Pope Gregory the Great (d. 604 AD). His *Moralia in Job* was one of the most popular texts of the Middle Ages. It provided commentary on the Book of Job, but also engaged with the inner spirituality of the believer and explored the question of how one created a Christian soul. While these issues would have been of tantamount importance

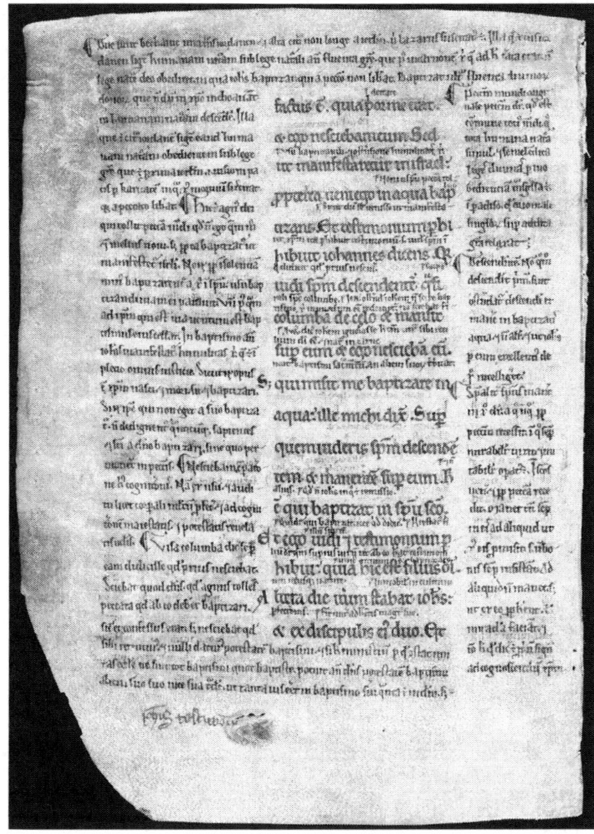

Figure 6.4 Glossed Bible, featuring text for the Gospel of John 1:25–35, with commentary attributed to Anselm of Laon and his school. Eastern France, ca. 1125–1150. This twelfth-century French glossed Bible is similar to the ones used by the community of Notre Dame de Beaugency. The text is in the center of the page, with the glossed information on the side. This type of bible was developed by the schoolmaster Anselm of Laon for use at his cathedral school. © The Ohio State University Libraries, Rare Books and Manuscripts Library, Spec.Rare.MS.MR.Frag.1.

to the monks, I believe they would also have been of great interest to any young noblemen who were being educated in the monastery. The state of their soul was something that concerned the noble born and they spent considerable time and energy trying to ensure that their soul (and those of their loved ones) was sufficiently prepared for the afterlife. Indeed a twelfth-century copy of Gregory's *Moralia* shows an armed knight battling the "monsters" that threatened his soul. Such an illustration would have resonated well with a secular audience and I would speculate that the copy from Notre Dame de Beaugency was similarly illustrated (Figure 6.5).

Figure 6.5 A knight fighting monsters in an initial starting a paragraph from Gregory the Great's *Moralia in Job*. © The British Library Board, Royal MS 6 C.vi.

The books in this collection reflect the role, needs and activities of a medieval religious community. Many of the books were clearly aimed at teaching and would have been used in the abbey school in training future canons as there are other standard teaching texts, particularly *Sentences* by Peter Lombard, the works on canon law by Huguccio and the *Tract on Virtue* by William of Auvergne, that would have been used in addition to the glosses to instruct those becoming members of the clergy. Other texts, however, I would suggest, indicate that the canons were teaching lay pupils in the abbey school.

As a community of canons, Notre Dame de Beaugency was not cut off from the secular world. While the Beaugency canons took vows like monks, they were not enclosed from the world. Rather, their vocation meant that they ministered to the laity and providing an education would have certainly fallen under their religious call. There are texts from "the little cupboard" that the canons could have used to educate secular pupils, such as the sons of the lords of Beaugency and their peers (as well as for the canons themselves to study). Gregory the Great's *Moralia* gave guidance for the soul, something of interest to both monk and future lord alike. Peter of Riga's *Aurora* presented the Bible in poetic form, which made it a hugely popular text during the Middle Ages with over 450 copies surviving today.[9] Such a text would have had clear appeal to a secular audience and could be used to teach young men about the Bible. The "Small Summary on Rhetoric" might also have been a useful text for training boys who would become lords the arts of communication and argument, as lords held courts and had to evaluate legal pleadings.[10] Lord Ralph I's correspondence with the bishop of Chartres and the abbot of Vendôme indicates a level of education. Moreover, the preambles to charters demonstrate the laity's familiarity with Scripture. Lord Lancelin II quoted the psalms and the writings of St. Paul when he donated St. Sepulcher to the monks of Vendôme (see Lancelin's donation of St. Sepulcher later on pages 207–209). These noblemen likely received all or part of their education from the neighboring canons.

The inclusion of the foundational works of medieval theology mirrors the canons' dedication to the spirit, prayer and reflection. The collection of sermons, however, signals their concern and vocation in preaching the word of God – both within the abbey and on those occasions when the laity would be in attendance. The "sermons appropriate for certain times of the year, like Lent," reflects both the seasons of the ecclesiastical year and the canon-preachers' concern that their sermons relay the appropriate message. The "Book of Medicine" and Marbode of Rennes' treatise on the medicinal use of stones is also indicative of the health care monks provided to their own, but also their outreach to the secular community. The books from the "little cupboard" are in keeping with the vocation and mission of a community of medieval canons.

The library at Notre Dame de Beaugency, I would posit, reveals an orthodox and traditional approach to Christianity. Yet there were others in medieval Europe who held different interpretations of Christianity and were often condemned as heretics for these beliefs. It is possible that a resident of Beaugency may have encountered a heretic, given there was an outbreak of **heresy** in Orléans in the 1020s and the twelfth-century heretic Henry of Lausanne preached at Le Mans around 1116, as well as traveling throughout France. But, as far as I know, there were no instances of heresy in Beaugency.

9 For information on this manuscript, as well as a clickable version of it, see https://library.osu.edu/innovation-projects/omeka/exhibits/show/the-king-james-bible/sections/item/7.

10 These texts would also have been consulted and studied by the canons themselves.

The eleventh-century incident of heresy in Orléans is particularly interesting because this group – unlike the later heretic Henry of Lausanne – ascribed to a series of beliefs that were not replicated anywhere else in Europe.[11] Also of interest is the role that the knight Aréfast played in detecting this heresy and bringing the heretics to justice. The account of this outbreak of heresy was written by Paul, a monk of St. Père of Chartres, who was well placed to know what had happened since Aréfast later became a monk at the same house. This incident of heresy is important in the larger scope of Christian history because it was the first time anyone was burned for heresy in Western Europe.

Paul of St. Père related that Aréfast's manservant returned home after spending some time with the canons in Orléans. He regaled his master with their teachings and Aréfast immediately became suspicious that they were practicing heresy. He swiftly contacted his lord, the duke of Normandy, and asked him to tell the king about the nest of vipers in Orléans. Aréfast also requested the king give him the aid he would need to root out this heresy. The king, "thunderstruck by the news," agreed to provide Aréfast with whatever assistance was required. Aréfast then traveled to Orléans, where he ingratiated himself with the said canons. They revealed that they did not think Christ was born of Mary and denied the resurrection. Key to their celebrations was the "heavenly meal" that the group regularly shared. As described to Aréfast, it consisted of some sort of sexual orgy where women were "put to ill use. Without regard to sin, whether it were a mother, or a sister, or a nun, they regarded that intercourse as a holy and religious work."[12] Children born of these unions were burned, their ashes collected and revered by the community and given as a sacrament. Aréfast arranged for the king and queen to come to Orléans, along with a group of bishops. After he reported his findings, a council was called for the next day and the canons were interrogated by the assembled body. Perhaps not surprisingly, the canons were not eager to share the secrets of their community and Aréfast played the role of getting them to confess all. They were condemned for their beliefs and summarily burned. Intriguingly, one of the canons had been the confessor of Queen Constance, who poked out his eye as he was being led from the council to outside the city walls where he was burned.

The contemporary evidence for the Orléans heretics is somewhat problematic, but as R.I. Moore suggests the account of Paul of Chartres is the "least inaccurate." Part of the problem is that we do not have what the "heretics"

11 Although another account of events by Ademar of Chabannes said they were Manicheans, a dualist heresy that had been around for centuries.

12 This information comes from Paul of St. Père of Chartres' account of the Synod at Orléans. For a translation of this source, see R.I. Moore, "The Synod of Orléans, 1022," in *The Birth of Popular Heresy*, Documents of Medieval History I (New York: St. Martin's Press, 1975) pp. 10–15, esp. p. 13.

themselves thought. Instead, we have to rely on the accounts of those who accused them of heresy and who had a vested interest in sensationalizing events or demonizing those who did not conform. Moreover, many accounts of heresy share the elements of sexual orgy and sacrificed infants – to the point that they become "tropes" or a common theme that runs through heresy accounts rather than an accurate description of what happened. Many of those writing about heresy were familiar with other accounts of heretics and may have borrowed elements for their own rendering of the heterodoxy. But in spite of these limitations, I believe that Paul of Chartres' account can be useful to understanding medieval belief as it holds interesting insights into aristocratic piety.

The hero of this account is Aréfast, a knight who was well-versed enough in the Christian doctrine to be able to detect heresy. He was also able to learn the teachings of the heretics, who "taught him by citing texts from the Holy Scriptures, and by employing certain figures of speech," a clue as to how medieval elites were educated. Indeed, according to the account he was a "perfect pupil."[13] Aréfast was also able to convince his lord, the king, the queen and the bishops of the realm that this was a serious case of heresy. Moreover, they trusted him to act as a spy to find out about the community and their teachings. All of this evidence leads me to conclude that nobles had a considerable grasp of the ideals and theology central to Christianity, but also a dedication to the faith. Aréfast was both appalled and threatened by these heretics and took action to wipe them out. His actions would have resonance with the lords of Beaugency, who undoubtedly heard of the incident and were faithful supporters of St. Croix of Orléans hence concerned about the presence of such deviants in their community. Paul of Chartres' retelling of these events shows that aristocrats were both dedicated defenders of the church and that they understood the nuances of their faith. This is reinforced by examples of the nobility including references to holy writings in their charters. The incident also indicates that the Beaugencys were certainly aware of heresy and that they – like Aréfast – needed to take action to be sure it did not spread. Indeed, it is possible that Aréfast was given the role as hero of the piece to encourage aristocrats in their faith and in rooting out heresy.

At the same time that another "heretic" called Henry of Lausanne began preaching heresy in northern France around 1116, profound economic changes were taking place that dramatically affected those living in medieval Europe. In the early decades of the twelfth century, the medieval economy was transitioning from a gift economy to one based on commerce and profit. While the economic change itself was significant, the impact of this transformation on religion was also revolutionary.

13 "The Synod of Orléans" in Moore, *Popular Heresy*, p. 11.

Religion and socio-economic change

The economy of early medieval Europe was based on subsistence. People grew enough to support their community, with perhaps a little left over that could be used in local trade. Importantly, the ethos undergirding the economy was one of survival, not profit. Gifts were a prominent feature of this economy and were used to create alliances, reflect social status and make statements about power and piety; but they were made not because someone expected a profit from the gift. Certainly, a donor hoped that making a gift to a monastery might improve her chances of getting into heaven. Similarly, a lord who granted a gift to a subordinate hoped it would ensure loyalty. But the fundamental principal was not to make a financial profit from what they gave; rather, it was to build a relationship. Starting in the eleventh century, this underlying premise began to change due to the fact that more goods were being produced, which meant a surplus was available to trade and perhaps make a profit. Improvements in farming technologies at the same time meant there was more to eat and the population grew. With three times as many people living in Europe in 1300 as in 1000, not as many people were required to till the land, allowing some to seek out opportunities in trade and move to a town. Towns and villages that had once held seasonal fairs – like Beaugency - became places of permanent economic exchange. Trade itself also metamorphosed from local or regional trade to international trade. Important factors in this transformation were the more common use of coins, a desire to make a profit and investors who had both the money and desire to do so. Italy was the seedbed of this change due to the fact that urban centers which had access to both goods and cash from the Mediterranean had remained strong even after the fall of the Roman Empire.

By the twelfth century, we can see evidence that those living in Beaugency had adopted similar notions and practices. The description of the markets held in Beaugency in the twelfth century demonstrates that a variety of goods was available (see Document 18, page 236). Some were probably seasonal and locally produced, but others clearly came from outside the region and were luxury items – like cloth and metal work. Moreover, there were “foreign” merchants among the market stalls of Beaugency. Coins were also in circulation in and around Beaugency, as evident in the payment of rents, dues and tolls in cash (see Documents 18 and 19, pages 236–245). Indeed, the lords of Beaugency even struck their own coinage. The population increased as merchants and trades people moved into Beaugency itself. The walls of Beaugency had to be rebuilt in the twelfth century to accommodate this expanding population (see Map 1).

Scholars have argued that these socio-economic changes had profound consequences for religion and the church, and I would agree with their interpretation.[14] An economy centered on profit proved something of a

14 See the suggested reading section at the end of this chapter.

challenge to the medieval clergy. Initially, the church responded with hostility to those involved in the profit economy based on their stance against **usury**, or making a profit from lending money, which was seen as un-Christian and taking advantage of people in difficult circumstances. Money, for many clergy, was viewed as a polluting and corrupting force. It could be used to purchase church offices; it engendered greed and distracted monks and priests from their spiritual calling. In response to the newly formed commercial society, new forms of Christian piety developed. To avoid these dangerous influences, Lester Little has argued, some escaped to the wilderness to flee secular corruption that the commercial economy represented and have a more direct connection with God.

Robert of Arbissel was one such cleric. Well educated and prominent, he was even asked by Pope Urban II to preach a sermon advocating for crusade in 1096. Robert was a proponent of monastic reform who traveled about western France preaching and living as a hermit. His piety and dedication attracted many to his circle. By 1101, Robert had established a community of religious women, which would eventually develop into the abbey of Fontevraud.[15] Robert's deliberate rejection of wealth, hence the profit economy, and his embracing of apostolic poverty is apparent in one of his contemporary's account of him:

> They say you go into the crowd, having discarded your canonical dress, skin covered by a hairshirt and a worn-out cowl full of holes, your legs half-naked, your beard long and your hair trimmed at the brow, barefoot, offering a strange spectacle to all who look on such that you lack only a club to complete the outfit of a lunatic.[16]

Nor was Robert the only clergy member driven to the hermetical life. Bernard of Tiron, his friend and religious compatriot, also established a religious community deep in the heart of the Perche, a region that was densely forested, hilly and sparsely settled. There he founded a small community, which eventually grew into the abbey of Tiron – through support of some of the most powerful aristocratic houses in western France. Other, less famous clergy, also took measures to live apart from the world of money and trade. Abbot Geoffrey of Vendôme (who we will meet in the next chapter) wrote to the hermit Hervé advising him about what criteria to use in selecting monks to join his hermitage. While Bernard of Tiron and Robert of Arbrissel may have been two of the best-known hermits, there were clearly others who were propelled by the same desire to set up new communities of religious life that

15 Lord Simon I made a gift to Fontevraud in alms for his wife, Adenorde. See Document 19, page 239 in this book.

16 Marbode of Rennes, "Letter to Robert of Arbrissel" in *Robert of Arbrissel: A Medieval Religious Life*, ed. and trans. Bruce L. Venarde (Washington D.C.: The Catholic University Press of America, 2003) pp. 96–97.

embraced apostolic poverty and eschewed the preoccupations – and dangers – of the commercial economy.

Several new forms of monasticism developed during the twelfth century that emphasized poverty. The Premonstratensians, for example, did not accept gifts from the secular nobility to avoid accumulating wealth or any possible influence from the secular world. The new form of monasticism that became the most popular was that of the Cistercians. Founded in the late eleventh century at Cîteaux, they rose to prominence under the leadership of St. Bernard of Clairvaux in the twelfth. These monks insisted on a strict adherence to the Benedictine rule and established houses out in the more marginal and unsettled areas of France – such as marsh lands and rugged hill country – to avoid corruption and focus on their piety. In addition to founding new orders, older, traditional communities also underwent a period of renewal. At Beaugency, the monks of Notre Dame were reformed through the combined efforts of Bishop Ivo of Chartres, Countess Adele of Chartres and Lord Ralph I of Beaugency. The monks, who were seen as lax in their religious observance, were replaced with a community of Augustinian Canons, who were placed under the leadership of a new abbot, a dedicated reformer himself and friend of Bishop Ivo.[17] However, while the response to the profit economy caused new and reinvigorated forms of monasticism to emerge, other religious expressions that the church found outside of the norm also developed. While most of these heretical movements were confined to the urban centers, from about 1116 to 1140, the heretic Henry of Lausanne (or Henry the Monk) attacked the clergy for being too wealthy and turned the people against them.

Henry spent time in Le Mans, located in the heart of Maine where the Beaugency family first emerged and still had relatives. A contemporary's description of his appearance accentuates his extreme adherence to poverty, which I interpret as encapsulating some of the tensions concerning the profit economy and the wealth of the church:

> He was a wolf in sheep's clothing, with the haggard face and eyes of a shipwrecked sailor, his hair bound up, unshaven, tall and of athletic gait, walking barefoot even in the depths of winter, a young man always ready to preach possessed of a fearful voice. His clothes were shabby, and his life eccentric.[18]

Note the similarities between this account of a heretic and that of Robert of Arbrissel; an indication that medieval authors read other's accounts but also that the line between heretic and orthodox was rather thin. Unlike Robert, Henry attacked the clergy and preached openly against the church. He even

17 The monks who were "replaced" by the canons would find a place at another monastery. Alternatively, they could opt to join the new community of canons, if they were willing to give up their old ways and embrace the values of the new community.

18 "Henry of Lausanne: At Le Mans, c. 1116, " in Moore, *Popular Heresy*, p. 34.

went as far as to attack a delegation of monks who were sent to negotiate with him: "His heresy turned the people against the clergy with such fury that they refused to sell them anything or buy anything from them . . .".[19] This reveals that his religious ideas, indeed his person, were shaped by a hostile response to the profit economy and the church's place in it. Henry of Lausanne's heresy, as well as the impetus to create new forms of religious expression and reform old ones, was a byproduct of the changes wrought by the profit economy.

For the lords and ladies of Beaugency, this development of such a spectrum of ideas and ecclesiastical communities meant new and different opportunities to support religion and express their piety. As far as we can tell, these expressions centered firmly on orthodoxy and did not stray into heresy. In the eleventh century, the Beaugency family – like their peers – had supported Benedictine monasticism through their gifts. They sought association with these monks because they believed they had the ear of God, but also demonstrated their piety by going on crusade and pilgrimage. Lancelin II went on pilgrimage to Rome and was inspired by his journey to restore St. Sepulcher. Ralph I and one of his sons both forged careers in the Holy Land. Another of Ralph's sons, Simon I, traveled to the most popular of medieval pilgrimage sites, Santiago de Compostella in Northern Spain. Although they continued to be faithful sponsors of Benedictine monasteries like St. Trinité of Vendôme and Marmoutier, the Beaugencys were also generous benefactors of new ecclesiastical foundations and communities. For example, later lords of Beaugency and their kin made gifts to the Cistercians, but also the monks of Grandmonte, a new order of monks that was recognized for their austere life style.[20]

One of the more unique formulations of monasticism was the foundation of the fighting monks: The Templars. Initially created to help protect pilgrims on their way to the Holy Land, the Templars became an extremely popular order. Although they had to abide by the traditional vows of a monk – i.e. poverty, chastity and obedience – instead of praying in a church they were armed combatants. Founded in the 1120s, with the support of St. Bernard of Clairvaux, the Templars became one of the most popular – and wealthy – orders of the Central Middle Ages. The appeal of this order to men like the lords of Beaugency, men who were trained to fight, must have been enormous, as they could express their piety through what they were born and raised to do without contradicting the central precepts of Christianity. Moreover, when one became a Templar it was not necessarily for life. Many men joined only for a short period of time. So they might journey to the Holy Land where they would fight in God's service for several years, but then return to their home and pick up their old lives. While there is evidence that some of the

19 "Henry of Lausanne: At Le Mans, c. 1116," in Moore, *Popular Heresy*, p. 35.

20 AD Loiret H 10, folio XXVII verso; *NDB* no. 91, pp. 107–108; *ChV*, no. 170, pp. 205–206.

Figure 6.6 Templar commanderies, like this one in Arville, housed communities of Templar knights. Structures were built to house the Templars, but also to provide for their spiritual and practical needs. Spaces at the Arville commandery include dormitories, kitchens, a church, but also tithe barns and a forge. Author photo.

later lords of Beaugency supported the Templars, it does not appear that any of them became Templars themselves. One of their very distant cousins, Robert II the Burgundian, however, did become the Master of the Temple, the highest office in the Templar order. The lords and ladies of Beaugency also supported some of the Templar commanderies in the region of the Loire such as the one at Arville[21] (see Figure 6.6). In addition to knowing friends, family and peers who joined the Templars, those residing at Beaugency – humble and lordly – may have encountered these knights at the market, in court or even in church.

While some scholars have seen the twelfth and thirteenth centuries as being defined by increased intolerance and persecution, this view has begun to be modified. Instead of the birth of a persecuting society, as argued by the eminent scholar R.I. Moore, others, notably Adam J. Davis, have argued for

21 Although there is a twelfth-century house called "the house of the Templars" in Beaugency, regrettably there is no evidence that a Templar ever lived there. Moreover, it appears that the residence got this name long after the Middle Ages.

the beginning of a compassionate society.[22] This compassion is evident in the new foundations established primarily in the burgeoning new cities that were aimed at caring for the unfortunate. For example, almshouses were created to provide charity for those who were too poor to support themselves. Concern for the sickly is also apparent in the foundation of civic hospitals and leprosaria. However, this compassion only extended so far, as the Jews living in France experienced increased – and more violent – persecution. The Beaugency family was eyewitnesses to these very changes and practiced both compassion and intolerance. To give voice to how these larger economic, social and religious transformations affected the lives of individuals, let us turn to the last will and testament of Lord Simon I (c. 1105–1154).

Witness to change: The will of Lord Simon I

Some time between 1146 and 1153, Lord Simon I of Beaugency sat down to record how he wanted his property to be distributed at his death (see Map 3). He did so in the presence of the bishop of Orléans and the chapter of St. Croix of Orléans. Although this will is concerned with the distribution of worldly goods, I will argue that it can be used to gain insight into aristocratic piety and how it was changing in the twelfth century. This is an unusually rich, detailed and long document that demonstrates the wealth of the lords, but also provides glimpses into how the lives of medieval elites were shaped by the broader economic and religious changes taking place in the twelfth century (see Document 19, page 239).

This lord of Beaugency made bequests to a total of fourteen different religious houses. Many of Simon's endowments had much in common with what earlier lords of Beaugency had done. The first clause of this document, for example, reflects a traditional pious benefaction made for the salvation of Simon's children, father, mother, wife and ancestors in general to the venerable house of St. Croix, which had been established in Carolingian times:

> So that my sins obtain absolution from the will of God, and for Ralph, my father, and Mathilda, my mother, and domine Adenorde [my wife] and of my heir who will have conceded this gift about to be confirmed, and for all the souls of ancestors . . .[23]

22 R.I. Moore, *The Formation of a Persecuting Society: Authority and Deviance in Western Europe*, 2nd edition (Oxford: Wiley Blackwell, 2007); Adam J. Davis, "The Social and Religious Meanings of Charity in Medieval Europe," *History Compass* 12 (2014): 935–950; "Hospitals, Charity, and the Culture of Compassion in the Twelfth and Thirteenth Centuries," in Sharon Farmer, ed., *Handling Poverties: Complexities, Contradictions, Transformations, c. 1100–1500* (Turnhout: Brepols, 2016), pp. 23–45.

23 *Cartulaire de Sainte-Croix d'Orléans*, ed. Joseph Thillier and Eugène Jarry (Paris: A. Picard et fils, 1906), no. 5, pp. 7–15. Hereafter, *SCO*.

He specified a gift of land so that the anniversaries of the deaths of his father, wife and child would be remembered in the prayers of the monks annually on the day of their demise. Their names, he requested, should also be written into the martyrology of the monks. Simon's concern for the remission of the souls of these relatives – and himself – is apparent in the provisions made for the observance of the anniversary of their deaths at ten different ecclesiastical foundations: St. Croix of Orléans, the almshouse of St. Croix, St. Mesmin of Micy, the monastery of Cornilly, St. Sepulcher at Beaugency, the almshouse (or Hôtel Dieu) and the leper house at Beaugency, the hospital of Mary Magdalene at Orléans and the monks of Cîteaux, St. Evurte and Marmoutier. These houses range from the traditional to new monastic foundations like the Cistercians, as well as foundations that cared for the poor and unfortunate.[24] The diversity of the houses that Simon chose to patronize demonstrates the breadth of options open to benefactors as a result of the religious and economic transformations that occurred in the first half of the twelfth century.

Simon's will also suggests that he, like many in medieval Europe, was searching for a new kind of religious expression or experience. I interpret his patronage of almshouses, hospitals and leprosaria as a reflection of concern and compassion for those less fortunate – something not always apparent in earlier benefactions. Simon also demonstrated an interest in a more personalized form of piety. In his will, he made a bequest to support the chaplain responsible for holding religious services in the private chapel in the castle. Architectural and archeological evidence from the castle of Beaugency suggest that a grander private chapel was built in the thirteenth century. Written records confirm that Simon's nephew, Lord John I (d. 1218), donated food, wine and clothing to support a canon from the neighboring church of Notre Dame to lead the private services in this chapel.[25] Significantly, John also indicated that he and his family would be buried in the chapel and records show that tombs of the family of Beaugency rested in this chapel until they were destroyed in the seventeenth century.

What might the inside of Lord John's chapel have looked like? There would have been an altar, likely with a silver lamp on it as John had specified that one be lit in perpetuity for his wife Elizabeth, but also stone tombs containing the remains of the Beaugency family. There would be decorative items on the walls – perhaps tapestries illustrating the life of a saint – and bejeweled vessels of gold that were used in services. Ralph I might even have brought a relic or two home from the First Crusade. Or his father Lancelin or son Simon may have gotten a relic on their respective pilgrimages to Rome and Santiago de Compostella. It is also possible that Simon or John may have

24 Simon made gifts to three leper houses at Beaugency, Orléans and Feritas, as well as to three almshouses or Hôtel Dieux at Beaugency, Blois and Orléans.

25 AD Loiret H 10, folio XXX; *NDB*, no. 102, pp. 117–119.

owned a book of hours or a psalter that could have been used to guide the various church offices as literacy rates increased among the aristocracy during the course of the twelfth century. Both of Simon's parents were literate as evidenced by the letters written to and by them (see Documents 2 and 4, pages 223 and 225). As Martin Aurell has suggested, these books could also have been used by the Beaugency women to teach their children the alphabet and numerical literacy. Simon and his wife likely read some Latin, along with vernacular languages. It was also during Simon's lifetime that romances in French became a popular and prominent feature of court life. Simon himself may have been educated at the monastery next door to the castle. His will certainly demonstrates the importance he – and his peers – placed on the written word. Indeed, Simon or John may have been able to read the Scripture for himself and follow along with the offices conducted by his chaplain. In this way, these lords heralded the beginning of a new, more personalized spirituality for the medieval aristocracy.

In addition to changes in piety, the arrangements Simon made concerning his property reflect the impact of the commercial revolution. Like his ancestors, Simon donated his property to the church. In contrast to previous lords, however, by far the lion's share of Simon's benefactions consisted not of real estate, but money. For example, the rent he collected annually on the feast of St. Firmin was given to the leper house at Beaugency so they would commemorate the anniversary of his wife's death. Similarly Simon gave money from rent to several other religious communities for commemoration for himself and other family members. As the economy shifted to one based on the exchange of coin, so the relationship between lords and their serfs changed. Whereas in the eleventh or tenth century, a serf – or even a free peasant – might fulfill his or her obligation to a lord through labor, by the twelfth century these labor services were being converted into payments in coin. Simon used these collected revenues and rents from his demesne to fund his pious benefactions to a wide range of religious foundations. Simon was also the first lord of Beaugency to fund his patronage through the tolls he collected from ships on the Loire, which he gave to the canons of Notre Dame de Beaugency. Simon's interest in tolls and shipping going on literally in his backyard was spurred by the new, thriving market economy. Lords came to realize that to participate in this moneyed economy that they would need to commute their agricultural resources into coin. Hence, they were willing to accept rents or revenue instead of labor from their serfs and peasants. They also developed their landed holdings so that they could be used to generate revenue by building mills – wind and water – bridges and sluices. (Remember that there were six water mills in Beaugency alone – see Map 1.) Relationships between lords and vassals also transformed. Instead of granting warriors or vassals with land, lords gave money fiefs or a payment in return for military service. On the other side of the coin, a vassal might choose to make a payment instead of fighting for a lord. The ties of feudal tenure, thus, were also changed by the new economic realities of the twelfth century.

Simon's cash bequests reveal interesting insights into his piety, but also I would argue, the church's interaction with the new profit economy. Simon would often make a modest gift of a couple of shillings or a pound, but then he would specify how the money was to be used. When he gave 5 shillings to the almshouse in Beaugency he indicated that part of the money was to go to provide a meal of fish to those monks tending the poor on the day of the anniversary of his wife's death. The rest was to be put toward feeding a pauper (a poor person) on the same day. Simon seems to have been particularly interested in insuring that the humble servants of God who were looking after the poor and the sick had meat to eat. He also demonstrated concern for the poor by providing them with food – a concern that led him to make the same gift to St. Mesmin of Micy. Additionally, he provided clothing to the poor, as evident in his gift of a tunic to a leper living in the leprosarium in Beaugency. While medieval people had always given alms, the twelfth century saw a new interest in creating and supporting religious communities like almshouses, hospitals and leprosaria that could take care of the sick and unfortunate who were part of the new urban landscape. But donations of money could cause concern on the part of the ecclesiastical recipients as many viewed money as a sign of corruption or pollution. Making a donation with a specified use – to provide nourishment to the servants of God, for example – I believe allowed donors and recipients to sidestep any concern an ecclesiastical community might have about receiving a donation in coin. Pious donations that helped to support monks or the poor was one way the aristocracy could put their revenues to use that was acceptable to the clergy.

Simon's will records his direct involvement with the burgeoning commercial economy, for the rent that he gave to St. Mesmin to commemorate Adenorde came from a stall in the market at Beaugency. He also gave market rights during the fair of St. Biénheure at Vendôme to Notre Dame de Beaugency. The control of markets was a lucrative source of income for lords and provided them with not insignificant revenues. Simon also appears to have borrowed money and been charged interest on it (in spite of church prohibitions on usury). For example, a certain Peter Haimar gave Simon 71 pounds and 6 shillings with the agreement that Simon would pay back 100 shillings or 5 pounds within three months. Peter charged Simon an interest rate of 7 percent of the original loan for the use of this cash. The church was concerned that neighbors would take advantage of each other's misfortune and, much like a modern day loan shark, might charge excessive amounts of interest. Seven percent would perhaps not have been too over the top (it would be about twice the current thirty-year mortgage rate in the United States but considerably less than what credit card companies charge), but still not an insignificant payment. Simon was also in debt to others. In his will he indicated that 10 pounds be paid to the Jews of Melun (a town about 80 miles to the north) and 7 pounds and 2 shillings to Samuel the Jew.

The Beaugencys and the Jews

The profit economy also shaped the experiences of the small community of Jews living in Beaugency and with whom the Beaugencys interacted. Indeed, a renowned Jewish scholar of the twelfth century, Eliezer of Beaugency, was likely born and raised there. While details of Eliezer's personal life remain unknown, he was a prominent Jewish Biblical scholar and studied at the School of Rashi (Rabbi Solomon ben Isaac) in Northern France under the famous theologian, and Rashi's grandson, Rashbam (Rabbi Samuel ben Meir).[26] Given the trade that went up and down the Loire River, Beaugency may well have attracted Jewish merchants – some perhaps from the sizeable Jewish community at Orléans just a few miles to the north.

For the tenth, eleventh and the first half of the twelfth century, Jews in Northern France co-existed with their Christian neighbors peacefully. They shared in the economic prosperity, the political stability and intellectual rebirth that characterized France up through the first fifty-years of the twelfth century. Indeed, Robert A. Harris and other scholars argue that Christian and Jewish theologians were influenced by each other's writings as part of the twelfth-century Renaissance. Established Jewish communities grew, like the ones in Paris and Troyes, but new communities emerged in smaller towns, like Blois and Beaugency. Unlike the Rhineland in Germany, Jews in France did not experience the anti-Semitic violence that was the byproduct of the First Crusade in 1096. Robert Chazan, a preeminent scholar of medieval Jewish history, argues that there was a correlation between Jewish prosperity and peace with what he calls "immature" states. In other words, when medieval France was under the rule of local lords, like those at Beaugency, Jews were by and large left in peace.[27] But when monarchs successfully centralized and consolidated their power, the Jews tended to suffer. As the French monarchy strengthened under Philip II Augustus, Louis IX and Philip IV the Fair, kings began to see the Jews as a source for revenue and placed taxes on them. They would also expel Jews from certain parts of their realm, co-opt their wealth into royal coffers and resettle them elsewhere.

The profit economy held profound consequences for Jewish life. As their Christian neighbors needed cash to participate in this commercial economy, they often turned to Jews for loans. Because the Jews were already seen by

26 Eliezer of Beaugency was an exegete, meaning he wrote commentaries on books of the Bible, specifically commentaries on the books of Jonah, Amos, Isiah, Ezekiel and the Twelve Prophets. See Robert A. Harris, "Medieval Jewish Biblical Exegesis," in *A History of Biblical Interpretation, Volume 2: Medieval through the Reformation Periods*, Alan J. Hauser and Duane F. Watson, eds. (Grand Rapids, MI: Eerdmans, 2009); pp. 144–154; "Contextual Reading: Rabbi Eliezer of Beaugency's Commentary on Jonah," in *Bringing the Hidden to Light: The Process of Interpretation-Studies in Honor of Stephen A. Geller*, Kathryn F. Kravits and Diane M. Sharon, eds. (Winona Lake: Jewish Theological Seminary in collaboration with Eisenbrauns, 2007), pp. 79–101.

27 Robert Chazan, *Medieval Jewry in Northern France* (Baltimore: Johns Hopkins Press, 1973), pp. 14–22.

medieval Christians as damned, there were no theological or moral barriers to their involvement in commerce or lending of coin. Tensions and hostility toward the Jews increased as Christians borrowed money and began competing in the market economy. Horrific violence was done to Jewish communities. Sadly, France was not immune to these outbreaks of violence, which became more and more associated with accusations of ritualized murder of Christian children or what came to be called Blood Libel. In the year 1171, the neighboring town of Blois – a mere 19 miles from Beaugency – was the site of just such a tragedy.

The story has been reconstructed from letters from various Jewish communities and individuals who were drawn into the case.[28] One evening the manservant of a citizen of Blois was down by the river where he encountered a Jew, Isaac ben Elazar. Isaac was on his way back from a business transaction where he had purchased a bundle of untanned hides (these would have been bloody, raw animal skins). The serving-man mistook one of these hides, which had slipped loose, as a body of a Christian child, which he though Isaac had thrown into the river. He subsequently ran back to his master and raised the hue and cry. The count of Chartres, Thibaut V, acted promptly and put the Jewish community of Blois, which consisted of around forty adults and their children, in prison. On May 26, 1171, thirty-two Jews were burned alive even though no evidence of a crime was established or a body discovered. The rest, mostly children, were imprisoned or forcibly converted. The incident of Blois was unusual because no body of a murdered child was ever found and it was the first time such violence was displayed toward resident Jews.[29] News of the tragedy first traveled to the Jewish community of Orléans, likely by way of Christian traders who witnessed or heard of the event. The shock was profound. What must the few Jews living in Beaugency have felt? Did they lock themselves in their homes or did they flee to the larger community just up the river in Orléans? The Jews of the region did act quickly to try to pay a ransom for their imprisoned brethren, but to no avail. A certain Baruch ben David Ha-Cohen, a Jew from the county of Blois (as opposed to the town), had tried to intervene for his fellow Jews but was not successful. He was able, however, to broker a "ransom" of 1000 pounds for the safety of the rest of the Jews living under Count Thibaut V's jurisdiction. Not satisfied with this assurance, the Rabbis of the towns of Northern France were terrified that more violence might follow and appealed directly to King Louis VII (coincidentally Count Thibaut V's brother-in-law), who assured them such violence would not happen again. A similar

28 Susan Einbinder provides a translation of the Jewish Chronicle recording these events and other supporting documents in *Medieval Hagiography: An Anthology*, Thomas Head, ed. (New York and London: Routledge, 2000) pp. 535–560.

29 For analysis of this event, see Robert Chazan, "The Blois Incident of 1171: A Study in Jewish Intercommunal Organization," *Proceedings of the American Academy for Jewish Research* 36 (1968): 13–31.

appeal went to the count of Champagne, in whose territories several large Jewish communities lay, and he similarly provided reassurance that there would be no violence (he too was related to Count Thibaut; he was his brother). In addition to these reassurances, the Rabbis succeeded in restoring the children who had been imprisoned and forced to become Christian to the bosom of their community.

This ghastly event understandably had a profound impact on the Jews of Northern Europe and Rabbeinu Tam, a prominent local rabbi, commemorated the events by declaring May 26 a fast day. Sadly, it also marked the beginning of an increase in persecution and mistreatment of the Jews. The days of co-existence and prosperity of the early twelfth century were never to be replicated. Although, for the story of the murdered child to have taken hold so quickly in the region, there must have been some who already viewed the Jews with fear, distrust and hatred. Significantly, Susan Einbinder has argued that enmity toward a female Jewish moneylender who enjoyed the protection of Count Thibaut V of Chartres may have motivated the resident of Blois to bring this accusation against his Jewish neighbors.[30] Tensions over credit and competition created by the evolving economy, hence, likely played a role in the tragedy in Blois. Jews found themselves the target of suspicion, violence and aversion. Kings, while taking the Jews under their "protection," continued to exploit them and use Jewish money and property to bolster their coffers. In his attempt to show his authority over the countess of Champagne, King Philip II Augustus would himself burn eighty Jews in the Champenois town of Bray in 1192.[31] His grandson, Louis IX, would force Jews to wear a badge and use these badges as a source of revenue. He would also prohibit the use of the Talmud and Jews' participation in money-lending – thus striking simultaneously at the communal and economic life of the Jews. Philip IV the Fair (which refers to his good looks and not his sense of justice), forbade the inquisition to try Jews and stated only royal officials had jurisdiction over them. Yet this did not result in an improvement in their condition. By 1306 hostility toward the Jews was so fierce that Philip IV expelled them from France, lining his pockets with the proceeds from the property they were forced to leave behind.

How would the lords and ladies of Beaugency have responded to the plight of the Jews? It is difficult to know, but as products of their time they probably viewed the Jews with some hostility. We know Lord Simon was indebted to them but may have preferred not to have to repay what he owed. His will confirms that he interacted with Jews and that there was a small Jewish presence in Beaugency – meager though it may have been. The Beaugencys would have certainly have known about the violence in Blois. It is possible

30 Susan Einbinder, "Pucellina of Blois: Romantic Myths and Narrative Conventions," *Jewish History* 12 (1998): 29–46.

31 Robert Chazan, "The Bray Incident," *Proceedings of the American Academy for Jewish Research* 37 (1969): 1–18.

that preaching aimed at rallying enthusiasm for a new crusade in the early 1170s may have been the spark that ignited the fires of persecution in Blois. The tinder was certainly already present.

Ironically, the forces that shaped the lives of the Jews also shaped the trajectory of life for the lords of Beaugency. The commercial economy changed the lords of Beaugency from landed warriors to land lords who collected rents and revenue. Certainly, they would continue to fight to protect what was theirs, but this often took place at court rather than on the battle field. As royal consolidation and ascent in power spelled doom for the Jews, so too did it bring an end to the autonomous lords of Beaugency. By the early fourteenth century, the Jews were gone from Northern France and the Beaugency lordship ceased to exist as an independent lordship as it became absorbed into the royal domains.

Conclusion

Religion was the warp and weft of medieval society. It was woven so inexorably into daily life that it is virtually impossible to extract it from the other threads that made up the tapestry of medieval existence – as is evident in the interplay between economic change and religious transformations. As society changed, so too did religion and piety. During the course of the thirteenth century, the church would continue to respond to the criticisms of wealth and power. This would result in the creation of a third order of religious, the mendicant orders of the Franciscans and Dominicans. These men eschewed all wealth, owned only the robe on their back and begged for their dinner. Preaching was central to their mission and they took to the roads of Europe to preach the orthodox word to the residents of the bustling city were heresy often took root. Although there is no evidence that a mendicant ever set sandal in Beaugency, they likely did and their message would not have been lost on its residents for the lords and ladies of Beaugency had long supported many different types of religious foundations and individuals.

Monks, canons, nuns and priests all played important roles in the lives of the Beaugency family. But what was life like behind the monastery or convent walls? Let us now turn our attention to how those who dedicated their lives to God, "those who prayed," experienced life and expressed their piety.

Suggested reading

Malcolm Barber, *The New Knighthood: A History of the Order of the Temple.* Cambridge: Cambridge University Press, reprint 2012.

Constance H. Berman, *The Cistercian Evolution: The Invention of a Religious Order in Twelfth-Century Europe.* Philadelphia: University of Pennsylvania Press, 2010.

Robert Chazan, *The Jews of Medieval Western Christendom, 1000–1500,* Cambridge: Cambridge University Press, 2007; and *Reassessing Jewish Life in Medieval Europe,* Cambridge: Cambridge University Press, 2010.

William Chester Jordan, *The French Monarchy and the Jews: From Philip Augustus to the Last Capetians.* Philadelphia: University of Pennsylvania Press, 1989.

Lester K. Little, *Religious Poverty and the Profit Economy in the Medieval West.* Ithaca and London: Cornell University Press, 1983.

Robert S. Lopez, *The Commercial Revolution of the Middle Ages, 950–1350.* Cambridge: Cambridge University Press, 1976.

Joseph H. Lynch and Philip C. Adamo, *The Medieval Church: A Brief History*. London: Routledge, second edition, 2013.

Megan McLaughlin, *Consorting with Saints: Prayers for the Dead in Early Medieval France.* Ithaca and London: Cornell University Press, 1994.

Robert I. Moore, *The Formation of a Persecuting Society: Authority and Deviance in Western Europe, 950–1250.* Oxford: Wiley-Blackwell, second edition, 2007.

Colin Morris, *The Sepulchre of Christ and the Medieval West: From Beginning to 1600.* Oxford: Oxford University Press, 2008.

David Nicholas, *The Domestic Life of a Medieval City: Women, Children and Family in Fourteenth-Century Ghent.* Lincoln: University of Nebraska Press, 1985.

David Nirenberg, *Communities of Violence: The Persecution of Minorities in the Middle Ages.* Princeton: Princeton University Press, second edition 2015.

Thomas F.X. Noble and John van Engen, *European Transformations: The Long Twelfth Century.* South Bend: University of Notre Dame Press, 2012.

Richard W. Southern, *The Penguin History of the Church: Western Society and the Church in the Middle Ages*. London: Penguin: revised edition, 1990.

Jonathan Sumption, *Pilgrimage.* London: Faber and Faber, 2002.

Diana Webb, *Pilgrims and Pilgrimage in the Medieval West*. London: I.B. Tauris, 2001.

7 The Beaugencys, the abbess and the abbot

Some time between 1104 and 1105, Lord Ralph I of Beaugency received a letter from his kinsman, Abbot Geoffrey of Vendôme:[1]

> Geoffrey, servant of the monastery of Vendôme, to his very dear lord and intimate friend, Ralph, [hoping he may] cross through the world of temporal things in such a way as to obtain eternal blessings.
>
> We know that you love our monastery, built and consecrated in the honour and in the name of the Holy Trinity, with all of your heart. And we implore with all of our being [that] the blessed Trinity of the father, son and holy spirit, from the love for whom you act, so that the Trinity keeps your body and soul in its all-encompassing embrace in the present, and that in the future it will give you eternal life, and from the Trinity's heavenly piety and glorious intercession of Blessed Virgin Mary, that the Trinity absolves your father's soul, for whom we know you were very concerned, of all the bonds of his sins and his faults, and that the Trinity gives him [the ability] to see and behold in person his Lord God, who is the God of us all, He who is the remission of sins, the reward and the reparation of his servants.[2]

To secure a place in heaven and mitigate their sins, the Beaugencys and their peers turned to the monks and nuns of medieval Europe, who spent their lives dedicated to prayer and interceding on behalf of the faithful. Here Ralph was clearly concerned about the state of his and his father's eternal soul, and Abbot Geoffrey offered reassurance. The Beaugencys created ties through patronage to religious houses, which they came "to love," but also by providing protection and support. Falling out with the monks or nuns could have critical consequences as we can see in another letter where Abbot Geoffrey provided advice to a neighbor of the Beaugencys about the state of his soul:

1 Abbot Geoffrey of Vendôme was distantly related to the Beaugency family through their Maine cousins, but also by marriage through the counts of Nevers.

2 Geoffrey de Vendôme, *Oeuvres*, ed. and trans. Geneviève Giordanengo (Turnhout: CNRS Editions, Brepols, 1996) letter 59, p. 105. Hereafter, GV.

Visit the companion website: www.routledge.com/cw/livingstone

> In the present life, you have for a long time acted to do harm, but you are hardly able to act well because you do not wish to. Yet you have done several good deeds, but in comparison with your evil deeds, they are small in number or hardly worth mentioning. This is why, as you nearly arrive at your last hour, that I counsel you in advice and I advise you in counsel to redeem yourself with all speed to, at the very least, end the evil actions which you have carried out for so long, so that at the same time your body dies, your soul does not also die. The rest of your life, which is short, you should be certain to spend it living for God, your creator and your saviour because until this moment you have lived entirely or nearly entirely for the secular world . . . If, contrary to fate, your sins prevent you [from doing this] it will not be pleasing to God, and know truly that your punishment will be without end.[3]

In marked contrast to Ralph I's father, Lancelin II of Beaugency, whose soul was in good standing and who was residing with Jesus, this noble had behaved badly and as he neared the end of his life he desperately tried to make restitution. Abbot Geoffrey advises that he quickly mend his ways, otherwise he would face eternal punishment.

Monks and nuns played a crucial role in interceding for medieval society and helping believers atone for their misdeeds. As evident in the documents quoted above, aristocrats like the Beaugencys sought the assistance of monks and nuns to help them attain salvation. Donations and interactions with these communities also provided the members of the aristocracy with a place to demonstrate or experience their piety. Some chose to dedicate their lives to the church; others cultivated their spirituality by interacting with these communities as lay brothers and sisters or as pious benefactors. Monasteries and nunneries could also fulfil more quotidian needs for the Beaugencys and their peers, such as health care or education. As these communities were so vital to the lives of the Beaugencys, this chapter will explore two religious houses within the Beaugency orbit and their relationships with secular society. Specifically it will focus on the monastery of St. Trinité of Vendôme and one of its abbots, Abbot Geoffrey (who was a distant relative of the Beaugencys), and the neighbouring convent of St. Avit of Châteaudun and its abbesses. "The Medieval Church" is often treated as monolithic, when in fact clerical experience and communities could be quite diverse and nuanced.

Abbot Geoffrey was an important cleric and a prolific writer. Luckily, his correspondence has survived the centuries and it is through his letters, supplemented with charters from his abbey, that we will enter the walls of the monastery of St. Trinité of Vendôme. St. Avit was the closest nunnery to Beaugency with a daughter house just a few miles away and its members came from the same local nobility as these lords and ladies. Unlike St. Trinité,

3 GV, letter 15, pp. 29–31.

the convent of St. Avit was much more modest in size and scope, an indication of this being that its cartulary contains 147 charters compared to St. Trinité's 549. Comparison of these two communities, the nuns of St. Avit and the monks of Vendôme, will allow us to see these differences, but also what medieval clergy had in common. Moreover, analysis of the lives of the monks and nuns of St. Avit and St. Trinité will provide an idea of what life would have been like for a member of the Beaugency family who entered the church.

The abbey of St. Avit of Châteaudun

Nunneries populated the medieval landscape and provided medieval noblewomen like the Beaugency women a place to dedicate their lives to God. Some, such as the abbey of Fontevraud, came to be as sizeable and influential as the prominent male monasteries like St. Trinité. Similar to male monasteries, nunneries faced threats to their holdings and the abbesses were just as fearless and capable as their male counterparts in defending their communities. For example, one abbess insisted that a recent corpse be dug up because her nuns had the right of burial and not the monks who had buried the body. Another group of nuns rioted when the local bishop attempted to take away their rights and curtail their autonomy.[4] In addition to Fontevraud and St. Trinité, there were smaller, more modest, religious communities. The abbey of St. Avit of Châteaudun was one such foundation.

Charles Cuissard, the nineteenth-century historian who gathered and published documents relevant to this convent, bemoaned:

> [Hence] after intending to publish the cartulary of St. Avit in its entirety, I quickly abandoned this project . . . as there is no importance to this cartulary . . . This summary [of the cartulary], in spite of its dryness, constitutes the history of the abbey of St. Avit, where not a single important event occurred.[5]

Historians of Cuissard's time focused on great events and great men and he is correct in that no important battle took place here; neither pope nor king visited or held a council. Yet the simplicity or "dryness" of these documents, I would argue, provides valuable insight into the lives of religious women of a regional convent.

Unfortunately Cuissard's dismissal of women's communities – and his decision not to publish the convent's cartulary – was characteristic of many

4 Penelope Johnson, *Equal in Monastic Profession* (Chicago: University of Chicago Press, 1991) pp. 86–89, 168–169.

5 Charles Cuissard, "Sommaire des chartes de l'abbaye de Saint-Avit," *Bulletin de la société dunoise*, 9 (1897/1900), p. 170. Hereafter, *SA*.

historians' view of women religious up until the twentieth century.[6] Religious women, with a few exceptions such as Hildegard of Bingen or Catherine of Siena, were seen as unimportant to both the major events of the Middle Ages and to medieval people themselves. Because they were women, this argument went, they were not deemed as "holy" or as effective in interceding with the divine as their male counterparts.[7] As a consequence, historians saw their lives and the documents recorded by their communities as insignificant. Early in the twentieth century, however, historians began to shift their interest to the lives of ordinary people and on the margins of society. But it was not until the 1970s, when feminist scholars began actively weaving the history of women into the narrative of medieval Europe that nuns like those at St. Avit became the focus of serious scholarly attention. Since then, literally dozens of women's religious communities have been recovered and detailed. Moreover, historians have pushed back forcefully against an interpretation of the irrelevance of nunneries and have demonstrated that nuns had considerable influence within both the church and medieval society. My interpretation of nuns of St. Avit is informed by this scholarship and I will argue that these "dry" documents show that this community touched the lives of its donors and neighbors, like the Beaugencys, in profound and important ways.[8]

Foundation and donors

A vassal of the Beaugency family, Lord Ganelon of Montigny, "restored" the abbey of St. Avit in 1045. There had been a community of monks living at St. Avit for some centuries, but the monastery had fallen on hard times and was nearly abandoned. Ganelon replaced the monks with nuns, endowed the abbey with considerable property and placed it under the protection of the bishop of Chartres. The Montigny family would continue to support St. Avit throughout the Middle Ages, for three centuries later a descendant of Lord Ganelon made a gift to the nuns (see Document 22, page 249). Ganelon was

6 Significantly, the cartulary of St. Avit has never been edited or published but every male house in the region, small and large, has had its acts edited and published. This dismissal or neglect of female houses is not unique to the region of the Loire. For example, while the charters of the Premonstratensian male houses have been collected, edited and published, those for the female houses have not.

7 Ironically, medieval male clergy, such as Peter Abelard, placed a great deal of value on the prayers and intercession of women religious.

8 While there is a handful of original medieval charters of St. Avit extant in the archives, much of what we know about this community comes from eighteenth-century copies of the charters or short descriptions of the charters –which are preserved in the Mediathéque municipal of Orléans. These manuscripts are preserved in MS 556 (old reference number 435 b) and 489 (old reference number 394). MS 489/394 consists of an 1862 copy of *Pièces concernant l'histoire ecclesiastique du diocese d'Orléans, Les Abbayes*, by Dom. Jean Verninac. The title page indicates he copied these from copies by Daniel Polluche, a local historian, whose copies of the charters are contained in MS 556/435 b Verinac and provide both transcriptions of the charters and analysis.

a generous patron indeed and provided the nuns with a rich endowment for their support. First, Ganelon set aside a chapel next to Châteaudun for the residence of the nuns. He also gave the adjoining parishes to the nuns, including the tithes collected and the burial rights. He then endowed the nuns with tithes and vineyards around the towns of Chartres and Blois, as well as from other places, rent generated from other properties and forest rights – specifically the pannaging of pigs in the forest and collecting firewood. Personnel to serve the nuns were also provided as Ganelon transferred three serfs and their children to the convent. Support for a priest was also given so that he would be available to hear the nuns' confession.[9] This myriad of property, dues and rights, was bestowed by Ganelon to ensure the community's survival.

The first abbess of St. Avit was a woman by the name of Adelaide. The necrology of the abbey records that "In the tenth calends of October (October 5 or 25), Adelaide the abbess, died, who was the first mother of this house." Who was this first "mother" of St. Avit? I believe she was the niece of Lord Ganelon of Montigny, the abbey's founder. While Ganelon himself was childless, his two nieces – Adelaide and Agnes – are identified in the charters as his heirs. Agnes went on to marry twice to local lords. "Adelaide the nun" appears in the foundation charter with her uncle. Given the common practice of aristocrats founding houses for their relatives, the first abbess of St. Avit was very likely Adelaide of Montigny, Ganelon's niece. Adelaide's experience was one that would have been shared by a Beaugency woman who joined the church. She too would have started out as a daughter of a noble house and appeared in family charters. As she matured, she gave up the world and became a nun. Although living in a convent, Adelaide's dedication to her family continued as she managed her family's foundation and prayed for their souls.

Unfortunately, the extant evidence makes it difficult to determine how long Adelaide remained abbess and who succeeded her. The next reference to another abbess of St. Avit occurs in 1118. While it was not unusual for young people to become heads of religious houses (Abbot Geoffrey, for example, was quite young when he became abbot), it seems improbable that there was only one abbess for a span of seventy-three years (1045–1118).

The next act pertaining to the abbey comes in 1092 when Agnes of Montfort-le-Gesnois made provisions for her two daughters to become nuns at St. Avit. Agnes lived some distance from Châteaudun, about 50 miles due east. The nuns' reputation for piety clearly had reached her for she made an extensive donation (see Document 20, page 246).[10] Her donation doubled

9 Mediathéque municipal of Orléans, MS 556/435 b, pp. 225–228.

10 Significantly, Agnes states that donated all of this property with the consent and counsel of her vassals, an indication that a female lord had the same rights, prerogatives and power as a male lord.

St. Avit's holdings and expanded the convent's territorial scope since most of the donated property came from or nearby Montfort-le-Gesnois (see Map 6). Included in the gift were two chapels (those of St. André and St. Croix) located in the castle precincts of Montfort-le-Gesnois, as well as the churches of St. Victor in Montfort-le-Gesnois and St. John and the chapel of St. Mary in Vibraye (situated midway between Montfort-le-Gesnois and Châteaudun). Tithes, burial rights and the churchyard pertaining to these ecclesiastical foundations were also granted. Further, Agnes also donated the right to half of the crops at Montfort-le-Gesnois and a neighboring village and tithes from other agricultural products, such as those on calves, lambs, fleeces, vineyards, pasture, untilled land and three mills. The nuns were provided with pasturage for pigs, vineyards, gardens, land, pasture and wood to be used for heat or building and the rights to a fish pond. In short, the grant met just about every need the nuns might have: Chapels to act as priories or daughter houses; wood to keep them warm or help them to build at the mother house or priories; fish to eat; grain to make into bread, pottage or beer; wine to drink; fleeces that could be sold or turned into cloth for the nuns' habits. Furthermore, the abbey gained two nuns from a wealthy and pious family, which would continue to support St. Avit into the thirteenth century.[11]

By 1100, St. Avit was a well-endowed house. Since the nuns of St. Avit were under the episcopal jurisdiction of the bishop of Chartres they had a special relationship with him. About the same time Agnes of Montfort-le-Gesnois made her gift, that is around 1091–1092, Bishop Ivo of Chartres wrote to the nuns of St. Avit. I would speculate that his letter was in response to a request from the abbess, perhaps Abbess Adelaide, who wrote to the bishop for advice and instruction on how the community could follow the rule of St. Benedict.[12]

Recall that the one of the fundamental principles of the Rule of St. Benedict was separation from the world. The vow of celibacy, which emphasized focusing on the spirit and not the distractions of the flesh, was central to this lifestyle. Bishop Ivo's letter to the abbess reflects this concern as he stresses the importance of protecting their virginity. Specifically, he emphasizes that the nuns should not engage in any interactions – including conversations – with men. Ivo references the Virgin Mary "whose life is especially commended as a model for the virgins of Christ, [she] did not live in public and did not like conversations with 'gallants,'" as an example for the nuns' interactions with men. Other female saints, he reminds the abbess, also eschewed conversation with men, "except in those cases when [men] appealed to their charity to aid them in their morals or in their needs, or in those cases when they received the grace of holy exhortations." He reiterates that the wall

11 *SA*, pp. 177–178.

12 Yves de Chartres, *Correspondance*, ed. and trans Jean Leclercq, 2 vols (Paris: Société d'édition "Les Belles Lettres," 1949) vol. 1, no. 10, pp. 41–49.

around their convent is for their protection and to keep them safe. Male clerics were especially concerned that nuns preserve their chastity because they thought nuns could be susceptible to moral corruption. However, they were equally invested that male regular clergy remain chaste, as is evident in the Augustinian Rule adopted by the canons of Notre Dame de Beaugency:

> In your walk, deportment, and in all actions, let nothing occur to give offense to anyone who sees you, but only what becomes your holy state of life . . . Although your eyes may chance to rest upon some woman or other, you must not fix your gaze upon any woman. Seeing women when you go out is not forbidden, but it is sinful to desire them or to wish them to desire you, for it is not by tough or passionate feeling alone but by one's gaze also that lustful desires mutually arise.[13]

Monks and nuns were enclosed, meaning that they were to live out their life within the walls of their community, to avoid just these temptations. Hence walls were erected not so much to keep the religious in, but to keep secular influences out.

Benedictine nuns and monks were to dedicate themselves to prayer and not be concerned with worldly vanities like how they looked, what they wore, or what they ate. They were also to be obedient to their abbess or abbot, to live simply and be moderate in all things. Ivo emphasizes these values when he described an ideal nun to the community of St. Avit, who

> first of all has a humble heart, a face pale and withered by thinness, a skin dried up and scarred by a hair shirt and not subjected to frequent baths. That is to say reserved when she is moved to talk, obedient when she is moved to listen. Who is frugal in what she eats, sober in her drink, grave in her deportment when she walks, roughness in her clothes and not extravagant, who maintains the softness of the soul and who in this is the sign: In all of these things it is never necessary to consult sensuality, but rather necessity.

Moreover, Ivo recommends that nuns "always abandon themselves to prayer or reading or work," so that "the devil always finds you occupied and so your thoughts must not be exposed to evil or wandering thoughts." He also recounts the lives of the saints Cecelia and Agnes and exhorts the nuns to follow their example.

Bishop Ivo's advice to the abbess was very idealized and prescriptive – meaning this was how he thought nuns *should* live rather than how they *did* live. As a member of the medieval clergy, Ivo was fully invested in insuring that monks and nuns followed the Rule of St. Benedict, which informs his

13 *The Rule of St. Augustine*, Chapter IV.

portrait of an ideal nun. But Ivo's advice was also shaped by clerical attitudes toward women, specifically the idea that women were more sexual than men. This was an attitude that resulted from clerical interpretations of Eve and her role in the fall from grace. Eve was thought to have used her womanly persuasion to get Adam to eat the apple and was hence responsible for humankind's expulsion from paradise. This explains Ivo's emphasis on nuns staying within the cloister, not being concerned with their physical appearance (which could tempt men), and suggesting they eschew all contact with laymen. His letter thus reflects clerical attitudes toward women, his own preoccupations about nuns and an attempt to provide an idealized model of life in the convent rather than the nuns' actual experience.

Similarly, the oath that the abbess of St. Avit started taking in 1118 to the bishop of Chartres when she assumed office is also prescriptive in that it records how abbesses were supposed to behave: "I, [first name], abbess of the humble nuns of Holy Avit, promise you, father bishop, and your successors, and also the mother church of Chartres, that I give my subjection and obedience, following the rules of the Holy Fathers."[14] How should we interpret this oath? Cuissard believed that it indicated that the abbess and nuns were completely dominated by male clergy. I would challenge this interpretation. In her obedience to the bishop, the abbess of St. Avit was no different than an abbot and hence no more dominated than male clergy. Moreover, as I will argue in the discussion that follows, the extant charters indicate that these nuns exercised a great deal of autonomy and commanded the respect of both their secular and clerical neighbors.

The community of St. Avit

While valuable in supplying what a male bishop thought about nuns, Ivo's letter and the oath are limited in their usefulness in determining daily life behind convent walls for a woman of the Beaugency family who lived as a nun at St. Avit. As documents of practice, the charters of St. Avit are more realistic in their portrayal of how nuns behaved and better placed to reconstruct the lived experiences of these nuns.

So who were the nuns of St. Avit? Unlike other, larger or more prominent ecclesiastical foundations, the documents of St. Avit are rather few, even though the community survived long into the modern period, which presents certain obstacles to the historian. For example, it is not possible to reconstruct an entire individual life from these documents. As a result, I will use a prosopographical approach, meaning I will examine the lives of several nuns to piece together the experience of the nuns of St. Avit. Although it is difficult to determine how large St. Avit grew to be, at its largest it was probably a community of about thirty nuns. On average one would expect about fifteen to

14 *SA*, pp. 171–172.

twenty nuns to call the abbey home. But as St. Avit expanded it came to have five priories or communities founded around a chapel where a small number of nuns would reside (perhaps three to five). While connected to the mother house, these sisters lived apart although by the same rules for their behavior.

By tracing the gifts made to the convent, we can determine both the status of the nuns and the donors. Most of these women were local, which can be ascertained by their use of a cognomen or second name that reflects their geographic origin. This means that they are described as "of" a place; for example, "Hersend of Ludon, the nun." Most of St. Avit's patrons also were not from the higher echelons of the nobility, although the vicecomital families of Châteaudun and Chartres did make some minor benefactions. Similarly, the counts of Chartres confirmed gifts made by some of their vassals to the nuns, but gave relatively little themselves.[15] King Louis VII also made a modest donation to the convent – likely due to the urging of the count of Chartres who was his seneschal.[16] Some minor local lords supported the abbey through their gifts. But many of those making donations to the convent held the rank of knight and some were merely **squires**. Others were not lords at all, just land owners or vassals of lords. Pierre of the village of Pessonis, for example, made a modest gift of land and later donated property so that his daughter Ameline could become a nun in 1135. In 1190 Arnoul of Rochefort likewise endowed St. Avit with property, so his daughter could become a ***religieuse***.[17] Both of these men clearly controlled land but were not designated as a lord, so they would seem to be rather modest land owners. Unlike the lords of Beaugency and other higher placed lords who were benefactors of a wide range of foundations, families of more simple means tended to support religious communities that they knew. So their patronage was often limited to local houses – like St. Avit (see Documents 23 and 24, page 251).

But what did an "average" nun or monk do with their time? The main occupation of those living in convents or monasteries was to pray. Ecclesiastical communities kept books that recorded the names of people for whom the religious should pray for each day (often called a necrology, martyrology or obituary). Seven times from sunrise to midnight, the sisters or brothers would head to the church for their prayers. The nuns who celebrated these offices were designated as choir nuns, because they had been educated in Latin and thus able to sing these prayers. The day would begin at Matins (sometimes called Lauds), just before sunrise. The next service was Prime, which meant the first service that took place approximately one hour after the first hour of the day (perhaps around 7 a.m.). Roughly two hours later was Terce, held in the third hour of the day or at around 9 a.m. At noon, Sext, or six hours into

15 Count Louis of Chartres, for example, gave 20 shillings in rent to light the church. *SA*, p. 176.

16 Maurice Jusselin, "Un acte inédit du roi Loius VII," *Bibliothèque des chartes* 71 (1910): 466–467. Count Thibaut V also made a generous donation in 1189. AD Eure-et-Loir H 4462. Significantly, both gave woods from near the abbey of Bonneval.

17 *SA*, p. 172 and p. 76 respectively.

the new day, was celebrated. The next office was Nones held in the ninth hour of the day or around mid-afternoon (perhaps 3 p.m.). Vespers was the final office of the daytime and occurred at sunset. The nuns or monks would pray just before going to bed at Compline and then awake to celebrate the Night Office or Vigils. They would be up a few hours later to start the cycle all over again. Prayers and the offices often consisted of singing particular psalms or hymns. The precentrix was the nun in charge of insuring they were sung properly. The monks would have been under the direction of the cantor. For some high feast days – such as Easter for example – all-night vigils would be held.

For some nuns, entering the abbey was a family affair (see Document 23, page 251). The three daughters of Philippa of *Harenc* all entered St. Avit at the same time. When the daughter of Pagan of Frouville took her vows, she would have joined her grandmother who was also a nun at St. Avit.[18] Most sisters would have resided at St. Avit, but others, like Sister Odelina the prioress, lived at one of the dependent priories of St. Avit. These nuns carried out the same duties as their sisters at the mother house, just on a smaller scale. Nunneries and monasteries both had officers charged with specific tasks. The head of St. Avit was the abbess, who was usually chosen from among the nuns and probably had experience as a prioress at one of St. Avit's several priories: St. Agil, St. Martin in Meung-sur-Loire, Vibraye, Vitray and Fontenay-sur-Eure (see Map 6). The charters record several prioresses who oversaw these priories. For example in 1168, the Abbess Hildegard, Prioress Ermengarde and Prioress Adelaide of St. Agil, all confirmed a gift made to the nunnery. Half a century later, Sister Maria was listed as prioress, Agnete as subprioress and Adelaide as the third prioress. There was also likely a prioress resident at St. Avit who would be second in command to the abbess. In addition, a treasurer of the convent oversaw the nuns' chapter house where they conducted their business and had charge of the convent's charters. There was also a sacristan, who looked after the convent's treasure of relics and holy objects. By the mid-twelfth century, as a result of the socio-economic changes of the commercial revolution, the nuns had an almshouse to dispense alms to the poor and would have assigned a sister to oversee it. The nuns also had an infirmary and hence an infirmarian. Since the convent was surrounded by walls, as Bishop Ivo describes in his letter, there was also a nun who acted as porter to monitor who was able to come and go into the monastery. Given the bishop's words on preserving virginity and not engaging in casual conversation with men, this would have been an important position. By 1178 there was both a cellarer and a sub-cellarer assigned to supervise the abbey's food stores and keep the kitchen well stocked.

Unfortunately, no physical remains of the nunnery are extant today as a result of the sixteenth-century Wars of Religion and the French Revolution

18 *SA*, p. 174 and p. 177.

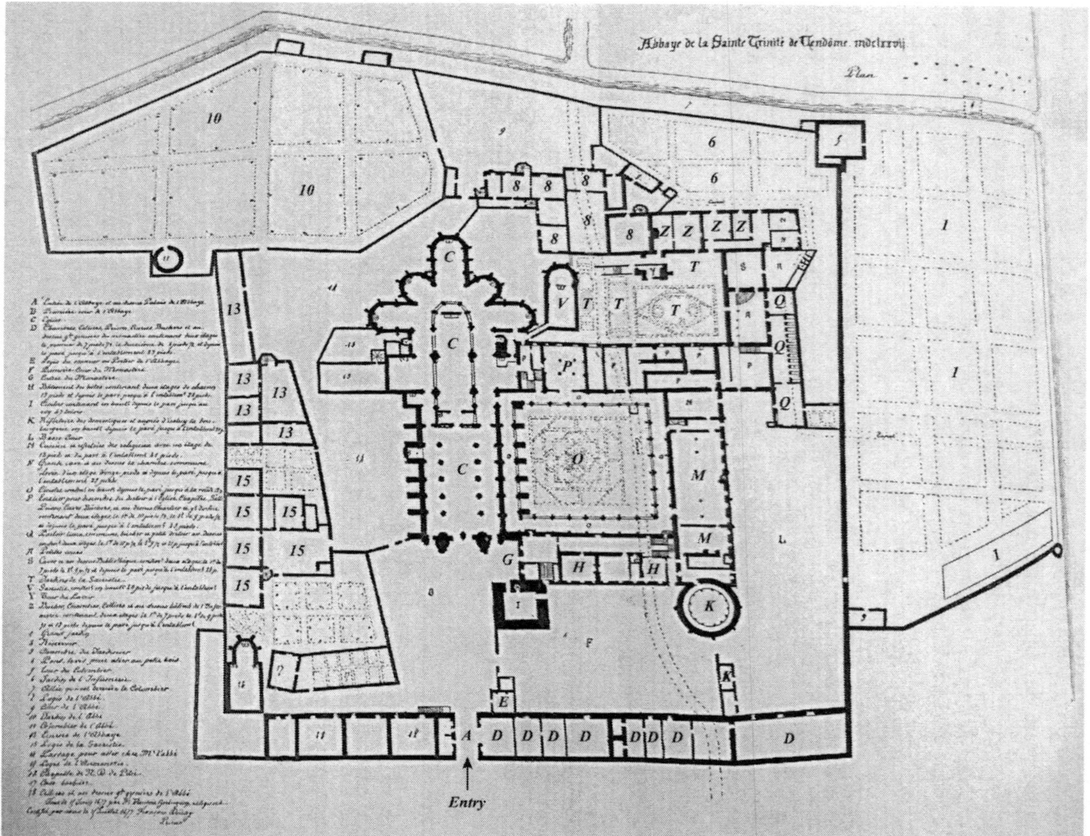

Figure 7.1
Plan of the Monastery of St. Trinité of Vendôme. The monastery included spaces for prayer, contemplation, a library, a sacristy, as well as living quarters and gardens.

A: Abbey Gate; C: Abbey Church; D: Rooms for servants and storage; E: Gate Keeper's House; G: Entry into monastic spaces; H: Guest Quarters; K: Refectory for Servants; M: Kitchen and Refectory for Monks; O: Cloister; P: Chapter House; Q: Monks' Dormitory; T: Sacrist's Gardens; V: Sacristy; Z: Infirmary;
1: Gardens; 6: Infirmary Gardens; 8: Abbot's Lodgings; 10: Abbot's Garden; 13: Sacrist's Lodgings; 15: Alms House.

Author Photo, *Cartulaire de l'abbaye cardinale de la Trinité de Vendôme*, éd. Charles Métais (Paris: Picard, 1893–1904), vol. 5.

of the eighteenth. But the physical layout of St. Avit was probably made up of spaces similar to those on the plan of St. Trinité, only on a smaller scale (see Figure 7.1). St. Avit had been founded in the Carolingian era and there is no evidence that any new structures were built once it became a nunnery in 1045. So the church and surrounding buildings were likely modest in size and perhaps a bit outmoded. As well as inheriting this physical space from the monks, the sisters also received several beautiful – and valuable – reliquaries. One was made of silver with images of the twelve apostles and St. Avit the patron of the community, in repoussé (a technique where the metal is worked by hammering from the reverse side to create a raised effect). The other reliquary was in the shape of the forearm of St. Avit, also in silver and encrusted with precious stones including rubies and emeralds. There was a glass window inserted into the reliquary where the arm bone of the saint would be clearly visible. On the opposite side of the arm-reliquary the name "Saint-Avit" was engraved. These were clearly very precious objects. Tradition held that they were given to the original house at St. Avit by their founder, the Merovingian King Dagobert.[19]

Examination of the plans of other religious communities can provide some clues as to what buildings and spaces would have made up the convent of St. Avit (see Figure 7.1). Inside of the walls would have been the nuns' church, the chapter house where they would meet and store their charters, a library, a sacristy or another space designated to hold the abbey's treasures (including the two reliquaries), a scriptorium where the nuns would write and copy texts (including charters), a dormitory where they nuns would sleep, a refectory where they would take their meals, kitchens, an infirmary, and a school for novices and local girls. The abbess may also have had a small house for her own use. There would also be what we might call "green spaces:" A cloister for nuns to study, pray and contemplate, as well as gardens for herbs, medicines and foodstuffs. In addition to the buildings for the nuns' use, there would also have been structures storing more mundane items, such as a stable for horses and other livestock. Since the nuns received donations of tithes of calves, pigs and lambs, they would have also needed pens and barns to house these animals. There may also have been a workshop where cloth was made for the nuns' use and perhaps a forge or blacksmith. The nuns' afterlife would also have been accorded space. Perhaps they, like the Carolingian monks of St. Gall, buried their dead in the orchard where their earthly remains could provide sustenance to the trees.

As well as the choir nuns, the walls of St. Avit embraced other women. Some were servants who helped the nuns with manual labor. Others were women who opted to join the convent late in life as *conversa*. In 1181, Pagan of Frouville made a gift to St Avit "in consideration of his mother, Aremburge,

19 Cuissard, *SA*, p. 198.

who was made a nun after the death of her husband."[20] Aremburge desired to pursue a religious life for the remainder of her days and did so as a member of this convent. This convent served an important function for local aristocratic families: It provided their female members with a space to pursue their religious vocation and/or a place where they could retire. Around 1200 the couple Odelina and Ragenfred made a donation to St. Avit with the stipulation that Odelina be able to retire to the convent at a later point.[21] Indeed, it seems that St. Avit was so overwhelmed with appeals to become a pensioner that Pope Innocent II gave them the right to be able to refuse such requests.[22] So when a daughter of Beaugency joined St. Avit, she would have been surrounded by women who had dedicated their lives to God, by those seeking a comfortable place to retire and pursue their piety, and those whose labor would help support the nuns.

In addition to dedicating their lives to prayer and singing the daily religious offices, the nuns of St. Avit also served the poor and sick. By the end of the twelfth century, St. Avit possessed two almshouses where the needs of the poor and destitute could be met. Even Bishop Ivo recognized that nuns would undertake charitable work and advised that nuns should not speak with men "except in those cases when [men] appealed to their charity to aid them." The sisters also kept busy with other pious work. Nursing seems to have been one of these occupations. In 1148 when the wife of a descendant of the founder Ganelon of Montigny became ill and recovered due to the nuns' nursing, he made a gift to the nuns "in return for care during her sickness"[23] (see Document 22, page 249). The ladies of Beaugency might also have engaged in charitable work in the convent, perhaps in taking care of the sick, as it was quite common for noble women to undertake such tasks as a demonstration of their Christian piety. The nuns' charitable work and piety earned them the respect of their secular neighbors – male and female. Perhaps they were, as Bishop Ivo suggested, pinch-faced, pale and scarred from wearing hair shirts.

Medieval people were anxious for intercession to help mitigate their sins and secure them a place in heaven. The thirteenth-century local nobility clearly believed these sisters had the ear of God and the saints, for Hugh of *Roleire* gave a measure of wheat so that the nuns would pray for him on the anniversary of his death.[24] Petronille and her husband Adam made a similar donation "for their anniversary"– meaning the nuns would pray for them on the anniversary of the day of their death.[25] In 1235 William of Ouarville granted four measures of grain from his mill for celebration of a daily mass

20 *SA*, p. 177.
21 AD Eure-et-Loir H 4275.
22 *SA*, p. 172.
23 *SA*, pp. 172–173.
24 *SA*, p. 180.
25 *SA*, p. 181.

Figure 7.2 The chapel of St. Pierre of Vouvray founded by Simon and Jeanne Lucé in 1239. Author photo.

and vigils in perpetuity.[26] Similar to the lords of Beaugency, the husband and wife, Simon and Jeanne of Lucé, founded private chapels. They made the grand gift of establishing a chapel in the church of St. Avit for the soul of their kinsman Peter of Bullou, who may have been Jeanne's first husband. They made a similar endowment of the chapel of St. Pierre of Vouvray for the soul of Odo of Bullou, perhaps Jeanne's son[27] (see Figure 7.2). Other elites sought proximity to the nuns after death. Lucy of Lancey gave the nuns six shillings of rent so she could be interred at St. Avit.[28] While not as large or lavish as other ecclesiastical houses, male or female, the nuns of St. Avit were clearly perceived to be spiritually pure and able to intercede with the divine.

Further testament to the nuns' reputation and piety are the benefactions made to St. Avit by fellow clergy. Robert the priest, for example gave a pasture in alms to the abbey.[29] Hugh the canon of Chartres cathedral made a gift of rent, on the condition that these revenues go to support his sister who was a nun at St. Avit[30] (see Document 23, page 251). Another canon of

26 *SA*, p. 182.
27 *SA*, p. 183.
28 *SA*, p. 179.
29 *SA*, p. 181.
30 *SA*, p. 179.

Chartres gave a cash gift to the nuns so they would pray for him yearly on the day of his death. But part of the gift, the canon specified, should also be put aside to support his niece, who had taken the veil at St. Avit.[31] These families must have had considerable respect for the abbey if they were willing to place their daughters there. This evidence clearly argues against the assertion that female religious were seen by medieval people as somehow inferior in their connection to the divine.

The abbess of St. Avit

The twelfth and thirteenth centuries would provide both opportunities and challenges for the sisters. What was it like being abbess of this community? What were the specific challenges and opportunities this community faced? After Adelaide of Montigny, the first abbess of St. Avit, the next appears in the records in 1118 when Adelais took the oath to Bishop Geoffrey of Chartres. She was followed in 1138 by Abbess Isabelle. There were very few gifts made in the early twelfth century and St. Avit seems extremely small at this point – perhaps only six to ten nuns. The second half of the twelfth century saw considerable growth, both in the size of the community and the number of gifts made by the local elites. By 1170, the abbey possessed several priories – three in the environs of Montfort-le-Gesnois and St. Martin at Meung-sur-Loire, a short distance from Beaugency. Shortly after, the pope issued a bull, or proclamation confirming and enumerating the possessions of St. Avit, which were described as "considerable." Examination of gifts made to St. Avit between its founding in 1045 and 1300 reveals some important patterns. For the first century of its existence, the abbey received a very modest number of gifts: Nine. The century between 1150 and 1250 was the time when St. Avit received the most gifts: A total of seventy-seven, which was nearly a ten-fold increase from the previous century. This was the peak of pious donations, as gifts decreased dramatically to twelve over the period between 1250 and 1400 (at least as far as the documents allow us to reconstruct).

The abbesses of St. Avit between 1150 and 1250 presided over the expansion of the abbey (see Map 6). Between 1150 and 1200 references to specific conventual offices appear such as prioress, cellarer, etc., indicating an increase in specialized management coinciding with the growth of the nunnery. The stature of these nuns is apparent in a donation made in 1178 where the Abbess Hildeard is called "the illustrious" and all of the sisters appearing with her are called "domina," a title of respect indicating lordly status.[32] In 1186, under the tenure of Abbess Avelina, the abbey expanded further when Lady Martha of Lanneray founded the priory of Fontenay-sur-Eure, where she built a house for the nuns.[33] Witnessing this gift was a young

31 *SA*, p. 185.
32 *SA*, p. 174.
33 *SA*, p. 175.

nun named Ada, who would eventually become abbess. It was during her time that St. Avit prospered, but also when indications of tensions and economic challenges begin to appear.

Ada of Touraille came from a well-established family. She was related to the vicecomital house of Châteaudun, although her exact connection to them is not clear. She likely entered the convent sometime in the 1170s as a young woman. Ada was clearly a woman of talent, since she worked her way up the ladder of offices within the convent – eventually becoming its abbess in 1201. By 1181, ten years after joining the sisters, she held the office of precentrix. "As a result of the supplications of their kinswoman Ada of Touraille, Viscount Hugh III founded the priory of Saint-Agil, which he magnificently endowed" in 1190.[34] This would be the fifth priory that St. Avit would control and added considerably to the patrimony of the nuns (see Map 6). Ada demonstrates that religious women were influential in appealing to their family for support of their convent. Although they were supposed to "leave the world behind" – as evident in Bishop Ivo's letter – this was more of an ideal than a reality. As the example of Ada shows, she continued to have contact with her relatives and secure their patronage for her religious house.

When Ada became abbess in 1201, she presided over a well-established community that probably had about fifteen to twenty nuns living in the central convent, but more in the priories. Abbess Ada spent much of her time dealing with managing and improving her abbey's holdings (see Figure 7.3).[35] As a daughter of a noble house, she had been educated and trained to do so. In 1201/1202 Ada was involved in resolving a problem that had developed when a causeway the abbey had built ended up causing harm to the residences on the riverbank, which were under the jurisdiction of the neighboring religious house at Chamars, once part of the Beaugencys' patrimony[36] (see Document 25, page 251). Ada met with members of this priory of Marmoutier to resolve this problem and recognized her abbey's responsibility for doing inadvertent harm to these residents. This resolution also indicates that the abbesses of St. Avit were developing their property and changing the environment so they could prosper and participate in the commercial economy – much as the lords of Beaugency had done with their holdings. The nuns had diverted water from the Le Loir River into one of the causeways for their mills.[37] Abbess Ada also had to work out a conflict with the abbot of Pontlevoy in 1204 concerning a gift of tithes made to both St. Avit and a priory of Pontlevoy, as well as appearing in ecclesiastical court to resolve a dispute

34 *SA*, p. 176.

35 Like secular lords, ecclesiastical lords also used seals as symbols of authority. Abbesses also had seals. For example, the abbess of the Cistercian convent of Beauville used a seal when she sold property to the canons of Notre Dame de Beaugency. AD Loiret H 10, folio XXVII verso; *NDB*, no. 91, pp. 107–108.

36 *SA*, pp. 176–177.

37 The nuns had also constructed a fishing weir that they were forced to take down as well since it interfered with the course of the water and made sailing on the Le Loir difficult.

with another cleric.[38] Neighboring clergy, appointed as delegates by the pope, were charged with arbitrating this dispute between St. Avit and a canon of Chartres cathedral. Ada never traveled the distances that Abbot Geoffrey did, but she did have to travel locally to appear in court and defend St. Avit's interests.

Gifts continued to be made to the abbey while Ada was abbess. Modest gifts, such as providing fishing rights in various mill ponds once a year, were granted. Others were more extravagant. Rotrou of Montfort, a descendant of St. Avit's early patron Agnes of Montfort-les-Gesnois, founded a chapel in a church at Vibraye, assigned a chaplain for the abbey's use and over whom the abbess would have authority (see Document 21, page 248). Consenting to this gift were Ada and three prioresses from the convent.[39] The abbey's membership increased along with its property during Ada's tenure. Ten new nuns joined St. Avit between 1201 and 1207 – each bringing some sort of endowment to add to the abbey's coffers. Overall Ada's tenure seems to have been a time of security, if not prosperity, for the nuns. However, coinciding with this prosperity were several lawsuits brought against the convent. Furthermore, at the very end of her tenure, Ada sold meadowland at Vouvray to the almshouse at Châteaudun, which was the first time the abbey had sold any of its property. How are we to reconcile this seemingly conflicting evidence of expansion and loss? Piecing together the charter evidence, I would postulate that the delicate balance between convent resources and population was out of sync.

If a Beaugency woman joined St. Avit in the first half of the thirteenth century, she would have found signs of economic tension increasingly apparent – in spite of the significant increase in gifts. In 1214, for instance, Abbess Ada's successor withdrew half of the tithes of a village which she had pledged to a local knight and promised to pay him recompense. But "because the abbey was unable to pay this amount, the brothers and friends of the sisters Agnes of *Verde* and Eustachia of Les Châtelliers-Notre-Dame stepped in to pay it."[40] The community of St. Avit did not have the cash to follow through on this transaction. In an attempt to generate revenue, later abbesses began leasing out their property. In 1225 they leased one of their farmsteads for 30 pounds and six measures of winter wheat. By 1240 some of the nuns' patrimony seems to have been in disrepair. In 1241 the abbess gave "mills in ruins and with no revenue" to Peter and his wife on the condition that they repair and restore them to a good state. In return, the couple would enjoy the mills for their lifetime, but upon their death the mills and their revenue would return to the abbey.[41] Two years later the same abbess and her nuns were forced to reduce the number of priests serving the abbey from three to only one because of "the misfortunes of the time and the losses that

38 *SA*, p. 177.
39 *SA*, pp. 177–178.
40 *SA*, pp. 178–179.
41 *SA*, p. 183.

Figure 7.3 The seal of an abbess. This seal dates from the second half of the twelfth century and is attributed as the "seal of Abbess Ada." Unfortunately, it is not clear which abbey this Ada headed. Our Abbess Ada of St. Avit likely had a seal very similar to this one – who knows? Perhaps this is her seal. © Archives nationales, Centre de sigillographie et d'héraldique, F 7238. Author photo.

the abbey had suffered."[42] The charter is frustratingly silent about these "misfortunes" and "losses," but several factors may have combined to cause the abbey difficulty. Although St. Avit did receive more gifts between 1200 and 1250 than it had received previously – or would receive the century after – these gifts were mostly modest and small. At the same time, the number of nuns at St. Avit increased. Indeed many of the gifts between 1200/1250 were made to endow or support a woman who desired to become a nun. So even though their patrimony grew through donations and management, these increases may not have kept up with the number of nuns needing support. Combined with losses of revenue or property due to legal proceedings, as well as an increasingly competitive and cash-based economy, the abbey of St. Avit

42 *SA*, p. 183.

seems to have lived on the margins. Moreover, with the advent of new communities, such as leprosaria and new monastic houses like the convent of Cistercian women of Notre-Dame de l'Eau in nearby Chartres, patrons had more choices as to what communities they would support and St. Avit may have been disadvantaged by this competition – contributing further to the economic tensions within the convent.

Unfortunately, the events of the following centuries would not improve matters. The Great Famine, when the kings of France gave a portion of their tithes from Chartres to the nuns because of "the misery of the time," followed by the Black Death, would have further stressed the abbey's resources in the fourteenth century. By 1490 the abbess and sisters were reporting to the king that their nunnery had fallen into ruin as a result of the wars, and if they had to pay any taxes, they would be forced to sell the chalices, books and other ornaments of the church. The king's commissioners recognized the desperate state of this house and were obliged to release the nuns from payment.[43] In spite of these challenges, however, the sisters of St. Avit persevered. During the French Revolution when religious institutions were under scrutiny and many disbanded, the abbess and her sisters declared "in one unanimous voice, protesting their firm resolution to live and to die in their house, that they were all very content and satisfied with their state."[44] Unfortunately, the eleven nuns were unable to return to their house at St. Avit. Rather, they lived out their days in the abbey of St. Nicholas of Verneuil. The last abbess died in 1837. Interestingly, the number of nuns at the end of this convent's life was about the same as when its first abbess, Adelaide of Montigny, began her tenure in 1045 – 792 years earlier.

Inside a monastery's walls: St. Trinité of Vendôme

Lancelin I of Beaugency was present in May of 1040 when St. Trinité of Vendôme was founded.[45] From its founding until the end of the twelfth century, Beaugency family members were generous benefactors of these monks. As such, the Beaugencys were frequent visitors and would have been well-acquainted with the abbey. The monks, in return, provided the Beaugencys with prayers and interceded for their souls. If a lady or lord of Beaugency had visited the monastery of St. Trinité, what would they have seen?

In contrast to St. Avit, we do have a physical rendering of the abbey for St. Trinité. Although drawn in 1677, the plan reflects the basic footprint of the medieval monastery (see Figure 7.1). The monastery was physically larger than the convent and home to probably at least three times as many religious. The community was wealthier as St. Trinité held property all over western

43 *SA*, p. 189.

44 *SA*, p. 197.

45 "Conventus Episcoporum ad dedicationem Vindocinensis monasterii S. Trinitatis," in *RHF*, vol. 11, nouvelle edition, ed. Léopold Delisle (Paris: Victor Palme, 1876), pp. 506–507.

France and could count some of the most powerful and prestigious men and women among its patrons. Yet these monks shared a common vocation with the sisters of St. Avit and while there were certainly differences between the two communities, they were perhaps differences of degree rather than kind. Indeed, one suspects that if Abbess Ada and Abbot Geoffrey sat down to a meal in the refectory, they would find that they had much in common both as heads of their respective communities and as professed religious.

The central role that the church played in the lives of the residents of St. Trinité is apparent in the organization of space as it is the largest central structure on the plan. Other areas were also dedicated to contemplation and prayer. Several cloisters, or squares surrounded by arcades, populated the monastery and were places where monks could go for quiet reflection. The other buildings also embody the occupations and communal living of the monks. At some distance from the main church was the dormitory, where the monks would sleep either in individual cells or dormitory style. Cells would have been small, plain and furnished only with necessities. Novices, or young men training for the clergy, might sleep together in a dormitory removed from that of the monks. The abbot had his own house or separate quarters as befitting his rank and where he could easily entertain guests or visitors – such as the lord and lady of Beaugency – to the abbey. In addition to living quarters was a refectory where monks would take their meals in silence, often while one of their fellowship read aloud. The cellarer would have been responsible for insuring that the monks had food. Nestled close to the abbey church was the treasury or sacristy where all the treasures and relics of the church were kept under the watchful eye of the sacristan. The library, where manuscripts were stored but also where monks would make copies of important works, was located opposite the cloister from the abbey church. The chapter house was where the monks would meet to discuss monastic business and where many of the monastery's charters were stored and penned. The chamberlain would have had oversight of this space and these documents. An infirmary was located in a building at some distance from the church. As Abbot Geoffrey references a *medicus*, or a medical monk, as well as an infirmarian in his letters, St. Trinité had monks in residence who specialized in medicine and the space to attend the sick. There was a garden where medicinal herbs could be grown. Other gardens were used to provide food for the poor (the almoner's garden) as well as for the abbot's table. There was also an almshouse where alms for those in need could be distributed, as well as a place for them to reside in the short term. The main form of transportation for the monks, like most other medieval people, was by horse. As a result, the monastery had its own stable, which was overseen by the hostler. The monastery itself was surrounded by a wall and gates. The wall was for the monks' safety – as it was for the nuns of St. Avit – but also to delineate the space of the monastery. Entrance to the monastery was through a gate manned by the gatekeeper. As a place of prayer – and considerable wealth – the monks needed to be able to regulate who went in and out of the monastery, as well as keeping corrupting influences out. Monks contributed to the life of their community in many ways. Some might copy manuscripts or teach the novices. While their day was centered on prayer, their labor also contributed to the life and success of their community.

Founded by the count and countess of Vendôme, the monastery rapidly became popular among the aristocracy of the region – including the Beaugency family. The comital couple, so the foundation legend goes, saw three stars falling from the sky and decided to found a monastery dedicated to the Holy Trinity where they fell. While a lovely story, the reality was likely far more pragmatic as the establishment of a monastic house was a way for nobles to demonstrate wealth and influence, garner support of the church and gain spiritual benefits. By the time Geoffrey became abbot in 1093, St. Trinité was a large and prosperous monastery with property all over western France. In his day the monastery was home to around ninety monks, as well as servants and workers. Like the nuns of St. Avit, the main occupation of the monks of St. Trinité was to pray, which they did seven times daily. In residence were three kinds of religious. First, there were the choir monks, who, like the choir nuns, were educated in Latin and entrusted with singing the daily masses. These brothers came from the elite families of the region. As St. Trinité did not allow child oblates to become monks until the early twelfth century – under Geoffrey's abbacy in fact – these monks were adults. Other brothers in residence included the lay monks who "converted" to the monastic life after having lived in the world for some time. The key difference between these monks and those of the choir was that they were not necessarily able to read Latin and hence could not participate in the liturgy. They served the monastery in other ways, however, perhaps by preparing vellum for manuscripts or tending the kitchen. Some lay brothers were those who converted *ad succurrendum*, meaning that they chose become a monk as they were at the end of their life or if they had suffered a grievous injury. Many perished shortly after they took the habit, but some survived to become permanent members of the monastery. (Remember the example of the Beaugency's vassal, Ascelin from Chapter 2, who joined the monastery after being wounded in battle.) Finally, there were the servants, or those of the *familia*, who helped the monks with various labors necessary for their support.

Ideally, a monastery was a self-contained and self-sustaining community with the brothers assuming specific duties or offices. Following the abbot in authority was the prior, who was in charge of the abbey whenever the abbot was not in residence. Given that Abbot Geoffrey traveled to Rome twelve times, as well as other places on monastic business, it was necessary to have a second in authority. In addition to the abbot and prior were ten other offices: The cellarer, the hosteller, porter, cantor, sacristan, almoner, treasurer, librarian, chamberlain and infirmarian, whose responsibilities ranged from insuring the monks had enough to eat (the cellarer) to someone to ensure alms were provided to the poor (the almoner) to someone who regulated who could come into the monastery (porter). The generosity of donors meant that

St. Trinité held lands over an extensive area. In order to exploit these somewhat far-flung resources, the monastery established priories, cells and chapels. The population of St. Trinité peaked in the twelfth century and began a slow decline in the thirteenth. Similar to Abbess Ada, Geoffrey was head of his monastery when it was perhaps at its most powerful and influential.

Abbot Geoffrey of Vendôme

We know that Geoffrey was born into an aristocratic family with holdings in the counties of Maine and Anjou. He was related to the lords of Beaugency through their cousins in Maine and had several interactions with members of this family. Aristocratic families frequently secured ecclesiastical careers for their children and the church provided opportunities for sons and daughters alike. Geoffrey's family placed him in the church in the hopes of deepening their relationship with the monastery, while at the same time furnishing Geoffrey with a career. Many elites found their true vocation or calling – like Geoffrey of Vendôme – but others were less willing to give up the trappings of the secular life, including a posh lifestyle, sex and even a family. Geoffrey, however, seems to have embraced the religious life with enthusiasm, if not zeal. Abandoning his family does not seem to have been a problem for Geoffrey, for he makes scant mention of them in his letters. Geoffrey became the abbot at Vendôme at a young age and may have been concerned that his elevation was assumed to be tainted by undue family influence – a practice known as **simony**. At the time of his appointment, the church had begun reforming such practices and any suggestion that an office was awarded on anything except the candidate's merits could result in the label of a simoniac, which would have threatened Geoffrey's stature as abbot. Geoffrey himself was dedicated to this reform (the Gregorian Reform Movement) which may have resulted in him consciously downplaying family connections.

Geoffrey was abbot of St. Trinité for almost forty years from 1093 to his death in 1131 (Figure 7.4). He was educated at the Cathedral School at Angers and the pupil of some of the most famous intellectuals of his day. By the time Geoffrey became abbot, St. Trinité of Vendôme was respected as a place of learning and home to an impressive library. Starting around 1120, Geoffrey himself authored many treatises on a variety of theological subjects, as well as writing several sermons and prayers. He was an advocate of reform and was himself invested with his office by Bishop Ivo of Chartres – one of the vocal proponents of reform. Indeed, the Gregorian Reform Movement would play a central role in Geoffrey's life.[46] These reformers, Geoffrey among

46 For Geoffrey's life as an abbot, see Geneviève Giordanengo, "La fonction d'abbé d'après l'oeuvre de Geoffrey de Vendôme," *Revue d'histoire d'Eglise de France* 76 (1990), pp. 165–184. For the Gregorian Reform Movement at St. Trinité, Hélène Tourbert, "Les fresques de La Trinité de Vendôme, un témoinage sur l'art de la réforme grégorienne," *Cahiers de civilisation médiévale* 26 (1983): 297–326.

Figure 7.4 This portrait, at the start of the collected works of Geoffrey of Vendôme, depicts Abbot Geoffrey in his abbatial vestments to the left, kneeling before Christ. While a "portrait" in the sense that it depicts Geoffrey, he is rendered rather generically and the portrait is not individualized. © Bibliothèques Territoires vendômois, fonds ancien du Parc Ronsard, Vendôme, Ms 193 f.2 v R.

them, believed that the church had been corrupted by secular influence. This corruption took several forms: Lay possession of ecclesiastical property, the ability of secular leaders to appoint clerics to their offices and simony (the purchase of church offices). The proponents of reform were also dedicated to ensuring the pope's power was supreme. This assertion by the reformers, and the popes themselves, led to several dramatic conflicts between popes and kings – that between Pope Gregory VII and Emperor Henry IV of Germany for instance. But conflicts also arose within the church, as powers and privileges enjoyed by bishops and abbots, which the reformers believed were the purview of the office of the papacy, were wrested away and deemed the sole privileges of the pope. Geoffrey's own commitment to church reform drew him into a dispute over the election of the bishop of Angers around 1100, who he believed to be a simoniac and corrupt. His interest in reform created close ties to the papal see and Geoffrey traveled to Rome many times in his life. Just after his appointment as abbot, Geoffrey went to Rome to help advise Pope Urban II on how to handle the threat posed by a rival to the throne of St. Peter. To both discuss and enforce matters of reform, church councils were held all over Europe. Geoffrey, as abbot and advocate for reform, attended several church councils locally and in Rome, including the Lateran Council of 1116.

Abbot Geoffrey was also friends with several important clerics of his day, such as the abbots of Cluny and Bonneval. We know of these relationships, and the events of Geoffrey's life, through the corpus of his letters. One hundred and ninety-five letters of Geoffrey's survive, which allow his voice to be heard – unlike many medieval people, such as the abbesses of St. Avit, who remain in the shadows. Unfortunately, as is often the case with correspondence, we do not have the response to Geoffrey's letters – except in rare instances. These letters provide a treasure trove of information as Geoffrey corresponded on a variety of subjects with a variety of people, including popes, archbishops, abbots, monks, priests, dukes, lords and even hermits. Through careful analysis of this correspondence, we can hear Geoffrey's voice telling us what it was like to be an abbot, his preoccupations, challenges and joys, as well as his life as both a member of the clergy and an aristocrat.

Let us begin by seeing what Geoffrey's correspondence reveals about life as a monk. Entering a monastery was no small matter and the monks wanted to be sure a candidate was suitable for entry. One of Geoffrey's clerical colleagues, a hermit, wrote to him about a possible candidate for the cloister. There was some question of this man's suitability for the monastic life and Geoffrey advised:

> You are concerned that if his conversion was too quick and he may have quit the world in an inappropriate manner . . . [but] if he seems to you to live a saintly life, take care to send him to us and do not delay to confer to us all the clerics of the honorable life that you find.[47]

One of the concerns about this potential monk seems to have been his wealth. Abbot Geoffrey had a somewhat pragmatic response to this: "We prefer in this a house of men of honorable poverty to those of proud riches. But if they have them [e.g. riches], it is not necessary to reject them, because they also have their place." Given that medieval monasteries were full of sons from wealthy and powerful families, like the Beaugencys, this would have been a

47 GV, letter 45, pp. 80–81.

concern or question that abbots would have often confronted. Other letters demonstrate that not all monks were suited to the monastic lifestyle – an issue that Geoffrey, as head of his house, confronted regularly.

Lord Ralph I of Beaugency wrote to Abbot Geoffrey about a family who wanted to know if their son, who had recently entered Geoffrey's house, could abandon his monastic vestments when he was visiting his family and engaging with the secular world. The abbot affirmed that this young brother could be returned to his family, but he could not put off his robes – even though he had not taken final vows.[48] Clearly this young aristocrat was having difficulty transitioning to the life of a monk. Some who found the religious life not to their liking actually fled from the monastery and became fugitives. Geoffrey wrote to the bishop of Chartres about one of his own monks who had fled St. Trinité because he was so unhappy. He requested that the monk return to the monastery so he could repent his actions in front of his brothers.[49] Unfortunately the letter does not make explicit what had caused this monk to leave. Geoffrey was not the only abbot to deal with monks-on-the-run, for he wrote to a fellow abbot instructing him on how to receive a monk who had run away and then returned back into the community. He advised that his fellow abbot be merciful toward this wayward monk and that he receive him "as a father" would a prodigal son.[50] One wonders if Geoffrey followed his own advice.

When confronted with an unhappy monk, however, Geoffrey did try to find ways to help him find his way in the religious life. Brother Herbert, Geoffrey feared, was too consumed with the affairs of the world. So he sent him to his "venerable brother" Prior André, who was in charge of one of St. Trinité's more remote houses, so that he could be schooled in his pastoral duties[51] (see Document 26, page 252). An indication that Geoffrey was respected by his fellow clergy is the letters he received asking for guidance. Monks struggled with their vows of poverty, chastity and obedience. When asked about the ideal spiritual life, Geoffrey emphasized two key elements.

First, was distance from the secular world. The concerns of terrestrial life, including family and wealth, were the main distractions to attaining ideal spirituality. Geoffrey speaks candidly, indeed almost coldly, about removing oneself from family. Second, he stressed obedience to God through chastity. Geoffrey wrote to the monks at Château-la-Vallière expressing concern that they were having too much contact with the opposite sex (here he voices the same concern that Bishop Ivo had for the nuns of St. Avit). He pleads with them to reform their ways so that they do not "provoke our [Geoffrey's] anger against you."[52] Similarly, Geoffrey's letter to Robert of Arbrissel criticizing

48 GV, letter 59, pp. 104–107.
49 GV, letter 24, pp. 42–43.
50 GV, letter 29, pp. 52–53.
51 GV, letter 82, pp. 158–159.
52 GV, letter 90, pp. 170–171.

him for his interaction with women is well known to scholars.[53] Robert was famous (or to Geoffrey's mind, infamous) for establishing a community of women at Fontevraud. Robert lived among women, with whom he shared quarters and worked closely in spiritual matters. Geoffrey believed that Robert had gone too far in his associations with women and feared he would succumb to temptation, for he says of a woman "when this [female] sex is good, there is nothing better than her; but when it [the female sex] is bad, there is nothing that is worse."[54] For Geoffrey, moderation was the watch-word. He was uncomfortable with Robert of Arbrissel's piety because he thought he went too far. Similarly, Geoffrey advised another monk about being over-zealous in his understanding of his vows and was fasting three days out of the week.[55] While Geoffrey praises the impulse, he chides the young monk saying that food is necessary to nourish his soul as well as his body. Geoffrey cautioned his brethren both when he thought they were overly lax in their adherence to the Rule of St. Benedict and when he though they were overly zealous in their application of its ideals. Perhaps not surprisingly, maintaining this equilibrium was a struggle for many monks throughout their lives.

The abbot as manager

Geoffrey spent a great deal of time and energy dealing with St. Trinité's assets. In these duties, he resembles a modern-day CEO. While the monastery grew as a result of aristocratic benefactions, these same men and women also asserted rights to St. Trinité's property. Sometimes, noblemen and women simply contested what their relatives or lord had given and the matter was settled in court. In other cases, however, Geoffrey had to go further than calling the offenders to task. For example, Geoffrey wrote to the bishop of Le Mans demanding justice for the actions of some of the local nobility. Around 1104 Hamelin of Montoire was excommunicated for rustling the monks' cattle. Although excommunicated by both the bishop of Le Mans and the papal legate (the pope's direct representative in France), Hamelin was eventually absolved. This did not, however, sit well with Abbot Geoffrey, who was apoplectic that the sentence of excommunication had been lifted and wrote to the bishop to tell him so[56] (see Document 27, page 253). What seems to have angered him most was that Hamelin was absolved "without him yet making any restitution to us" for the crimes he had committed against the abbey. Geoffrey was willing to take his complaints about the local nobility to the very top of the church hierarchy. A few years later, Geoffrey once again appealed to the bishop of Le Mans because Hamelin's son, Peter,

53 GV, letter 79, pp. 148–151.
54 GV, letter 90, p. 171.
55 GV, letter 5, pp. 10–11.
56 GV, letters 40 and 41, pp. 72–75.

"violently sacked one of our cemeteries and destroyed nearly entirely two of our farms."[57] Getting no justice from this bishop, Geoffrey took his case to the bishop of Angers. Frustrated once again, Geoffrey took the ultimate step of writing to the papal legate. Since Geoffrey does not write of this problem again, it seems that his monastery received adequate compensation for the damages done by the Montoire family.

In another instance, the abbey of St. Trinité was involved in a protracted dispute with Countess Euphronia of Vendôme between 1103 and 1105.[58] Geoffrey recounts that the countess claimed the church of Savigny from his monastery and had gone as far as to break into the church with her men and steal the tithes stored there.[59] It may seem odd that a member of the laity controlled a church, but throughout the eleventh century nobles had built churches on their land as a sign of their piety. Recall Lancelin II of Beaugency's construction of the chapel of the Holy Sepulcher in the mid-eleventh century. Often – but not always – nobles gave these churches to local monasteries once the church began to assert that ecclesiastical property should not be in lay hands as part of the Gregorian Reform Movement. Geoffrey wrote the bishop to set a date for a court to be called to hear this case and even asked that he be provided an escort because he feared the countess might do him further violence. Geoffrey wrote a second letter probably several months or a year later where he voices his astonishment that the bishop has rendered a verdict on this matter which Geoffrey clearly sees as favoring the countess. He then goes on to accuse the bishop of "loving a woman" more than seeing justice done for a member of the church.[60] Not satisfied by the response he had gotten from this bishop, Geoffrey wrote directly to Pope Pascal II:

> To his very dear and venerable father, the Pope Pascal. Geoffrey indignant minister of the monastery of Vendôme, with due obedience and affection. The allod of St. Peter, known as the monastery of Vendôme, is menaced in this world as if in the middle of the sea by a very dangerous tempest. It no longer suffices that it, as is normal, is ravaged by secular power; but now it is to be maligned equally by the attacks and negligence of prelates, who are supposed to be the defenders of the church.[61]

Papal intervention in the matter seems to have done the trick and the countess confirmed St. Trinité's possession of this church shortly afterwards.[62] This letter reveals much about Geoffrey's personality. He was a stalwart

57 GV, letter 117, pp. 226–227.

58 This was the wife of the count of Vendôme who was imprisoned by Lancelin II of Beaugency.

59 GV, letter 32, pp. 58–61.

60 GV, letter 33, pp. 61–65.

61 GV, letter 53, pp. 92–95.

62 *STV*, no. 405, vol. 2, pp. 159–160.

defender of his abbey and was not afraid to call out his superiors for what he saw as a failure of duty. Disentangling the church from the secular world, particularly from the influence of the nobility, was a central tenant of the reform movement – and one with which the Beaugency family was familiar as they, like their neighbors, restored ecclesiastical property to the church from their domains. Geoffrey had very little patience with his fellow clerics who did not see matters as black and white as he did.

As Geoffrey noted, not only did he have to protect his monastery's property from the secular nobility, he also had to deal with other ecclesiastical communities regarding St. Trinité's prerogatives. He sent a letter to the pope to detail his grievances against the abbey of St. Aubin of Angers because the bishop of Saintes had seized rights from Geoffrey's monastery and given them to his adversaries even though the bishop had no right to do so.[63] Geoffrey was also upset with this bishop over the tithes from the salt pans located at Oléron – an island 200 miles to the southeast of Vendôme.[64] The patrimony of the abbey of Vendôme was extensive indeed, much of it gained through gifts but then developed due to the monks' own labor and management. As well as land, the monks also controlled winepresses, windmills, forges and bridges. Like the abbesses of St. Avit and lords of Beaugency, St. Trinité constructed these structures to exploit natural resources, but also as sources of revenue needed for the burgeoning commercial economy. Evidence of Geoffrey's interest in enriching his monastery through building is apparent in two letters that he wrote to the bishop of Le Mans requesting that he return his monk, John, who was a mason, to St. Trinité. The bishop – who was probably refurbishing the cathedral at Le Mans or his own episcopal palace – was hesitant to send John back and Geoffrey eventually had to resort to seeking excommunication for poor John.[65] Overseeing such an extensive real estate portfolio was a full time job, and Geoffrey undoubtedly relied upon his prior and other officers for assistance.

The personal side of Abbot Geoffrey

It might seem from this recitation of complaints against the nobility and fellow clerics that Geoffrey's relationship with them was fraught. This is not the entire picture, however, for in many of his letters to his own monks, penned while he was away, he expresses his genuine love and affection for his brothers: "Brother Geoffrey . . . to his dear sons and brothers."[66] Geoffrey could also be a thoughtful friend and colleague. When his "intimate friends" or clerical colleagues fell ill, Geoffrey dispatched the monk-doctor from

63 GV, letter 53, pp. 93–95.
64 GV, letter 177, pp. 406–409.
65 GV, letters 145 and 146, pp. 312–315.
66 GV, letter 164, pp. 360–361.

St. Trinité to attend them.[67] Abbot Geoffrey enjoyed a particularly close relationship with Abbot Bernier of the nearby monastery of Bonneval. He invited Bernier to the festival of the Holy Trinity at his monastery in Vendôme. Before attending the court held at Angers over the dispute with the Countess of Vendôme, Geoffrey wrote to Abbot Bernier for his help and counsel. In turn, Geoffrey also provided support to Bernier. He sent several letters to Bernier encouraging him to stand fast in his position against simony in spite of the criticism he was receiving.[68] When Bernier experienced serious difficulties with the monks in his charge, Geoffrey wrote to him:

> Very dear father of Christ, I particularly desire to know of your state, because I am not able to be present in person, I am forced to interrogate you via the present letter, beloved of God and dear to men, to know how your congregation is behaving toward you, because I have no doubt that you are comporting yourself in the best way toward them.[69]

The problems between Bernier and his monks eventually were resolved, for in the next letter to him dated a few years later, Geoffrey writes to inquire if he could borrow a mule for his upcoming trip to Rome.[70]

As an abbot of a prestigious and privileged monastery, Geoffrey often found himself traveling and his letters contain nuggets of detail of what it was like to travel in the Middle Ages. While many of his journeys were overland, travel by water was also an option. When Geoffrey wrote to his prior, he indicated that he would be making the journey to the priory "half by water, half by horse."[71] Travel was also costly, as Geoffrey communicated to the abbot of St. Jean of Angély that he "did not have the silver" to travel to his monastery.[72] As well as visiting the abbey's priories, Abbot Geoffrey also voyaged to cities for legal proceedings and to meet with his fellow clergy.[73] Geoffrey was on the road quite a bit on the abbey's business and in several

67 GV, letter 52, pp. 92–93. Medieval letter writers often used flowery language to describe relationships. "Intimate friends," although suggestive to modern ears, meant not men with whom Geoffrey was physically intimate, but rather his closest and dearest friends. Bernard of Clairvaux in particular was known for using the language of what appears to be secular love in writing to his colleagues and friends. For an example of the sense of intimacy that his letters reflect see Bernard's letters to Countess Ermengarde of Brittany on *Epistolae: Medieval Women's Latin Letters:* https://epistolae.ccnmtl.columbia.edu/letter/244.html and https://epistolae.ccnmtl.columbia.edu/letter/245.html. For analysis of this correspondence, Shaun Madison Krahmer, "Interpreting the Letters of Bernard of Clairvaux to Ermengard, Countess of Brittany: The Twelfth-Century Context and Language of Friendship," *Cistercian Studies Quarterly,* 27 (1992): 217–250.

68 GV, letter 111, pp. 214–217.

69 GV, letter 119, p. 231.

70 GV, letter 132, pp. 270–271.

71 GV, letter 171, p. 399.

72 GV, letter 149, pp. 324–325.

73 GV, letter 47, pp. 84–85.

of his letters he commented unfavorably on his lodgings. When traveling south to Saintes – perhaps to deal with the claims the bishop of Saintes made to his monastery's rights – Geoffrey sought lodging at a priory of St. Aubin of Angers. He sent a messenger ahead to request a place to stay and in response was treated very rudely. Upon returning home, Geoffrey wrote to the abbot of St. Aubin to express his displeasure over the treatment he received at another monk's hands.[74] Geoffrey reminded him that the Rule of St. Benedict specified that hospitality is to be provided to fellow monks. Nor was this the only time Geoffrey experienced a less than hospitable welcome. When he and his entourage found themselves in the midst of a violent storm, they sought refuge at a nearby priory. However, the cellarer was reluctant to provide hospitality because the prior was away and protested that he did not have space enough to house Geoffrey and his party. Geoffrey wrote to the insubordinate monk's superiors strongly expressing his displeasure, attributing the cellarer's reluctance to his being a "slave to avarice" and unwilling to share his priory's resources with his monastic brethren.[75]

As well as visiting monasteries around France, Geoffrey also journeyed to Rome several times. As a dedicated reformer, the abbot went to Rome to meet with the pope, but also to seek his assistance in bringing unruly clergy and nobility to heel. His letters reveal that he was sometimes reluctant to leave Vendôme and feared the dangers a trip to Italy might entail. In 1118 Geoffrey traveled with the archbishop of Tours to see the pope. On another trip that was likely his last trip to see the pontiff, Geoffrey wrote to the archbishop of Reims to ask that he be able to join his party.[76] Travel even around the Touraine could be dangerous, as Geoffrey frequently indicated he was reticent to make a journey and often requested guarantees of safe conduct from his ecclesiastical superiors.

Abbot Geoffrey's correspondence also reflects many of the important ecclesiastical questions and developments of his day. Geoffrey wrote about issues central to those clergy who were committed to reforming the church in the late eleventh and early twelfth century. To expunge lay influence, reformers insisted that all ecclesiastical property, including churches, tithes and other revenues, must be the exclusive province of the church. This meant that those aristocrats who controlled such property were encouraged to restore these properties to the church (and threatened with excommunication or damnation if they did not). In spite of Geoffrey's long and impassioned letter to the bishop of Chartres chiding him for not doing more to ensure that church property was restored, the preambles to many charters from the Chartrain indicate that aristocrats understood this tenet of reform and were

74 GV, letter 76, pp. 142–145.

75 GV, letter 54, pp. 94–97.

76 GV, letter 204, pp. 510–511. This journey was at the end of Geoffrey's life, so he may have been concerned about the rigors of travel as he was aging.

coming to recognize that possessing church property was a serious transgression.[77] Lord Lancelin II demonstrated his understanding of both Scripture and church doctrine when he restored the chapel of St. Sepulcher to St. Trinité around 1080.

> In the name of the father, and the son and the Holy Spirit, the one and only true and almighty God, I, Lancelin the knight who is called of Beaugency, often pondering and being lured by the fragility and intransigence of human affairs, reflect that absolutely nothing of man's gifts of transitory things prevails to endure for a long time, except for those [things] that are [given] for the love of God's poor or the churches or the monasteries, only those that are bestowed through the grace of fraternal compassion and the pure intention of pleasing God [and] have been given generously in this world; in consideration of these things, so it appears to me, not in unthoughtful agreement, as I hold in great esteem the words of the Apostle Paul who said this: "We brought nothing into this word and we certainly do not carry anything out;"[78] and that: "Time is short, it remains that they also who have wives be as if they have none, and they that weeps as though they wept not, and they who rejoice as if they rejoiced not, and they that buy as if they possessed not, and they who used this world as if they used it not; for the fashion of this world pass away."[79] But also that the Psalm: "He has distributed freely, he has given to the poor, righteousness remains His forever."[80]
>
> Therefore considering these words, to which I am so strongly dedicated, weighing which is right for me: All the good of the grant for Lord against that of the good for the temporal world, [I] not deserving reward and always conceding virtue in this world, however little, not only do I give but I also restore for the redemption of my sins and for the health of my soul [and the souls] of my relatives and also my son Ralph, the church namely which is situated among the walls of my castle, and is consecrated in the name and honor of the holy tomb of our Lord God Jesus Christ, and Holy Mary mother of the same God, and our Lord and Saviour of the world and all the saints, I bestow to the monastery of St. Trinité of Vendôme, so that it is held and possessed by law in perpetuity and quietly, under the name of the monastery, thoroughly out of touch from all men and every controversial false claim.[81]

Lancelin was concerned about the corruption that worldly goods could have and determined that the best course of action was to give them to the church.

77 GV, letter 182, pp. 416–423.

78 First Epistle to Timothy.

79 Epistle to the Corinthians, chapter 7, lines 29–31; www.latinvulgate.com/verse.aspx?t=1&b=7&c=7

80 Psalm 112.

81 *STV*, no. 279, vol. 1, pp. 431–436.

For, he concludes, material things can only be of benefit when they are working for the good of the monks or the church. The charter also indicates that he was familiar enough with Scripture to reference it in his gift. Implicit in his struggle was that Lancelin possessed a church, which he eventually "both gave and restored" to the monks. The use of the verb, restore, is particularly significant here as it signals that Lancelin realized on some level that this property rightfully belonged to the church. While it is true that Lancelin's hand did not write the charter – a monk did – he would have likely dictated it and had final approval of the written document. As a consequence, I believe this document can be interpreted as a reflection of what a nobleman knew about church reform, but also Scripture. Abbot Geoffrey may have been concerned that the reformers' stance on church property had yet to be fully accepted by secular society, but Lancelin's benefaction demonstrates that the message was in fact getting through.

This abbot also violently opposed clerics whom he believed had gained their office through lay influence or lay investiture (the granting of an ecclesiastical office by a lay person). Between 1116 and 1118, Geoffrey sent a blistering criticism of these practices to the newly elected bishop of Angers, whose election Geoffrey had fought tooth and nail because he believed he was unfit for church office.[82] The abbot of Vendôme also fiercely defended the right of the papacy. In letter after letter, he continually dressed-down bishops who thought their authority exceeded that of the pope. In particular, Geoffrey seems to have taken umbrage with Bishop Hildebert of Le Mans, who lifted sentences of excommunication even though it was not his place to do so – which Geoffrey forcefully pointed out[83] (see Document 27, page 253). Abbot Geoffrey of Vendôme was well schooled in the tenets of reform and a dedicated reformer who did his best to ensure that all clergy complied with them.

Geoffrey's letters reveal much about his personality, as well as issues of the day. Clearly this was a man who was uncompromising in his beliefs – be it the obligation of a monastery to provide hospitality to fellow monks or the elevation of a bishop. Geoffrey was sure he was in the right and was fearless in defending his ideals. While Geoffrey's sometimes ferocious defense can make him appear inflexible, he brought the same dedication and loyalty to caring for the monks in his charge and his friends. He was smart, politically astute and eloquent. Geoffrey was also every inch the aristocrat. His letters convey his sense of superiority and expectation that things will be just as he wants them. In this regard, he was similar to the Beaugency lords. Aristocrats were entitled, powerful and used to getting their own way (as the dispute over Ohlem and Hilducia in Chapter 5 illustrates). Geoffrey was as fearless, and skilled, in defending the church as his kinsmen were in defending their secular lordships.

82 GV, letter 142, pp. 300–309.

83 Abbot Geoffrey's issue here seems to be that excommunication could not be lifted by a sole bishop. Rather only an episcopal synod could commute this sentence.

Conclusion: Abbot Geoffrey and Abbess Ada

Their lives separated by almost a century, Abbot Geoffrey and Abbess Ada had much in common but they also speak to the diversity of experience for those who entered the church. They both lived through a time of considerable change as the twelfth and thirteenth century saw religion and monasticism evolve. As abbess and abbot of Benedictine houses they were responsible for the spiritual lives of their flock, but also insuring their communities had sufficient resources for their support. Moreover, both started life in aristocratic families and while each chose to dedicate themselves to God, their lives continued to be affected by their noble neighbors and kin. Abbot Geoffrey battled to prevent lay control of ecclesiastical property and to defend St. Trinité's holding from aristocratic intrusion. Abbess Ada sought out noble born patrons to help support her convent and appealed to her relatives to make gifts to St. Avit. She, too, protected her abbey's property from those who would usurp it. While much of their time was taken up with asserting their rights and defending their community, Geoffrey and Ada were unquestionably dedicated to the religious life. As a nun and a monk, they spent much of their time in prayer and contemplation. Like their brothers and sisters, they too were called to pray seven times a day. The communities of St. Trinité and St. Avit demonstrate the rigors of religious life that those members of the Beaugency family who dedicated their lives to God would experience.

Suggested reading

Alison I. Beach, *Women as Scribes: Book Production and Monastic Reform in Twelfth-Century Bavaria*. Cambridge: Cambridge University Press, 2010; "Listening for the Voices of Admont's Twelfth-Century Nuns." In *Voices in Dialogue: New Problems in Women's Cultural History*, eds. Kathryn Kerby-Fulton and Linda Olson, pp. 187–198, South Bend: University of Notre Dame Press, 2005.

Elizabeth Dachowski, *First among Abbots: The Career of Abbo of Fleury.* Washington D.C.: Catholic University of America Press, 2008.

Jacques Dalarun, *Robert Arbrissel: Sex, Sin and Salvation in the Middle Ages,* trans. Bruce L. Venarde. Washington D.C.: Catholic University of America Press, 2006.

Adam J. Davis, *The Holy Bureaucrat: Eudes Rigaud and Religious Reform in Thirteenth Century Normandy.* Ithaca and London: Cornell University Press, 2006.

Penelope D. Johnson, *Equal in Monastic Profession: Religious Women in Medieval France.* Chicago: University of Chicago Press, 1994.

Anne Lester, *Creating Cistercian Nuns: The Women's Religious Reform Movement in Thirteenth-Century Champagne.* Ithaca and London: Cornell University Press, 2011.

Megan M. McLaughlin, *Sex, Gender and Authority in an Age of Reform, 1000–1122.* Cambridge: Cambridge University Press, Reprint 2014.

Kathleen Hapgood Thompson, *The Monks of Tiron: A Monastic Community and Religious Reform.* Cambridge: Cambridge University Press, 2014.

Bruce Venarde, *Women's Monasticism and Medieval Society: Nunneries in France and England.* Ithaca and London: Cornell University Press, 1999.

8 Conclusion: From warrior to administrator

The evolving nature of medieval aristocratic life is recorded in stone and mortar in the castle at Beaugency, in parchment and ink in the cartulary of Notre Dame de Beaugency and manifest in the flesh and blood of the later Beaugency lords.

The *donjon* at Beaugency was constructed some time in the eleventh century, likely started by Lancelin I. The remains of the *donjon* demonstrate it was designed for defensive purposes: The walls were thick, there were few windows and the majority of the space was designed to house a military force and provide public access to the lord (see Figures 1.4 and 1.7). Some smaller spaces were interspersed throughout that could be used solely by the lord's family. The twelfth century saw profound changes to the *donjon*, as windows were added and enlarged. Ralph I may have overseen the addition of the handsome twinned arch windows to the second story of the tower. These were considerably larger openings and far more decorative than earlier efforts. These modifications improved living in the *donjon* and reflect a time when defense was not as paramount and comfort was more of an objective. Under the lordship of Lancelin III the castle witnessed another impressive set of renovations. A third floor was added to the tower to provide additional space, with areas that could be used as private rooms. Two watchtowers were also constructed, as well as the crenellations. Perhaps, like Lord Arnold of Ardres, he commissioned "a certain architect or carpenter" to build a "three storey structure" and to help with these renovations.[1]

By the turn of the thirteenth century, the castle at Beaugency had transformed from a military fort to the home of a prosperous lord. While the military character and function of the tower was maintained, just like the lords themselves maintained their position as "those who fight," there were other additions to castle that provided for creature comforts and the appropriate setting for a lord who not only commanded men, but also considerable wealth. The lords, like the fortification from which they took

1 Lambert of Ardres, *The Counts of Guines*, p. 146. Recall that Lord Arnold of Ardres' new castle was also three stories. For this description, see Chapter 1.

Visit the companion website: www.routledge.com/cw/livingstone

their name, underwent change. By the dawn of the thirteenth century these people were not simply warriors, but literate businessmen and managers of considerable estates.

Early in the fourteenth century, the canons of Notre Dame de Beaugency decided to collate and organize the records of the property, revenues, rents and tolls that made up the abbey's patrimony. This would have entailed copying (and perhaps redacting) the information contained in the abbey's original charters (see Figures 0.1a and 0.1b). The timing of the construction of the cartulary was not accidental; rather it coincided with King Philip IV's taking over of the lordship of Beaugency. Understandably, the clergy of Notre Dame de Beaugency wanted to have a clear record of what the abbey possessed in the face of increased royal presence – particularly since the king was interested in accruing as much land, revenue and power as he could muster. It was in the abbey's best interest to have a strong sense of what they owned and what was owed to them. Significantly, when deciding how to organize their records, the scribe who put together the cartulary opted to start with acts issued by King Philip IV, all dating from the early fourteenth century, rather than beginning chronologically with the earlier acts of the lords of Beaugency. This choice at once signals royal dominance, but also the change in status of the lords who had once reigned supreme. Here ink and parchment bear witness to the important shifts in political power that characterized France from the time of Louis VII (1137–1180) to that of his great-great-great grandson, King Philip IV (1285–1314).

Flesh and blood: The last lords of Beaugency, c. 1180–1300

The last will and testament of Ralph I's two sons, Lancelin III and Simon I, help to crystalize some of the important changes in lordship from the beginning of their father's tenure as lord around 1090 to the death of Lancelin III about one hundred years later (1182). Throughout his life, Ralph made gifts of land to traditional Benedictine monasteries (St. Trinité and Marmoutier) and some of the new monastic houses in the region (the abbeys of Tiron and Notre-Dame de Josaphat), as well as conferring fiefs. His patronage was representative of what lords granted out in the late eleventh and early twelfth centuries: Land and revenue. In contrast, that of his son Simon, who died around 1154, was quite different. In his will, Simon did not donate any significant amount of property (only two mills, some pasture and vineyards). Yet his will is extremely long and detailed and designated gifts to nearly a dozen different religious institutions – as well as recording his debts. Most of his donations were cash gifts – dues, rents, tolls and rights. Moreover, he did not grant out any of his land as fiefs. This signifies an important change from what his father had given a generation earlier and testifies to the economic, but also political, changes of the 1120s–1150s.

Simon's will indicates that the tenor of lordship had changed. Unlike his predecessors, Simon was not concerned with building fortresses or defending against hostile neighbors or lords. Rather, he was involved with developing the resources of his lordship, which were considerable, and finding ways to make money in the emerging commercial economy. The rift between the Beaugency family and King Louis VI and King Louis VII meant that Simon did not participate in any wars for the king or count. Yet this did not mean that his power had diminished as he spent his time holding courts, maintaining peace and overseeing the resources that made up his lordship. Tools of governance developed during Simon's tenure that helped him to rule his lordship more effectively. Like many of their class, the lords of Beaugency had started using a seal as a symbol of their power and to authenticate documents –hopefully preventing forgeries and disputes. Simon was the first to employ a seal (see Figures 8.1a and b). The closing of an 1149 charter recording Simon's gift to St. Lomer of Blois reads "Hervé the chancellor of Lord Simon wrote this."[2] This indicates that Simon had a personal chancellor and that the lords of Beaugency had their own chancery or record-keeping office by the mid-twelfth century. Lordship was becoming more bureaucratic, more formalized, and the Beaugency lords used these tools to govern their lordship well.

Figures 8.1a and b The seals of two Beaugency lords – Lord Simon I, c. 1150 (left) and Lord Ralph II, c. 1280 (right). Note how the seal has developed from the mid-twelfth century to the mid-thirteenth century. It has gone from rudimentary to quite elaborate detail. Some of Simon I's charters indicate that he sealed the document and he was the first Beaugency lord to use a seal. This is likely what his seal looked like, if not the seal he used. Archives nationales, Centre de sigillographie et de héraldique, BM 157 and S 8759. Author photo.

2 Mediathéque d'Orléans, MS 489.

Simon's brother, Lancelin III, succeeded him as lord by 1154 and died in 1182. Many of the realities that defined Simon's experience as lord of Beaugency continued under Lancelin. As he was approaching death, Lancelin set his affairs in order by issuing a charter that would act as his last will and testament[3] (see Document 28, page 254). In contrast to his father's movie-star-hero life, Lancelin remained at home to help govern the family holdings and attend to the collection of rents, oversee peasants and provide justice to vassals. Nor did he ever appear in any royal acts. Unlike his father's day when being a lord meant defending your castle and fighting for your king or count, Lancelin did not participate in any wars or even local battles. While such a life experience hardly attracted the comment of contemporary chroniclers, in many ways such a peaceful life was something of a triumph in itself and reflective of the influence that the lord of Beaugency commanded.

The years spanning the reign of Louis VII (1137–1180) and the lives of these lords of Beaugency were important ones. During these decades, profound transformations took place. Sometimes these changes manifested themselves dramatically, but more often they took place quietly and without fanfare. That Lancelin III was able to rule his lordship without repelling enemies from his castle gate suggests that this was a time of political stability – and this stability is evident in the orderly landscape in the second illustration of the three orders (see Figure 1.3). In contrast to his father and grandfather, whose main objective was to acquire and defend land combined with fighting for their lords in the wars that raged in the Loire Valley, Lancelin and his brother spent their energies preserving what they had and developing their holdings to generate revenue. Significantly, the only vassal provided for in Lancelin's testament did not hold land from Lancelin. Rather he held a money fief from tolls exacted from the bridge at Beaugency, which Lancelin gave to the church to have the anniversary of his vassal's death celebrated (see Document 28, page 254). Although the lord of Beaugency had granted revenue rather than land to his vassal, there were still strong bonds of affinity between them as Lancelin donated revenue to provide for the spiritual health of his vassal.

While he might not have controlled as much territory as his progenitors, Lancelin III ruled over a rich lordship (see Maps 3 and 4). His wealth – and his power – came from the exploitation of the bounty of the land. His social world was changing too. Families like the Beaugencys no longer populated the inner circle of counts and kings. New families had taken their place, but also new men whose skills extended beyond bravery in battle as they could read, write and figure too. Indeed these changes to the aristocracy are apparent in the two depictions of medieval society discussed in Chapter 1. In the earlier rendering (see Figure 1.2), the military function of the aristocracy is clear: The knight is wearing chain mail and carrying a weapon. But in the

3 AD Loiret H 10, folio XXI verso; *NDB*, no. 75, pp. 86–88.

later rendition (Figure 1.3), the chain mail has been traded in for elegant clothing lined with fur – a sign of both wealth and status. And while one of the aristocratic group is wearing armor, it is largely ceremonial rather than something a warrior would actually wear in battle. These men have been transformed from warriors into courtiers and administrators.

The trends evident in the last testaments of Simon I and Lancelin III continued to develop and evolve over the next three generations of Beaugency lords and Capetian kings (see Genealogy 1). Lord John I succeeded his father, Lancelin III, as lord of Beaugency in 1182. John continued improving the castle precincts by building a small personal chapel for the family's use (see Map 1). Like his predecessors, John made many gifts of anniversary masses for his kin to several ecclesiastical communities, which similarly consisted of revenue or gifts in kind rather than land. Indeed, John's most extensive gifts concerned granting half of what he collected from the fair of St. Nicholas, testament to both the changing nature of the economy and lordship: Markets and revenues had taken the place of land as the currency of power.[4] John I also had a chancellor and used a seal. The charters record that both Simon I and Lancelin III sealed their charters, but Lord John I (1182–1218) was the first to make habitual use of the seal and his successors would follow his lead.[5] The thirteenth-century documents reveal other important changes in governance of the Beaugency lordship.

In February of 1221, the bishop of Orléans wrote a letter outlining the settlement of a dispute over what Lord John II (the son of John I) had given to Notre Dame de Beaugency. The parties involved were John II's widow Mathilda and her second husband, Robert of Courtenay. Robert, it appears, had claimed more than what Mathilda had a right to through her dower grant from John II.[6] A court was convened where Robert's lawyer and agent presented a letter he had penned outlining what he asserted were Robert's and Mathilda's rights to this property, which consisted of revenue from tolls, wheat ground in the mills and bottles of wine from the annual grape-pressing. Robert's representatives made his case and a compromise was reached. To indicate her consent to the compromise, Lady Mathilda sent a letter of patent (meaning a letter with her seal) to the bishop and the abbot. In contrast to previous contestations, this one has more of a bureaucratic sense to it. Robert did not assert his rights to this property through violence or invading the land as Lord Lancelin II had in the eleventh century when he sent armed men

4 AD Loiret H 10, folio V; *NDB*, no. 10, pp. 18–19.

5 Archives nationales, Centre de sigillographie, BM 157 and S 8759. There are modern models of the seals of Simon I and Ralph III, but none of the other lords. The Centre de sigillographie identifies seal BM 157 as being that of Lord John I of Beaugency. It is possible that this is his seal, but I however think it is more likely to be Simon I's seal. See footnote 13, Chapter 3 and Figure 8.1 for an explanation.

6 AD Loiret H 10, folio VI verso; *NDB*, no. 15, pp. 25–27.

to occupy lands that had been granted to the church, property which he believed belonged to him. Robert and Mathilda behaved quite differently. Instead they sent their lawyer and representative with documents to argue their case. Their twelfth-century predecessors, Lord Ralph I and Mathilda were also clearly literate, and the ability to read and write had become essential to being a lord by the thirteenth century. Moreover, these thirteenth-century lords employed agents who ran their estates, advocates to represent their interests and chancellors to pen letters of patent outlining their rights and positions. In the next generation, when Lord Simon II, John II's brother and Mathilda's brother-in-law, was entangled in a dispute with the monastery of St. Avit of Orléans, he too sent one of his officials to represent his position and argue his case. The issue in dispute was rights of justice and punishment. Again, a compromise was reached through the mediation of the monastery and lord's representatives.

In spite of earlier attempts by count and king to assert their dominion over the Beaugency lords, the Beaugencys had maintained their independence – even when they faithfully served the counts of Chartres. This balance of power shifted, however, under Simon II.

In 1222, Simon II of Beaugency took an oath to the count in which he recognized the count's suzerainty over himself and his lordship (see Document 29, page 255). This was unprecedented. When an earlier count had tried to establish his dominion over Ralph I, Ralph offered to fight a judicial duel against the count himself to protect his independence.[7] Two prominent bishops intervened to prevent the duel and Ralph retained his autonomy. By the early thirteenth century, however, the scales had tipped in the favor of those lords who controlled large regions of France – in addition to the county Blois, the comital house of Blois (which had split with that of Chartres to create two separate counties) also held extensive territory in the north of France. Simon swore in front of all of his vassals that the tower and fortress of Beaugency were now under the count's control. Hence, when Ralph II succeeded his father as lord in 1253, the lordship he inherited was no longer independent, but titularly under the dominion of the count of Blois. The intrusion of higher placed lords into the lordship of Beaugency would escalate during Ralph II's tenure.

Shortly after he became lord, Ralph II issued a document that clarified all of the dues and revenues that the canons of Notre Dame de Beaugency had received from his ancestors in gift. In this regard, Ralph II was much like previous lords of Beaugency. However, Ralph's acts reflect a new reality of lordship. In 1272, Ralph II was summoned by King Philip III to fight in his

7 Charles Métais, *Fréteval, Beaugency, Saint-Aignan: Châteaux jurables et rendables aux comtes de Blois, 1220 à 1252,* (Châteaudun: J. Pigelet, 1889), p. 156. Insistence on taking an oath may have been the situation that caused the rift between Ralph and Count Thibaut IV in the early twelfth century. Recall that Bishop Ivo of Chartres wrote to Ralph about his involvement in a judicial due (see Document 2, page 223) and advising him to reconcile with his lord, the count.

campaign against the counts of Foix.[8] But Ralph never went on campaign. The royal account recording the lord of Beaugency's summons states: "The Lord of Beaugency appeared for himself; he was excused due to poverty."[9] By 1272, the Beaugency family had been reduced to dire straits (or at least claimed to be) to the point where they could not afford to provide military service even when asked by the king. This represents a dramatic decline from the time when Ralph I set off on crusade with his retinue in 1096.

Starting in 1280, Ralph II began issuing his charters in French. This signifies a cultural as well as a mental shift. Latin was phasing out as the language of politics to be replaced by the vernacular languages – meaning that potentially anyone could understand the document if it was read aloud to them. Ralph was active as the lord of Beaugency up until the mid-1290s. He issued charters, made gifts and confirmed alienations of property by his vassals. He also allowed the canons of Notre Dame de Beaugency to cut through a passage in the wall between the castle and monastery to provide them better access to their buildings – a clear indication that this lord of Beaugency did not feel particularly threatened and a testament to the peace that had been established by the Capetian kings. Yet the increased power of the Capetian monarchy also undermined Beaugency autonomy. King Philip IV was committed to bringing all regions of France directly under his control. He accomplished this through submission and conquest, but also the more practical approach of purchasing lordships. In 1291 King Philip paid Ralph II of Beaugency the hefty sum of 5400 pounds for the lordship:[10]

> To all who see and hear this presently, Dreux Pellerin, the **prévot** of Orléans, [sends] greetings.
>
> All should know that the noble man, Sire Ralph, lord of Beaugency, knight, sells, abandons, to the very high lord, Philip, king of France . . . This is to be all that is known as Beaugency, i.e. all of the barony

8 Simon II was also summoned in 1236 and 1242 by King Louis IX. There is no evidence to indicate that Simon actually fought for the king in 1236 and the charters demonstrate that he was in Beaugency in 1242–1243. So even though he may have been summoned to fight, Simon remained at home. The king, apparently, did not look askance at Simon's lack of participation in the military expedition since there is no indication that Simon was punished or fined in any way – a sign of royal benign neglect. See *RHF*, vol. 23, eds. Natalis de Wailly, Léopold Delisle and Charles Jourdain (Paris: H. Welter, 1894), pp. 725–726. Similarly a later rendition of Joinville's history of St. Louis' crusades lists a "Simon of Beaugency" as going on the Tunis campaign in 1270. However, Lord Simon II of Beaugency was dead by 1253. *RHF*, vol. 20, nouvelle edition, ed. P.C.F Daunou and J. Naudet, (Paris: Royale Impremerie, 1840), p. 308. It is possible that the entry might refer to Ralph IIIs son, Simon. But given this is a later addition, even this identification is dubious.

9 "Ce sont les noms de ceux qui tiennent a nu du roy en la bailli d Orliens, qui son semons a Tours a la quinzaine de Pasques par le commandement du roy," in *RHF*, vol. 23, p. 762.

10 P. Bouvier, "L'acquisition de la seigneurie de Beaugency par Philip le Bel," *Le Môyen Age* 26 (1913): 266. Archives nationales, J 162 no. 7.

> and castellany with all that pertains to them . . . At St. Lorenz des Aireux, at Briou, at Chaumont, etc . . . and all of the other things which make up the property, that is in chattels, in villages, in bourgs, in the fortress, from the water [e.g. rights to rivers, streams, ponds, mill races, sluices], in rent, in land, in vines, in pasture, in wood, in gardens, in the roads, in houses, in pasturage, in justice, in the seigneury and in all other things, and in all of the fiefs and other rear-fiefs, and the aforementioned Sire Ralph retained for himself while he lives, for his support, accommodations at Beaugency, the rooms and gardens of the same place.[11]

Evidence of the newly established royal control emerges in the documents shortly after the sale. In 1297 Ralph II's son, Simon, was described as "Simon of Beaugency, Lord of Jouy." While Simon is described as coming *from* Beaugency, he was not called the lord *of* Beaugency. Rather he was the lord of a lesser neighboring lordship, that of Jouy. Two years later in 1299, King Philip IV himself issued a charter concerning the lordship of Beaugency. Specifically, he spelled out what dues previous lords of Beaugency had given to the abbey of Notre Dame de Beaugency. The cartulary of Notre Dame de Beaugency places this act as one of the first in the collection – tangible evidence of this power shift. A royal official now managed Beaugency and the former lords were relegated.

Populating the landscape over which the lords from Simon I to Ralph II reigned were peasants who had become increasingly free over the course of years since the time of Lancelin II. They had benefitted from the commercial economy as their labors were commuted to payments and opportunities for additional income through trade – or even moving to a town and adopting a trade – became realities. By the end of the thirteenth century, there were more of them and they were better fed through the combined use of new technologies and protein rich crops. Forests had been cleared and more land was under cultivation. Their houses were larger and some of them might even be built of stone and have windows. The commercial economy also meant a wider array of goods was available to them. They no longer had to wait for seasonal markets to purchase their wares, rather they could visit local markets that were held if not daily then several times a week.

Stepping outside the castle walls, a thirteenth-century lord would encounter a structure that was not present when Lancelin II ruled over Beaugency: The current abbey church of Notre Dame de Beaugency. Although there had been a community of monks present in Lancelin II's time, by about 1104 the monks and their church were both in decay. Ralph I acted to replace the monks with newly reformed canons and under Simon I or Lancelin III a new

11 Translated from Pellieux, *Beaugency*, p. 130.

Romanesque church was completed to replace the old monastic church.[12] It is an impressive structure and a testament to the importance of the abbey, town and lordship. New ecclesiastical structures and communities had been founded all over the lands that the Beaugencys called home and the places where they worshipped. As a result of its increased population and concomitant concern for the wellbeing of its poorer residents, an almshouse was built in Beaugency. So too were places for the sick, such as hospitals and leprosaria. Alongside these more modest structures were larger, newly reformed monasteries. Like the castle and the land itself, the ecclesiastical landscape had changed significantly since the time of Lancelin I and Lancelin II.

The village of Beaugency had also transformed. It was larger both in population and area than it had been in the eleventh century. A market place dominated the center of town – and was just a short walk from both the castle and abbey. A new set of walls delineated the boundaries of the town. There were more streets and more residences. Some belonged to merchants, other buildings provided shops and homes for craftsmen practicing a range of occupations. Markets were held and people from all over the region came to buy and sell. Jews and Templars could be counted among the town-village's residents, with the occasional foreign merchant or itinerant preacher making a stop. The merchant may have been looking for new markets for his cloth, while a Franciscan brother stood in the market place and spoke of the dangers of greed and avarice.

By the end of the thirteenth century, the Beaugencys were either willing, or compelled by royal autocracy and declining finances, to give up their right to rule as independent lords. Over the course of the thirteenth century, the kings of France had become more and more powerful – a fact that is well illustrated in the later depiction of medieval society in Figure 1.3 (Chapter 1) that was created during or shortly after the reign of King Philip IV. The king is at the center of the upper register, seated on a throne bedecked in glorious robes against a backdrop of blue tapestries emblazoned with the royal symbol of the fleur-de-lys. He is the center of attention – and power – while the church and aristocrats stand obediently at his side. Governance came to be centered in Paris, with a trained bureaucracy overseeing justice and the collection of revenue. Contributions of kings like Philip II Augustus and Louis IX provided a strong, centralized kingship for their successors. The lords of Beaugency, while sidelined from the politics of the royal court, did benefit from these changes as the economy flourished and peace reigned. They themselves contributed in no small part to this peace and prosperity through their able management of the Beaugency patrimony. As the year 1300

12 The church was started during Ralph I's lifetime, but finished during his sons. The twelfth-century abbey church was damaged during the Wars of Religion and during World War II, however, and there have been some modern additions. But overall the size and space of the church is much as it would have appeared to people of Simon I's time.

approached, however, King Philip IV sought to further strengthen and consolidate royal power by bringing lordships like Beaugency under his direct control. Hence, he purchased the lordship from the Beaugencys and it became part of the **royal demesne** – granted out to support various royal children or their spouses. The Beaugency family continued to live comfortably in their château, call themselves "lord," and enjoy local prominence. But they were no longer autonomous lords. Although they provided local justice occasionally, they did so as agents of the king. The age of independent feudal lords had come to an end.

Suggested reading

John W. Baldwin, *The Government of Philip Augustus: Foundations of French Royal Power in the Middle Ages.* Berkeley: University of California Press, 1991; *Paris, 1200.* Palo Alto, CA: Stanford University Press, 2010.

Joseph R. Strayer, *The Reign of Philip the Fair.* Princeton: Princeton University Press, 1980.

William Chester Jordan and Jenna Rebecca Philips. *The Capetian Century: 1214 to 1314.* Turnhout: Brepols, 2017.

Documents

No. 1: Charter from St. Trinité of Vendôme recording the establishment of a settlement by Ralph I of Beaugency at Montfollet, April 26, 1085

Translated from *Cartulaire de Sainte-Trinité de Vendôme*, ed. L'Abbé Charles Métais, 5 vols (Paris: Alphonse Picard et Fils, 1893), vol. 2, no. 325, pp. 32–35.

We and our successors are led by the certainty and necessity to relate perpetually by the recording of letters the faithful memory of how Ralph I, son of Lancelin II of Beaugency, gave to the Lord God and the Monastery of Vendôme the church of the fortified settlement that is commonly called Montfollet. Accordingly, he gave from these and other of his properties [from] what appears to be his at present, and even promising in the future he would give [from] what will seem to be his, with the condition that the monks would build a church in the fortified settlement, where, [as] he showed them, presently [stands a church constructed] in wood. Truly so that they would begin building this church in stone, he made clear and designated, following the estimate of the monks, how much land there will be for the construction work around the location of the church for many outbuildings in addition to all of the other buildings that would appear to need to be built.

In addition he gave land for making a burg [a settlement], however much will be necessary, conceding to the monks all of every revenue from the same burg, and all of the customs for selling as well as buying, or any business of any craft or occupation. Also in the same burg even in all of the property pertaining to the jurisdiction of the monks, he himself will do nothing while he lives, nor will he agree to anything to be done; he will quarrel with no burghers' credit or loan or hospitality in their houses for his men or for foreigners; however of the goods that will be bought or sold in his market, he will hold his just rights and nothing more; if he will wish to buy something from them [there will be] no oppressing the merchants so that so he would take the best for himself or give any to another so he or she is able to have it; unless due from a rope merchant;

no tolls or dues will he charge them [the monks and those living in the burg] in his market, and not in all of the monks' land, nor question these revenues no matter who or what or anybody of his or the monks will concede voluntarily. Of the men of the monks he will do nothing to collect the ban or the *corvée*, but if armed men or some other strong force will come to plunder or invade his land, or if any enemy wishes to seize the castle in his land around them, only in these two times of trouble will our men come with him. If however he himself will wish to go further [to fight with] others, in this kind of trouble they [the monks' men] will not go with him, nor with his men, and thereupon moreover neither his prévot nor his vicarius will not call up the monks' men to battle, rather the monks alone will say [whether their men can go to battle]; he himself through one of the servants of his men will make the call to battle.

Here at every point these things have been recorded, having consulted with us, and besides equally they have recorded the aforementioned agreement with [consulting] these men whose lands are held around this place[1] whose names are these: Willer son of Frodon of *Sancto-Victore*,[2] and Simon his brother give land consisting of two carrucates, Robert and Ingebald give land of two bovates at *Cergi*. Walter gives land of two bovates at *Cergi*. Hervé gives half of his land at Puteolis, Odo Paganus and Hubert his brother give land from *Pesotum*, which they call *Adsames*, from four bovates; Ralph of Beaugency, son of Lancelin, gives all of the tithes and burial rights of the entire fortified settlement, which he acquired, giving sufficiently in exchange [for these rights], to Otbert Tenerio who possessed these same tithes as if through custom of inheritance, [Ralph gives] even all of the tithes of St. Martin, which he holds around the fortified settlement of Montfollet, and the land for the construction of the out buildings of the monks and he provides enough for buildings of the burg, with all of the customs that he holds in perpetuity, from all of the inhabitants of his burg, and all **pannage**, rents, sales, agreements, and strictures; and in addition, gardens, land, mill pond, if he is able to do so, and all pannage not only of our pigs but all, for the monks' [pigs] will be brought to the woods at that time when the trees in the woods abound in acorns. And also payments and all other customs, if he holds these in our land, by which means we hold these; our land we hold by this means; but even in those, which we had acquired through purchase or gift, in all of his castle grounds, he dedicates to St. Nicholas and us; even land he promised for the building of vines to

1 Meaning close to Ralph's fortress and burg at Montfollet and where the church will be constructed.

2 Reconstructing medieval place names can be challenging as names of places have changed and been modified over the centuries. Place names in italics are in the original Latin because I have not been able to track down a modern equivalent. The documents also do not include Roman numerals after the names of the Beaugency lords. I have inserted them to provide clarity.

all of us and our burghers, and many others, he promised and he singled out. He did all of this not for any gain but only for seeking the mercy of God. We still said to him that we would build the church of Montfollet, when we think it is possible, in honor of St. Nicholas, [and] he gave and will have given the tithes of the pelts from all of his hunters besides. Witnesses: William son of Frodo and his brother Simon Archembald. The illustrious count Stephen, Thibaut [IV] son of the most noble count, through the request of Ralph I, son of Lancelin II of Beaugency, gave his assent to the monks of St. Trinité to construct in this place in honor of God and St. Nicholas at Montfollet. Witnesses: Fulcher son of Nivelon, Rainard the forester of Count Stephen; others; Pagan seneschal of lord Ralph. This is done in the plateau, which is between the woods of trees at *Oscareacum* in the year of the incarnation of the lord 1085 in the month of April, on the day of the Sabbath close to Easter.

No. 2: Letters of Bishop Ivo of Chartres concerning Ralph I of Beaugency, c. 1115

Translations of letters no. 248 and 249 from *Lettres de Saint Ives,* ed. and trans. Lucien Merlet, Mémoires de la société archéologique d'Eure-et-Loir, 8 (1885), pp. 446–448.

Bishop Ivo wrote to his fellow bishop, John of Orléans about an incident involving Ralph I of Beaugency*:*

> Recently, our clergy, returning from Orléans where they have attended the trial of Count Thibaut [IV], reported to us that a knight of Lord Ralph provoked a knight of the count into trial by combat, and that your church approved this provocation by a judgement and fixed a day for this duel. This news has greatly astonished us, because trial by combat hardly ever ends without the spilling of blood: Yet the venerable and unchangeable authority of the Fathers prohibits clergy from taking part in judgements which might result in the spilling of blood, and the Roman Church does not admit trial by combat as a method of proof . . .

Unfortunately the letter does not indicate what caused the knight of Lord Ralph to enter into a judicial dual with the count's knight. Clearly there was some serious matter of dispute between them. Ivo followed up this letter with one to Lord Ralph himself.

> Your well-being demands of me discussion, or a consultation by letter, which could guide you in this difficult situation in which you find yourself. I wrote immediately to the bishop of Orléans of the affair that involves you, [as] it seemed to him that communicating this [information] to me would be useful for him and for you. You are able to learn from

him my opinion on the conflict which rose between you and the count, and the conduct that I counsel you to take here and now. Nevertheless, I respond to your request by urging you, whatever the situation which would occur between you and the count, to show to him always the honor which he is owed and at no point to attempt to inflict any suggestion of infamy on him. Because the Apostle says: "Honor to the one who ought to have.honor, fear to the one who ought to keep fear." And moreover: "All men must submit to the powers who are above him."[3] This is just as David, who had yet to be king, brought honor to the treacherous King Saul; for one day when David found the opportunity to kill him, he satisfied himself by cutting the edge of Saul's coat, and however he repented such a slight insult and beat himself in the chest. Although Saul did not cease the persecution, David honored him always while he lived and wept at his death. Take this example, and imitate this model of peace and of fidelity toward your lord. If you receive an insult from by him, recall this by this reasoning, reject the words of reproach and injury, because these words breed hate without end; pride humiliates, humility elevates. Adieu.

No. 3: Charter recording the entrance of the boy Gaufred into the monastery of Marmoutier, 1037–1064

From *Cartulaire de Marmoutier pour Vendôme*, ed. by M. de Trémault (Paris: Picard et Fils, 1893), no. 29, pp. 321–322.

A certain man of the castle of Lavardin, named Hildebert, putting things in order, bestowing one of his sons to God, surrendering [him] at the monastery of Marmoutier and to the knight of heaven so that the child may so greatly entreat for the salvation of his relatives [so] that nothing of the mundane world will hold them and they conquer the bondage of the chains of [worldly] care. Moreover the boy named Gaufred was received by Lord Abbot Albert and the other brothers, because of the power of the love of God, and his own salvation, and friendship of his father, and showing the customary fear in God than for any advantage of the world. So the aforementioned man gave to Saint Martin, in the assembly of the brothers, land in Varenne situated in the Vendômois, one carrucate of unplowed land, two shillings of rent, paid to Salomon of Lavardin in the summer festival of St. Martin. Hence, so that the gift would be in perpetuity and stable, Salomon, from whom Hildebert himself [held the land], and Count Thibaut, from whom Salomon himself held the land, agreed with joy. And [Hildebert] added one arpent of

3 These quotes seem to be from Romans 13:1a and 13:7. Thus the "apostle" to whom Ivo refers is Paul, author of the Epistles to the Romans.

arable land at *Melchim*, from the fief of the aforementioned Salomon, himself also assenting. The already mentioned Hildebert in addition assigned to the brothers of Marmoutier, twenty pennies of rent from one arpent of his kinsman Archambert, namely so that rent to which is referred, the same Archambert each year in solemnity renders the aforementioned [rent] to the same St. Martin, paying at the same time of celebration.

All of this his wife named Hersend and sons, namely Hildebert, Salomon and Drogo, freely enough authorized, and whose generosity they [the witnesses below] can bear testimony, if it becomes necessary, are noted: Warin major, Rotger, Hildrimus, Gislebert, Raynald.

No. 4: Letter of Lady Mathilda of Beaugency to King Louis VII of France, c. 1140[4]

Translated from *Recueil des historians des Gaules et de la France*, vol. 16, ed. Michel Jean-Joseph Brial (Paris: Imprimerie Royale, 1814), p. 20.

To Louis, king of the Franks, her lord and kinsman. M [Mathilda] of Beaugency, [sends] greetings.

Believing in the loftiness of your reputation, I write these letters [to you] by messenger. Due to the counsel and assent of my sons, Simon, Lancelin and Ralph, I gave in alms to the church of Semoy [just north of Orléans], land which I have bought, and from where I paid rent, and other land which I had wished to develop I [also] release to them, by the agreement, so, while I live, they would pay the land rent on each property; [but] after my death they would hold it freely. And further I solemnly testify to you that Lancelin[5], soon would have made redress [paid the revenue] for the woods of St. Jacob, [but] he brought word to me because the monks might have excommunicated me specifically for the revenues from this land and his counsel [was] to secure an agreement with them. Now however, he whose counsel I followed in this matter, has violently seized the pious gift itself, namely the land rent. For this reason, I mercifully call upon your charity so that you would make my pious gift remain for the love of God, because I am prepared to swear by my hand, or by another of my commands, so as I wrote to you, so that it would be done.

4 The editor of the *Recueil des historians des Gaules et de la France* dated this document around 1160. This date is problematic for several reasons. First, it is unlikely that Mathilda lived until 1160 as she was born around 1080. Moreover, two of the sons she references in the charter – Simon and Ralph – were not alive in 1160. Simon died in 1154 and Ralph was dead by 1148. I would place this letter closer to the start of Louis VII's reign, that is around 1140.

5 Unfortunately Mathilda does not identify who Lancelin was. Given she references her sons above, it is possible that this was her son Lancelin, whose advice she had received earlier.

No. 5: Lady Adenorde's dower, 1150

Translated from *Cartulaire de Sainte-Trinité de Vendôme*, ed. L'Abbé Charles Métais, 5 vols (Paris: Alphonse Picard et Fils, 1893), vol. 2, no. 526, pp. 364–365.

> Let it be known in the present and future that Simon I, lord of Beaugency, gave to us of Holy Trinity the market fairs of Saint-Bienheuré, on behalf of a certain knight who served him in hope of a gracious gift, namely the son of Ridellus of Rillé, who died among us in our hospital [and who] we buried with honor in our close. But this gift, Adenorde, wife of the same Simon, by no means wished to concede then at the time, because Lord Simon had given her the aforementioned fairs of Saint-Bienheuré in dower. After some time the same Adenorde, imprisoned by a grave sickness of the body, becoming aware that she was embarking on the journey of all flesh, now freely relinquished the fairs to us, and she humbly entreated Lord Simon, so that he could restore them to us, for the fairs he himself held in his own hand. Whose requests Lord Simon voluntarily granting in good will, this and many others, for the redemption of the soul of the same Adenorde and his relatives, he gave to us and others. All of which gifts Lancelin III, Simon's brother, at the request of the same Simon, conceded. And so Lancelin granted to us the fairs of Saint-Bienheuré at Beaugency in the court of the monks, before the Galilee gate of St. Sepulcher in the presence of Lord Abbot Robert, the lord abbot sitting on his palfrey, Lancelin truly standing on his feet before the court. Everyone who heard and saw this, on the part of the monks: Lord Abbot Robert, Hylarius the sacrist, Evrard who was then the prior [of the priory of St. Trinité] in Beaugency, Guimund the librarian, Martin of Blois, Martin of Beaugency; of the servants: Evrard of Coulommiers-la-Tour, Eschivard, Russell of the hospital, Robin of Beaugency; on the part of Lancelin III: Lancelin himself, Tebaud Morinus, who was sitting on a certain horse while holding a silver cup in his hand, circumspectly in a suit of armor. This is done at Beaugency, in the court of the monks, in the year 1150 from the incarnation of the Lord.

No. 6: A gift for Lady Elizabeth, 1201

Translated from *Cartulaire de Notre-Dame de Beaugency*, ed. G. Vignat (Orléans, Herluison, 1879), no. 66, pp. 77–78. Archives départmentales du Loiret, H 10, fol. XXII, verso.

> In the name of the holy Trinity, so that the present and future know, since I, John I, lord of Beaugency, for the love of God and also for the redemption of my soul and my ancestors, but most especially for the soul

of my most beloved wife Elizabeth, [and] with the consent of my heirs, John, Ralph, Mathilda, Agnete, Adelicia and Lucia, I gave and conceded to the cellarer of Notre Dame de Beaugency, dues of twelve measures of wheat and twelve measures of oat, which I held in the land of the deceased John of Poisseaux, rendered and collected in perpetuity in the octave of the Feast of St. Remigius.[6] For this pious gift, therefore, the canons of Notre Dame de Beaugency will observe the anniversary of my most beloved wife each year; which truly the cellarer himself of the same canons will solemnly administer on the day of the anniversary [of her death]. In addition, my most beloved wife, Elizabeth, gave and conceded for her soul, four shillings of rent in perpetual possession to the sacrist of Notre Dame de Beaugency; therefore the sacrist himself will arrange one silver lamp [to be lit] in perpetuity. To the greater benefit of the confirmation of these pious gifts, I confirm the present charter with the impression of my seal. Delivered through the hand of Bohemund, my chancellor and chaplain. Done in the year of the incarnation of the lord 1201, in the reign of Philip.

No. 7: Noblewomen doing homage, 1226 and 1252

Lady Alix of Fréteval does homage to Countess Blanche of Champagne, 1226

Translated from *Chartes Vendômoises,* ed. Charles Métais (Vendôme: Société Archéologique, Scientifique et Littéraire du Vendômois, 1905), no. 269, p. 296.

I, Alix of Fréteval make known to all inspecting this present charter . . . [that] Lady Blanche, countess of Champagne, has promised to me, that I and my heirs will hold from her that which will fall to me or come to me from the inheritance of the county of La Perche or what pertains to it, because it moved from [the authority of] the count of Chartres, and I give my fealty to confirm this. Truly, the countess herself will pay the feudal relief of twenty to the aforementioned count for me [so that I am freed from my obligations to him]. Further, so that the present charter will remain fixed and permanent, I affirm the charter by making my seal. Done in Chartres, in the year of the lord, 1226, in the month of April.

6 "Octave" refers to the eighth day of the feast of St. Remigius, which would be the first week of October; corresponding roughly with the fall harvest.

Confirmation by Mathilda of Fréteval of the homage that she owes to the Count of Blois, 1252

Translated from *Chartes Vendômoises,* ed. Charles Métais (Vendôme: Société Archéologique, Scientifique et Littéraire du Vendômois, 1905), no. 367, pp. 383–384.

> To all who inspect this present charter, Mathilda, a noble woman, a widow, lord [domina] of Fréteval, [sends] greetings in the Lord. It will be known by all that I hold and secure the castle of Fréteval with all that pertains [to it] in fief from that noble man, the count of Blois, and [what] my ancestors similarly held in liege homage and the aforementioned castle and [that] pertaining [to it] I have held [in] legal standing so that all of my complaints [go] to court of the noble man, the count of Blois, my lord mentioned above, and always I have had legal standing itself at the court as long as I held the aforementioned castle with all that pertains to it and of all that pertains to the castle, as my predecessors similarly [did]. Dated in the year of the lord 1252.

No. 8: Documents concerning the gift by Robert of Moncontour and his son Bertran's dispute of this gift, 1081–1098

Translated from *Cartulaire de Sainte-Trinité de Vendôme*, ed. L'Abbé Charles Métais, 5 vols (Paris: Alphonse Picard et Fils, 1893), vol. 2, no 361, pp. 105–107; no. 340, pp. 63–66 and original manuscripts, AD Loir-et-Cher, 21 H 69, nos. 4 and 5.

In 1081, Lord Robert of Moncontour made a gift to St. Trinité of Vendôme:

> The men now living will know, as well as those living in the world in the future, that Robert of Moncontour, at the request of Lord Abbot Oderic of Vendôme, gave to St. Trinité and the monastery of Vendôme, for the redemption of his soul as well as his parents, all of his property and which land he held from Coulommiers-la-Tour, namely in houses, vines, in woods, in water [i.e. streams or ponds], mills, in servants and serfs, in fiefs, in fields and all revenues, and whatever he would hold there from Lancelin II of Beaugency. This is done in Vendôme, in the year of the incarnation of the lord 1081 in the chapter house of St. Trinité, Lord Abbot Oderic, and all of the chapter living there, and in the presence of Fulcher of Turre, and praising this, and Vulgrin the son of Domitilla [Vulgrin was Fulcher's son too, but here is referred to as the son of Domitilla]. Moreover Lord Lancelin II of Beaugency and his son Ralph I confirmed this, from whom the benefice was [held].

Eleven years later in 1092, the monks of St. Trinité recorded the following:

> Our successors knowing but also retaining steadfast memory that after Robert of Moncontour relinquished to us of what he held [with] Lancelin II of Beaugency and his son Ralph approving, whose property it was, unjustness allowed Bertran the son of the aforementioned Robert to make a false claim to the same gift of his father; but with his own men he could not take away from us the aforementioned gift; but at *Sanctonicum*, therefore he was able to take more than this [from] our estates; he inflicted many injuries on us; and frequently made complaints about us to Count Geoffrey Jordan, who then ruled the honor of Vendôme, [because] many barons of this castle were the count's vassals, he made himself a supporter of the same count rather than us. Then it came to pass, as we who do not know God's providence, so that the same count G[eoffrey] fell into the hands of the aforementioned Lancelin II [of Beaugency], who threw him into prison just as hostilely as he savagely seized him. In remittance of his sins [and] under oath, at a court convened by Lancelin with his son Ralph, from whom at that time Bertran sought to absolve [the dispute], at that same court and [with] many witnesses, Bertran swore that the villa of Coulommiers-la-Tour, just as the aforementioned Robert gave to us the same confirmation, [and] Bertran freely restored [the property] from [his] false claim and swore he would defend our church against all mortals who [might dispute this]. Who, after that was resolved, fearing the oath that he had made, it was sworn by the aforementioned Bertran that he quietly declared to us the aforementioned gift he had claimed, so that in the court of Lord Lancelin by this he resolved the plea with us . . .[7] Ralph I angered by the false claim for the same reason that because it was his property and from himself [that] Robert held earlier, and so too did his son Bertran so that it seemed Bertran owed the right to hold [this property] to him [Ralph] . . . he violently seized Coulommiers-la-Tour. Truly not long after, partly from fear of God creeping over him, partly from advice of counsel, himself recognizing he has not done right by the church, at the court of Lord Abbot Bernon . . . [and the monks] . . . in the presence of the witnesses noted below, [Ralph abandoned] the claim to the aforementioned villa in our chapterhouse . . . he promised [to make claim to] nothing in the same villa against the monks or [to] what Bertran himself had claimed. Therefore this by the sign of the holy cross, formed by his hand, he affirmed, so that the whole gift . . . and pact, that with Bertran we agreed upon, authorizing, so that anything from that time the monks . . . who were of the church St. Trinité, of land, of woods, of serfs, and all other revenues . . . Done in the year 1092 of the incarnation of the Word.

7 The charter is badly damaged here and below.

> Witnesses who saw and heard: Ralph I himself and his four knights, Peter of Thaurciis . . . Girard son of Dudene, and Ralph I of *Boola*, Vulgrin son of Ingelbaud Brito . . .

Six years later in 1098, Bertran was again in court with the monks:

> Bertran truly first-born son of the aforementioned Robert was not present when this gift was made,[8] therefore what his father justly gave, he himself later unjustly falsely claimed. After some time Bertran himself, aroused by divine inspiration, when he arranged to go to Jerusalem, and this journey for God he believed certainly that nothing would be useful for himself if he did not dismiss this false claim to the gift which his father made from piety, he sent for Lord Abbot Geoffrey the successor of Abbot Bernon, so that he would come to him; because Lord Geoffrey was [now] made abbot. In whose presence, Bertran publicly recognized his wrongdoing against his father's gift, which he himself should rather to augment rather than to decrease, and peacefully, this namely which his father had given before, [with] his wife Domitilla, and his sons Peter, Philip, Robert and William, present and conceding, he conceded [what he had claimed from his father's gift] to the monastery of Vendôme. Accordingly, Lord Abbot Geoffrey took Bertran himself, and his wife and his sons, into the benefit of the society of his monastery and he gave Bertran eighteen hundred shillings of Anjou for this concession, his wife Domitilla 100 shillings, [and] his sons, Peter four pounds, Philip 12 pennies, Robert 12 pennies, William 12 pennies, Abbot Geoffrey similarly gave for this concession. Because they saw and heard this matter: Bertran himself, Domitilla his wife and their four sons. Of Bertan's men: Scallatinus, Tracatinus, Obrannus, Haimeric Flocellus. This is done at Moncontour, before the church situated in the castle itself, indictione vi, in the year of the Lord 1098. This truly Lord Ralph I of Beaugency conceded for a second time, at Poitiers, where he was then, in the presence and at the request of Bertran.

Signed by the cross +: Bertran. S. + Peter. S. + Philip. S. + Robert. S. + William, sons of the same Bertran.

No. 9: Lord Ralph I's gift for Landric Malasherbes, 1086

Translated from *Cartulaire de Sainte-Trinité de Vendôme*, ed. L'Abbé Charles Métais, 5 vols (Paris: Alphonse Picard et Fils, 1893), vol. 2, no. 329, pp. 43–44.

> A command of God, the universal ruler, befell a certain knight named Landric, cognomen Malas Herbes [Malesherbes], to die at Beaugency,

8 The gift of 1081.

who was very familiar[9] and a friend of Ralph I, son of Lancelin; Whose death having made Ralph not a little sad, shortly thereafter the body was conveyed slowly by his men for burial here [St. Trinité at Vendôme], promising to us many good things from that time forward, if only we would respectfully grant [Landric's] burial [at the monastery]. The burial was done at the crack of dawn, beginning with counsel [with] his men, Ralph came to our chapter house and he gave to us and perpetually conceded that we would hold all of that from his lordship which he held from the church of St. Bienheuré, by irrefutable right, namely all of the cemetery, and all the feasts that pertain to it, and immediately this [was recorded] in a letter of testimony, in the presence of his court [entourage] and all who were attending the chapter, and it was read out loud. Truly [by] such a pact he [also] granted this: for the soul of the aforementioned Landric, his vassal and friend, so that one pauper will be perpetually clothed each Easter in the almshouse of the monastery of St. Trinité. Done in the year of the incarnation of the word 1086, XIIII kalends of January [December 19][10] as these witnesses saw and heard this to be written: Ralph himself, Odo Malas Herbes the brother of the deceased, Fulcher of Turre, Vulgrin son of Ingelbald Brito, Gervase son of Lancelin, Peter Chotard, Bodellus his brother, nephews of Lancelin of Beaugency [Ralph's cousins], Tetbald son of Leterius, Hugh son of Salomon.

No. 10: A crusader's donation, 1096

Translated from *Cartulaire de Marmoutier pour le Dunois*, ed. Emile Mabille (Châteaudun: Lecesne, 1874), no. 152, p. 141. AD Loir-et-Cher H 544.

Let everyone know that Hugh Guernonatus, who was prévot of Blois, and his son were falsely claiming from us [the monks of Marmoutier] the land of Rhodon and of Bergerioux, and of Perthehuiset, and from *Villa Trochiae* pertaining to the priory of Villeberfol.[11] However, in the year of the incarnation of the Lord 1096, which is the year of the dedication of the church of Marmoutier by Pope Urban [II], when the same Hugh and his eldest son, named Warin, would have wished to go to Jerusalem with

9 This is to say that Landric and Ralph were close friends. This could also be translated as intimate friends. I believe the idea here is to emphasize that Landric and Ralph were extremely, close, personal friends. A bond that often developed among men who spent their lives together and in battle. Some might read this as suggestive of a homosexual relationship. To me, this reads more as a strong, particularly close, personal friendship.

10 Medieval people followed the Roman practice of reckoning dates backwards from certain fixed days. The kalends is the first of the month; ides is the fifteenth and nones is nine days before ides or the seventh of the month.

11 Recall that the lords of Beaugency were the protectors or advocates for this priory.

the army of Christians[to fight] against the pagans, [they] abandoned to God and Holy Martin and also us, his monks, all [that was claimed] of the aforementioned false claim for his soul and for the soul of Prasae, his wife. And also two of his sons, that is the aforementioned Warin and Peter, similarly abandoned the same false claim for the soul of Prasae, their mother, but also for their souls, and at that time all three accepted for themselves, from the charity of Holy Martin, six pounds of money from Blois from Lord Odon, then at that time the prior of Villeberfol. And who promised that they would make certain that all of their brothers [would] concede [to abandoning the claim]. For which the aforementioned Peter was to stand surety [for the agreement], he who remained on his father's offices and holdings and he [who] will protect [them] until his father himself or his brother Warin would return from Jerusalem; namely he who discharged all false claims and also those of his brothers to us and any fine for the same false claim that may be brought to us or anything hereafter, he himself would restore all to us, and moreover certain of his brothers who were then absent, he would make them dismiss the same false claim when they would return. The witnesses to these matters are: Hervé the prévot of Blois cognomen Belonius, Teodoric Avaray and his eldest son, Ingelbald the cellarer of Blois, Burdin the count's cook, Clamohocus the servant, Astho the boy, son of the aforementioned Hugo Guernonatus from another wife, who thereupon had two shillings, Gion the monk of Pontlevoy who wrote this same [list of] witnesses.

No. 11: Lord Ralph I's donation upon his return from crusade, 1101

Translated from *Cartulaire de Sainte-Trinité de Vendôme*, ed. L'Abbé Charles Métais, 5 vols (Paris: Alphonse Picard et Fils, 1893), vol. 2, no. 362, pp. 108–109.

Since God, the creator and giver, is all things by which man is sustained, he who is known by extreme ingratitude and diseased by deadly avarice will be destroyed; even a generous donor who possesses the tithes on the goods who does not give all voluntarily, that which was being given must be emended, so that the gift works for eternal salvation. Weighing this very carefully, Ralph I of Beaugency gave in perpetuity to the monks of St. Trinité serving God, all of the tithes on his grains and vines, [both those that] he will hold from any place as well as at Beaugency, [and] in the place near the castle itself constructed in honor of the Holy Sepulcher. And so he made this pious gift for the soul of his father and his mother and himself and all of his friends, and the gift he released into the hand of lord Abbot G.[eoffrey], with great devotion, on bended knee, and next also brought this [symbol of the gift] to the altar of St. Sepulcher. Here are the witnesses who affirmed: Hainric, [Lord Ralph's] seneschal, Garner Bisolus, Odo Malas Herbes, Adrald Mala-Terra, Guanilo infans [the child], Peter of *Caorciis*, Simon of Montfollet, Bernard, Guillelm the tradesman, Rainer son of Grossinus, Arnald the merchant, Milo of Jerusalem, Robert the monks' librarian, Ingelbaud of *Talitio*, Walter of the Holy Sepulcher, Bernern the servant of Haimeric, Malger the servant, Achard son of Rainer Largus, Girard son of Odollus, Odo son of Theodoric Gubulcus, Rivalon, Hugo Calvus, Gosbert of Jerusalem and many others.

No. 12: Raher the fisherman is made a serf, 1095

Translated from *Le Livre des Serfs de Marmoutier*, ed. André Salmon (Tours: Imprimerie Ladevèze, 1864), no. 40, pp. 164–165.

All will know that Raher the fisherman, when he was free and before he wished to serve us zealously, that he wished to be close to us and to serve us well and faithfully. And also accepting in marriage from our serfs a certain sister of Landric the cook, he first came into our chapter and became a serf of St. Martin and his monks, that is [of] Marmoutier. We also gave him a certain one of our houses which had been Hildemar the cook's, accepting yet thereupon from him sixty shillings; [from] which house he is able to sell food or drink freely, if it might become necessary for him. But yet first, he should offer the house to us for sale and then, if we wish to buy it, so much the better. But if not, he will be able to sell the house to one of our men. But if he dies without legitimate heirs, the house itself will remain with us and it will also be ours. Which if Peter Barba, brother of the aforementioned Raher, would wish to buy [the house] from us, it will be sold to no other, if yet he will wish to give as much for it as anyone else. Nevertheless, the wife of Raher will possess the house, beyond his life time, even if she does not have children with him. The witnesses to this matter are these: Hubert the cellarer, Landric the cook, Peter Barba, Girard fisherman, John the warden of the hospital, Ernulf of Ruilly, Sancelin the cellarer, Ansegisus the butcher.

Done in the year of the incarnation of the lord 1095. Our community under the dominion of Abbot Bernard in the twelfth year of his ordination.

No. 13: Bertran Agnellus is made a serf, 1032–1084

Translated from *Le Livre des Serfs de Marmoutier*, ed. André Salmon (Tours: Imprimerie Ladevèze, 1864), no. 3, p. 5.

Let it be known that Bertran Agnellus is making himself a serf of St. Martin, for this therefore we allow him to buy a certain house in our burg, which he bought from a certain serf of ours named Hademar. He himself and his wife Ermentrude and son Rigald came into our parlor and there placed, following custom, four pennies on their heads, they all three surrendered themselves and all of their descendants [posterity] to [be] the serfs of our prior, Lord Odo: These people witnessed this: Odo the cook, Girald the cook, Hervé the cook, Ingelbert the mayor, Guido the mayor, Walter of *Chinsi*, Esgared son of Walter the porter.

No. 14: Of a certain youth named Adam who was made a serf, 1081

Translated from *Le Livre des Serfs de Marmoutier*, ed. André Salmon (Tours: Imprimerie Ladevèze, 1864), no. 125, p. 116.

Our present and our posterity will know that a certain youth, named Adam, skilled in carpentry, born from free stock, wishing himself to be made a serf of St. Martin and us, and from custom placing four pennies on his head, he and all of those who come from his line, to be surrendered in serfdom to St. Martin and us, his monks of Marmoutier, for the present and also for the future, through the hand of our lord abbot [who] at this time [is] Bartholomew, in the year of the incarnation of the lord 1081. These witnesses: Odo the cellarer, Martin the cellarer, Ledald the chamberlain, Algiso the cook, Bernard the cook, Durand the baker, Abram the porter.

No. 15: About Vitalis becoming a serf, 1032–1064

Translated from *Le Livre des Serfs de Marmoutier*, ed. André Salmon (Tours: Imprimerie Ladevèze, 1864), no. 98, p. 92.

We wish our posterity to know that Letard a certain cowherd of ours, due to approaching death, summoning [his] son, a minor named Vitalis, conferred [him] to St. Martin and us in servitude, so with the assent of this boy himself and the rest of his brothers. And so that he [Vitalis] cannot refuse this joining or attachment of this kind at any time whatsoever, the father surrendered him into the hand of a certain of our monks named Ernald. These witnesses: Martin priest, Dodo and Isembert our servants.

No. 16: Chirograph *of the daughter of Maria Conversa, made free, January 22, 1069*

Translated from *Le Livre des Serfs de Marmoutier*, ed. André Salmon (Tours: Imprimerie Ladevèze, 1864), no. 76, p. 73.

Let it be known by our brothers, namely those monks of the monastery of Marmoutier, that Otbert who was the mayor of St. Martin, held certain land at *Cedentum*, from St. Martin, because he himself was a serf of St. Martin. However, after his death, his wife Maria Conversa, without her children being present with her, neither her only son or her only daughter, on account of [them] being in mourning, asked Lord Abbot Bartholomew, that he might make her daughter free, so that she might be able to be given in marriage to a free man. And thus the Lord Abbot himself promised to create such a pact: That the daughter herself and her brother abandon to St. Martin the aforementioned land of their father, because they were themselves serfs, so yet that the brother of the girl would remain a serf, and if ever she herself weds a serf or a colibertus [she] would return to original servitude. Therefore they came into our chapter house, the mother with her children, and because the Lord Abbot was not able to attend, his mandate and his agreement is confirmed by the prior, with assent of all of the chapter to this pact, namely that which is described above, clearly this woman and her brother dismissed the aforementioned land to St. Martin wholly and quietly, and she herself is made free by the pact above, her brother, named Gausbert, remaining in servitude and she herself moreover is called Cecilia. Act of the sixth year of the Lord Abbot Bartholomew, month of January in the festival of the Holy Martyr Vincent. These witnesses: Walter the archdeacon, Vivian the cleric, Ebulono the brother of the same girl by another father [her half-brother], Girald the cook, Odo the cook, Gausbert the cook, Johan conversus [either a monk who took his vows later in life or a layman who was living in the monastery without taking monastic vows].[12]

No. 17: About the serfs of Tavers, 1203

Translated from *Cartulaire de l'abbaye de Notre-Dame de Baugency*, ed. G. Vignat (Orléans: Herluison, 1879), no. 12, pp. 20–21. Archives départmentales du Loiret, H 10, fol. V, verso.

I, Lord John I of Beaugency, make it known for the present and future that Berion, wife of Peter Berion, acknowledged herself in my presence to be a serf of the canons of Notre Dame de Beaugency along with her heirs, just as her ancestors had been serfs. Because truly the same Peter, [who] led Berion to marriage without any agreement and without approval, acknowledged namely his wife to be a serf of the same canons along with her heirs. But, let it be clearly understood that with the assent and will of the same canons, Aelez, wife of Geoffrey Gautier, daughter

12 The use of "Conversa" to refer to this family is interesting, given that Maria is the only one who uses this cognomen. It could refer to her or a member of her family from who she adopted the cognomen joining the monastery as a layperson without taking the vows. It is possible that the John conversus listed at the end of the charter could be a kinsman with the same cognomen. Given the fluidity of the status of serfs, "conversa" could have another meaning: Someone who converted not the religious life, but who changed their status from free to serf.

of the very same Berion, along with her heirs, remained a serf of myself and my heirs. And let it be known that as many years the same Peter will hold the tenement from my custom, so as many years of customs he pays back to me, and all who will hold the tenement after him. So that a dispute is not able to arise to any of the above, I order this charter to be written by means of a divided chirograph which I reinforce through the authority of my seal. Done in the year of grace 1203.

No. 18: List of merchants and their wares at the markets and the Quasimodo Fair and what they owed to the monastery of Notre Dame de Beaugency c. 1150–c. 1300

Translated from *Cartulaire de Notre-Dame de Baugency*, ed. G. Vignat (Orléans, Herluison, 1879), pp. 204–206. Archives départmentales du Loiret, H 10, fol. LV recto and verso.

These are customs of our market days and the first of the Quasimodo fair

From the butchers of the village, for the market stall, 2 denarii[13] or pence.

If foreign [butchers], for the stall 2 pence, and for the plot,[14] a half-penny.

For fresh pigs, 2 pence; for salted 1 penny.

For the sale of fresh hides, a half a penny; for the sale of a cow from the stable as well, 4 pence.

From apothecaries, if they sell pepper and such like, if from the village, 2 pence.

If foreign merchants, 2 pence and for the plot, a half-penny.

The same [plot and stall] for the drapers, 4 pence.

For the selling of tapestry, if they have a stall, 2 pence; if they display their merchandise on the ground, a half-penny.

The same for the sale of spears if the merchants are foreigners, a halfpenny.

13 Medieval coinage was based on the denarius, or penny, and it was the only coin minted in medieval France at this time. A solidus or shilling was worth twelve pence, and a pound was worth 20 shillings (or 240 pence). An obol was half of a penny and was a silver penny cut in half. Shillings and pounds were money of account, meaning that they existed for accounting purposes but were not actual currency. Significantly the dues exacted for marketing goods at the fairs taking place within the jurisdiction of the abbey of Notre Dame de Beaugency did not get up to the value of a pound, but consisted of four or five pence at most.

14 "Plot" designates the space where the stall would be set up, in addition to the materials that made up the market stall itself.

From the foreign fripperers [ragmen], a halfpenny; if from the village, nothing; if they have one of our stalls, 2 pence.

From the sale of feather mattresses or pillows with a coverlet, as above, 2 pence; for those with only a coverlet, as above, a halfpenny.

From the selling of ointments and the like, if from the village, for the stall, 2 pence; if foreigners, 2 pence; for the stall and for the plot, a halfpenny.

From the sale of cooked meat from the village, for the stall 2 pence; if foreign 2 pence for the stall and for the plot, a halfpenny.

For those above who sell pork, namely raw pork, 2 pence.

From the selling of reliquaries, cases or chests, for the plot, a halfpenny.

From the selling of glass, for the stall, 2 pence; if they display their merchandise on the ground, a halfpenny or glass.[15]

From the sale of foreign knives, 2 pence and one halfpenny; if from the village 2 pence.

From the selling of swords, nothing.

From the selling of iron and other implements, if they display their merchandise on the ground, a halfpenny.

From the sale of plates and tripods and the like, a halfpenny; From a master, 2 pence and one halfpenny.

From foreign mercers, 3 halfpence.

From the goblet makers, one drinking vessel will suffice.

From the rope maker of the village 1 penny; from foreign rope makers, three halfpence.

From the selling of leather, if from a stall, 2 pence and one halfpenny; if they display their merchandise on the ground, one halfpenny.

From bootmakers, a halfpenny.

From those who sell bows, 2 pence.

From the sale of vegetables one half penny or one halfpenny of vegetables.

From the selling of apples, halfpenny; or one halfpenny of apples.

From the selling of dishes, one dish will suffice or a halfpenny.

15 In other words, they would pay the fee in kind with the merchandise they are selling. This arrangement was on objects or products that were particularly valued, like glass, goblets and dishes, or essential, like vegetables, apples, wool and salt. For the examples of goblets, vegetables, apples, dishes, wool and salt, see below.

From the selling of buckets or urns, one measurement from the bucket or urn.[16]

From the sale of hemp, a halfpenny; and similarly from selling flax, one more halfpenny.

For six fleeces sold by the slaughterhouse, as above, a halfpenny; but if the fleeces are from dead sheep, nothing.

For spun wool, two measures [of spun wool]; unless it is able to be conveyed from within a mile of the market by one man alone without rest.[17]

For the sale of a horse, 4 pence; and if two men exchange [a horse], whichever, 4 pence.

For an ass, a halfpenny; for 4 sheep, 1 penny, by whomever.[18]

For a cow, 1 penny by whomever, for a pig, 1 penny; for a pack horse, 2 pence.

For 12 spades or hoes, 3 halfpence.

From the sale of other things, a halfpenny. From the foreign ropemakers, 1 penny.

From ploughmen [selling their labor] halfpenny; if they bring their own team, 1 penny.

For pigs with piglets, if lactating, 1 [penny]; if not lactating, one halfpenny for both buying and selling.

From buying and selling goats, by whomever, one halfpenny.

From the sale of salt, as much as one can hold in a hand [one handful of salt].

For the selling of bed frames, if they bring their cart, 1 penny.

For the sale of chair frames, if they bring their cart, 1 penny.[19]

16 Presumably, this could be a measurement of liquid, like wine, or a measurement of solids, like grain or fruit.

17 This may indicate a local wool merchant rather than someone coming outside of the community.

18 "Whomever" indicates if the merchants were either local or foreign.

19 These last two items appear as French words, chesières and chasliz, respectively. Determining their meaning was difficult and required consultation with a scholar of medieval French. I would like to thank Kathy Krause for her help in translating these two words. This also demonstrates that the vernacular was becoming more common when these customs were recorded in the thirteenth century and exemplify how medieval scholars depend on many specializations to do their scholarship. "From their cart," I believe indicates that they were selling these items from the bed of the carts on which they transported these items.

No. 19: Lord Simon I of Beaugency's will, 1146–1153

Translated from *Cartulaire de Sainte-Croix d'Orléans,* edited by Joseph Thillier and Eugène Jarry (Paris: Picard et Fils, 1902), no. 5, pp. 7–15. The original document existed until the 1940s, but perished when Orléans was bombed by the Allies in World War II.

Because they who are in time, as with time, are often changed and fade away, it pleased our predecessors so that those things that might be done [e.g. recorded], for truly it is old age that is the mother of forgetfulness for at any time old age and oblivion are able to erase [these words], but through belief and continually resisting [time and oblivion], the words of this charter might be commended [e.g. written down]; wherefore I, Simon lord of Beaugency, so that no long lasting interval of succeeding time would vanish the certainty of truth [of what is recorded here] from sinuous memory from the darkness of not knowing, [and so] that our posterity would not be led to the error of ignorance, I decree this charter to be bequeathed to memory, so that my sins obtain absolution from the will of God, and for Ralph I, my father, and Mathilda, my mother, and domine Adenorde [my wife] and of my heir who will have conceded this gift about to be confirmed, and for all the souls of [my] ancestors, I donate in perpetuity to God and the church of St. Croix and Lord Manassas, Bishop of Orleans, the custody of a knight which I used to hold in the grange of Cravant, moreover so that certain gifts which are contained in this testament, I donate and concede in perpetuity for me and all of the aforementioned souls. In addition, for the aforementioned souls, I similarly concede the gift of one measure of barley which Ralph, my father, gave perennially to the priest of the church of Cravant, and therefore will I not hold less of my custody of the vassals of the bishop of Orléans at Cravant [than he did].

Let it also be noted that I give Warin of Cravant to St. Croix, a free man, so that he can be a dependent of St. Croix at Cravant. Furthermore I, Simon of Beaugency, for the same souls I affirm and I concede the freedom namely as written which my grandfather [avus] and Ralph my father gave to Hubert of *Noyem* and his sons and daughters of which liberty the aforementioned Hubert was [granted] during the lifetime of domine Adenorde, Hubert truly agreed to that because of the gift domine Adenorde made to have 200 masses to be sung and to feed 100 paupers.

In addition, I, the aforementioned Simon, give to God and the church of St. Croix for the souls of me and Ralph, my father, and domine Adenorde and my heir who will consent to this gift all of that which I hold in the daughter church of a certain man of the sextons of the church of St. Croix and because [of] this, the aforementioned sextons[20] will bang

20 A sexton was in charge in taking care of the church and church yard. He was often also charged with ringing the bells and digging graves.

a drum on the anniversary [of the death] of myself and Ralph, my father, and domine Adenorde and my heir who consented to this gift.

Moreover, I, the aforementioned Simon, donate annually in perpetuity two pounds of wax to be made into two candles to illuminate the altar of St. Croix at the same time, namely the fifth ides of May [May 11], from which [time] they will be lit [and] at no time are they to be extinguished as long as they are able to last, and these candles are to be delivered to the chaplain in the castle of Beaugency who pays forty shillings in rent, which I have in the feast of Holy St. Firmin, VII kalends of October [September 25].

Let it also be noted[21] that the land of *Ostentio* is free and peaceful of the church of St. Croix, and yet if the men of the lord of Beaugency would remain in his servitude, they and the men of the same villa are able to remain there in which place there is ancient custom, without controversy. Let it be the final agreement because Lord Simon asked the lord Bishop Manassas of Orléans and all of the chapter of St. Croix so that for God and his love and for these gifts that he has enumerated for himself, his father Ralph, and domine Adenorde, and the heir of Lord Simon who will concede the gifts above, so that the day of the anniversary [of their deaths] be celebrated annually in the church of St. Croix [and] to be written in the martyrology of the same church; this petition moreover all unanimously conceded because Lord Simon asked the community of monks, they promised to do this.

Moreover, I, Simon of Beaugency[22] also for the aforementioned souls and for my heir who will concede this gift, donate two shillings of rent annually in the feast of St. Firmin in perpetuity to the poor of the Alms House[23] of St. Croix so that they themselves and the priest of this house will procure meat when they will celebrate the anniversary of domine Adenorde. Besides likewise I, Simon, also give for the aforementioned souls to the Leper House of Orléans two shillings of rent annually in the feast of St. Firmin for procuring for them and their priests meat on the day of the anniversary of domine Adenorde which they will celebrate annually. Let it also be manifest furthermore because I, Simon of Beaugency, namely the aforementioned [donation] is for the souls of myself and Ralph, my father, and domine Adenorde and my heir who will concede this gift, I give annually to the church of St. Mesmin de Micy three shillings of rent in the feast of the Saint Firmin, that is in

21 The language of the charter switches here away from Simon's first person voice to third person. This clause may have been inserted later by a monastic scribe. Since the original no longer exists, it is not possible to determine if this section was in a different hand or merely inserted as Simon was giving his testimony. This version could also be based on a redacted copy.

22 Here the charter switches back to the first person, with Lord Simon as dispositer.

23 I have elected to leave Alms House and Leper House capitalized in the translation as that is how the charter was reproduced. However, for modern references almshouse and leper house will be used.

September, in a market stall of Beaugency for procuring fish for the monks on the day of the anniversary [of the death] of domine Adenorde, which they celebrate annually and also they will feed one pauper.

Moreover I, Simon, accept into my custody the donkeys which will carry firewood from the woods of domine Beatrice to the cooks of the monks and to the Hôtel Dieu according to the customs of old that they hold there.

I, Simon, furthermore, for my soul and the souls of all the abovenamed and for my heir who will concede this, give to the monks of Cornilly annually thirteen pence [1s, 1d] in rent paid in the feast of St. Firmin for making an anniversary for me and my father and domine Adenorde and my heir who concedes this. Let it also be noted that I, Simon, give to the Leper House of Beaugency three shillings in rent paid in the feast of St. Firmin from the sale of meat procuring [fish] for them and their priests on the anniversary of [the death of] domine Adenorde which they will celebrate annually and for the anniversary [of my death] and my father and my heir who will concede this and for us they will feed one pauper.

Moreover, this, I, Simon give to the monks of St. Sepulcher of Beaugency two shillings of revenue for procuring [fish] for the monks on the day of the anniversary [of the death] of domine Adenorde as with all of the aforementioned anniversaries so that whatever happens they will celebrate [it]. I, Simon of Beaugency, for me and my father and domine Adenorde and for my heir who will concede this, give in perpetuity five shillings in revenue to the abbot of the Alms House for the procurement of fish for the monks on the anniversary of domine Adenorde. Themselves will celebrate every of the aforementioned anniversaries whatever happens [and] they will feed one pauper.

I, Simon, for the same and in the same way give to the nuns of Holy Mary of the Hospital two shillings of revenue for procuring fish for the ladies [dominas] on the day of the anniversary of domine Adenorde so that they will celebrate [her anniversary] annually and moreover on the aforementioned anniversary and in the same way the revenue to be paid in the feast of St. Firmin. I, Simon, give annually for my soul and [those of] Ralph, my father, and domine Adenorde and my heir who will concede this, a silver marc to the monks of Cîteaux for the purchase of fish for the whole convent when they hold their chapter meeting. Truly they themselves will observe annually all aforementioned anniversaries and for me and for us they will feed one pauper.

I, Simon, for me and the souls of Ralph, my father, and also my heir who will concede this donation and for domina Adenorde, that which I hold in two mills of La Ferté-Saint-Aubin, I give in perpetuity to the church of Holy Euverte, and for the work of cooking, the largest logs in my woods, accepting completely that which is sufficient to their own use of two mills, but not the use of the sluice; I even donate to the same church an area next to this mill in which there may be a house for a miller who may be a free man and not bound by custom as [are] the men of the lord of Beaugency. Truly, they will celebrate annually mine and all of the aforementioned anniversaries and they will feed one pauper for us in perpetuity.

Next, I, Simon, give to the church of Marmoutier the church of Notre Dame of Bonnes Nouvelles of Orléans. So that the monks themselves [of Marmoutier] will celebrate annually in all of their churches my anniversary and [those anniversaries] of Ralph, my father, and Adenorde, my wife, and my heir who will concede this gift and they will feed in perpetuity one pauper and similarly in alms from the same churches they will support another pauper.

Let it be noted, moreover, that I, Simon, donate to the abbot of Notre Dame de Beaugency a measure of salt on each ship carrying salt from which I take as my tolls and I concede to the same [monks] one measure[24] at Montigny freely and peacefully in which I took whatever I wanted.

I, Simon, give and concede in perpetuity the market rights, namely [those] during the fair of Saint-Biénheure of Vendôme, except the right of the administration of justice and fiefs of my vassals. I, Simon, for myself and R[alph], my father's, soul and for the souls of domine Adenorde and my heir who will concede this benevolence, I accept into my lordship at Moret[25] all of those properties which are from their own men and pertain to the abbot of St. Lomer [of Blois]. Those truly will not come to Blois during the war that might be between Blois and Beaugency except through the permission of the lord of Beaugency and they swear allegiance to the same lord.

Furthermore, I, Simon, accept into my custody all property except the serfs which the canons of St. Mary of Blois have in their dominion.

I, Simon, give and concede in perpetuity to the Alms House of Blois one measure [of land] at Suèvres freely and peacefully and hay of two arpents of pasture until I would give them two arpents of pasture.[26]

When[27] the Lord Simon went on pilgrimage to Santiago de Compostella[28] he owed the Lord Barbe of *St. Cerano* 100 pounds of coin of

24 The charter does not indicate a measure of what. However, since Montigny was located on the Le Loir River, this could refer to a measure of salt taken from ships transporting salt on the Le Loir river. Or it could be a measure of land, as it is below in the donation to the almshouse of Blois.

25 Commune of Rouvray-Saint-Crois in the Loiret.

26 Simon is giving them the hay from two measures of pasture until he is able to give them the pasture itself.

27 The footnote to this edition says that the following represents the second column of the original act.

28 The Latin reads literally "went on the road to St. Jacob." This indicates that he went to visit the shrine of St. James the Great in Northern Spain: Santiago de Compostella. This was the most popular pilgrimage route in Western Europe. Moreover, the document again shifts into the third person and starts the next section of Simon's settlements: his debts.

Anjou to be paid completely on the eighth day after the feast day of the birth of St. John the Baptist which are the first days of July and seven times 100 shillings [700 shillings or 35 pounds] of Angevin coin to be paid completely on the eighth day after the feast day of the Birth of the Lord [Christmas]. And from the other part Simon owed to the same Barbe, [that is] fifty-nine pounds of Angevin coin and four silver wine ladles[29], and for this fifty-nine pounds and four silver wine ladles, Lord Barbe has in pledge [from Lord Simon] to meet this debt, forty measures of winter oats, namely wheat, and eighteen pecks and five dry measures of corn by the measure of Tours.

Simon of Beaugency then owed to Peter Haimar seventy-one pounds and six shillings of coins of Orléans from which he agreed to pay him one hundred shillings [5 pounds] of Orléans within three months, which debt is to be paid from the lordship of Beaugency.

Simon at that time owed to Theobald Marin 1000 shillings [50 pounds] which will be paid to him from the lordship of Reginald Affixius.

Lord Simon then owed Jolduin Mirapedem one hundred pounds of tolls from over the Loire, of this he paid back one hundred pounds from Orléans.

Simon then owed to Gaufred Passerellus ten pounds of coin from Orléans and ten pounds of Angevin coin which will be paid from the prefecture[30] of La Ferté-Aurai and from the prefecture of Chaumont.

Furthermore, Lord Simon owes Matthew Hermenard forty pounds[31] and he promised to send to him ten measures of oats of the measurement of Tours.

Besides this Lord Simon owes to Eschivard, son of Mellerius, ten pounds of Orléans which is to be paid from the prefecture of Archembald Nigrius and he promised him that he would make him free from all exactions or customs and that he gives to him [in compensation] a suitable house in the suitable place of Beaugency and two arpents of vines.

And also Lord Simon owes to Odo of *Bestisy* forty shillings which he kept as payment of the dues from his land.

Likewise Simon owes to Simeon of the Alms House [*Karitate*][32] eighteen pounds and four shillings of Orléans which he will accept from the

29 If the original debt was 100 pounds and Simon paid 35 pounds (or 700 shillings), that would leave 65 still owed. Simon seems to have paid this with 59 pounds of coin and four silver ladles. Apparently four silver ladles were worth 6 pounds or just over 1 pound a piece.

30 "Prefecture" refers to a portion of Lord Simon's holdings that were under the supervision of a prefect, or in French, prévot. The prévot would have been responsible for providing revenue from rent and other exactions to his lord. Lords like Simon – but also counts and dukes – divided their lands and placed officers in charge who were responsible for overseeing the land and insuring the proper revenues were paid to the lord. In addition to being responsible for revenue, prévots could also have legal duties.

31 The document uses "talenta" instead of libra for pounds here.

32 Simeon is of *Karitate*, which would seem to be a misinterpolation of "Caritate" which means charity or likely almshouse.

prefectures of Avary and Suèvres. Moreover Lord Simon B[of Beaugency] owes to the Jew of Melun ten pounds of Orléans to be paid forty days after the day of the adoration of Jove. Besides Lord Simon owes to Robert of *Gaudo* twenty pounds of Orléans which are to be collected from the prefecture of *Jahannes* and Lord Simon promised him to be free from all exactions or customs for ten years so that the lord of Beaugency in this time would take nothing from his property.

The same Lord Simon owes twenty shillings to a certain peasant who placed two cows with the wife of Hervé of *Joona* which Simon seized to pay the dues on his land.

As yet besides, the same [Simon] owes Robert Feet-on-the-Ground ten pounds from Orléans which will be paid completely from the prefecture of Archembald Nigrius on the feast of St. Remigius.

He also owes the same [Robert] two measures of wheat which he gives to him. The same [Simon] also owes to Peter Buclerius seventeen shillings which he took to pay the dues on his land.

The total of all that written above that is owed is eleven thousand and one hundred shillings [555 pounds]; from this however four times a thousand [4000] shillings and four pounds [204 pounds] are in coin from Anjou. The sum of this debt that Lord Simon commanded to be redressed to the butchers and to other men by the hand of Hernulf of Avary is twenty-eight pounds and six pence. The sum of the expenses made by Hernulf for the use of the cook midway through Lent until Easter is sixty pounds and nine shillings. The sum of the debt by Simeon is four [pounds] and thirteen shillings. The sum of the debt by Robert of *Gaudo* is twelve pounds and a half. The sum of the old debt by Peter the panetarius is eight pounds and fifteen shillings of Orléans and all was pardoned. The sum of the debt by the same Peter to Natalis that is always [paid] in the feast of St. Albinus is six pounds and twelve shillings. Likewise the sum of eleven pounds [is paid] by the same person at the festival of St. Albinus always on the Tuesday after Easter. Of these that are owed, thus far four pounds and seven pounds are paid. The sum of the debt by Gaufred Dray is thirty-one shillings. The debt of Christian Guinebert and Peter Escornant is the sum written below. And the total of all of that of the debts that they owe to all of the panetariuses from whom Lord Simon first held the land is twenty-five pounds and forty shillings. Likewise the sum of the debt to Robert of Avaray and Entelm of *Tefaugio* is thirty-two shillings and three pence. The sum of the debt to Odo of *Valnosia* is seven pounds and twelve shillings and a half. The sum of the debt to Raginald Affliche is sixty [pounds] and seventeen shillings and three pence. The sum of the debt to Rainard the chamberlain is seventeen shillings and a half. The sum of the debt to Michael the butler is nine shillings.

The general sum total of all of the revenue that Lord Simon owed[33] to his poor men[34] for all of their services is eighty-seven pounds and five shillings and six pence and eight measures of wheat. And it is known that Lord Simon ordered Hernulf of Avaray and Peter the panetarius [that] all of these debts to poor men [to be] first paid from the revenue from the mills on the Loire and at Choisel, and the dues from the transport of salt, and half of the tolls and duties of Beaugency and from the portion of domina Mathilda [his mother] if by chance she will allow this to pass to the lord of Beaugency, except that which is paid from her benefice, and after receiving this payment, the same of any of the same payments are paid back to Lord Barbe of *Sancto Cerano* because Simon owed him, and from the likewise one thousand shillings handed over to him in gifts for a single year during which time [when this] was owed, ten pounds would have been paid back. In addition, Lord Simon bequeathed to the church of Notre Dame de Beaugency and the church of Holy Firmin twenty marcs [160 pence or 13s 4d] of silver that will be paid from the [revenue generated from the] oven of Choisel and moreover he bequeathed to Robert the Hermit forty shillings for the alms for Theodoric Orchenellus which he received from payment from the revenues from his land. Moreover he bequeathed to the Hôtel Dieu of Beaugency thirty shillings and from the bridge at Beaugency, seven pounds which he received in revenue. Further, he owes Samuel the Jew seven pounds and two shillings of which thirty are coins of Provins. Finally Lord Simon wishes all to make note that he gave perpetually each year to the chapel of his castle, two measures of wheat from the tithes of his granary and two measures of wine from the tithes of his cellarer. In addition, Lord Simon gave from the same tithes for the chapel of St. Martin of Tavers two measures of wheat and this all of the wheat and all of the wine to be paid annually in the commemoration of the deaths of the granger and the cellarer of the lord of Beaugency.

Moreover, Lord Simon bequeathed twenty shillings in alms for domina Adenorde to the Leper House of Feritas, twenty shillings to the nuns of *Chauforneso*, twenty shillings to the nuns of *Glatigny*, twenty shillings to the monks of *Cunaut*, to the chapel of St. Michael of Fontevraud five shillings, to the monks of *Burgel* one silver chalice, to the Leper House of Meung-sur-Loire one chalice, to the Leper House of Châteaudun five shillings, five shillings to Notre Dame of Étampes, to the Leper House of Orléans five shillings, to the Leper House of Beaugency forty-four shillings, to supply a certain man with one tunic.

33 In this case "owed" does not refer to being in debt, but rather what Simon bequeathed to these clergy for their spiritual services.

34 Meaning clergy.

Let it be known that from the alms of domina Adenorde [that] will be paid are forty-eight pounds and nine shillings of coins of Orléans and of all of this is to have been paid from half of the tolls and dues from Beaugency. And from what is owed by domine Adenorde, which sum is seventy-four pounds of money of Orléans, twenty-two pounds are paid, before Lord Simon would have gone on pilgrimage, Jelduin Mirepez received through the hand of Robert Falcille, and another fifty-two pounds remaining to this point will be paid back from that which Lord Simon will hold at Feritas.

All of this, one at a time, at the court of Lord Simon the counting up by Simeon Hernulf and Robert of Gaut, was known that the sum of all of the recorded debts/bequests was fifty thousand shillings [2500 pounds] and ten pounds and ten shillings [2510 pounds, 10 s], from which five thousand-one hundred shillings [255 pounds] were coin of Anjou.

Lord Simon ordered that this charter, through the hand of Lord Bishop Manassas of Orléans and all of the court of the chapter of St. Croix, be handed over to the abbot of St. Euverte and to be strengthened by the seal of the aforementioned bishop, so that he ordered the charter absolutely will remain firm, and if anyone will presume to challenge this they will be struck down by the sword of the divine.

No. 20: Foundation charter of the priories of St. Aegid[35] *and St. Victor of Pont-des-Gennes by Agnes of Montfort-le-Gesnois, 1092*[36]

Translated from *Instrumenta, Institut des provinces de Frances, tome premier: Géographie ancienne du diocèse du Mans* (Paris: Derache, Librarie, 1865), pp. lxxv–lxxvi.

I, Agnes, wife of Hugh of Pont-des-Gennes, reflecting that the flesh and blood of progeny to be fragile and perishable, and desiring to propagate the fruitful spirit begotten in Christ so that it endures and advances, I marry my two daughters, Petronilla and Hadrilda, to Christ and I wish [them] to be surrendered and dedicated to the state of holy virginity in perpetuity. Because truly I recognize their corruptible flesh will be beset by illness and, I determine, will not be able to survive in any way without the body's sustenance of nourishment without being surrendered into marriage, whose virginity I ordain to be joined to the bed of the immortal bridegroom. Therefore I give to my aforementioned daughters and Saint Avit in whose monastery I consecrate them, these domains to be transferred [and] will be possessed in perpetuity [by them] these things that are contained below:

35 Although the title says St. Aegid, the chapel donated was called St. André.

36 The village of Montfort-le-Gesnois was created in the modern era by combining the two smaller communities of Montfort-le-Rotrou and Pont-des-Gennes.

Namely the church of Saint Victor of Pont-des-Gennes with all appurtenances, with such an agreement, except those who would dwell at that place, either they sold or acquired the revenue, and they paid the customs, and all that pertains to the parish itself, even in tithes which are from burial. Moreover, I give the chapel of St. André and the chapel of the Holy Cross, which are located in the castle precincts, and half of the half tenancies that are situated in front of Montfort, which Fulcrad and Theobald and Johannes hold, the tithes on wheat, sheep, fleeces/wool, pigs, calves, and in addition the tithes of all the lands which I hold today in lordship at Montfort, and of that which is gained [meaning anything added to the lordship], let that be turned into gain, whether woods or vines or deserted [land, i.e. not cultivated]; also the tithes of the half-tenency of *Branla*, which namely the half-tenant Hibard, who has the cognomen of Mala Musca, holds [and] agrees to [this] presently. In addition to give bountifully all water from three mill sluices which are behind the monastery of Pont-des-Gennes [and run] all the way to the stream/channel of *Diceicum,* the tithes of the three mills which are next to the church so that they are divided between the priests and the nuns.[37]

Furthermore, I give the woods of Montfort for the building of their houses and for heat, and also for the pannaging of pigs and certain animals, eliminating all customs utterly. Also I add to these gifts, two adjoining vineyards, one while I live, the other after my death. I give in addition the tithes on the vineyard of my father, however these [will transfer to the nuns] after my death, [and also] that vineyard and house that I had built at Montfort. Because if my daughter Lucia wishes to have this house in her dominion after my death, she pays to the aforementioned place of Saint Avit ten pounds and a third of the part of the tithes on gardens which are in common between the nuns themselves and the priests. Moreover, I increase all of the tithes of the earth of Herbert Vacariae which are contained across the water to be in the dominion of these [nuns] and the garden of Vitalis with hedged meadow measuring two sextaria which [are] for the work of the gardeners.

In addition, I give to these [nuns] the church of St. John of Vibraye with all appurtenances and the chapel of Notre Dame [Holy Mary] having been arranged with the good pact so that they would pay the customs, if those who wish to live in that place or even all who buy or sell at that place. Further, I donate to those [nuns] all of the tithes from the land which today I hold in dominion at Vibraye, equal measure of woods and field set out in this agreement. If I or another used to assign anything from or of this land itself, the possessor would always pay these tithes most peacefully, and also the profit from the building of houses

37 Presumably meaning between the priests who have charge of these churches and the nuns of St. Avit.

and from charcoal burning, and of themselves and the men of the nuns themselves, and the pannaging of their own pigs and the tithes of pannaging of all of the forest.

I also give to those [nuns] land of Fulcher of Dives and all the customs of those lands namely [that] I hold presently in my hand and meadow of the aforementioned man with the additional agreement that they would pay the customs for those who made their homes there. In addition I give the fishpond at Braye for their use. Truly Hugo of *Floreia* gives his granddaughter Petronilla[38] three measures of land in alms on the other side of the fishpond of Braye. And I, Agnes, hence gave to him forty shillings; Moreover, all of this I did with the counsel and approval of my daughter Lucia and our noblemen.

If truly anyone wishes or raises a false claim to any of all of these things that are written here, I have been prepared to set it aside no matter what it would be and to consider it entirely; or if I am not able to resolve the dispute, I or our heirs [will] strongly restore to them in equal exchange.

Truly the witnesses to this largesse are those who are written here: Bishop Hoël, Wicher the deacon, Geoffrey Mulot magister [teacher], Geoffrey Brito, Guandelbert, Gosbert son of the cantor, Fulcon son of Guandicus, Gradulph from the monastery of St. Julian and Turgius of *Taceyo*, Richard of *Mereio*, Alberic of *Milesia*, Avesgastus of *Conerario*, Hibard Mala Musca and his two sons Drogo and Fulcon, Johannes of *Capella*, Fulcon of *Morterio*, Patrick his son, Hugo of *Morterio*, Odo of Noens, Fucon of *St. Michael*, Hugo of *Montibus*, Hubert son of Anogerius, Hebert Vacariae, Hoilerius son of Albert, Guetenus son of Hedeberti, Odo son of Algerius and Fulcon his brother, Herbert of *Mall*, Walter the forester, Richard the servant, Robert Adamus and son Walter.

+ Signed Domina Agnes + Lucia, her daughter + Hugon, her son.

This aforementioned gift, Rotrou junior confirmed with his seal, in the year of grace 1092.[39]

No. 21: Charters of the convent of St. Avit of Châteaudun: Rotrou of Montfort's donations, 1206 and 1213

Foundation of the chapel at Vibraye, dated 1206

This foundation is pieced together from three references in MS 556/435bis from the Mediathèque d'Orléans, p. 191, 204 and 229:

38 This could be Agnes' father-in-law, as one of her daughters was named Petronilla. But it seems strange that Hugo did not also make provision for the other granddaughter. Perhaps he was closer to Petronilla than Hadrilde, or Petronilla and Hadrilde could have been half-sisters and had different paternal grandfathers. Or it could be a gift for another nun named Petronilla.

39 Rotrou junior would have been either Agnes' son or her lord, Rotrou of La Perche.

Rotrou of Montfort, son of Rotrou[40] and Agnes, founded at chapel at Vibraye, with the consent of Abbess Ada of St. Avit, and Marie the prioress, and Agnes the subprioress, and Adelaide the third prioress.

Rotrou of Montfort, son of Agnes of good memory [and] the daughter of Domina Duchisse of Brou, for the remedy of his soul and that of his mother and ancestors, assigns a chaplain to the chapel of Notre Dame of Vibraye, with the consent of Abbess Ada and the convent of St. Avit, whom the abbess of St. Avit will have the right of nomination and whom will be dependent upon the convent. With the consent of his father and Marguerite, his wife, and her daughters Agnes, Inogentia, Heloise, Alicia, Burgonia, and Aliena, he gave many things [to St. Avit]. Done in the chapterhouse of St. Avit, in the year 1206 under the reign of King Philip in the month of September. [In the presence of] Prévot Geoffrey of La Ferté, Bernard, Reginald of *Buris*, Hugo of *Ortelo*, Maria the prioress, Agnes the subprioress.

Rotrou of Montfort's gift of 1213:

Rotrou continued to make gifts to the nuns of St. Avit. In 1213 he made a modest donation that is recorded in a manuscript in the Archives départmentales d'Eure-et-Loire, H 4455. It is a small and tattered parchment, which accounts for the elisions within the text:

> Rotrou of Montfort, son of another Rotrou and Agnes of good memory, let those in the present but also the future make note, therefore accepting and holding from my estates and fiefs, tithes . . . and pigs, with rights to pannage in the woods, with revenues from pannaging from the dwellings, I give to the church of St. Avit of Châteaudun . . . namely what they hold each year and I donate from the *Villa Goeti* namely woods and surrendering . . . and from Raginald of Montmirail and Count Hervé of Nevers from his holdings. So that this charter will remain firm and stable, I corroborate it with the strength of my seal. In the year of grace 1213.

No. 22: Charters of the convent of St. Avit of Châteaudun: Garnier Bisolius' gift to the nuns for nursing his wife, 1148

This gift is pieced together from an entry in MS 556/435bis from the Mediathèque d'Orléans, p. 219 and Cuissard's short description. Cuissard, in his article, essentially provides a very brief snapshot of the various donations

40 This Rotrou would have been the grandson of Agnes of Montfort-le-Gesnois, one of the earliest patrons to St. Avit.

made to St. Avit. Unfortunately he leaves out some important details contained in the modern copy of the charter. Here is Cuissard's description:

> Garnier Bisolius, son-in-law of Odo of Montingy, gave "at St. Gemma" land consisting of the labor of two oxen, ten pence of rent in the coin of Orléans, three measures of wheat in the measure of Vendôme, three loaves of bread and three capons,[41] in recognition of his wife recovering her health. The act was done "at *Villa Bersadi*," under the seal of Count Thibaut IV of Blois. [Note that Thibaut calls himself Count of Chartres in the charter below. As he was count of both places, he employed both titles. In spite of the two different titles, this was the same count/person.]

The nineteenth-century copy of a presumably medieval charter from which Cuissard got this description reads as follows:

At St. Gemma:

> I, Thibaut, Count of Chartres, wish that all men in the present and future to make note that Garnier Bisolius gave to God and the church of Châteaudun where the nuns serve God in that very place, anything he held at St. Gemma, namely land sufficient to support the labor of two oxen, ten pence of rent in the coin of Orléans, and three measures of wheat in the measure of Vendôme, three pence worth of bread, and three capons, to be paid annually, for his wife the daughter of Odo of Montigny,[42] to the aforementioned church in return for care during her sickness and then later for her death there. However, Hugh, the son of Garnier Bisolius, contested the aforementioned pious gift. But in the end he was forced by no one [and] from my request he conceded what had been given to the aforementioned church in perpetuity at a certain of our assemblies at *Villa Retfondi* in the month of September the Sunday after the feast of Holy Mary. Many holy witnessing that indeed neither the aforementioned Hugh nor another [is able] to bring [a false claim] to this pious gift or to harass by false contestation, hereafter I affix my seal of authority to this charter truly confirming the concession of Hugh made above. These witnesses: Odo of *Vivvardo*, Aubert of *Monteannis*, Robert his son, Herbert Senex [the Elder] of Prunay, Garnier Bisolius the brother of the aforementioned Hugh,[43] and others among *Villa Bersadi* in the year 1148.

41 A capon is a rooster that has been neutered to improve the quality of its meat.

42 This would have been a great grandniece of the original donor, Ganelon of Montigny.

43 This Garnier could have been another of Garnier's sons and Hugh's brother. Or the scribe could have made an error and this Garnier should be Hugh's father, the original donor.

No. 23: Charters of the convent of St. Avit of Châteaudun: Donations by Nicholas and Hugh of La Bruyère to support their sisters who were nuns, 1210 and 1217

These gifts are pieced together from an entry in MS 556/435bis from the Mediathèque d'Orléans, pp. 190 and 211 and Cuissard's short description.

In May 1217, Hugh of Bruyère, canon of Chartres cathedral, gave to the abbey of St. Avit a rent of 30 pence on the condition that his sister, Odelina, a nun at this house, will benefit [from this gift] during her life.

In the year 1210, Nicholas of Bruyère, knight and lord of Bois-Ruffin, for Aalis his birth sister, assigns eighteen shillings and eleven pence each year from his revenues collected at Brou, the same for his sister Odelina, both of whom are nuns at St. Avit.

No. 24: Charters of the convent of St. Avit of Châteaudun: Donations for Ameline by her family, 1215

These gifts are pieced together from an entry in MS 556/435bis from the Mediathèque d'Orléans, pp. 190 and 209 and Cuissard's short description.

In the month of July, 1215, William of Mémillon, a knight, confirmed to St. Avit two setiers of wheat and two of oats to be taken each year from the small holding at Taillepied in the feast of St. Remigius, which he gave to St. Avit for his sister, Amelina of Le Verger, of good memory, with the consent of her husband, Nivelon of Martel, and of their children Nicholas, Jacqueline and Fulk, and Robert of Freschot, Ameline's son-in-law, and Mathilda, his wife. These witnesses: Froger, Judicaël, Ernaud and William, the chaplain of St. Avit, Bernard of Bullou and Adam of *Bardilleriis*, knights.

No. 25: Charters of the convent of St. Avit of Châteaudun: Conflict between the nuns of St. Avit with the monks of Chamars over the construction of a causeway, 1201

Translated from *Cartulaire de Marmoutier pour le Dunois*, ed. Emile Mabille (Châteaudun: Lecesne, 1874), no. 209, pp. 193–194.

In the name of the holy and indivisible Trinity. Dean Hugh and Master Girald, canons of Paris, and Master Girard of Poissy, to all whom the present letter will have reached, greetings. Let it be known to all involved in your joint case, that is between the prior and the monks of Chamars on one part and the abbess and nuns of St. Avit on the other part, was heard by our lord pope, through distant appeal; [the resolution] was as follows. He declared accordingly in the portion [of the property] of the monks in a certain glade, which is transected by the river Le Loir, [where] the nuns had a causeway to be made, and which usually changes the flow of the water and the customary practices of sailing in the aforementioned glade, so much so the monks themselves as well as others who possessed estates in adjacent places, as they had become accustom to have, so that it [the causeway] would hinder [the flow of water] and the water moreover flowing into the pastures of the monks making the area flooded, from which the monks themselves and their men suffered many losses. [F]or that reason they petitioned so that the now mentioned causeway of the nuns [they] will join together to destroy, and of the losses sustained, they [the nuns] will be brought together [with the monks] to make amends. Moreover, they themselves [the monks] justly asserted to make the claim to them with the greatest reason that it is not allowed for anyone to build anything on the public bank of the river which would harm the path of navigation.

Also because when the nuns built a fishing weir in another part of the same glade which they took from the monks, through [the order of] Count Thibaut, following the judgement of good men who from antiquity had held freely the course of the water and the right to sail in the aforementioned glade, the nuns were forced to destroy the same weir; . . . Therefore we who heard this testimony and evidence, and having diligently examined the rationales and allegations, in addition to having the counsel of prudent men, we pass judgement on the abbess and nuns of St. Avit and their agent, so that they must destroy the aforementioned causeway, and not otherwise make another weir in the glade, so that it is possible for both the use of public navigation and so as not to impede the convenience of the monks,[it is] permissible and also just, if they [the monks] will wish by their right to ask for damages. Therefore together in resolution and the memory of this sentence, we who are present do ourselves corroborate and through the strength of our seals, and Master Geoffrey of Poissy, colleague, does not have a seal, did not affix his seal. Public act of Paris, year of grace, 1201.

No. 26: Letter of Abbot Geoffrey of Vendôme to Prior André, 1106–1107

Translated from *Geoffrey de Vendôme: Oeuvres,* ed. and translated from the Latin by Geneviève Giordanengo. CNRS Editions (Paris: Brepols, 1996), pp. 158–159.

Geoffrey, humble servant of the monastery of Vendôme, to his venerable brother André, remembering by heart, "not to do my own will, but to do the will of Him who sent me."

We have sent along to you, very dear friend, our dear brother Herbert, who we know to be very farsighted in the affairs of the world, and we have recommended to him to act wisely and on your counsel as to how he ought to conduct himself with the outside world, especially impressing upon him to love you with all of his heart and to obey you with zeal deserving of your virtue as a prior. For your part, be an example for him and the other brothers confided to your direction in your pastoral charge so that the Eternal Pastor is not able to find in them [just] one small perfection. If you show yourself to be worried, as a result of our admonition, about the souls confided to your trust, believe very fervently and doubt nothing that you cannot excuse due to a lessening of your means. Because God, by my mediation, by me his unworthy servant, will make up for your misery and on his part you will receive an eternal recompense for the flock well-guarded.

No. 27: Letters of Abbot Geoffrey of Vendôme to Bishop Hildebert of Le Mans concerning the lords of Montoire, 1104

Translations from *Geoffrey de Vendôme: Oeuvres,* ed. and translated from the Latin by Geneviève Giordanengo. CNRS Editions (Paris: Brepols, 1996), pp. 72–75.

To Bishop Hildebert of Le Mans, 1104

To Hildebert, bishop of the good life, Geoffrey, servant of the monastery of Vendôme, sends greetings.

We have learned and we know that Hamelin of Montoire, excommunicated by you and the legate of the Roman Church for the evil deeds that he has perpetrated against us, has been absolved, without him yet making any restitution to us. Also, we especially appeal to your goodness so that he quickly makes restitution of that which he took from us or submit anew to the excommunication which it seems he has illicitly avoided, for let it not be annulled that which has been carried out publically against him by you and by the vicar of the apostolic see.

To Bishop Hildebert of Le Mans, 1104

To Hildebert, bishop of the laudable life, his dear father in Christ, [from] Geoffrey, the smallest of the servants of the monastery of Vendôme, to always live holy lives, and not rely on anything else.[44]

You have learned, as you have made known to us, that your clergy have anew accorded to Hamelin the communion that was prohibited to

44 Giordanengo indicates that this is a quote from John 4:1.

him, because our brothers did not wish to receive justice from him. The brothers, whose word is true, they deny to have acted in this way and affirming that you offered to them neither justice nor an assurance that justice would be rendered to them. It is why, preserving your peace, we ourselves state sadly that you had to know of such deeds, just as you must have had knowledge of them, [we are] completely troubled [by the fact that] that you had to believe your clerics on this point, as well as the circumstances which were causing the delays that deprive us of our property and which are absolutely contrary to canonical rules. For it is held through the establishment in the decrees of the Fathers, you know this very well, that "the judges of the Church carefully ensure to not pronounce judgement in the absence of those who are debating the case." And, as well as the punishment to which he had been condemned does not follow immediately after the accusation, if he is absent, likewise the excommunicated must not secure the remedy of absolution as long as the claim by those who submitted it have suffered an injustice from his part.

This being the cause, we ask in great astonishment for what reason Hamelin's acquittal is accepted, he against whom our injustices call out again and complain. And no less surprising to see someone seek absolution or to be already considered absolved, he who the Roman Church has bound by a sentence of excommunication. He should not have been legally acquitted or to have obtained a reprieve, under the pretext of the law that it is said to have been proposed. In effect, he who is at once rejected from the church by the order of a bishop is not able to be reconciled by a discussion or any grounds except making restitution. You are not ignorant, in our opinion, that these things have been thus defined at the Council of Toledo. These words are sufficient to the clerics who, if greatly fearing God, would never have trampled upon His justice with two feet.

Excellent bishop, we beg you with total devotion to your dignity, to put an end to our complaint and do not put off any longer redressing the situation of your justice changed by the clergy. Farewell and aid us, your servants, for the love of God, so that we do not lose all in your diocese on account of faulty justice.

No. 28: Lord Lancelin III of Beaugency's will, 1160–1182

Translated from *Cartulaire de Notre-Dame de Baugency*, ed. G. Vignat (Orléans, Herluison, 1879), no. 75, pp. 86–88. Archives départmentales du Loiret, H 10, fol. XXI verso.

Let not hostile intervention surrender care of this vineyard to oblivion nor this faithful institution be purged by perverse malice, [so] for the present and also for posterity this present charter [is] to be commended to writing, because I, Lancelin III, lord of Beaugency, concede and confirm by the authority of my seal, in honor of Holy Mary and the saintly martyrs Fuscian and Victor and Gentian, for the anniversary of my father Ralph and my mother Mathilda, [the following]:

For the good works of the church of Notre Dame [of Beaugency] five shillings; for cooking meals for the canons, five shillings; from St. Firmin, five shillings and five shillings from the bridge, under this condition that the servant, who receives the tolls from the Loire, will promise faithfully that henceforward in the nativity of St. John the Baptist, [even if] anyone has paid nothing from that place, so that these aforementioned pious gifts would be paid, except the ten pennies which Matheus of *Carta* had in fief from me [a money fief] and I give for him as a pious gift for his anniversary; half to Hôtel-Dieu and the other half to the good works of the church of Notre Dame and to the cooking for the canons.

Furthermore, I concede for the anniversary of my brother Lord Simon I and Adenorde his wife, one measure of salt in toll from the Loire, from each ship carrying salt, except a ship from the bridge . . .[45] an alleviation was done, in accordance with custom, which Lord Simon had in the land of the canons at Montigny, and in addition twenty pennies in revenue from the oven of Choisel; and truly for the anniversary of Hersend, my [second] wife, five shillings in revenue from the market stall of Aalard the butcher. For the anniversary of Aalise, my [first] wife, I concede the customs which I hold in the vineyard of the canons at *Ereos*.

The witnesses to these things are: Manassas, bishop of Orléans; Gauter, precentor of St. Liphard of Meung-sur-Loire, Harduin then abbot; Hoderic prior, with many others. Farewell.

No. 29: The oath of Simon II of Beaugency to the count of Blois, 1222

Cartulaire de la Chambre des comptes, fol. 35, r et v, charte no. 71. From "Fréteval, Beaugency, Saint-Aignan: Château Jurables et Rendables aux Comtes de Blois," Charles Métais, Châteaudun, J. Pigelet, 1889, pp. 161–162.

I, Simon [II] of Beaugency, wish to make note for the present and future that I did liege homage to that noble man, Lord Walter of Avesnes, count of Blois, in front of the men, the men of the tower of Beaugency, and all that held fiefs from it, and I swore to that same lord that I am rendering to him the tower and fortress of Beaugency from its greatest strength to its weakest, as often as I will have need of himself or by a specific order at any time.

45 The manuscript is blank here, but the editor suggests it could have been from the bridge at Blois. This would mean that those ships disembarking from Blois and sailing by Beaugency would be free from this toll.

This lord truly ordered that one knight swear an oath to me for his life time, so that the tower and fortress therefore would remain as it was when I surrendered it to him; he would render service to me within forty days after this agreement. In these matters, as testimony and strength, I placed my seal to the present charter to corroborate them. Dated in the year of the Lord, 1222 second mense of July.

Glossary

Abbey A complex of buildings (church/chapels, dormitory, kitchen, refectory, library, etc.) which comprise the community dwelling of an order of monks or nuns.

Abbot/abbess The heads of an ecclesiastical community usually selected by members of that community. For monks, this would be an abbot; for nuns, an abbess.

Almshouse See entry for Hôtel Dieu.

Alod Property not held in return for feudal service. Can be personal property, moveable or immoveable property, or inherited property.

Aula A hall, generally used by a lord for public proceedings and occasions, such as holding court and homage ceremonies. At the castle at Beaugency, this appears of have been an open-air hall.

Ban A set of powers and privileges exercised by lords which allowed them public authority to command, provide justice, adjudicate disputes, punish and collect exactions from those living under their authority. It signified not only their control and dominion over people, despite class, but also their control over land.

Benedictine A monk or nun who followed the rule created by St. Benedict, who wrote the *Regula Benedicti* which sets the guidelines for Benedictine monasticism.

Bishop The highest ranking clergy member in a diocese, a district entrusted to his care, supervision and administration.

Canon There were two types of canons: Regular and secular. Regular canons lived by a rule, like the Augustinian rule, and were sometimes cloistered. Secular canons lived in the world, often in their own houses and were not cloistered, and interacted with secular society. Some canons served secular officials as chancellors.

Canon Law The laws created by the church to regulate the lives of believers, but also to govern the hierarchy of the church.

Capetian The royal dynasty that ruled France from 987–1328.

Cartulary A collection of documents called charters (see below) that were created to organize an ecclesiastical community's property – like the cartulary of Notre Dame de Beaugency. Sometimes cartularies include histories of the foundation.

Charters Documents of practice that record transferal of property – usually, but not always – to the church.

Château French for castle.

Chevage A tribute or "head-tax" that serfs paid to their lords.

Cluny A monastery in Burgundy that became one of the largest monastic orders in medieval Europe. Founded in 910 by Duke William I of Aquitaine.

Cistercian Refers to the monastic order founded by Robert of Molesme at Cîteux, France, in 1098. Required a stricter observance of the Benedictine rule. Became one of the most popular forms of monasticism. St. Bernard of Clairvaux played a key role in the order's expansion and popularity in the twelfth century.

Cognomen A name in addition to the first name that could denote geographic association (Lancelin de Beaugency or of Beaugency) or a personal charateristic (Geoffrey the Red). Often passed down hereditarily.

Commercial Revolution A change in economy during the late eleventh and early twelfth century from subsistence and bartering to cash-based, profit motivated commerce.

Consanguinity Being from the same line of kinship as another person. Degrees of consanguinity or kinship determined who could marry. In the twelfth century, seven degrees of kinship were used to determine if a marriage could take place. If the couple was related within seven degrees, they were not supposed to marry.

Corvée Unpaid labor a peasant owed his lord.

Count/countess A man or woman who controlled a region of a county. He or she held courts and called upon their vassals to provide them with counsel and military service. Also provided military service to their lord, often a duke/duchess or a king/queen.

Donjon French term for tower or castle. Also the root word for the modern term of "dungeon."

Dower The share of his holdings that a husband gave to his wife upon marriage. It was used for her support when she was widowed. In northern France, most wives received one-half or one-third of their husband's property as her dower.

Dowry A portion of family property, or cash, or goods, given to a woman by her natal or birth family when she married.

Duke/duchess A man or woman controlling a duchy, which could consist of several counties and/or lordships. Usually received the duchy directly from the king and had jurisdictional and legal rights over it. Often provided military service to the king or queen.

Fief Land or property given by a lord to a vassal in return for military service and counsel, as well as certain feudal aids like providing castle guard or cash for a lord's ransom or a cash gift at the time of the marriage of his daughter.

Foremariage A fee paid by serfs to their lords if they wanted to marry a serf from a different lordship.

Gregorian reform movement Reforms named for Pope Gregory VII (r. 1073–1085) that dealt with the moral integrity of clergy members and establishing the independence of the church from secular control. Key ideals of the reform were prohibiting lay investiture, simony, pluralism and clerical marriage. Also asserted church oversight of which relatives the laity could marry.

Hagiography The life of a saint, written by a member of the clergy, that focused on their piety, martyrdom, as well as their posthumous miracles and interventions.

Heraldry A system of heraldic symbols and coats of arms designed to designate aristocratic families.

Heresy/heretic A belief or practice that was not approved by the church or not considered orthodox. A heretic is a person who adheres to heretical belief or practice.

Homage A ceremony where a vassal pledges fealty and loyalty to his/her lord.

Historiography The study of how history has been studied, how it has evolved as a discipline and how it has been written over the centuries.

Hôtel Dieu Often synonymous with Almshouse. A building staffed by clergy where the poor and ill could find health services, food and shelter.

Leprosarium/Leprosaria (plural) A house or community specifically for lepers to live and receive care. Staffed by clergy. Developed in the twelfth century.

Liberal Arts The curriculum at cathedral schools and medieval universities consisting of the trivium (study of grammar, rhetoric and logic) and quadrivium (arithmetic, geometry, astronomy and music).

Lord A man or woman who controlled a lordship, including juridical authority, and the right to hold a court and collect revenue. Often entailed control of a castle and military service.

Lordship Land, territory or estate over which a lord (male or female) held authority or jurisdiction.

Mainmorte Fee paid when serfs passed their property from generation to generation.

Martyrology See entry for "Necrology or Obituary."

Monk Refers to a man who has taken the monastic vows of poverty, chastity and obedience. Lives in a monastery.

Noble Generally synonymous with aristocrat. Indicates a person of high status and elite family. Can be applied to those who were of the rank of lord, viscount/viscountess, count/countess or duke/duchess.

Necrology or Obituary A list of the souls for whom the monks or nuns would pray for on the anniversary of the person's death. Can include members of the community or church, as well a lay patrons, friends or relatives.

Oblate Children who were given to the church, usually by an aristocratic family, who were taught and raised to join the clergy.

Ordeal (Judicial ordeal) An "ordeal" used to settle a legal dispute. Ordeals included those by fire, water and combat. Trial by fire entailed grasping a hot iron rod, bandaging the wound and then checking the wound after three days to see if had healed. Ordeal by water used a similar premise, but instead of grasping a hot iron, the person submerged their hand in boiling water. A judicial duel was another ordeal, where the two parties – or their representatives – would battle one another. Whoever won the duel won the dispute. The underlying assumption to all judicial ordeals was that God would intervene on the side of the just.

Pannage The turning out of pigs usually in a forest for them to forage for food.

Patrimony The land that had been the traditional territorial base of a noble family.

Patronage Financial support of an organization or individual – in the case of the Beaugencys, ecclesiastical foundations. Patronage played an important role in medieval culture as it was often used to create relationships and networks of power and influence.

Pilgrimage The journey to visit a saint's shrine (oftentimes visiting several along the way) at a church or cathedral which housed relics, to seek intervention, grace or miracles on the pilgrim's behalf or that of a family member.

Popular Crusade or People's Crusade Part of the First Crusade. Led by the charismatic leader Peter the Hermit, and consisted of peasants and common people who were inspired by the message of crusade to leave their homes and go fight in the Holy Land. They were slaughtered by the Seljuk Turks shortly after crossing over from Constantinople into Anatolia in October 1096.

Potestas Latin term meaning power.

Prévot Officer in charge of a prefecture. Lords divided their lands into prefectures and prévots were responsible for collecting revenue from rent and other exactions to his lord, as well as providing peace and supervision over the lord's lands.

Priory A smaller dependent house of a monastery or nunnery, governed by a prior or prioress.

Regular Clergy Clergy who live by a rule or *regula*: Monks, nuns and some canons.

Relics A remnant of a saint's body, clothing or other such artifact that was considered to have sacred powers to heal and grant miracles. Typically housed in a shrine or reliquary in a church or cathedral. Objects of veneration. Many made pilgrimages to visit relics, as they were a physical and tangible way of connecting with the divine

Religious/Religieuse Man or woman who commit their lives to the church – for example, a monk or nun.

Romance A type of literature that developed in the twelfth century, usually centered on Arthurian legends. Instead of focusing on battles, as the *Chansons de Geste* – the other common type of medieval literature – romances explored emotions, human motivations and developed more well-rounded characters. Chivalry was often a common theme.

Royal Demesne The territory belonging to the French king centered around Paris.

Saint A person who was venerated, usually after their death, as particularly holy, virtuous and pious. Some saints had been martyred or persecuted for their faith. A saint was generally believed to be connected to God, and medieval people prayed to saints asking for their intercession. Saints were also believed to perform miracles.

Secular Clergy Refers to clergy members who participated in the secular world and resided in a community outside of monastery or abbey, including priests, canons and deacons. These are the clerics who are often in charge of education, preaching, administering the sacraments and interaction with the laity.

Seneschal Officer who was in charge of an aristocratic or royal household. May have had judicial, administrative and military duties.

Sepulcher A tomb that usually houses the body of the deceased and maybe decorated with a sculpture of the tomb's inhabitant. The Holy Sepulcher in Jerusalem is the perhaps the best known and is the church built around the purported tomb of Christ.

Serf An unfree agricultural worker who performed labor for his/her lord and paid certain fees like *mainmorte* and *foremariage*. Attached to a piece of property that he/she worked and was able to pass along to his/her descendants for them to work.

Squire An apprentice to a knight or a lord with some distant connection to the nobility.

Simony The buying or selling of church offices.

Taillage/Taille A tax collected by lords on the peasantry living in their domain.

Three Field System A type of crop rotation utilized to increase crop production. Arable land would be divided into three fields and two of the fields would be in use for a season, allowing the third to "rest" or remain fallow. Hence bringing two-thirds of the arable land under cultivation. A practice that replaced the two field system where only half of the arable land would be cultivated.

Tithes One-tenth of income or produce paid to support the church. Part of the Gregorian Reform Movement was to ensure that the laity did not control ecclesiastical tithes. If they did, they were encouraged to restore them to the church.

Usury The practice of charging interest on a loan. The church was hostile to usury on the grounds that lenders who charged interest took advantage of a fellow Christian's misfortune.

Vassal A male or female member of the nobility who held a fief from a lord. In return for they fief, they provided their lord with military service, certain feudal aids (like castle guard) and counsel. A vassal may have held fiefs from several different lords.

Viscount/Vicountess A viscount or viscountess controlled a viscounty, which was usually a portion of a county. They administered the viscounty by holding courts, collecting taxes, providing protection and military service.

Index

Entries in *italics* denote figures; entries in **bold** denote maps; * indicates a place name.

Taylor & Francis eBooks

www.taylorfrancis.com

A single destination for eBooks from Taylor & Francis with increased functionality and an improved user experience to meet the needs of our customers.

90,000+ eBooks of award-winning academic content in Humanities, Social Science, Science, Technology, Engineering, and Medical written by a global network of editors and authors.

TAYLOR & FRANCIS EBOOKS OFFERS:

A streamlined experience for our library customers

A single point of discovery for all of our eBook content

Improved search and discovery of content at both book and chapter level

REQUEST A FREE TRIAL

support@taylorfrancis.com